The Experimental Arabic Novel

SUNY series in Middle Eastern Studies
Shahrough Akhavi, editor

The Experimental Arabic Novel

Postcolonial Literary Modernism in the Levant

Stefan G. Meyer

State University of New York Press

Published by
State University of New York Press

Printed in the United States of America

For information, address the State University of New York Press,
90 State Street, Suite 700, Albany, NY 12207

Marketing by Fran Keneston • Production by Bernadine Dawes

Cover photograph by Jens-Uwe Rahe. The photo originally appeared in *Kleine Libanesische Bibliothek* (Beirut: Orient-Institut der DMG, 1977), and is reprinted with permission of the artist.

Library of Congress Cataloging-in-Publication Data

Meyer, Stefan G., 1949–
The experimental Arabic novel : postcolonial literary modernism in the Levant / Stefan G. Meyer.
p. cm. — (SUNY series in Middle Eastern Studies)
Includes bibliographical references and index.
ISBN 0-7914-4733-2 (alk. paper) — ISBN 0-7914-4734-0 (pbk. : alk. paper)
1. Arabic fiction—20th century—History and criticism. 2. Modernism (Literature)—Arab countries. I. Title. II. Series.

PJ7577 .M49 2001
892.7'3609—dc21

00-041338

1 2 3 4 5 6 7 8 9 10

Dedicated to my father,

Alfred G. Meyer,

former professor of political science at the

University of Michigan,

and to all those who helped me along the way

Contents

Acknowledgments

The Ph.D. dissertation that formed the basis for this book was begun on a Fulbright fellowship in Amman and Damascus in late 1994 and early 1995. The bulk of the reading for the dissertation was done while I was affiliated with the Institut Français d'Études Arabes de Damas (IFEAD) in Damascus in 1995. I completed the dissertation in Ann Arbor in the spring and summer of 1996, and received a Ph.D. in Comparative Literature from Rutgers University in October of that year. The manuscript was then revised for publication in the fall of 1997 at the American Center of Oriental Research (ACOR) in Amman on a grant from the Council of American Overseas Research Centers (CAORC). Late revision was done as a visiting scholar at the University of Michigan in 1998 and the spring of 1999. The work also involved travel for interviews and consultations in Latakia, Beirut, London, New York, Ramallah, and Tel Aviv from 1995 to 1997.

My greatest thanks go to Hassan Abbas, at IFEAD, who finally got me pointed in the right direction, helped me narrow and organize my research, and oversaw the reading for the dissertation. Without his help I would still be at ground zero. The process of revision from dissertation to publishable manuscript owes the most to Fakhri Salih in Amman. Thanks also goes for the kind tutoring of Mu'ayyad al-'Atili at the Al-Abraj Center in Amman. Anton Shammas of the University of Michigan in Ann Arbor provided key help with the early stage of revision, and Nora Kalliel, also in Ann Arbor, gave equally valuable assistance in the final stage. I also received important feedback at crucial points in the revision process from Maarten van Delden at New York University, Hannan Hever at Tel Aviv University, and Nancy Roberts in Amman.

Three authors whose insights were important in helping me get on the right track early in the period of the dissertation research were Nabil

Sulayman in Latakia, Elias Khoury in Beirut, and Abdelrahman Munif in Damascus. I also benefited from early conversations with Fakhri Salih and Murid Barghuthi in Amman, and later talks with Yumna al-'Eid, Mona Amyuni, Abduh Wazin, Hassan Daoud, and Rashid al-Da'if in Beirut and Hanan al-Shaykh in London. There were several authors in Amman with whom I conducted productive and informative interviews in the early stage of my research, including Jamal Abu Hamdan, Ibrahim Nasrallah, Mu'nis al-Razzaz, Mahmud al-Rimawi, Suhayr al-Tall, Basmah al-Nusur, Elias Farkouh, Taher Riyad, Ramadan Rawashdeh, and Ziyad Barakat.

The project could not have begun without help from the members of my dissertation committee at Rutgers. These included my chairperson Abena Busia, my graduate director Josephine Diamond, Roger Allen of the University of Pennsylvania, and Janet Walker. Other people to whom I am grateful for assistance during my period in New Brunswick are Elise Salem Mangonaro of Fairleigh Dickinson University, Lillian Farhat, and Ann Lipovsky.

There were many people who were of general assistance to me during my first visit to Amman. These included Aida Dabbas, Alain McNamara, and Hoda Qasim of the Fulbright Commission, Ibrahim al-Sa'afin of Jordan University, Nuha Kassis Nafal of the Al-Abraj Center, As'ad Abdelrahman of the Shoman Foundation, Maher al-Kayyali at Dar al-Faris, Widad Adas, Suhayr al-Tall, and Rima Irani. Thanks also go to fellow Fulbrighters Eliot Goldberg of George Washington University and Brian Katulis of Villanova University. People of assistance during my second period in Amman included Pierre and Patricia Bikai, Kathy Nimri, and Bob Mittelstaedt of ACOR, Mufideh al-'Atili at the Al-Abraj Center, and Amin Odeh at Al al-Bayt University in Mafraq.

In Damascus, thanks for interview opportunities go to Mamduh Adwan, Shawqi Baghdadi, and Nihad Sirris. Thanks go also to Zulfa Samman at USIS, and fellow Fulbrighters Najjat Rahman of the University of Wisconsin, Layla Hudson of the University of Michigan, and Nezar Andary, as well as to Suhayl Chabat and Eric Gautier at IFEAD, Marlin Dick, and Hussein Maxos. Thanks for similar assistance in Beirut go to Maher Jarrar and Hassan Krayem of the American University in Beirut, Suhayl Idris at Dar al-Adab, Samah Idris, Samia Tabari, and the staff of the Orient Institut.

At the University of Michigan, thanks go to Ernest McCarus, Raji

Rammuny, and James Bellamy, of the Department of Near Eastern Studies, as well as to Jane Hansen, the department manager. Thanks also go to Lemuel Johnson, of the Department of English, and graduate students Moulouk Berry, of the Near Eastern Studies Department, and Neil Doshi, of the Program in Comparative Literature. Elsewhere, thanks go to David Damrosch at Columbia University, Salma Khadra Jayyusi in Cambridge, Massachusetts, Fadi Allaouie of Miami Beach, Florida, and May Jayyusi in Ramallah. Final thanks go to Zina Lawrence at SUNY Press and Don Herdeck at Three Continents Press.

The author gratefully thanks the following publishers for permission to use previously published material in the compilation of this book:

Material from Samira Aghacy, "Elias Khoury's *The Journey of Little Gandhi*: Fiction and Ideology," *International Journal of Middle East Studies* 28, no. 2 (1996), reprinted with the permission of Cambridge University Press.

Material from Mona Takieddine Amyuni, "Style and Politics in the Poems and Novels of Rashid Al-Da'if," *International Journal of Middle East Studies* 28, no. 2 (1996), reprinted with the permission of Cambridge University Press.

Material from Elias Khoury, *Little Mountain*, translated by Maia Tabet, foreword by Edward Said, 1989, reprinted with the permission of Carcanet Press Ltd., Manchester, England.

Material from *Anthology of Modern Palestinian Literature*, Salma Khadra Jayyusi, 1992. Republished with permission of Columbia University Press, 562 W. 113th St., New York, NY 10025. Reproduced by permission of the publisher via Copyright Clearance Center, Inc.

Material from Samira Aghacy, "Rachid El Daif's *An Exposed Space Between Drowsiness and Sleep*: Abortive Representation," *Journal of Arabic Literature* 27, no. 3 (October 1996), reprinted with the permission of E. J. Brill, Leiden, Netherlands.

Material from Hoda Barakat, *The Stone of Laughter*, translated by Sophie Bennet, 1994, reprinted with the permission of Garnet Publishing, Ltd., Reading, England.

Material from Ibrahim Nasrallah, *Prairies of Fever*, translated by May Jayyusi and Jeremy Reed, introduction by Fedwa Malti-Douglas, 1993, reprinted with permission from Interlink Books, Northampton, Massachusetts.

Material from Edwar al-Kharrat, *Girls of Alexandria*, translated by Frances Liardet, 1993, reprinted with permission from Quartet Books, London, England.

Material from Ghada Samman, *Beirut Nightmares*, translated by Nancy N. Roberts, 1997, reprinted with permission from Quartet Books, London, England.

Excerpts from *Cities of Salt* by Abdelrahman Munif, translated by Peter Theroux. Copyright © 1987 by Cape Cod Scriveners Company. Reprinted by permission of Random House, Inc., New York, and Wylie Agency, UK, London.

Material from Ghada Samman, *Beirut '75*, translated by Nancy N. Roberts, 1995, reprinted with the permission of The University of Arkansas Press, Fayetteville, Arkansas.

Material from Elias Khoury, *The Journey of Little Gandhi*, translated by Paula Haydar, foreword by Sabah Ghandour, 1994, reprinted with the permission of University of Minnesota Press, Minneapolis, Minnesota.

Material from Elias Khoury, *Gates of the City*, translated by Paula Haydar, foreword by Sabah Ghandour, 1993, reprinted with the permission of University of Minnesota Press, Minneapolis, Minnesota.

Material from Emile Habiby, *The Secret Life of Saeed, the Ill-Fated Pessoptimist,* 1985, reprinted with the permission of Salma Khadra Jayyusi and Trevor Le Gassick.

Material from Sonallah Ibrahim, *The Smell of It and Other Stories,* 1971, reprinted with the permission of Denys Johnson-Davies.

Preface

This study aims to introduce English-speaking readers to the modern and contemporary Arabic novel and to stimulate their interest in drawing comparisons with Western modernist texts. The book is primarily meant to serve the needs of students and general readers who may have little or no familiarity with Arabic language or literature. To these ends, I have made prominent use of texts translated into English, turning to nontranslated works when faced with a significant gap in my survey of the experimental Arabic novel that could not otherwise be filled. The geographical focus is on the area known as the Levant, or "Greater Syria," comprising Lebanon, Syria, Jordan, and Palestine. Some discussion of selected Egyptian novels is included, to provide the broader context of literary development in the region as a whole. The novel in North Africa is excluded, due in part to the extent of European, particularly French, literary influence in this region, which tends to set it apart from the rest of the Arab world.

To make this study more accessible to English-language readers, I have rendered the names of authors, characters, and place names into anglicized form. This has omitted the plethora of diacritical marks used in transliteration that would otherwise clutter the text. The names of authors with significant works in English are rendered according to the form in which they tend to appear in their English-language publications. This sometimes goes against phonological good sense, for example, Nawal el-Saadawi, for Nawāl al-Sa'dāwī (even though Nawal al-Sa'dawi would be a more accurate representation of the name). The forms of other authors' names have been dictated by common usage.

In the case of the name of an author, character, or place name that appears in the text of a translated work, I have retained the spelling of the name as rendered by the translator. Sometimes this results in the appearance of the same name in different works rendered with different spellings, such as Zakariyya in Gamal al-Ghitani's *Zayni Barakat* and Zakaria in Ghassan Kanafani's *All That's Left to You*. In the case of a nontranslated text, the fully transliterated name of an author is given the first time the author is quoted or when the author's work is specifically introduced in the text. The Arabic transliteration is given in parentheses following the anglicized form, for example, Elias Khoury (Ilyās Khūrī). In the case of an author, character, or place name that occurs in a quoted passage of a nontranslated text, the transliterated form is given in brackets, following the anglicized form, the first time the name is mentioned, for example Sarhan al-Beheiry (Sarḥān al-Buḥayrī).

To make the text easier for English-language readers to use, I have given the title of the English translation first. This is followed by the original Arabic title, given in transliterated form, thus: *Death in Beirut* (1976; *Ṭawāḥin Bayrūt,* 1972). Such works are thereafter referred to exclusively by their English titles. Works that have not been translated into English are introduced by the Arabic title in transliteration, followed by a translation in nonitalicized form in parentheses, for example, *I'tirāfāt Kātim Ṣawt* (Confessions of a hit man, 1986).

In the notes and bibliography, the author's name is rendered in either anglicized or transliterated form, depending on whether the work is in English or Arabic. Thus, for example, *Gates of the City* (1993; *Abwāb al-Madīnah*, 1981) is attributed to Elias Khoury, while *Al-Wujūh al-Bayḍā'* (The white faces, 1981) is attributed to Ilyās Khūrī. Occasionally, critical references to authors' names deviate from the most acceptable anglicized form. In such cases, the form of the name is given as cited by the third party, with the preferred anglicized spelling given in parenthesis, for example, Mureed Barghouthy (Murid Barghuthi). In notes or bibliographic citations, the preferred spelling is similarly given, in brackets, following the nonpreferred form.

In transliteration, the reader will encounter symbols representing sounds that are not represented in English. The *ā, ū,* and *ī* are differentiated from the *a*, *u*, and *i* to denote the three long vowels, as opposed to their corresponding short vowels that are not represented in the Arabic alphabet. The *ṣ*, *ḍ*, *ṭ*, and *ẓ* are differentiated from the *s*, *d*, *t*, and *z* to represent the velarized consonants, which do not occur in English. The *ḥ* is differentiated from the *h* to represent the voiceless pharyngeal fricative as opposed to the consonant found in English. The ' is differentiated from the ' to represent the voiced pharyngeal fricative *'ayn* as opposed to the glottal stop *hamzah*. The consonants *th*, *kh*, *dh*, *sh*, and *gh* are rendered with the '*h*' as a helping symbol, as are their common equivalents in English.

Like the aforementioned pairs of letters, the *'ayn* (ʻ) and *hamzah* ('), while differentiated in transliteration, are not distinguished from one another in the anglicized forms of names. Thus Ibrāhīm al-Saʻāfīn is anglicized as Ibrahim al-Sa'afin. At the beginning of anglicized words or names, the custom of dropping the *hamzah* in transliteration is extended to the *'ayn*, as well. Thus, the name ʻArabī is rendered in anglicized form as Arabi.

With respect to the definite article, *al-*, where the names of authors contain the definite article, the article is represented when the whole name is given, but dropped when reference is made only to the last name. Thus, the last name of Mu'nis al-Razzaz is given simply as Razzaz. The definite article is capitalized when it appears at the beginning of a sentence or the beginning of a title, e.g.: Al-Mutanabbi, *Al-Hadaf.* When the definite article of a last name appears together with the individual's first name, however, it is rendered in lower case, for example, Gamal al-Ghitani, *Ḥadīqah al-Ḥawāss*.

A number of appendices have been supplied for ease of reference. A glossary of Arabic transliteration symbols is provided, paired with the names of their corresponding letters in the Arabic alphabet. A glossary of authors' names is also provided, with the anglicized form of the name given first, followed by the transliterated form. The anglicized and transliterated forms of authors' names are cross-referenced the first time they appear in the bibliography, with anglicized forms of the names given in parentheses, and transliterated forms in brackets. The bibliography is divided into three sections, and features a list of Western texts that hopefully will stimulate comparative inquiry.

Arabic Transliteration Symbols

alif	*ā*	*ṭā'*	*ṭ*
bā'	*b*	*ẓā'*	*ẓ*
tā'	*t*	*'ayn*	*'*
thā'	*th*	*ghayn*	*gh*
jīm	*j*	*fā'*	*f*
ḥā'	*ḥ*	*qāf*	*q*
khā'	*kh*	*kāf*	*k*
dāl	*d*	*lām*	*l*
dhāl	*dh*	*mīm*	*m*
rā'	*r*	*nūn*	*n*
zāy	*z*	*hā'*	*h*
sīn	*s*	*wāw*	*w, ū*
shīn	*sh*	*yā'*	*y, ī*
ṣād	*ṣ*	*hamzah*	*'*
ḍād	*ḍ*		

Glossaries of Arabic Names

GLOSSARY OF ARABIC WRITERS

Tawfiq Yusuf Awwad	Tawfīq Yūsuf 'Awwād
Hoda Barakat	Hudā Barakāt
Salim Barakat	Salīm Barakāt
Murid Barghuthi	Murīd Barghūthi
Rashid al-Da'if	Rashīd al-Ḍa'īf
Hassan Daoud	Ḥasan Dāwūd
Khayri al-Dhahabi	Khayrī al-Dhahabī
Gamal al-Ghitani	Jamāl al-Ghīṭānī
Kahlil Gibran	Jubrān Khalīl Jubrān
✓ Emile Habiby	Imīl Ḥabībī
Fawaz Haddad	Fawāz Ḥaddād
Yahya Haqqi	Yaḥyā Ḥaqqī
Mohammed Hussein Haikal	Muḥammad Ḥusayn Haykal
Sonallah Ibrahim	Ṣun' Allāh Ibrāhīm
✓ Yusuf Idris	Yūsuf Idrīs
Rabi' Jaber	Rabī' Jābir
Jabra Ibrahim Jabra	Jabrā Ibrāhīm Jabrā
✓ Ghassan Kanafani	Ghassān Kanafānī
Edwar al-Kharrat	Idwār al-Kharrāṭ
Elias Khoury	Ilyās Khūrī
Fu'ad Kin'an	Fu'ād Kin'ān
✓ Naguib Mahfouz	Najīb Maḥfūẓ
Hanna Mina	Ḥannā Mīnā
✓ Abdelrahman Munif	'Abd al-Raḥmān Munīf
Ibrahim Nasrallah	Ibrāhīm Naṣr Allāh
Hani Rahib	Hānī al-Rāhib

Ramadan Rawashdeh	Ramaḍān al-Rawāshidah
Mu'nis al-Razzaz	Mu'nis al-Razzāz
Nawal el-Saadawi	Nawāl al-Sa'dāwī
Tayeb Saleh	Al-Ṭayyib Ṣāliḥ
Ghada Samman	Ghādah al-Sammān
Hanan al-Shaykh	Ḥanān al-Shaykh
Nihad Sirris	Nihād Sirrīs
Taysir Subul	Taysīr Subūl
Suhayr al-Tall	Suhayr Salṭī al-Tall
Abduh Wazin	'Abduh Wāzin
Faris Zarzur	Fāris Zarzūr

GLOSSARY OF ARABIC CRITICS

Adonis	'Alī Aḥmad Sa'īd
Mahmud Amin al-Alim	Maḥmūd Amīn al-'Ālim
Muhammad al-Baridi	Muḥammad al-Bāridī
Faysal Darraj	Fayṣal Darrāj
Kamal Abu Dib	Kamāl Abu Dīb
Ceza Kassem Draz	Sīzā Qāsim
Yumna al-Eid	Yumnā al-'Īd
Sabry Hafez	Ṣabrī Ḥāfiz
Muhammad Kamel al-Khatib	Muḥammad Kāmil al-Khaṭīb
Shakir al-Nabulsi	Shākir al-Nābulsī
Ibrahim al-Sa'afin	Ibrāhīm al-Sa'āfīn
Fakhri Salih	Fakhrī Ṣāliḥ
Anjil Butrus Sam'an	Anjīl Buṭrus Sam'ān
Sami Suwaydan	Sāmī Suwaydān
Faruq Wadi	Fārūq Wādī
Ahmad al-Zu'bi	Aḥmad al-Zu'bī

Introduction

The Experimental Arabic Novel and Comparative Modernisms

> You can't make a typology of Arab literature today. Modernism in the Arab world does not mean that the premodern has disappeared. It coexists with the premodern and the postmodern. The reason for this is related to the way knowledge is produced in the Arab world. It is not produced by the culture itself, but is imported from without.
>
> —Elias Khoury

> For the modern artist the past imitates the present far more than the present imitates the past. What we have to deal with here is a major cultural shift from a time-honored aesthetics of permanence, based on a belief in an unchanging and transcendent ideal . . . to an aesthetics of transitoriness and immanence, whose central values are change and novelty.
>
> —Matei Calinescu

This book represents an attempt to trace the development of experimentalism in the modern and contemporary Arabic novel, focusing on the Levant region (Lebanon, Syria, Jordan, and Palestine). At the same time it uses the experimental Arabic novel as a model or case study by which to examine and interrogate the Western notion of modernism, challenging the tendency on the part of some literary theorists to discuss this body of literature according to distinctly Western ideas. The basic premise of this study is that it is inadequate and misleading to speak of modernism or postmodernism as we understand these concepts in the West and expect them to apply to Arabic literature. Alternatively, however, it is possible to speak of distinct literary modernisms that have each evolved with a different set of characteristics, depending upon the nature of their historical antecedents. This offers us a way of speaking about the experimental

Arabic novel and similar trends in postcolonial literature in a manner that allows us to both compare and contrast them meaningfully with Western literature. While it is possible to speak of successive modernisms throughout history, those that are of relevance to this discussion belong to the twentieth century, or perhaps more accurately to the postindustrial age.

To approach this subject, we have to start with some general definition of postindustrial literary modernism or at least some salient characteristics that we can identify with it. In *The Modern British Novel*, Malcolm Bradbury states that

> Somewhere around the turn of the century there occurred a great "turn of the novel." The powerful tradition of Victorian fiction—moral, realistic, popular—began to die, and something difficult and more complex began to emerge. The novel was aspiring to become a more "self-conscious" form, which sought to be taken seriously as "art."[1]

While concerned specifically with the British novel, Bradbury states that he considers the novel to be an international form and does not regard British fiction as having been isolated from developments elsewhere. He sees the British tradition as in some sense international, linked as it is with travel, exile, emigration, and exterior influence. Concerned as he is with both the avant-garde modern tradition of the first half of this century and the more socially conscious modern tradition of the contemporary era, he invites the possibility of extending the concept of modernism to more recent developments in the non-Western world.

A second element in this comparison can be found in the following observation of Matei Calinescu in his book *Five Faces of Modernity:*

> Literary modernism is . . . both modern . . . and anti-modern: modern in its commitment to innovation, in its rejection of the authority of tradition, in its experimentalism; anti-modern in its dismissal of the dogma of progress, in its critique of rationality, in its sense that modern civilization has brought about the loss of something precious . . . the fragmentation of what was once a mighty unity.[2]

These general characteristics of literary modernism—its artistic self-consciousness, its ambivalence toward modernity, and the increasingly complex and fragmentary nature of literary form reflected in both these trends—can be clearly discerned to varying degrees in the experimental Arabic novel from its inception to the present. In the 1950s and early 1960s, writers in both Lebanon and Egypt, influenced by the French existentialists, produced works that were clearly more psychologically and existentially self-conscious than those of their predecessors. Throughout the 1960s, the works of writers such as Naguib Mahfouz and Sonallah Ibrahim in Egypt, Ghassan Kanafani in Palestine, and Jabra Ibrahim Jabra in Iraq represented an even more artistically self-conscious and radically ambivalent attitude that arose in the context of an increasingly politicized social atmosphere. In the 1970s and early 1980s, writers like Emile Habiby in Israel, Salim Barakat in Syria, and Abdelrahman Munif represented a fully politicized generation that sought to refashion the novel on the basis of distinctly Arab cultural, linguistic, or historical characteristics. Finally, the late 1980s and 1990s saw the advent of the so-called "new" Arabic novel, centered mainly in Lebanon, whose practitioners, such as Elias Khoury and Rashid al-Da'if, have produced highly fragmented narratives devoid of the "Arabizing" tendencies of their immediate predecessors.

In their introduction to literary modernism, entitled *Modernism: 1890–1930*,[3] Bradbury and Thomas McFarlane refer more specifically to what they consider to be the four main preoccupations of the modernist novel. These include concerns with the complexity of its own form and particularly with freeing narrative from the determination of plot. They also include a focus on the representation of inward states of consciousness and the examination of what lies beneath the surface of life and reality. Of these four preoccupations, the first two are essentially concerned with formal innovation, and the last two with the expression of subjectivity. Realism, to the modernist, thus represents a problem in terms of both form and consciousness. The "fragmentary" nature of modernist form tends to break down some of the totalizing assumptions of realism and, conversely, the breakdown of such assumptions can be seen as expressed through modernist formal innovation.

While Bradbury and McFarlane generally limit Western canonical modernism to works written before 1930, in *The Art of the Novel*, Milan Kundera extends the range of Western modernism by distinguishing between two distinct traditions in European modernism. Locating his own work within what he sees as a Central European novelistic tradition whose progenitors were Kafka, Musil, Hašek, and Broch, he contrasts this with the Western European tradition of James, Conrad, Joyce, and Proust. He differentiates between these two modernist traditions by noting that in Kafka's writing the interior life of the characters is absorbed by the situation in which they find themselves. Similarly, for Kundera, external determinants in the world have become so overpowering that internal impulses no longer carry any weight. In his book *Postmodernist Fiction*, Brian McHale uses this same reference point to distinguish between modernism and postmodernism, referring to what he sees as the epistemological bias of the former, and the ontological bias of the latter.[4]

According to McHale, modernism's primary thrust is to question: to seek answers, definitions, and boundaries. Life or reality is seen as a process of becoming, and the individual is seen as responsible for creating his or her own conditions and circumstances. In postmodernism, on the other hand, reality is accepted with its limits perceived as preexistent and imposed from without. Another way of saying this is that the nature of modernism is dialectical, while that of postmodernism is dialogic. Similarly, the predisposition of modernism is psychological; that of postmodernism, existential. Whether we see this dichotomy as distinguishing modernism from postmodernism, or one school of modernism from another, it points to the main difference between canonical Western modernism as defined by Bradbury and McFarlane and its Arabic counterpart. The modernist Arabic novel has never developed a "psychological" viewpoint to the degree that we find in its Western counterpart. Virtually from its inception, it was politicized, and represented a viewpoint closer to the "postmodern" view of man as a socially determined entity. This is understandable in an area of the world where national identity has been shaped to a large degree by its reaction to Western influence and, indeed, domination.

In order to put the experimental Arabic novel into greater perspective, however, it is first of all necessary to note that it is essentially an adopted form. Unlike in the West, where it was the natural outgrowth of a culture that developed over a four-hundred-year period, the novel has never been the preeminent literary form in the Arab world. This distinction belongs to poetry, and perhaps secondarily to the short story. Furthermore, the novel has generally been viewed as a literary form somewhat akin to rhetoric. As such, it has long remained primarily a vehicle for the expression of ideas and ideological viewpoints. The first novels in Arabic appeared only in the second decade of the twentieth century.

From this point on, however, the Arabic novel has followed a pattern of development that has echoed or paralleled the development of the Western novel, moving roughly from romanticism to realism to modernist experimentalism, albeit within a historically different time frame and at a highly accelerated rate. Of course, just as in the West, different literary styles coexist with one another today and (even more than in the West) vary from country to country, according to prevailing social, cultural, and political conditions. So that today in Syria, the realist novel is still the preeminent form, while in nearby Lebanon novelists are increasingly writing in a style more heavily influenced by current global literary trends.

We also have to keep in mind that the Arabic novel is a genre that is highly restricted in terms of its audience. Moreover, the experimental novel is an even more specialized type of literature reflecting for the most part the interests and concerns of the upper intellectual strata of society. Roger Allen has noted that the novels published in the Arab world within the last three decades "share with those of other world traditions an intense preoccupation with the concerns of intellectuals in society."[5] He adds that, in the case of the more cosmopolitan Arab novelists, "the demands on the Arab reader reflect . . . the experience and erudition of the writer."[6] While modernist experimentalism in the West also represented the artistic movement of an avant-garde with a limited audience that put it in the category of "highbrow art,"[7] the gap between Arab novelists and the reading public has been more stubbornly enduring, and may even be widening.

In the face of this situation, Arab writers have tended to cling to a patriarchal conception of their role in society. Pierre Cachia's characterization of the early Arab modernists has not lost its relevancy today:

> For all its democratic zeal, the generation of modernists that flourished between the wars never assumed it had to be guided by the will of the people, only by what it was convinced was the common good. . . . The new elite was . . . dedicated to the spread of enlightenment to the masses and convinced that when this was done the masses would inevitably be one with it. Its attitude was one of collective paternalism. . . . Most Arab writers look upon themselves as nothing less than cultural and social guides for their contemporaries. . . .[8]

The paternalistic attitude of Arab writers is also a result of an alienation that is somewhat different from that experienced by Western writers.

In the West, alienation has been characterized by the individual's feeling of anonymity within society, the urge to escape, and to justify this escape. It is, in a sense, the destiny of the individual, something that is accepted and even embraced. Alienation in the Arab world, however, is commonly felt to have been forced on the individual against his or her will, and the instinct is to combat it, to find a cure for it, rather than to escape by fleeing, dropping out, or turning inward. Thus, alienation in the contemporary Arab could be said to be less a matter of the alienation of the individual from society, than of the alienation of society from the individual. For the most part, writers in the Arab world have never felt themselves to be bohemians, social rebels, or misfits, as has been the case in the West. The Arab writer's alienation has stemmed from his or her inability to find harmony within the society due to the weakness and failure of society's institutions.

Although alienation in the Arab world has been tempered by social commitment, the type of alienation that Arab writers have suffered has paradoxically been far more severe than that experienced by writers in the West. Arab writers have been alienated fundamentally from political processes and institutions. They have been censored, exiled, and their books have been banned. In discussing the general topic of writers' freedom in the Arab world, Roger Allen has noted that those "who cross the line of officially established acceptability may suffer still worse fates: life imprisonment and even death, sometimes announced, sometimes not."[9] This has created a further rift between the artist and the reading public. Allen notes that "Faced with such situations . . . it has been the lot or choice of many modern Arab writers to leave their natural and most immediately accessible publics and go into exile." He quotes Jabra Ibrahim Jabra, who was himself an exiled Palestinian novelist, on this subject: "If alienation is both obvious and painful when one is absent from the homeland, then it is even more so when one is physically still here."[10]

A specific gap that exists between Arab writers and their public is that the spirit of irony, paradox, criticism, and particularly self-criticism within the society as a whole is still severely restricted. In a culture in which the privileges of ironic distance are not available, there is a significant hindrance to the development of more complex forms of the novel. This is a problem endemic to Third World literature in general, where one finds many of the most sophisticated and cosmopolitan writers producing largely for a readership outside their homeland. Such was the case with Salman Rushdie, whose *The Satanic Verses*[11] caused such outrage in the Islamic community because it was meant to be primarily understood by Westerners. "Sadly," as Edward Said has noted, "that the novel dealt with Islam in English and for what was believed to be a largely Western audience was [for the Islamic community] its main offence."[12]

Experimental Arab writers have thus suffered from two immense strains in their literary practice—the weight of Western influence and literary precedent, on the one hand, and the traditionalism and political coercion existent in their own society, on the other. Working within the constraint of social preoccupations, they have focused their experimental efforts on the attempt to break down certain specific conventions of realism, particularly the construction of narrative to fit an ideological viewpoint. They have reacted to the formal unity, ideological bias, omniscient viewpoint, and heroism of realist narratives and countered these with narratives that are fragmented, artistically determined, multiple-voiced, and that reflect a sense of cultural crisis, while still working from a standpoint that reflects the values and priorities of the *engagé*. In her article "Opaque and Transparent Discourse in Sonallah Ibrahim's Works," Ceza Qasim Draz offers a definition of avant-garde art that reflects this interconnection between art and social engagement:

> Firstly, it negates the traditional forms . . . and secondly, by negating the traditional forms, it defamiliarizes reality and evokes in the reader a different feeling, an experience that is quite unprecedented. . . . The rejection of traditional forms implies the rejection of the society that produced these forms, and the aim of this rejection is to awaken the reader to a new reality or, at least, to the necessity for a new reality. Avant-garde literature . . . is . . . deeply rooted in the social reality, a literature which is *engagée*.[13]

Similarly, Shakir al-Nabulsi (Shākir al-Nābulsī) expresses a modernist viewpoint regarding the primary importance of a personal perspective in literature, yet he is unable to express this without linking it to its social orientation:

> Personal experience is the most important subject of the modern novel. And personal experience, as Henry James says, cannot be transmitted

> directly or superficially, but must be converted to an artistic viewpoint.[14]
>
> And herein is concealed the quality and genius of the artist, by whose means direct, personal impressions are translated and transformed into a form that transcends the individual and personal.[15]

To understand the relationship between the modernist Arabic novel and its Western counterpart, it is of great aid to focus on the influence of existentialist writers on the modern Arabic novel beginning in the 1950s, and continuing through the 1960s. In the West, existentialism can be said to represent the point of balance between the Western and Central European modernist traditions. It also could be said to represent the last gasp of modernism, or the point of transition between modernism and postmodernism, since it presents the introverted modernist sensibility in a state of suspension, caught at the point of being overwhelmed by the power of external determinants. In the Arab world, however, exposure to existentialist literature played a very different role in facilitating the transition from realism to modernism. This underscores the fact that the experimental Arabic novel of the 1960s represented a strain of modernism that emerged in a very different world from the canonical Western modernism of the turn of the century, sixty years before. It was a world that had been profoundly changed by, among other things, modernism itself. This gives an indication of the extent to which the experimental Arabic novel represents a unique form of modernism, distinct from its Western counterpart.

Equally important as distinguishing between the experimental Arabic novel and the modernist novel in the West, however, is to distinguish it from the Arabic novel that preceded it. Students, scholars, and critics of Arabic literature will rightly point out that, as a non-native literary form, the Arabic novel has always been experimental. We can, however, note a distinct change in the approach to the Arabic novel beginning in the 1960s (most strikingly in such works as Naguib Mahfouz's *Miramar (Mīrāmār),* Ghassan Kanafani's *All That's Left to* You *(Mā Tabaqqā Lakum),* or Jabra Ibrahim Jabra's *The Ship (Al-Safinah).* That a watershed similar to that described by Bradbury with respect to the British novel occurred in the Arabic novel in the 1960s is attested to by the following observation of Walid Hamarneh:

> The Arabic novel until the 1960s was dominated by the "realistic" tradition that produced its best results in the works of Najib Mahfuz [Naguib Mahfouz]. Novels were mostly narrated through either the editorial omniscient third person narrator or the first person as protagonist. . . . The 1960s witnessed the proliferation of a new experimental phase in Arabic fiction that was manifest in the works of both the younger and older generation of writers.[16]

Hamarneh, then, recognizes the 1960s as a turning point in the Arabic novel, and as the beginning of a new type of experimentalism. The formal experimentation in these works was concerned mainly with a change in the modes of narration. While this ultimately involved many different techniques, the earliest and most common type of experimentation was with the "democratization" of narration, or polyphony. The change is a significant one because, as Hamarneh notes, this experimentation challenged the rhetorical tradition of the Arabic language itself in a way that the realist novel that preceded it had not. Language itself, and the way of thinking that it represented, became the subject and focus of the experimental Arab novelists. Their work can thus be differentiated from that of their predecessors by the greater degree of self-consciousness with which they have approached the problem of adapting the Arabic language to the novel form.

At the same time, Hamarneh explores the broader implications of this change:

> The writing of the history of the Arabic novel was dominated by a conception of the genre . . . that . . . was grasped as the culmination of a process of development that began with importing and imitation and moved on to domestication and maturity. . . . It looked at the novel as a genre characterized mostly by the conventions of the mainstream realistic novel in Europe. . . . This is not the appropriate place to criticize the histories of the Arabic novel. . . . What is important is that such histories grasped the novel as a genre with a single unitary tradition that was originally imported from the West. The attempts to go beyond Mahfuzian [Mahfouzian] realism since the late 1960s have been characterized by an attempt to surmount the generic conventions associated with the genre, much more than its realism.[17]

Hamarneh's observation regarding the view of literary historians is suggestive of the attitude of writers themselves. The more fundamental change that occurred in the Arabic novel in the 1960s had less to do with a shift in style than it did with the very self-image of writers and their conception of their work. Beginning in the '60s, Arab novelists ceased to think of themselves as importers, imitators, and domesticators of a Western genre of writing. Rather, they began to view themselves as experimentalists in their own right, striking out on their own, cultivating their own varieties of narrative, and adapting the novel for their own purposes. Hamarneh makes the important point that the realist Arabic novel had made use of an imported genre while still maintaining a rhetorical tradition embedded in the native Arabic culture. With the change in narrative mode that he describes, the emphasis is shifted to an attempt to use the same genre to undermine this rhetorical tradition.

This paradoxical attempt to become more independent of Western influence and simultaneously carry out a revolution against Arabic literary convention represents the expression, in Arab terms, of modernism's ambivalence toward modernity. The issue of modernity in the Arab world had always been seen as inextricably bound with that of its relationship to the West, as synonymous with Westernization, but this ambivalence was a new development that set the experimental Arabic novel of the 1960s apart from its predecessors. Literary critics have been slow to recognize this change because "modernism" in the Arab world has generally been viewed as concerned exclusively with the pursuit of modernity. To speak of "modernism" *(ḥadāthah)* that is somehow inconsistent with or antagonistic to "modernity" *(taḥdīth)* has not really been a part of Arab literary discourse. It has thus been axiomatic in the Arab literary criticism that all modern literature is modernist in the broad meaning of term. Thus, Pierre Cachia could write as recently as 1990:

> The programme which Arab intellectuals have been proclaiming for about a hundred years is modernity, broadly understood as the realization of the values of Western civilization.[18]

This also points up another contrast between modernism in the Arab world and the West. The ambivalence toward modernity was always implicit in Western modernism, since modernity in the West had been a thing already achieved. Western modernism was thus from its inception concerned with exposing the internal deficiencies of a preexisting modernity. In the Arab world, however, modernism had to develop this ambivalence even as it was evolving toward modernity. Elias Khoury represents this changed view of modernism when he states:

> Modernism only emerges in contemporary Arab culture in a form native to it. It has not been a copy of Western modernism, but rather an Arab attempt to integrate modernity into a cultural structure with its own particular historical characteristics.[19]

For Arab novelists, this significantly more complex task has implied a much more self-conscious, analytical approach to writing, comparable to that initiated by the canonical Western modernists of the early part of this century. At the same time, the issues involved in changing approaches to literature reflect those faced by society at large, and these issues of language, aesthetic form, social class, and gender are of even greater magnitude in the Arab world today than they were in the West sixty years ago. The issue of which Arab novelists are most aware is that of language. According to the contemporary Lebanese novelist, Rashid al-Da'if (Rashīd al-Ḍa'īf),

> The main problem of the Arabic novel has been the fashioning of a "historical language." Until the advent of the novel, the Arabic language had been ahistorical, unchanging, depending largely on the tradition of rhetorical style *(balāghah)*.[20]

Elias Khoury similarly explains the whole problem of the Arab quest for a new self-image in terms of the gap between the *langue* and *parole* in Arabic. He has emphasized that the essential problem is not one of being merely progressive, creative, or experimental in style, but of fashioning a language of artistic expression in order to "recreate present reality."[21] One of the main obstacles to this is the problem of "diglossia," the gap that exists between the literary and spoken forms of the language, a disparity that is far greater in Arabic than it is in European languages. Experimentation with the colloquial in narrative was a fundamental characteristic of the work of Western modernist writers such as William Faulkner, James Joyce, and Gertrude Stein. Yet, apart from its use in dialogue, the Arabic novel so far has not significantly experimented with this form of the language in narrative, nor is it likely to do so. The literary language *(fuṣḥah)* is simply too well entrenched as distinct from the colloquial for this to occur. Thus, while the modern Arabic novel seems from the Western point of view to be implicitly socially engaged, hence progressive, because it possesses a collective sense, a desire to speak for the whole that is lacking in Western literature, from a linguistic standpoint this is far less true.

The Arabic novel also has not exhibited many of the social themes central to Western modernism. Western modernism has always been connected with the rise, dominance, and decline of the bourgeoisie and the intelligentsia. One of its primary literary themes has been the movement from one class to another and the difficulties of adjustment to a change of status, as well as to modernity itself. These conditions have prevailed to a considerably lesser degree in the case of the Arab word, where the rise of a bourgeois class has been a recent phenomenon. The movement between classes has also been less fluid than in the West. As a result, Arabic novels have tended to focus more on social conditions experienced *within* a particular class—whether bourgeois, peasant, or urban—and the relationships among members of the various classes, than on the movement of individuals from one class to another. Within this framework, Arabic experimentalism has focused on exploring ways of reconciling its deeply embedded cultural heritage *(turāth)* with modernity, as well as on a quest for a renewed cultural and historical self-image. Elias Khoury has expressed this by defining modernism as "an attempt to search for future legitimacy, after the past has lost its legitimacy."[22]

The attempt to reconcile tradition and modernity also has had an impact on the formalism of the experimental Arabic novel. In his book *Forms of Disruption*,[23] Neil Donahue discusses abstraction in German modernist prose as connected with abstraction in art. A visible disparity exists between Arabic and Western literary modernism in this case, for while there is clearly a tendency toward narrative abstraction in the work of experimental Arab novelists, in the Islamic world art has been essentially abstract from the beginning. The iconoclasm of Arab culture, deriving from the prohibition against depicting the human form and features, according to Islamic tradition, presents a powerful contrast to the iconographic tendencies of Europe. Thus, whatever abstract tendencies there are in experimental Arabic prose would tend to refer back to, rather than rebel against, the inherited culture, and might even represent a strain of cultural conservatism. While experimental Arab novelists may have thus felt free to experiment with techniques of narrative fragmentation, this may not necessarily be read as reflective of progressive thinking in other respects.

An example of this gap between formal innovation and ideology can be seen with respect to the expression of male Arab writers regarding gender issues and sexuality. In her book *Rich and Strange: Gender, History, Modernism*, Marianne DeKoven sees the formal experimentation of Western modernist texts as an expression of "profound ambivalence concerning the radical changes in society and culture promised by the 'revolutionary horizon' [of] feminism." These changes, she adds, were "overtly desired" by women and "overtly feared" by men.[24] DeKoven finds in modernist form a paradigm that challenges the masculine self-representation that was predominant in Western culture. In the case of contemporary Arabic literature, however, we find that male and female novelists are stylistically far more polarized than is true within the tradition of Western canonical modernism. Formal experimentation is the particular obsession of male writers in the Arab world, and this experimentalism is used more as a way of avoiding issues of gender and sexuality than as a vehicle for expression on these topics.

In summary, we can say that the experimental Arabic novel can be both distinguished from its predecessors and allied with Western modernism by virtue of its self-conscious revolt against Arabic narrative tradition and its ambivalence to modernity. Stylistically, experimental Arab novelists absorbed the fragmentary narrative techniques of Western canonical modernism and applied these for the similar purpose of challenging an embedded rhetorical tradition of realism. Just as significant, however, are the ways in which the experimental Arabic novel has had to grapple with both the weight of Western literary precedent and the highly resistant forces of tradition in Arab culture. This has produced a genuine literary distinctiveness while at the same time has left much room for potential expansion within the broad framework of modernist literary development. In subsequent chapters, we will explore this development from the 1960s to the present day, and in the conclusion, we will specifically address the question of the relationship of the contemporary Arabic novel to both modernism and postmodernism.

Chapter 1

Modernist Ambivalence and the Beginnings of Narrative Experimentation

"Have you ever read the novel *The Plague*?" I asked her. I felt that much depended upon the answer she gave.

—Sonallah Ibrahim, "The Smell of It"

The difficulty of making one's way through a world which is jumbled in this fashion is one that is freely acknowledged. However, it is clearly unavoidable if the novel is to tell its story, as I fully intended that it should, in a single burst.

—Ghassan Kanafani, "All That's Left to You"

EXISTENTIALISM AND THE FRAGMENTATION OF NARRATIVE VOICE

We can trace the origin of the experimental Arabic novel directly to the social ferment in Egypt and the Levant during the '60s. In Egypt, writers were confronting the effects of the 1952 revolution, while writers in the Levant were reacting largely to the occupation of Palestine. At the same time, since literature itself participates in creating the cultural conditions for its continued development, we must also consider the influence of the reigning literary trends of the time. In the Arab world at this time, social realism was the dominant novelistic form, while in the West, the most important experimental literary trends were French existentialism and the "theater of the absurd."

The importance of French literary influence in presiding over the "birth" of the experimental Arabic novel cannot be underestimated, especially in the context of the comparative study of Arab and Western modernism. Existentialism, in particular, not only lent to the experimental Arabic novel an orientation that differed from that of the Western modernist novel, but this difference in orientation has persisted to this day. In the West, literary existentialism came at the tail end of the period of high modernism. It represented the confluence of modernist sensibility and political engagement, and served as a bridge between modernism and postmodernism. In the Arab world, existentialism appeared at the end of a period of social realism, and served as the foundation for the transition from realism to modernism.

In his *Form and Technique in the Egyptian Novel, 1912–1971* (1983), Ali B. Jad notes that the disenchantment with the Egyptian revolution "resulted in a shifting of emphasis to universal issues and the so-called 'human situation' as opposed to local sociopolitical subject matter." This coincided with "the growth of a process of popularization of the ideas and works of people like Sartre and Camus and the rise of the theatre of the absurd in Beirut and then in Cairo, in the late 1950s and early 1960s."[1] The influence of the French existentialist writers on the Arabic novel was far greater than that of the modernists who had preceded them. Jad writes that the French novel and theatre of the absurd (Sartre, Camus, and Ionesco) exercised "a degree of influence which (in Egypt, but not in Lebanon) was much out of proportion with familiarity with French language and literature in general."[2]

By the early '60s, the Nasserist revolution had already produced a disillusioned sense that the dreams and expectations that it had engendered would not be fulfilled. *The Smell of It* (1971; *Tilka al-Rā'iḥah*, 1966), written by Sonallah Ibrahim (Ṣun' Allāh Ibrāhīm) in 1964 but published only in partial form two years later, reflects the dual preoccupations of the avant-garde novel of the time. It realistically depicts political repression and surveillance, while at the same conveying a feeling of existentialist ennui. As Roger Allen notes in *The Arabic Novel: An Historical and Critical Introduction* (1995), *The Smell of It* is a portrait of the effect that political "imprisonment has not only on the imprisoned person, but on everyone around him. All motivation vanishes, and minutiae assume an extreme importance; the entire day seems taken up with mere survival."[3]

To express what Allen calls this "atmosphere of oppressive surveillance and hopelessness,"[4] Ibrahim employs a prose that is deliberately simple and free from causal connectives:

> I went up to my room. I put the key in the lock. . . . I entered and undressed, putting my trousers on the clothes hanger and hanging them up on the wall. I had a bath. Then I returned and sat down in front of the desk. I turned on the transistor radio. I saw the roll of cloth in front of me and opened it up. I found it to be a length for a pair of pajamas not a suit. I lit a cigarette. My sister came along and asked how much of the fifty piastres was left. I calculated the fares, but didn't have the courage to mention the ten piastres for the taxi. Her fiancé came and said he'd stood for two hours in front of the Co-operative to buy meat.
>
> "The situation is quite unbearable," he said. (26)

The style is remarkably similar to that of Camus's *The Stranger (L'Étranger)*.[5] Ibrahim recounts the most mundane actions—putting a key in a lock, putting his trousers and clothes on a hanger, sitting in front of a desk, turning on a radio, lighting a cigarette. At the same time, however, he puts these actions on par with more complex events, such as the statement by his sister's fiancé that he had stood for two hours in front of the Co-operative to buy meat. There is a distinct effect of enlargement and compression of time that is achieved by this means within each paragraph. Moreover, within his paragraphs Ibrahim follows a similar pattern of beginning with the most mundane, even banal actions, and leading to a more complex conclusion:

> Suddenly the bell rang. I took up the book and dawdled about a bit, lit a cigarette, and took the packet along with me. Again the bell rang. I hurried to the door and opened it to the policeman to whom I gave the book, while I extracted the packet of cigarettes and gave him one. He left.
>
> I returned to the room and threw the book on to the desk. I looked out of the window and found that the other window had grown dark. I lay down on the bed, smoking till I had finished the cigarette, when I threw it out of the window and went to sleep.
>
> In the morning I went out and bought a newspaper, a small bottle of milk, and some bread. I returned, boiled the milk, put some sugar in it, then dipped the bread in the milk. I read the paper. Then I went out again. I took the Metro. It came to a stop before the First Aid station and all the passengers got off. I found that there was a carriage turned over on its side near the rails and that its black entrails protruded. I walked to the café in which Magdi used to sit. He was sitting in a corner by himself.
>
> "We must affirm our existence," he said. (27–28)

The passage begins with the appearance of a police officer who monitors the former prisoner. This type of surveillance is described in an offhand, almost casual, manner, yet is repeated throughout the text, so that the ennui becomes insidious, as if the narrator has not escaped the prison at all. In the rest of the passage, we can once again see how Ibrahim begins with a recitation of very simple actions—he buys some milk and bread, returns to his apartment, boils the milk, puts sugar in it, dips the bread in the milk, reads the paper, and so forth. Near the end of the paragraph, however, he describes the sight of a carriage turned over on its side from which "its black entrails protruded." This type of narrative is deceptive in a way typical of existentialist literature. By focusing on the small, mundane aspects of existence, it appears to represent an attempt on the part of the narrator to objectify himself. Yet behind this veneer of objectification is outrage and disgust, ironically emphasized by the detached quality of the narration:

> "Let's go to the cinema," said my sister, and off we went. It was a film about birds that grew in number and size until they became savage, chasing people and attacking children. I was conscious of having a bad headache. . . .
>
> Morning came and I got up, washed, dressed, and went out. I had a sandwich and bought all the morning papers, then I took a Metro-train. I watched the carriage doors as they closed. I stood alongside the apartment reserved for women and began scrutinizing them one by one. They had elaborate hair-dos and their faces were heavily made up. I got down at the First Aid stop. A man was lying on the pavement beside the wall covered over with blood-spattered newspapers, while on the tram-stop platform in the middle of the street a number of women in their black *milayas* had gathered, gesturing towards the man and wailing. (6)

In these passages, suggestions of violence—Alfred Hitchcock's *The Birds*, the man lying covered with blood-spattered newspapers—are reported by the narrator in a deadpan, on an equal emotional pitch with the most mundane events. Allen refers to this as a "contrast between the sheer ordinariness of so many incidents in the novel and the . . . psychological tensions pent up inside its narrator."[6] At the same time, the narrator displays curiosity that is aroused by the commonplace (the women with elaborate hair-dos and made-up faces). The reader's awareness is shaken by this intermingling of fear and apathy, curiosity and ennui, suspense and monotony, which gives the text as a whole the power to instill in the reader a feeling of heightened sensibility.

Sexuality is also treated on a level of equality with everyday experience. The narrator mingles his fantasies, and even his sexual activity, with the mundane:

> I closed my eyes. I imagined yesterday's girl with her white body lying before me on the bed, full and rounded, her hair fresh and fragrant, while I kissed every part of her, passing my cheek along her thigh and resting it against her breast. I put my hand down to my thigh and began playing with myself. At last I gave a deep sigh. Tired, I sprawled back in my chair, staring vacantly at the paper in front of me. After a while I got up and gingerly stepped over the traces left by me on the floor under the table. I went to the bathroom. I washed my socks and shirt and hung them up at the window. (32)

Not surprisingly, Jad writes of Ibrahim's work that its "resemblances of attitude and idiom . . . recall Camus' *L'Étranger*." He notes that Sonallah Ibrahim was interested in the theme of revolt in modern fiction, and wrote a somewhat detailed essay on its emergence and development in American novels in the 1950s and 1960s. This was at a time when Camus's work had been introduced to Arab readers in abundance and had also been popularized in Arab literary journals. Jad sees a close similarity between Sonallah Ibrahim's work and that of Camus:

> [It is] reticent, both social and metaphysical, and induced specifically by a tragic sense of apparently meaningless human existence. As such (the tragic tone apart, since there is no place for tragedy in Camus' utterly indifferent universe), it is an essentially existentialist revolt rather than a defiant, usually violent, revolt against the social "system."[7]

The Smell of It also possesses other broad modernist characteristics. The narrator is engaged in writing, and his narrative often touches on his writerly preoccupation:

> I tidied up the desk and wiped away the dust that had gathered on it. I seized hold of the pen but was unable to write. I took up one of the magazines. There was an article about literature and the sort of things

> that one should write about. The writer said that Maupassant said the artist must create a world that is simpler, more beautiful than ours. He said that literature should be optimistic, throbbing with the most beautiful of sensations.
>
> I got to my feet and went to the window and looked out at yesterday's window. However, it was closed. Again I sat myself at the desk. I seized hold of the pen but was unable to write. (17)

Ibrahim's concern with narrative subjectivity seems to conflict with the "objectified" effect that the text also conveys. He alternates between a primary narrative voice, of which the previous quotes were examples, and a narrative voice printed in italics, which conveys a sense of heightened subjectivity. The narration printed in normal type seems to represent the words that the narrator is committing to paper, while the narration in italics represents the thoughts, memories, and fantasies that crop up in between:

> Beside her I spotted a little girl. My heart missed a beat when she turned her whole face in my direction. I saw her dark brown complex ion. Her face was without kohl or make-up. Suddenly I found myself looking right into her eyes. They were wide and limpid. For an instant I was lost.
>
> *Her eyes were two stars in silent space. I was swimming in space, lost. It was night-time when our eyes met. Her two eyes gleamed in the light. I saw my image in their vast whiteness and I saw it in their deep blackness.* (35–36)

Memory, as well as fantasizing, plays a significant part in the narrative, and reflects a nostalgia that at times contradicts the very "detached" narrative of earlier passages:

> *We would come by tram. We'd take it from the Square before it turned off into Zahir Street. I used to love this quiet street because it was full of trees whose dense branches used to meet high across the middle of it, shutting out the light. I used to love the sound of the trolley-arm thrusting its way with difficulty between the branches overhead.* (51)

Punctuating this narrative are the regular visits of a policeman who functions as a parole officer. Repeatedly, there is a knock on the door, the narrator opens it, hands the officer a book, the policeman signs it and leaves. This occurs with the same lack of drama as all the other events in the narrative:

> I opened the peep window of the door and found the policeman in front of me. I opened the door to him. I took the book from my pocket and handed it to him. He signed and left. (48)

The regularity with which these visits are recorded in the narrative, however, acts as a frame for the narrative itself. They are like horizontal prison bars set at regular intervals, circumscribing the entire text, as well as the narrator's existence.

Given the constrained existence of Egyptian writers at this time, it is not surprising that they began to experiment with circumscribing narrative itself. This change in literary technique is embodied in the later work of Naguib Mahfouz (Najīb Maḥfūẓ) as in that of no other Arab novelist. While Mahfouz is best-known for his trilogy, which marks the apogee of the realist novel in the Arab world, Mona Mikhail refers to Mahfouz's pioneering efforts at modernist narrative technique in *Children of Gebelawi* (1981; *Awlād Ḥāratinā*, 1959).[8] In this work, she explains, Mahfouz is "clearly more interested in ideas and concepts rather than in depicting faithfully life in the city. . . . Symbolism becomes more pronounced in his writings." Mikhail notes that the seeds of this new style had already been sown in his novel *The Beginning and the End* (1985; *Bidāyah wa Nihāyah*, 1949),[9] whose "stream of consciousness and cinematic techniques successfully explored the psyche of his tormented heroes."[10]

These experimental tendencies came together in a pioneering work entitled *Miramar* (1978; *Mīrāmār*, 1967).[11] Combining symbolism and stream-of-consciousness technique, this work is divided into five sections, representing the viewpoints of four different narrators. The narrative viewpoints are each constrained by limitations in knowledge, perception, and viewpoint that symbolically represent different strata of society. Set in Alexandria in a *pension* of the same name, *Miramar* involves seven main characters. Amer Wagdi, the primary narrator, is a retired journalist who comes to the *pension* to live out his retirement. The landlady, Mariana, is an old acquaintance of his. Tolba Marzouq is a former landowner, whose lands have been confiscated by the revolution. Zohra, a young woman who has escaped from her village after her relatives tried to marry her off to an old man, comes to work as a maid at the *pension*. Finally, there are three young men, Sarhan al-Beheiry, Hosny Allam, and Mansour Bahy who come to live at the *pension*, each one of whom becomes in some way involved with Zohra.

Miramar was clearly influenced by a translation of William Faulkner's *The Sound and the Fury*[12] published by the Palestinian writer Jabra Ibrahim Jabra (Jabrā Ibrāhīm Jabrā)[13] in 1963. This translation influenced a number of key Arab writers of the time, causing them to break with the traditional realist technique of omniscient narration and to substitute multiple narration, or polyphony. Like *The Sound and the Fury*, *Miramar* is a work that is concerned with social change and disillusionment. Its focus is a contrast between generations, with the younger generation depicted as comparatively rootless and devoid of values. The *pension* provides a microcosm of Egyptian society, just as Faulkner's Yoknapatawpha County did of the American South. The Lebanese scholar and literary critic Yumna al-Eid (Yumnā al-'Īd) notes that

> The world of *Miramar* is a network of relationships . . . confined within the spatial borders, the microcosm, of the Pension, and extending to the borders of the outer world, from which the patrons of the Pension come.[14]

Anjil Butrus Sam'an (Anjīl Buṭrus Sam'ān) makes the point that the novel is both realistic and symbolic, meant to represent the period after the 1952 revolution. Each character is meant to represent a different stratum of the society, with the character of Zohra, for instance, representing the rural poor.[15] Hosny Allam, from a landowning family and trying to start a business, is cynical, arrogant, and without charm. Sarhan al-Beheiry, from a family that benefited from the revolution, is an outgoing, opportunistic playboy. Mansour Bahy, a radio broadcaster, is ethical, introverted, and tormented. Caught between these personalities, Zohra must somehow fend for herself in a social milieu that affords her far less protection that the village from which she has run away. Primarily, she must fend off the advances first of Hosny Allam, then of Mahmoud, a newspaper vendor who proposes to her. Finally, she falls in love with Sarhan al Beheiry, who calculatingly seduces her and then drops her to pursue her tutor. Mansour Bahy, the only one of the young men not in love with Zohra, is so outraged by Sarhan's behavior that he vows to kill him. In the end, Sarhan is found dead, but by his own hand, not that of Mansour Bahy.

Amer Wagdi narrates the first and last sections, with each of the three intermediate sections narrated by one of the young men. This narrative division is the primary innovation of *Miramar*. Its kinship to Faulkner's *The Sound and the Fury* lies mainly in the fact that all of the narrators focus on the same series of events, each providing a different perspective. At the center of these events is a woman, Zohra, who, while she does not have a narrative voice of her own, is nevertheless the character around which the events revolve. Similarly, in *The Sound and the Fury*, Benji, Jason, and Quentin all are concerned with narrating roughly the same series of events, each has a very different perspective, and these events all revolve around Caddie.

Sabry Hafez (Ṣabrī Ḥāfiẓ)[16] claims to see even closer parallels between *Miramar* and *The Sound and the Fury*, not only between Zohra and Caddie, but also between Sarhan al-Beheiry and Jason, Mansour Bahy and Quentin, and Hosny Allam and Benji. The basis for such comparisons is very slender, however, and in any event far less essential than a comparison in terms of structure and technique. The interest in Hafez's analysis is that it is a comparative one, and that he recognizes the clear link between *The Sound and the Fury* and *Miramar*. Yumna al-Eid has less of a comparative orientation, but possesses a more sophisticated critical sense. When we combine their perspectives, we can recognize the debt that Mahfouz owes to Faulkner in the basic construction of the novel.

Amer Wagdi, for instance, is clearly the primary narrator. His narration is used as a framing device, both beginning and concluding the work. Eid sees Amer Wagdi as clearly representing the authorial viewpoint:

> *Miramar* is dominated . . . by the viewpoint of Amer Wagdi, who appears to play a role that distinguishes him from the other narrators in the novel. Amer Wagdi is the one who opens and closes the narrative. . . . He is the first one [to enter] the Pension. . . . He [represents] the authorial voice.[17]

Eid is suggesting that Mahfouz lets go of the most obvious manifestations of narrative control, yet still exercises an influence over the reader's viewpoint by making certain characters more sympathetic and allowing them to speak for him. In fact, there is a whole group of "favored" characters in the novel, with Amer Wagdi at their center. It is true that the reader tends to feel that Amer Wagdi, and the characters allied with him, have the favor of the author. These characters include Zohra, the landlady Mariana, and Mansour Bahy, who is a younger version of Amer Wagdi, but more flawed and troubled. A revealing point in the narrative occurs during Mansour Bahy's narration, when he makes clear that Zohra, Mariana, and Amer Wagdi are the people he prefers:

> I was very fatigued from traveling, so I stayed in the pension and joined the group around the radio. Luckily they were my favorites, Amer Wagdi, Madame, and Zohra. (101)

At the same time, Eid points out that although Amer Wagdi has both the first and last say, he is just one of four narrators, one of four points of view. She notes that Amer Wagdi does not appear to possess complete knowledge, but rather only a certain degree of it. Hosny Allam also has a certain degree of knowledge, but from a different viewpoint.[18] Moreover, Eid notes that Amer Wagdi's knowledge is restricted to what he has seen, and that in this sense he is at the same level as the other narrators. Amer Wagdi, for instance, does not know the reasons for the quarrel that occurred between Zohra and Sarhan al-Beheiry:

> He knows . . . nothing . . . beyond the boundaries of what he is able to see. . . . The narrator does not convey anything other than what he sees, the scene limited by his angle of spatial and temporal vision.[19]

If any of the narrators has a privileged position, in fact, it is Sarhan al-Beheiry. As in the case of Faulkner's *The Sound and the Fury*, the central events of *Miramar* are shrouded in ambiguity. Those events concern Sarhan's relationship with Zohra, just as in *The Sound and the Fury* they concern the past incestuous relationship between Caddie and Jason. Sarhan's viewpoint is the key to these events, and thus, as Yumna al-Eid points out, his is a more "interior" viewpoint than that of the other characters:

> Sarhan al-Beheiry [Sarḥān al-Buḥayrī] [represents] an interior viewpoint. . . . His knowledge is the knowledge of someone who understands the relationship between the parties [involved in] the event. Sarhan al-Beheiry knows more, then, about the quarrel than the others who only see one side of the situation. . . . None of the other narrators

> was able to enter Sarhan al-Beheiry's room in the Pension Miramar, and see or hear the intimate and secret things that occurred between him and Zohra [Zuhrah].[20]

Like *The Sound and the Fury*, *Miramar* is concerned with a change in generations. The characters are divided, as Sabry Hafez points out, between two groups of old and young—Amer Wagdi, Mariana, and Tolba Marzouq, on the one hand, Zohra and the three young men, on the other. At the same time, they are divided between those who are favored by the implicit authorial viewpoint and those who are not. Mansour Bahy is, in some ways, the young generation's equivalent of Amer Wagdi—a political radical, combining Amer's moral sensibility with an almost fatal instability. Mansour, more than any of the other young males in the novel, thus encapsulates Mahfouz's reservations and misgivings about the "younger" generation. In Sam'an's opinion, the main aspect of the book is its viewpoint toward the revolution. Amer Wagdi and Zohra are the only two who believe in the revolution. For Amer Wagdi it was a dream; for Zohra it is an experience for which she is striving.[21]

Another technique that Mahfouz uses is to insert pieces of internal monologue in the narration, which he indicates by means of italic print, in the same way that Faulkner does in *The Sound and the Fury*. A typical example is the following pair of sentences that occur near the end of Hosny Allam's narrative:

> I ought to clear my head, with a wild drive from one end of Alexandria to the other. *White clouds sail slowly above my head, almost within reach, drenched with colors; the air is light and sharp.* (86)

Such passages represent a deeper or more intensified level of consciousness or awareness. Via this technique we learn not only of Mansour Bahy's intention to kill Sarhan al-Beheiry, but that he has already killed him in his thoughts. Having been privy to these thoughts, we are not surprised that he confesses to having killed Sarhan al-Beheiry, even though the latter was already dead when he found him. Like *The Sound and the Fury*, *Miramar* is constructed somewhat like a mystery story. There is a central core of events about which our information is incomplete. Each narrator augments our information through the perspective from which they perceive the world, revealing their differing obsessions, motivations, and values. We also see the interior lives of the characters as only imperfectly mirrored in their actions. The world is presented as a stage on which people's lives intersect, with only a transitory and partial expression of their true feelings coming into the open.

The most important difference between Mahfouz and Faulkner is that Mahfouz utilizes multiple narration, or polyphony, for a more limited purpose. He is concerned with eroding the convention of omniscient narration mainly in order to give the reader a 360-degree view of events. He concentrates on conveying the limitations of each character's range of awareness in order to build a composite picture of those events. Sam'an refers to this as "selective awareness."[22] Each narrative voice is given more or less equal weight. Mahfouz does not attempt to deal with the validity of the different types of perception on the part of his different narrators. In Faulkner, on the other hand, the emphasis is as much on the quality and nature of the narrators' awareness as on how each one contributes to building a complete picture of events.

Thus, while Sam'an maintains that the disappearance of the traditional narrator in *Miramar* allows for the existence of several competing points of view,[23] Walid Hamarneh disputes this conclusion, insisting that

> One cannot maintain that the narrators in *Miramar* are liberated from a force which stands above them. What we have here are relativized narrators rather than democratic narration. We get different perspectives and voices. But these are still regulated by a force that maintains the checks and balances between the different narrators in order to provide a comprehensive picture of a reality that is representationable.[24]

In Palestine, the early and mid '60s represented a period of deepening political tensions that presaged the June War of 1967, mirrored most effectively in the work of Ghassan Kanafani (Ghassān Kanafānī). A spokesman for the Popular Front for the Liberation of Palestine, and the editor of its weekly, *Al-Hadaf*, his family fled Palestine in 1948, settling finally in Damascus. Later he moved to Kuwait, and then to Beirut. He was killed in the explosion of his booby-trapped car in 1972, thought to be the work of Israeli agents. As Hilary Kilpatrick states in her introduction to his most famous work, *Men in the Sun* (1978; *Rijāl fī al-Shams*, 1963),[25] Kanafani's work is remarkable, given his position as a lifelong Palestinian refugee and activist. Unlike most politically committed writers of the time, he did not resort to polemicism or to imposing an ideological scheme on his fiction except in a general sense. Instead, he reworked his overtly political themes to give them a profounder, universal meaning.[26]

Men in the Sun is a short and powerful allegorical novel. Three Palestinians, each representing different generations and areas of life, attempt the difficult journey across the desert from Iraq to Kuwait, in an attempt to escape from their past existence. The driver of a water truck picks them up and agrees to take them over the border inside the closed tank. The conditions inside the tanker as it travels under the blazing desert sun are life threatening, and the fate of the passengers depends critically on the time it will take them to cross the border. A delay at the Kuwaiti post caused by the officials' refusal to sign the driver's papers and their foul jesting causes fatal minutes to pass for the men in the oven-like tank. By the time the driver has crossed the border and is able to open it, his three passengers are dead. In the ignominious conclusion, he takes the corpses to the municipal dump and, after departing a moment, returns and removes their valuables.

The story of the disaster that befalls the three passengers represents the larger tragedy that has befallen the Palestinian people. In particular, it can be read as an exposé of the weakness of the Palestinians, depicting them as weak-willed and preferring the search for material security to the fight to regain their land. The driver, Abu Khaizuran, represents the ineffective Palestinian leadership that has ultimately betrayed its own people and led them along the road to disaster. A eunuch, whose name means "bamboo," he symbolizes an individual who seems impressive on the outside, but is weak and hollow within.

While the political message is important, the structure of the work, its narrative technique, and its degree of interiority mark it as highly innovative. The novel is divided into four parts, each of which is titled after, and focuses on, a different character in turn, and which is centered in that character's individual consciousness. For instance, the book begins with the narrative of the first passenger, Abu Qais, who has come the long way from Palestine to the Shatt al-Arab waterway in the southern part of Iraq, near the Kuwaiti border. The stream-of-consciousness element in the narrative emphasizes the existential quality of his situation:

> Abu Qais rested his chest on the damp ground, and the earth began to throb under him, with tired heartbeats, which trembled through the grains of sand and penetrated the cells of his body. Every time he threw himself down with his chest to the ground, he sensed that throbbing,

> as though the heart of the earth had been pushing its difficult way towards the light from the utmost depths of hell. . . .
>
> He turned himself over and lay on his back, cradling his head in his hands. He started to stare at the sky. It was blazing white, and there was one black bird circling high up, alone and aimless. He did not know why, but he was suddenly filled with a bitter feeling of being a stranger, and for a moment he thought he was on the point of weeping. No, yesterday it didn't rain. We are in August now. Have you forgotten? Those miles of road speeding through a void, like black eternity? Have you forgotten it? The bird was still circling round alone like a black spot in the blaze spread out above him. We are in August. Then why this dampness in the ground? It's the Shatt. Can't you see it stretching out beside you as far as the eye can see? (9–10)

It is its ending, however, that gives *Men in the Sun* an absurdist flavor that goes beyond mere tragedy. Kanafani's intent is to pose the existential question of whether or not one can have control over one's destiny with respect to the issue of national will, purpose, and destiny. The conclusion is open-ended. We do not know why the passengers choose to die rather than possibly be discovered and imprisoned. Abu Khaizuran's questioning, however, transcends issues of individual and collective guilt, bringing the novel to a close on a subjective note of despair and questioning:

> As he returned to the lorry and lifted one leg up, a sudden thought flashed into his mind. He stood rigid in his place, trying to do or say something. He thought of shouting, but immediately recognized what a stupid idea that was. He tried to finish climbing into the lorry, but didn't feel strong enough. He thought that his head would explode. . . . He turned to look back to where he had left the corpses, but he could see nothing, and that glance simply set the thought ablaze so that it began to burn in his mind. All at once he could no longer keep it within his head, and he dropped his hands to his sides and stared into the darkness with his eyes wide open.
>
> The thought slipped from his mind and ran on to his tongue: "Why didn't they knock on the sides of the tank?" He turned round once, but he was afraid he would fall, so he climbed into his seat and leant his head on the wheel.
>
> "Why didn't you knock on the sides of the tank? Why didn't you say anything? Why?" Why? Why? (56)

The nature of this ending is comparable to that in such short existentialist fiction as Sartre's "The Wall,"[27] or Camus's "The Guest."[28] In "The Wall," the narrator is a political prisoner who faces immediate execution. An interrogator enters his cell and questions him about the whereabouts of a partisan, warning him that he will be executed in fifteen minutes if he does not reveal the fugitive's location. The prisoner knows the whereabouts of the man, but refuses to divulge it—not out of heroism, loyalty, or patriotism, but out of pure stubbornness. He makes up a story intended to lead the them on a wild goose chase, just to watch them make a spectacle of themselves. After half an hour, they return, but do not shoot him. It turns out that the fugitive was in the very spot to which the prisoner had inadvertently led them. In "The Guest," the main character is a teacher who is charged with handing an escaped prisoner over to the authorities. Instead, he lets the prisoner go, only to see him walk toward the prison of his own volition.

In each of these works, the authors play with the fatalistic notion that man has limited control over his destiny. In Sartre's story, the prisoner exercises a curious, paradoxical, control over his fate at a point when he has relinquished all control in his mind. In the stories by Camus and Kanafani, there is a similar relinquishing of control, with ambiguous or disastrous consequences. The consequences themselves are less relevant than the way in which they fly in the face of expectation. Not surprisingly, Kilpatrick notes that "Kanafani was accused by enraged compatriots of 'throwing Palestinians on the garbage heap.'"[29]

While the most innovative aspect of *Men in the Sun* is the combination of an existential tone and a political theme, the novel also is experimental in formal terms. Although written in the third person, the narrative focus that Kanafani puts on each character in turn comes very close to a division of the text into different narrative voices. In this respect, Kanafani anticipates the polyphonic narrative technique that was to become a central feature of early experimentalism with the form of the Arabic novel.

Another major work of this period that also seems to have been heavily influenced by Jabra's translation of Faulkner's *The Sound and the Fury* is Kanafani's *All That's Left to You* (1990; *Mā Tabaqqā Lakum*, 1966).[30] Sabry Hafez refers to its "heavy indebtedness"[31] to the American work. The short novel concerns a brother and sister living in Gaza, who were separated from their mother in 1948. The mother now lives in

Jordan. The sister, Maryam, has lost her virginity, become pregnant, and been forced to marry the father, who is a married man with five children. To make her humiliation complete, her husband is a known coward and traitor, "a personification of betrayal of the Palestinian cause from within," according to Roger Allen.[32] Driven to despair by this situation, the brother, Hamid, sets out for Jordan in search of his mother.

All That's Left to You possesses a different type of structure than *Miramar* or *The Sound and the Fury*. The text is a dual one, narrated in turn by Maryam and Hamid. The period of time is that of Hamid's journey, yet during this period Maryam makes a simultaneous journey of an inner nature, following her brother's progress in her thoughts and imagination. In the climax, as Roger Allen remarks, "brother and sister are both face-to-face with the enemy, without and within." Hamid captures an Israeli border guard and realizes that he will have to kill him, while at the same time Maryam's husband, Zakaria, threatens her with divorce if she does not have an abortion, and starts to beat her. At this point, she stabs him to death "in a gesture," as Allen points out, "which is made to suffice for both situations."[33]

Thematically, *All That's Left to You* is linked with both *The Sound and the Fury* and *Miramar* by the centrality of the heroines, Maryam, Caddie, and Zohra, and particularly with the placement of the issue of a woman's honor at the core of each of these texts. A related theme that the two works have in common is the implicit focus on the feminine as a repository of values. There is an implied criticism here of the male viewpoint, although the interest and value attached to the feminine is done without investing in any female characters a direct narrative role.

In each of these three novels we find a triangle relationship at the center of the plot. This consists of the heroines (Caddie, Zohra, Maryam), the men who threaten their honor (Dalton Ames, Sarhan al-Beheiry, Zakaria), and the men who wish to defend that honor (Quentin, Mansour Bahi, Hamid). In each case, there is a symbolic connection between the woman's honor and larger social issues. The men who threaten the women's honor to a certain degree represent a substratum of corruption at the core of the society. Kanafani, however, does something additional with the motif. He creates a dual structure, in which the issue of honor is reflected in both national and personal terms.

Roger Allen notes that in *All That's Left to You*, Kanafani makes use of different typefaces to differentiate changes in the mode or person of narration. There is a certain similarity here to Mahfouz's use of italic type to set off interior monologue from the more formal narratives in the text, a technique also used by Faulkner. Kanafani alternates between standard and bold text not to convey a deeper level of consciousness or awareness, but merely to differentiate Maryam's narrative from Hamid's, since the two are interwoven. Kanafani's narrative is also stylistically complex, however, since he changes person at will, moving from third person to first and back again within a single narrative sequence.

In the original Arabic, two different typefaces are used. The first represents Maryam's narrative, the second (in bold type) Hamid's. In the English translation, a third, italicized typeface is used to represent Maryam's interior viewpoint, as she follows Hamid's progress through the desert via her imagination. The italicized narration in the English translation makes clear how these portions of Maryam's narrative function as a bridge between her own experience and Hamid's. Clearly, Kanafani's primary concern in structuring the narrative in this way was to use every means to heighten the parallel between Maryam's and Hamid's narrative. In thematic terms, Maryam and Hamid both confront an unknown enemy—Hamid confronts an Israeli who doesn't speak his language, and Maryam imagines a confrontation with Zakaria's first wife:

> It was then that I decided to see her, next morning, before I did anything else. I'd knock on her door, and say, "I'm his second wife." It didn't matter how she'd react; only that I just wanted to meet her and see what she was like, and then I'd know how to handle myself with both of them. It seemed pointless just to sit and wait. I'd be denying myself life if I allowed him simply to use me as an alleyway between his school and my house, planting his sperm in me before he left. (33)

> *They remained sitting in that vast, open space like two ghosts separated by a blade. They appeared unreal as they waited, with the icy wind of death circling around them, for the single moment of truth to come, an event that seemed as distant as their shoulders were close. Their coming together in that infinite expanse seemed partly an accident, partly an ineluctable decree of fate. They were so numbed by it that they had to sit down together to absorb it.* (34)

> **At last I asked him, "Where have you come from?"**
>
> **I nudged him with the point of the knife I held against his stomach, and asked him again.**

> **"Perhaps you only know Hebrew, but that doesn't matter. But really, isn't it amazing that we should meet so dramatically here in this emptiness, and then find that we can't communicate?"** (34–35)

These two "events," one imagined, the second both imagined (as narrated by Maryam) and "real" (as narrated by Hamid), are placed next to each other in the text in order to emphasize their kinship to one another. The italicized text not only links the two events thematically, but also serves as a bridge between reality and imagination.

There are other thematic parallels between the two narratives. Hamid feels possessive of his sister's virginity, and at the same time is obsessed by his family's dispossession from Jaffa. The blood bond between brother and sister is stronger than the bond created by marriage. Here, there is a direct parallel between Zakaria's position vis-à-vis Maryam and that of the Israelis vis-à-vis the Palestinians. Once again, Kanafani positions Maryam's and Hamid's narrative to bring out the parallel:

> "If only my mother was here, Zakaria, if only my mother was here. But there's no one, only you, and Hamid would kill me if he knew—and I think I'm pregnant." You smiled and . . . looked at my belly as though you could see the child twisting in my entrails, hidden illicitly, viewing the world with two small eyes. Later on . . . you said, "Your body's a fertile land, you little devil, a fertile land, I tell you!" (13)
>
> **A fertile land, sown with illusion and unknown prospects. . . . All the steel blades of the world could never hack down one root off your surface.** (14)

Supporting this dual thematic structure is another structure consisting of what Sabry Hafez refers to as two types of time: "natural time" and "subjective time."[34] The combination of these two types of time creates a dual movement in the text—toward Hamid's confrontation with the Israeli enemy on the one hand and Maryam's confrontation with her husband on the other. Kanafani's use of this technique, reflecting both a political preoccupation and a preoccupation with the individualized consciousness, makes a highly charged statement about Palestinian disenfranchisement while avoiding what Roger Allen calls "the magnified realism that marks or even disfigures the works of less artistic commentators on the Palestinian cause."[35]

Both Roger Allen and Sabry Hafez refer to the very significant key to the work that Kanafani provides in his introduction, in which he speaks of his intention to do more than create thematic parallels:

> The five characters in the novel, Hamid, Maryam, Zakaria, Time and the Desert, do not move along parallel or conflicting lines. In this work we find instead a series of disconnected lines which occasionally come together in such a way that they seem to be making just two strands and no more. This process of fusion also involves the elements of time and place, so that there appears to be no clear distinction between places and times that are far removed from each other, or indeed between places and times at a single moment.[36]

Here we can see that Kanafani is not as indebted to Faulkner for the overall structure of *All That's Left to You* as Mahfouz was in *Miramar*. Rather, as Hafez notes, Kanafani is more influenced by certain features and portions of Faulkner's text, most notably the use of symbolism in the "Quentin" section, which is dominated by the theme of time and images of water. Hafez sees Kanafani's use of the desert as equivalent to Faulkner's use of water as a symbol:

> The Quentin section . . . is the section that influenced Kanafani more than any other section of Faulkner's novel. . . . We find that the desert is Kanafani's formulation of the water symbolism in the Quentin section of Faulkner's novel. For Quentin—who waits by the water at the end of this section, water symbolizes innocence, purity, peace, and tranquility, or, more precisely, death. It also symbolizes danger, temptation, and mystery. . . . And in the Quentin section, the incessant sound of time has the function of a marker that gives events meaning and context. . . .[37]

Kanafani, Hafez states, uses the desert to symbolize the same things for which Faulkner uses water as a symbol: innocence, purity, peace, calm, and, at the same time, danger, mystery, and to some extent death. The motif of the desert is combined with that of time in Maryam's narrative, as described by Roger Allen:

> Throughout the long night of Hamid's traversal across the frontier, Maryam is unable to sleep. She feels inside herself the pulsating beat

> of his footsteps, a sound mingled with the ticking of the clock and the movements of the baby which she is carrying. Initially, Hamid is linked to her too by the ticking of his watch, but when he discards it, the sound is replaced by the pulsating of the earth beneath them.[38]

Maryam's narrative is filled with references to both the clock and to Hamid's footsteps, and the link between the two is another link between the real world and the world of Maryam's imagination:

> I'm counting his steps, one by one, with the subdued metallic strokes on the wall in front of me. It's like a death march. (8)

> "I can't sleep, I can't . . . his footsteps fill my head, they never stop."
> "Whose footsteps?"
> "His footsteps, Hamid's. Have you forgotten him?"
> "You're crazy. Are you listening to his footsteps?"
> "I can hear them, I tell you. They keep pace with every beat of the clock." (43)

The purposes for which Kanafani puts the technique of multiple narration to use are complex, involving not only the telling of separate events and the thematic juxtaposition of those events, but also the interconnection between different "levels" of reality. Yet this technique was subsequently abused by a host of writers who aped this modernist narrative formula without integrating it with their artistic purpose. This is at least to some extent the case in Jabra Ibrahim Jabra's *The Ship* (1985; *Al-Safinah*, 1969).[39] A Palestinian who lived for most of his career in exile in Baghdad, Jabra was less of a political activist than most of his literary contemporaries. He was Western-educated, married a woman from an aristocratic family, and lived in relative comfort throughout his life. Baghdad, at this time, was also removed from the center of the Palestinian political struggle.

Jabra's novelistic career was a long one, yet his novelistic preoccupations remained largely the same throughout his life. Faruq Wadi (Fārūq Wādī) sees the main theme in his writing as a concern with the problems of the "enlightened bourgeoisie":

> We can get a sense of the common thread between all these novels. . . . We are faced with an artist who was capable of sustained development, yet he remained bound to roots that he coveted . . .whose ideas

> developed from a specific intellectual and class orientation, and whose personality developed from this orientation—the orientation of an "enlightened bourgeois" with cultural aspirations. . . .[40]

Similarly, in discussing Jabra's novel *Al-Baḥth 'an Walīd Mas'ūd* (In search of Walid Mas'ud, 1978),[41] Mattityahu Peled notes that the love affairs it describes

> All follow a similar pattern: educated men and women, considering themselves free of old-fashioned prejudices, aspire to find happiness in life but settle for something less. . . . Unhappy and unsatisfied, they search for sexual satisfaction, depicted . . . as the paradigm of human passions. . . .[42]

It is thus not surprising that, although written in the wake of the 1967 War, Jabra's chief response in *The Ship* is an escapist one. Ahmad al-Zu'bi (Aḥmad al-Zu'bī) notes that

> The site of the ship is the meeting place of the characters in the novel, as well as the point of departure toward the unknown, toward nothingness. . . . It is a means of escape from a reality that the characters in the novel are no longer able to endure.[43]

Roger Allen notes in his introduction that, while the setting is a cruise at sea, the thematics of the novel are concerned with "the metaphysical yearnings of the major characters,"[44] which are toward the land. The characters discuss the situation of the Palestinians, in particular. Some of the characters are political activists. One of the two main characters, Wadi, has a fierce attachment for the land that has been lost, and is haunted by the death of a close friend at the hands of the Israelis, and his subsequent revenge.

One could, however, quarrel with this interpretation by asserting that political issues really provide only the background, the motivation for certain characters, as well as the subject of their dialogue or debates. It is important to keep in mind that, despite the preoccupation of the characters with issues of land, their journey is by sea, which is conveying them steadily farther and farther away from the realm of political conflict. Virginia Woolf's *The Voyage Out*[45] offers a model for cross-cultural comparison. Woolf's characters carry their cultural baggage with them into an "exotic" setting, yet this journey ultimately provides a pretext for self-investigation and dialogue unavailable to them in their native environment.

While Jabra was an ardent Palestinian nationalist, in *The Ship* he converts the problem of the dispossession of the Palestinians to a "universal" theme of exile, with the characters approaching their predicament somewhat like the ancient Hebrews on their way to Babylon. The two main characters, Wadi and Isam, differ in that the former's exile is voluntary, the latter's involuntary. One is attached to the land; the other is not:

> "Yes," I said, "I'm running away from it. I reject it. I reject the destructive, useless struggle for it."
>
> "It's strange, Isam," Wadi reflected. "No matter where I go, no matter what fancies possess me, I'm forever running toward my land, which has been separated from me by a thousand kilometers of barbed wire. I run toward it carrying a hand grenade. Yet you reject your land?"
>
> "I was delighted to sell most of it," I said. "I had no regrets." (75)

At this point, Wadi interrogates Isam about his motivations:

> Wadi drew close and stared at me with his deep-set eyes. "What exactly are you running away from?" he asked.
>
> "From Luma," I answered, without reflection. (75)

Wadi then argues that land is much more important than women:

> "Land, land, that's the secret in your life, with or without Luma. The land will drag you back to it no matter how much you resist, no matter how far you go. Luma is the soil, the trees, the water. She is the land, no matter how much you imagine otherwise." (76)

Isam replies:

> "Land interests you," I said, "because you were forced to leave it. . . . People who are deprived of women think about women all the time. You, on the other hand, are deprived of your land." (76)

This is Jabra's theme. There is no difference, for Jabra, between Wadi's loss of a homeland and Isam's sexual and emotional starvation. Throughout the novel, the world of women is connected with the theme of exile and dispossession. Women represent an escape, illusion, or forgetfulness—as does exile. The novel does not represent the viewpoint of an *engagé,* but rather that of an escapist who finds solace in pondering his escapism. The sea is a counterpoint to the theme of dispossession for the land, symbolic of the transient state:

> In the final analysis, you and I are nothing but small particles of dust floating within this great music, particles in the vast nebula of the universe.
>
> Everything is transitory, except these waves. (22)

In *The Ship*, Jabra experiments with narrative perspective in a way reminiscent, if not imitative, of Mahfouz's *Miramar*. Roger Allen notes in his introduction to the novel that "*The Ship* invokes the specters of Faulkner, Durrell, and Joyce on the technique of the multiple narrator."[46] In *The Ship*, there are ten chapters, five narrated by one character, four by another, and one by a third. As in *Miramar*, the action in *The Ship* takes place largely in a restricted area, which offers a microcosm of a portion of society. The main characters in the novel belong to the same fraternity of upper-middle-class intellectuals, socialites, nouveaux riches, and remnants of aristocratic families found in Jabra's other works. It is a more restricted microcosm than that of *Miramar*, a circle of people who, whether they hail from Baghdad or Beirut, all have connections with one another of some kind.

The plot of *The Ship* has a soap opera–like quality. Isam has boarded the cruise in an attempt to escape his love for a married woman named Luma. She, however, has found out about his intended departure, and booked passage on the same cruise with her husband, Falih. The husband, in the meantime, has brought his secret lover, Emilia, on board with him. The other main protagonist, Wadi, has similarly left his lover, Maha (a close friend of Emilia), behind in Beirut and come on board with another woman, Jacqueline. Essentially, no character is with the partner that they really wish to be with—each has been inveigled aboard by another, and all are connected with each other in some way, even if they're not aware of it.

Via this melodramatic plot, we find Jabra experimenting in an indirect way with form. Each character is responsible for another character's being aboard the cruise. A causal chain connects Isam, Luma, Falih, Emilia, Maha, Wadi, and Jacqueline. This experimentation with causality, however, is an example of a purely mechanical use to which the technique of multiple narration can be put. It allows Jabra to hide the various coincidences that bring the characters together, but contributes little else to the narrative.

While the purpose of the technique of multiple narration in the hands of Faulkner, Durrell, and even Mahfouz, is that the same events are seen and interpreted quite differently by the various participating characters, this is not really the case in Jabra's *The Ship*. The narrators make little use of their narrative positions to talk about themselves or express their points of view. Just the opposite—most of their narration focuses on the actions and speech of others. The bulk of the text's narrative is in the third person or quotes, and the change in narration only serves to shift the point of observation, not the perspective itself. Walid Hamarneh comments: "There are virtually no linguistic markers as to the differentiation among the different characters."[47]

Moreover, Jabra is more of an armchair philosopher than a storyteller. The text has a "shapeless" feel, a discursive quality that, in itself, might recommend it if used for different artistic aims. As it is, Hamarneh notes that Jabra

> Merely uses techniques that provide for more complex ways and means for representing consciousness, yet remains complicit with the traditional authoritarian mode of narration based on the possibility of omniscience. Moreover, the abundance of literary, artistic, and intellectual allusions and discussions have . . . contributed to the further monologization of the whole work.[48]

Thus, instead of a dialogue between distinct voices, we have merely an authorial voice in dialogue with itself. While Mahfouz's characters in *Miramar* are crisply drawn, distinct, Jabra's merge with one other. Wadi may be fixated on land, Isam on love, and Falih (Luma's husband and the eventual suicide) may be more pathological in his escapism, but they are all variations on the same type. The same is true of the female characters in the novel. Luma is more of a temptress, but all the women depicted in the text are cut from the same cloth. They share a sisterly bond, even as rivals, in the pursuit of men. Roger Allen notes that Jabra told him and his co-translator that he regarded their translation as the best version of the novel, precisely because they each took one of the two main characters and translated every section narrated by that character. In Jabra's words, they were able to achieve something that he felt he could not.[49]

THE DEFAMILIARIZATION OF NARRATIVE

The end of the '60s signaled a profound change in the Arab world and, by extension, in Arabic literature. Ceza Kassem Draz (Sīzā Qāsim) comments on the change in mood in the latter part of the decade, marked by the failure of the Nasserist revolution, culminating in the defeat of the Six-Day War in 1967 and Nasser's death in 1970. She notes that these events created "a deep feeling of frustration and triggered an era of suspicion, a suspicion not only of . . . traditional society, but also of the present society and its self-expression in language."[50] While novelists up until 1967 focused on the erosion of the omniscient voice of realism by means of polyphony, the years following witnessed the beginnings of experimentation the actual breaking up or fragmentation of the thread of narration itself.

An early example of this tendency is the novel *Anta Mundhu al-Yawm* (You as of today, 1968),[51] by the Jordanian poet Taysir Subul (Taysīr Subūl). In this work, the fragmented nature of the narrative form reflects the similar sense that the writer is trying to convey with respect to state of the family, political parties, and society as a whole in the Arab world at this time. The novel is made up of short narrative segments that switch from one situation to another, often alternating between first and third person, time frames, and dialogue and interior monologue. The reader is caught off balance, not really knowing where the text is leading. The placement of the various narrative fragments, however, is carefully done to accentuate the feeling that the author wishes to convey—the harsh, almost dictatorial oppression felt in almost every aspect of the society.

The first chapter opens with a brutal family scene in which the father of the main character, Arabi ('Arabī), kills a cat for taking a piece of meat that had been reserved for dinner:

> I saw him through the window, waiting by the kitchen door with a stick in his hand. He was looking north, the direction from which the white cat was coming with a measured gait, still smacking its mouth. I was afraid that it was going to enter the hall, and decided to leave. He

> saw me slipping away and motioned to me by putting his finger in front of his lips. With the other hand he ordered me to stay where I was. Something moved next to us, and I knew that the cat had entered and that the operation was going to begin. I didn't want to witness it. I heard him open the door. It crossed the room. There we were, the three of us, with no possibility of getting out. It searched the corner and gave a fearful meow. He followed it and hit it hard, aiming for its head, but hitting its back. It rolled its body into a ball a couple of times and took refuge by the window. I heard the sound of its claws scratching at the glass. Then it jumped. He swung and struck it on the head. Its blood swelled and spurted on the ground. It sagged against the window a second time and let out a loud meow, rubbing its claws against the glass and tensing its head to forestall another blow. I heard the sound of its breathing muffled by the flow of blood. It shivered violently and rubbed its cheekbone on the ground. Its nose twitched, full of blood. Then it went to sleep . . . its eyes still open. (7)

This is immediately followed by a brief passage that describes the family getting ready to eat at the sound of the signal to break the daily fast during Ramadan:

> In the courtyard, between two tall grapevines, they gathered in a circle, waiting for the cannon to sound. I watched the last shard of the sun's disk drop below the western horizon. Much of its red glow still remained. I saw the muezzin standing on a rock at the top of the mountain waiting for the hour for (the sun) to return to its bosom. And I watched my mother crossing the courtyard carrying a platter of rice, the steam wafting in her reddened face. I heard my mother calling me, "Come and eat, Arabi." Then I saw the muezzin cup his hands around his mouth and call: "*Allāhu Akbar, Allāhu Akbar*." The sound of the cannon exploded. (7–8)

The two passages appear to have little relation to one another, yet there are some subtle connections. The first passage is meant to convey the harsh paternalistic way in which the father rules over the household. There is a similar inflexible control exercised in the tradition of Ramadan. No one is allowed to eat until the sun goes down. At the same time, there is another subtle connection between the two scenes in that they both have to do with food. The family is prevented from eating before the muezzin calls and the cannon sounds, while the cat is killed for stealing a piece of meat.

In the next passage, the family sits down to dinner. Subul uses this scene to reinforce the severity of the father's paternalistic rule in the family:

> The meat was cooked with yogurt. He put it back in its place on top of the rice with an air of severity. His short, white beard mimicked the movement of his sharp, brittle face. I looked at the wrinkled face of my mother, the skin between her eyes squeezed into two distinct lines. All the meat was on top of the rice. It wasn't the whole thing; a piece of the shoulder was missing. . . . My father took hold of the tongue . . . a part that he liked the best. How could a cat like that have swallowed a whole piece of that size? (8)

The action on the part of the father of grasping the tongue is symbolic. It does not refer merely to the fact that he is choosing this part of the meat for himself, but is also a sign to the family that they are to say nothing. That this is his favorite part of the meat is also symbolic of the fact that he has absolute sway in the family, that his "word" is law. The tongue, therefore, is a sign of paternalistic rule or dictatorship. Here also, Subul mixes interior monologue ("How could a cat like that . . . ") with his description.

The following scene jumps to a different time and place. The narrator meets a friend and the two of them agree to attend a gathering sponsored by a political party. This is followed by a brief passage of two lines, in which Arabi sees the body of the dead cat the day after it was killed. This time, the narrative is written in the third person:

> The next morning its head was severed from its skinned body. Arabi saw it when he opened the door, and it turned his stomach. (10)

This is followed by several short scenes, which follow one another in rapid succession. In the next scene, Arabi and his friend go to a bar and observe the stinginess of the bar owner. In the next, he has a conversation with his friend about his father. The father is described as fearsome, strict, unyielding, and abusive to his wife (Arabi's mother). He is supposed to have been a fighter in the war, but Arabi never saw him in this role. His observation of the father's tyrannical role in the household is meant to suggest doubt on his part that he could, in fact, have been a brave fighter (since cowardly people tend to abuse those who are weaker than they are). A passage of interior monologue in inserted, in which Arabi dwells on the sight of the skinned cat and wonders who could have skinned it. A scene from the political party gathering follows this, narrated in the third person:

> Arabi said that he hated to go to listen to poets who stamp the ground with their feet. . . . Imperialism is not to be found under their feet. (10)

The reference here is to the recitation of verse during these party gatherings, highly political in tone, and delivered in a pompous and bombastic manner. Fakhri Salih (Fakhrī Ṣāliḥ)[52] notes that this "cut and paste" technique is meant to create an overall effect that comments on society as a whole. He adds that the selection of seemingly unrelated scenes interspersed with one another is intended to make the specific ideological point that the problems they depict are all essentially part of a single phenomenon.

While Subul's work represents an early and modest effort both in greater narrative experimentation and more direct societal criticism, a far deeper, ambitious, and more exhaustive effort in this direction was Sonallah Ibrahim's second novel, *Najmah Aghusṭus* (The star of August, 1970).[53] In her article, "Opaque and Transparent Discourse in Sonallah Ibrahim's Works," Ceza Draz explains that *Najmah Aghusṭus* was conceived as the negation of a text written previously by Ibrahim and two other writers, Kamal al-Qilish and Rauf Mis'id. The text in question was a reportage of their visit to the Aswan High Dam, published in 1967, and entitled "Insān al-Sadd al-'Ālī" (Man of the High Dam). In this article, Draz analyzes *Najmah Aghusṭus* as an experiment in the "demystification" of the language used in the prior documentary. In the documentary, Draz explains, the authors "consciously or unconsciously worked toward the 'mystification' of their readers by processes familiar in the discourse of fiction."[54]

Draz speaks of an interchange between the two texts in which the fictive discourse becomes factual, while the factual discourse become fictive; art is truth, while reportage is deceit. The public discourse of the original text is mystifying, while the private discourse of art is demystifying. In the former work, the discourse itself replaced the object, thus blurring the vision of the reader and distorting reality. In the latter work, Sonallah Ibrahim attempted to disentangle the object from the discourse surrounding it, reinstating it in reality. Thus, Draz characterizes *Najmah Aghusṭus* as a "negative" text, which instead of claiming to represent truth admits to being fictive. She writes that in the text "the self-defense mechanisms against illusion are restrained [and] the process of allegorical interpretation accompanying the reading of fiction is cast aside" (135).

Draz specifically identifies the processes involved in creating the two texts as those of familiarization and defamiliarization, and shows how the mystification of the reader is produced in the reportage of the article by means of describing the familiar in terms of the unfamiliar, particularly through personification. As the title "Man of the High Dam" indicates, the text tends to reconcile the object and the subject through a process of personification and humanization. From the very start, the narrators are careful not to dislocate their fellow travelers; they start from the familiar and guide them very carefully to the unfamiliar. What is valorized in the text is permanence as opposed to change. The narrators are careful at every step to assure the reader that what he is about to experience is not different from what he has experienced before. Metaphor is used to change what is not agreeable or acceptable into something acceptable; by transforming a reality that is alien and novel into a reality that is familiar and everlasting. The world of the High Dam is thus the perfect world, a utopia.

In the demystified, defamiliarized text of *Najmah Aghusṭus*, on the other hand, Sonallah Ibrahim attempts to present objects without mediation. The very star of title, "The Star of August," as Draz notes, appears only at the end of the novel, and does not stand for anything but itself (142). At the same time, Draz notes that the various functions of language are set aside to allow only the referential function to be assumed by the text. The text is taken over by the referent to such an extent that it becomes iconic, that is, it becomes a diagram of the object (143). The ultimate object or referent in question is the High Dam, and Ibrahim seeks to represent this object in two ways. First of all, he represents it via descriptive narrative that focuses on its most basic constituents, such as steel, concrete, and the sweat and effort of the workers who built it. Secondly, he represents it in the structure of the text itself.

Draz notes that this very structure tends toward an iconic representation of this object. This can be represented by the shape of a step pyramid, composed of three parts, with four chapters in the first part, the second part consisting of a single chapter and four chapters in the third part. The first four chapters describe the various steps in the High Dam's construction: excavating, blasting, moving, and dumping, with the subject of each of these operations a piece of equipment: excavators, dynamite, bulldozers, and dump trucks. The second part covers only twenty pages, and consists of an uninterrupted interior monologue. The third part reproduces the four operations of the first part, but in descending order (143–44).

The narrative voice is that of the author in his role, but not in his function, as journalist. Despite Draz's claim that Ibrahim is trying to be completely "objective," the text has a distinct point of view, even a social and political message. The message, however, requires the author to keep his interpretation at a minimum, and allow the reader to make interpretations for himself. This, in fact, is the message itself, over and above the book's social and political content.

Throughout the novel, the narration alternates between description of the author's observations of the building process, and other thoughts, recollections, and experiences that are not connected with this process. Draz refers to the sections that deal with the construction of the High Dam as the surface level of narration, and the other sections as the undercurrent, or subtexts. The latter sections are consistently short, one-paragraph sections. Draz sees this as evidence of repression. The subtexts represent the repressed dreams of society, and concern subjects such as art, social conflicts, the totalitarian state, and the cult of personality. While the transitions from the surface level of narration appear to occur randomly, some conceptual association usually sparks them. This is often merely a single word, which acts like a tripwire, causing the narrative shift. In the following passage, for instance, the narrator and his friend are stranded on the road and looking for a ride:

> The car continued on its way . . . and we approached it. We tried to climb on the rear, but the passengers prevented us and shouted for the driver to get moving. But the situation confused the driver and he stopped the motor. A long argument ensued between us and ended with him agreeing to take us with him. We jumped on the outside of the car but couldn't find any free space on the two long facing seats which were taken up by a number of workers. So we sat down on the floor. (64)

This is immediately followed by a flashback passage in which the narrator, as a political prisoner, is being transported in a police lorry. The linking word here is *iqta'ada* (to sit down), and the connecting thought is that of sitting on the floor of a lorry, and being transported in cargo- or freight-fashion:

> They ordered us to squat down and bend our heads until we couldn't see anything on the road. And in the dark of the night the procession of lorries drove into the heart of Old Cairo. . . . (64)

Another example occurs as the narrator is traveling in a bus. They come to a billboard that keeps track of how much of the High Dam project has been completed:

> One of the military policemen stopped us and then let us pass. The minaret of a mosque appeared in front of us and beneath it was a crowd of people too numerous to count. There I saw the famous sign that kept a daily record of how much remained according to the project plan until the end of the first stage. Now the sign contained an expression of thanks to the workers, wishing them success with the second stage. The writing was in both Arabic and Russian and was signed by both Abdel Nasser and Khruschchev. (48)

This is immediately followed by a transition, once again, to the narrator's memory of prison. The prisoners smuggle in the daily paper, and there too, a space is reserved that tells each day how much time remains until the project is completed:

> The papers arrived covertly and were read covertly. The copy concerned the building of the Dam: 375 days left until the current of the Nile would be transformed . . . 300 days left . . . 260 days left. Beyond the walls of stone and barbed wire the desert surrounded us on all sides. But Sa'id's towering stature appeared each morning, extending his sight far beyond, as if he could see everything. He said that he wanted to see that day. But he was never able to. (48)

The individual named Sa'id (Sa'īd) is a fellow political prisoner of the narrator, whose gaze metaphorically goes far beyond the prison walls—that is, he is depicted as farsighted and highminded. He looks forward to the day when the Dam will be completed, but dies before this occurs. The irony here is not directed at the High Dam project, but at the government, which was getting help from the Russians in building the dam, but at the same time was persecuting its native communists at home. Mahmud Amin al-Alim (Maḥmūd Amīn al-ʻĀlim) comments, "Here we see a clear contrast between the notion of progress, represented by the sign and the notion of backwardness represented by the imprisonment of the Egyptian communists."[55]

Alim's point is that the whole novel is built on contrasts of this sort, such as progress/backwardness, freedom/oppression, wealth/poverty, and abundance/hunger. The High Dam is built out of this very dualistic principle; it is a contradiction in and of itself. There is irony here, but not the irony of ambivalence or even resistance. It is clearly a Marxist sense of irony, which takes the notion of progress represented by the High Dam very seriously, yet sees the government as betraying this ideal even as it works to carry it out. Alim argues that, unlike *The Smell of It*, which was primarily concerned with conveying a feeling of existential *Angst*, *Najmah Aghusṭus* is essentially an intellectual work, which is trying to communicate an idea or viewpoint (114). Ibrahim's didactic point is that, at the same time that Egypt was pursuing the progressive path of technological modernization represented by the High Dam, it was socially and politically backward. The High Dam project was at odds with Egypt's political and social development, and as such represented not only an ideal, but also a contradiction.

How is such a sociopolitical contradiction connected with the ambiguity of the text itself? Here we come up against a major difference between Arabic and Western modernism. Both the High Dam project and Ibrahim's text represent change. The text is allied with the project that is its subject. From Ibrahim's point of view, the average reader can no more easily understand his text than the average citizen can understand the High Dam. The High Dam is not something easy to fathom. It is something immense and complex, which represents change that cannot be readily grasped. Readers in a society dominated by such contradictions do not readily grasp political and social contradictions, such as those embodied in the High Dam. Thus, while textual ambiguity in Western modernism is rarely overtly political, in the Arab world, it is nearly always political in its intent and effect.

Draz refers to this, stating that "in societies where truth is concealed, distorted, and repressed, literature's function becomes the revaluation of this truth and its disclosure" (145). The function of the experimental novel is to defamiliarize reality. Yet the reality of the society depicted in *Najmah Agusṭus* is a contradictory one, caught between the striving for modernity and a state of consciousness that is utterly incapable of making such a transition. The writer is therefore in a situation that is unambiguous to him yet highly ambiguous to the average reader. There is no easy solution to such a problem. Readers will be disoriented by such a text, and the bulk of them will not understand it and even be hostile to it. It is important to stress that, as a novel that appeals primarily to the avant-garde or intellectual elite, it has to be seen as on a par with the works of Joyce or Faulkner, in terms of its accessibility to the reading public at large.

The most disorienting aspect of *Najmah Aghusṭus* is not the lack of narrative subjectivity, nor the shifts from surface text to subtext, nor even the iconography of the novel's structure as a whole, but rather the interior monologue that makes up the brief second section of the novel. This section differs starkly from the rest of the narrative. It is also an alternate mix of description and interior monologue, but in a compressed form. There are no paragraphs, no sentences. The whole chapter is in the form of a single sentence. Mahmud Amin al-Alim distinguishes between what he calls the vertical structure for the first and third parts, which consists of a series of scenes and vignettes, and what he calls the horizontal structure of the second part, which is simply an uninterrupted stream of narrative (103). More importantly, for Alim, "the second part of it [is] that which gives the novel its particular literary flavor, which in fact saves the novel in literary terms, and raises it from the level of mere *reportage*" (100).

The subjects of this narrative are the same as those in the first and third parts. There is a surface text concerned with a description of the High Dam project, which alternates with various subtexts. In this case, however, the transitions from one type of narration to another do not occur from sentence to sentence or from paragraph to paragraph, but from word to word, and cannot be grammatically separated at any particular point. For instance, in the following passage, the narrator is examining a particular portion of the dam project. He climbs down a ladder into a deep hole. He is in darkness. Suddenly there is a transition to a memory of lovemaking, which similarly took place in darkness. The word darkness *(ẓalām)* provides the point of connection:

> . . . I held onto the narrow iron ladder attached to and tilted towards the wall of the tunnel and alighted on the steps with my back to the wall on which it descended while nearby water mixed with pieces of rock and cement dampened my clothes and the darkness grew bit by bit until the light which came from behind me went out and the tongue that extended from it in front of me faded just as the ladder and sloping wall stopped and the tunnel infinitely extended the mass of darkness across which her cries reached me while I watched her thighs around my waist persistently drawing me closer. . . . (226)

Another example is the following passage, in which the memory of prison is evoked by the machinery used in the project. The linkage is made via the common concept of a wound *(jaraḥ):*

> [L]ayers of soil poured from the metal claws leaving a long wound in the walls of the mountain which resembled the huge traces of the fingers of a giant prisoner who has tried in his moments of agony to climb the walls and whose nails have scarred masonry or like the dirty nails of the old guard whose hands inflicted wounds on us. . . . (219)

The highly politicized viewpoint of the novel is evident in passages such as the following, which subtly weaves description of the dam project with thinly veiled observations on the ruling class:

> [S]ome of the holes in the first masonry walls were filled but the undulation [of the water] created other holes which joined together to create a multifaceted syringe against which it pressed and squirted and squeezed, expanding the elastic which covered the holes just like the expanding skin covered by a layer of fat on the body of the contractor as he sat in the seat of his car with his fat wife beside him twirling the gold bracelets around her forearms these were the ones who ruled over us. . . . (224)

Passages such as these did not escape the censors, and were sufficient to have the novel banned in Egypt (the first edition was published in Damascus in 1974). In one of the key passages of the text, Ibrahim mixes images of the High Dam project with his own contemplations on ancient Egyptian religion. His point is the explicitly political one that the workers who believe that they are contributing to the project out of love are in fact doing so out of fear:

> [T]hree Sa'ayidis remained in the reservoir area slowly gathering slats of wood then packing them together and finally sitting and waiting for the cranes to carry them off and deposit them near me a Russian photographer waited patiently to take a picture of the moment when the water would pour out of the tunnel into the reservoir and from there outside where it would rush in constant profusion to newly irrigate the land until it was saturated with water and its fruitfulness would safely be doubled at the behest of Habi who was born with the sun while the rains poured down and after centuries became a god and the father of the gods when the priest announced amid the incense in the courtyard of the temple that He had come at this time after almost losing himself in the other world where the rest of the gods among whom Ramses had ordered that he be included in the holy of holies beside which were conducted the secret religious rites in the darkness far from the people and the artists passed the night by the light of the oil lamps working with their hammers and chisels and carving and polishing tools engraving with the stroke of a serpent from top to bottom their eyes trying to already discern the form contained within the rock whose art did not allow them to make a mistake and correct it He spoke to them saying before you is meat and drink and everything that people desire in order to say that your love belongs to Me he is the one who causes you to work for My sake and they added to the wrinkled face the names of the eternal youths and trembled in fear and religiosity before the light smile which their fingers carved upon the sensuous lips and immersed in their last breath wrote the name STALIN on the walls and set to engraving at his orders. . . . (234)

According to Alim, while part 2 is in the form of a single sentence, it is not really a single sentence, nor does it make the impression of a single sentence on the reader. If the narrative concerned a single subject or topic, it might be possible to write it as a single sentence twenty pages in length. In this case, however, in addition to the surface texts, there are many different subtexts, just as in part 1 and part 3. These concern observations on Michelangelo as a symbol of artistic creativity, lovemaking, and the heroic death of one of the political activists. No single sentence could contain, refer to, or reflect on all these different subjects, events, and interests (103).

From a grammatical point of view, then, the text of part 2 should contain periods, commas, and paragraphs. The question is, therefore, why did Sonallah Ibrahim write it this way? Alim notes quite simply that the purpose of this type of writing is to produce a condensed or concentrated text. He notes that Ibrahim himself referred to part 2 as the "solid nucleus" of the text as a whole (100). But what, in turn, is the purpose of producing such a concentrated text in the middle of the novel? The very lack of clarity, or confusion caused by reading such a concentrated text is obviously one of the main objectives. The fact that, apart from this condensation, the subject matter of part 2 is the same as that of parts 1 and 3 suggests that the middle portion of the novel is meant merely to reinforce what the author is trying to accomplish in the other parts. In particular, the alteration between surface text and subtexts, which becomes so entangled in the middle section, is meant to reinforce the intimate connection that the two types of text have with one another—that is, the connection between external space and internal space, between oppression and repression.

In this sense, the narration is not one entirely devoid of subjectivity, but one, rather, as Draz points out, in which subjectivity is suspended. The narrator—who is not named throughout the novel—is dehumanized, objectified, his minutest gestures described "as though he were an automaton" (144), yet the text is written in the first person, and many of the subtexts have a personal tone. Draz's notion of the subtext as "repressed" is the key to understanding this type of writing. Subjectivity is, then, repressed, rather than canceled, and is ultimately communicated through the tension and built up by means of the interrelationship between surface text and subtext. Mahmud Amin al-Alim hints at a subjective dimension to the text when he analyzes it as a threefold "journey" that takes place in terms of both time and space, as well as on an inner level via the narrator's memories, dreams, and reflections (68).

In general, the influence of *Najmah Aghuṣtus* on the Arabic novel in terms of narrative experimentation was not felt until years later. The only comparable example of experimentation on the part of another writer during this period can be found in *Al-Baḥth 'an Walīd Mas'ūd* by Jabra Ibrahim Jabra. Like *Najmah Aghuṣtus*, it contains a section of concentrated text, which functions as a nucleus of the work as a whole, and which creates a heightened effect. In this work, Jabra's narrative once more presents a number of characters representing a microcosm of bourgeois society in Baghdad. Again, he gathers his characters together in a single location in which they interact with one another, and their sentiments reflect the isolation and impotence that they feel in this position of remoteness from the center of the Palestinian conflict. This time, however, Jabra borrows a technique from Mahfouz's *Miramar*, by which the focus of his characters' attention is another character who has hardly any voice in the narrative.

In this case, the central character is even more radically absent from the narrative than in *Miramar.* He has, in fact, disappeared, leaving behind only a tape of his last words. The book opens with the narration of Dr. Jawad (Dr. Jawād), who has been entrusted with a tape that contains the last recorded thoughts of his friend, Walid (Walīd), which was found in his car, abandoned near the Iraqi-Syrian border. The doctor converses with Amir ('Āmir), another friend of Walid's, and tells him about the tape. Amir wants to gather a number of Walid's friends together and play the tape for them. Dr. Jawad expresses skepticism that anything could come out of such a hearing, since he says that Walid's words are meaningless . . . a mixture of happiness and sadness, nothing more. . . . Yet in the end he consents to Amir's proposal.

As in *Najmah Aghusṭus*, the core of Jabra's book takes the form of a section of concentrated text, in this case only a few pages in length. The section consists of the tape of Walid Mas'ud's last words. As in Sonallah Ibrahim's text, the narrative in this section is compressed. There is no punctuation. Words are simply strung together. The result is an intensified narration. There are, however, some major differences between the compressed sections of text in *Al-Baḥth 'an Walīd Mas'ūd* and that in *Najmah Aghusṭus*. To begin with, while there are connections in *Najmah Aghusṭus*—whether by a single word, or by association—between the different narrative sections that link them together. In *Al-Baḥth 'An Walīd Mas'ūd*, there are no such connections. Walid's "tape" consists of an interiorized stream-of-consciousness narrative that simply goes from one thought or memory to another.

Secondly, while in Sonallah Ibrahim's text, the concentrated section of narrative is meant to give an intensified sense of reality, in *Al-Baḥth 'an Walīd Mas'ūd*, it is meant to convey a heightened feeling of personal subjectivity and emotion. Dr. Jawad prepares the reader for this in the first few pages of the text, in which he describes Walid as having been angry, fierce, and excitable in his relations with others. By contrast, he describes himself as someone who always got along with other people. He narrates that Walid used to argue that he couldn't afford such a contented attitude, and urged him to adopt a more radical stance toward life (12).

Another of Walid's former friends, Ibrahim, makes a comment immediately after the tape has been played that "Walid mourned himself before he was mourned by others." This is the substance of the tape that Walid Mas'ud leaves behind. It provides no plot, no mystery—only a record of Walid's nostalgia, pain, sadness, and self-pity.

There are many levels of ambiguity in the text. First of all, there is an elusiveness surrounding Walid's identity. Clearly, he was a friend of all those who gather to mourn his apparent death, yet there is a dual sense that in their reflections on Walid, the other characters are merely reflecting on aspects of themselves, creating ambiguity with respect to authorial identity. In the opening pages, Dr. Jawad declares his desire to write a book about Walid, representing the self-reflective authorial viewpoint. At the same time, the material of the text contains elements that, with respect to Jabra himself, are clearly autobiographical in nature. Jabra, then, parcels out his identity between Dr. Jawad and Walid, just as Walid's identity is parceled out among his friends. In this sense, the characters reflect aspects of Walid, or of the ultimate authorial voice.

The ultimate tone of the book is highly reflective, Proustian, dominated by the desire to dwell on memories, to go back to the past. The central part of the text, which is Walid's "tape," focuses both on the importance of memory, as well as on feelings of disillusionment with respect to the present, which is perceived as a time of frivolousness and boredom. Walid's thoughts wander from his childhood, to a recent relationship with a mysterious woman, named Shahd, of whom none of his friends have been aware, to the heartbreak of losing his son, killed in the conflict of the Lebanese Civil War which was raging at this time. There is a lyricism to the text reminiscent of Virginia Woolf. At the beginning of the tape, he talks about his childhood as a schoolboy, the thoughts picked up seemingly at random and thrown together in a tumble:

> An olive green book satchel filled with books and notebooks and pencils and colored pens schooldays hanging from a strap bulging under the arm at the hip with childhood secrets a book of the acts of heroes strange names Hercules Ulysses Achilles Patroclus. (26)

Jabra also inserts an intruding voice without any punctuation to set it off from the preceding narrative:

> I took the satchel and emptied it of books on the window sill then Sulayman [Sulaymān] and Abid [ʻĀbid] and I ran . . . to the olive trees . . . the heavy bare olive trees you boys get away from those trees. (26)

Much of the tape narrative dwells on the new woman in his life, who is not named until nearly the end. Walid's voice switches from scene to scene, beginning with a memory of his lover sitting in a chair, then shifting to a scene at the beach, then to a train, and then from descriptive narration to declamatory form:

> She was sunk into a big chair her breasts like two ivory spheres illuminating her nudity around her hips and her thighs leisurely greeting the warmth of the blazing fire in a big black chair the days we went to the beach and felt the icy stormy wind and the whitecaps rising up from the middle of the sea racing to the shore and dissipating at our feet struggling in the soft wet heavy sand and her lips cold and fragrant and studded with droplets and her cheeks next to her flying hair her hair flying despite her fingers planted against it we stretched our necks out the window of the roaring whistling train rumbling across the green earth promise me do you promise me that you won't grow up and won't grow old and I promise you that I will remain as you see me now. . . . (26–27)

Eventually, Walid's tone become more urgent, more angry, and more despairing, until it reaches a crescendo of emotion:

> [S]he handed me the letter from her car as I was standing on the curb and she departed in the car saying escape before the time is gone and the time went time always goes always we arrive too late in any case a plane would be of no use nor wings the crows will attack us in broad daylight and in the darkness of night there is no difference no difference no difference no difference none none none none none none twenty years ago I spoke to her with pride and ten years before that I spoke to her with conceit and stubbornness and now I speak to her with indifference. . . . (33)

His anger spills out toward his friends, including those gathered listening to his words, and at this point it is clear that his feelings center around their political passivity compared with his own sense of urgency:

> [A]nd Ihsan [Iḥsān] is still debating with Ibrahim [Ibrāhīm] and his tongue is almost unable to keep up with his mouth and his hand trembles like Ibrahim's he reaches his peak when he shouts and his eyes become filled with tears they're all traitors all traitors. . . . (33)

This anger dissipates once again, and Walid returns to feelings of nostalgia, loneliness, and despair. The monologue ends on this note, with Walid expressing the sentiment that he has said nothing and that all his words have no meaning. The reaction of his friends is mixed. The women are crying, dabbing at their eyes, others feel that, indeed, Walid's confession was a waste of time, and that his words amounted to nothing. The paradox of the text as a whole is that, unlike *Najmah Aghusṭus*, in which the "concentrated" section of text sums up the book as a whole, in *Walīd Mas'ūd*, it is the inverse case. Walid's confession is a hollow core to the text, which simply serves to highlight the reactions of the various other characters.

Each character represents an aspect of Walid, in the sense that each talks about an aspect that they see in him. One character talks about Walid's relationship to women, another about his relation to art and literature. Yet, at the same time, Walid simply serves as a mirror in which these characters see themselves. Mattityahu Peled argues that Jabra intended *Walīd Mas'ūd* to be a polyphonic novel in the Bakhtinian sense, structured along the lines of "'a plurality of independent and unmerged voices and consciousnesses,'" in which the author is eliminated "as the dominant narrative voice."[56] Peled adds that "by choosing to write a polyphonic novel, Jabra . . . meant to write a 'novel of ideas' or an ideological novel" in the sense that "various consciousnesses confront each other with ideas in an open-ended argument. . . . The result is that the reader discovers a situation, not a narrative."[57] Clearly, if we view the novel in this way, we can say that Jabra's objective in *Walīd Mas'ūd* is the same type of polyphony that he attempts to achieve in *The Ship*. In *Walīd Mas'ūd*, however, he is far more successful in relinquishing the dominant narrative voice and creating independent narrative voices in its stead.

THE STRATEGY OF IRONIC DISTANCE

While writers such as Jabra concentrated on themes of exile and disillusionment, other writers were exploring another narrative strategy in the face of oppression and occupation, namely the use of thinly veiled irony and symbolic representation. Fakhri Salih[58] discusses the work one of the most important of these writers, the Egyptian Gamal al-Ghitani (Jamāl al-Ghīṭānī), in terms of his use of the form of the historical novel as a means of barbed comment on the present. Salih notes that the historical novel had long been a developed form in Egypt, but mainly as a form of escape from the present and its problems. By contrast, he maintains that the next generation of writers to experiment with the form of the historical novel used this form more as a way of examining and understanding the present. Although Salih concedes that their number was too small to consider them as having constituted a literary movement, he notes that their importance as experimentalists was considerable, and that their work, particularly that of Ghitani and Habiby, has had a lasting impact on the development of the Arabic novel.[59]

Ghitani's best-known work, *Zayni Barakat* (1988; *Al-Zaynī Barakāt,* 1974),[60] is acknowledged as a novel of great significance in the history of modern Arabic literature. Although innovative in several respects, its chief significance is its use of the form of the historical novel for the purpose of commenting on the present. While the book appears to take the form of a historical novel, virtually all the characters in the book spring from Ghitani's imagination. Salih notes that Ghitani works at grafting the form of the modern novel onto the material of the historical novel, using a veiled technique to comment on the present by confirming it in the past. The lack of characters that can be connected to historical record is a clue that this is a fictive text meant to present an image of present-day reality in veiled form.

The title character is the only one for which there is a degree of historical authority. Ghitani uses the historical figure of Al-Zayni Barakat Ibn Musa (Al-Zaynī Barakāt Ibn Mūsā) as the basis for the book, taking his information from Muhammad Ibn Iyas (Muḥammad Ibn Īyās), a major Egyptian Mamluk historian. Ibn Iyas mentions in his account of the defeat of the Mamluks by the Ottomans that Ibn Musa held the position of *muḥtasib*, or inspector of markets, a function analogous to treasurer and comptroller, as well as that of governor of Cairo and the adjacent province of Giza. Ibn Musa was a political survivor in an era of turbulent unrest. He served more than forty years in office, despite challenges to his authority, arrest, and imprisonment, and the implication of the text is that in order to survive for such a length of time, he had to be a clever political manipulator.

The text is polyglot, made up largely of sections of third-person narrative, usually headed by the names of the characters whose perspective they represent, in the fashion of Kanafani's *Men in the Sun*. Interspersed with these, however, are several sections of first-person narrative, consisting of the observations of a Venetian traveler, Visconti Gianti, as well as a bewildering array of fictionalized "documentary" passages. These include public announcements, decrees on behalf of the Sultan, and judicial decisions and decrees, but focus mainly on the activities of Zakariyya ibn Radi, the Head Spy of Egypt. They also include reports received by Zakariyya from his spies in the field, issued by his secretariat, and sent to the Sultan and emirs, as well as miscellaneous incoming and outgoing correspondence, or fragments thereof.

The character of Zakariyya is crucial for building the picture of a police state as all-pervasive as that which existed in the Roman Empire or, in the twentieth century, behind the Iron Curtain. When we first meet him, he has just kidnapped the favorite boy of the Sultan, and is torturing him in an attempt to find out for himself his true relationship to the Sultan, and particularly if the Sultan has a "preference" for young boys. After sexually violating the boy, he watches him harden, aging by dozens of years in a space of three days. Still failing to get any information, Zakariyya "regretfully" decides to have him choked and buried alive, since to allow him to live would leave open the possibility of his activities being discovered by the Sultan. He watches the strangulation himself.

Irony pervades the nature and methods of the police state run by Zakariyya. He is a perfectionist, dedicated to his profession, viewing it as both an art and a science. His ambition is to create the ultimate spy organization to serve the cause of the stability of the state, yet in the type of system which he imagines, the state itself would be subsumed by its own security apparatus:

> Zakariyya continues his meditations: what a system! And what splendid organization! That's how it is done; the whole of creation is ordered in such a way that not a single good deed or a single bad deed goes unrecorded. (83)

When Zayni, an unknown to Zakariyya, is appointed *muḥtasib*, Zakariyya immediately sets out to gather as much intelligence on him as possible, just as he did with the Sultan. From the outset, the reader is given the impression of a power struggle between Zakariyya and Zayni.

The figure of Zayni stands in a strong contrast to that of the Head Spy. He gives every indication of being a pure-minded reformer, at first declining the position, since, as he says, corruption is rampant, the people oppressed, the responsibility too great, and he would be held accountable for the injustice. Yet he soon accepts the position and embarks on a series of ambitious reforms. One of these reforms is to hang big lamps throughout the city to be lighted every night, for the purpose of ensuring greater security. The reform of the lamps is torpedoed by the religious clerics, fed by innuendoes circulated by Zakariyya's spies:

> Part of the Friday sermon delivered from the pulpits of mosques . . . delivered by all preachers, regardless of their rites. . . . People of Egypt! It never happened before that lamps were hung. The Noble Messenger has enjoined us to lower our eyes so that we may not see the nakedness of people. But the lamps reveal our nakedness. God has created night and day: dark night and lit day; God has created the night as a cover and a shield; do we remove the cover? Do we do away with the shield that God has given us? Do we give in to our arrogance and dispel the darkness of the night from . . . the city? This is heresy, which we do not accept. It is a deviation from the law and we reject it. (96)

At the same time that Zayni embarks on his reforms, however, he also apparently creates a special team of spies to work under his direct supervision. Later, he accepts Zakariyya as his deputy. Questions are raised in the reader's mind about Zayni's motives. Is he coerced into accepting Zakariyya in this position? Is he the reformer he seems to be, or is it possible that he is also a charlatan, an opportunist, and a sinister manipulator? This ambiguity is the major source of tension in the narrative. Even if Zayni is the reformer he appears to be, the text is dominated by irony. Regardless how influential Zayni becomes, and how far-reaching his reforms, these efforts are always balanced by a negative counterweight. The entire social and political system, the weight of tradition, and the avarice of men are like a morass into which any reformer steps at his peril. In order to survive in such a system, Zayni must adopt some of the same methods used by his opponents.

In the end, it turns out that Zayni never had a spy system of his own, that this was just a rumor that he allowed to be circulated to put Zakariyya on his guard. Yet this does not diminish the ambiguity surrounding Zayni, since it shows him to be a master tactician, equal to his adversary. At the same time, there is equal ambiguity regarding Zakariyya's nature. When the clerics kidnap and threaten to summarily execute Zayni, it is the Head Spy's intervention that saves him. Moreover, although Zakariyya has contemplated and planned Zayni's murder almost from the moment he took office, he never carries it out. The novel ends with the Ottoman conquest of Cairo, after which the voice of the Venetian traveler returns to tell about the vanquished city and the return of Zayni as ruler of Cairo after the victory of the Ottomans.

Ghitani does not attempt to represent specific figures on the Egyptian political scene in a veiled way in his novel, but rather only to create a general picture of a society that resembles the Egyptian society of his day. It is not so much that the repressive condition of his fictive historical Egypt is seen as equivalent to that of his present-day model. Rather, by means of his fictional account, the reader grasps the nature and mechanism of power, and the way it is used for repressive ends. At the same time, however, Ghitani builds a mood of uncertainty, gloom, and cynicism that is very "modern":

> Cairo today is like a man blindfolded, thrown on his back, and awaiting an unknown destiny. (20)[61]

> This is the age of perplexity, when doubt is master and certainty extinct. (92)

This uncertainty, perplexity, and doubt are represented by the status of Zayni as a largely absent character, which allies the text with Mahfouz's *Miramar*. Ceza Draz refers in an article on irony in contemporary Arabic fiction to the character of Zayni as "absent and present at the same time,"[62] while Walid Hamarneh notes that

> Al-Zayni's presence is always in the air, even though he never narrates and his voice is never heard, with the exception of some official documents that bear his signature. He remains the most enigmatic of all the major characters, and this is strengthened by the different contradictory reports about him that we get. It is true that we learn more about him in the latter parts of the novel, yet he remains as evasive as ever. In other words, he is the subject of the narrative, but . . . his presence becomes more manifest through his absence.[63]

Sizā Qāsim (Draz) also observes that the fashioning of such an absent main character is directly connected with the use of irony in connection with Ghitani's subject, which is the mechanism of power: "The *Muḥtasib* is the Law, and he is above the law; no one knows the truth about him."[64] In other words, irony depends upon the simultaneous presence of two conflicting features. In this case, it is the fact that Zayni embodies the Law, and yet that his power is reinforced by his very absence. In this sense, he represents the way in which power is exercised in a police state, secretly, furtively, and effectively. Hamarneh comments on Zayni's position in the narrative:

> [It] is analogical to the real center of the narrative, namely the nexus of power/knowledge. Power, or to be more accurate, the creation, perpetuation, and preservation of power centers, the relationship between power and authority, and the mechanisms of repression and domination, past and present, are what is central to the novel.[65]

Hamarneh analyzes the novel as being narrated through a multiplicity of modes of narration as well as narrators. Characters are portrayed and analyzed through their own voices, through what others "report" about them, or through the ironic juxtaposition of what they say and what we get to know from other "more reliable" sources. He further identifies several of what he calls "layers" of narration. The first layer is the first-person narration of the outsider, Visconti Gianotti, whose knowledge is limited to the appearances of what he sees, and to what his interpreters tell him. The second layer is the discourse of the general public of Egyptians, whose limited access to knowledge is determined by the fact that their sources of information are the official and quasi-official ones. The third layer is that of individuals who have limited access to some privileged information, but remain outside the actual decision-making process.

Zakariyya, who is near the center of political decision making and knowledge acquisition, represents the fourth layer. He holds a privileged position in the network of repression, power, and authority. Hamarneh also points out that these "layers" are also analogical to the relative proximity of their representatives to Zayni. Zakariyya is the closest to him, and eventually becomes his closest aide. Hamarneh also postulates a fifth layer, namely the discourse center associated with Zayni himself, but asks, "Who is he, and is it really possible to know within the fictional world created by the text?"[66]

The subtle irony of an Egyptian novelist like Ghitani gives way to a much more explicit, sarcastic form of irony in the hands of the Palestinian writer, Emile Habiby (Īmīl Ḥabībī). Living and writing as an Arab within the state of Israel, Habiby developed a unique style which reflected a wide variety of influences, including Arabic classical and oral literary traditions, Jewish humor, the twentieth century Central and Eastern European novel, and Latin American magical realism. He was one of the first Arab novelists to fully exploit the technique of pastiche, incorporating the forms of poetry, the short story, the folk tale, the memoir or autobiography, and other literary forms into the novel. Fakhri Salih refers to his "fusing of the *Maqāmah*, the news story, examples of poetry, jokes, and proverbs" into a single narrative structure.[67]

Implicitly comparing his style to that of magical realism, the Palestinian writer Ibrahim Nasrallah (Ibrāhīm Naṣr Allāh) has said of Habiby's work that it is "not magical *(siḥrīyah),* but skeptical *(sukhrīyah).*"[68] One could say that Habiby's technique is a melding of the magical or mythical with irony, skepticism, and black humor. What is important to understand here is the connection between Habiby's use of pastiche and reliance on folk tradition, on the one hand, and his black humor, on the other. Both of these traits are related to his status as a Palestinian within Israel. In the introduction to her *Anthology of Modern Palestinian Literature*, Salma Khadra Jayyusi makes the point that "Palestinian literature has achieved a particularity of its own, or at least differed in certain instances from other contemporary literature in the Arab world . . . . While one can say that all Arabic literature nowadays is involved in the social and political struggle of the Arab people, politics nevertheless imposes a greater strain on the Palestinian writer."[69]

Palestinian literature, by Jayyusi's definition, is resistance literature. As she notes:

> Whether in Israel, or in the West Bank and the Gaza Strip, or in the diaspora, Palestinians are committed by their very identity to a life determined by events and circumstances arising out of their own rejection of captivity and national loss. . . . The luxury of choosing one's own past, of selecting memories, of re-arranging relations that transcend events and external circumstances, is not theirs.[70]

While Jayyusi claims that this luxury does not exist for the Palestinians, this is precisely what Habiby attempts to do in working with the folk tradition in his novels. The purpose is to fill a vacuum, a void, created by the national loss, and this vacuum can be filled precisely with cultural memories even while the reality of this loss is lampooned with black humor. Habiby's ambivalence thus acts both in a critical and a restorative manner.

Habiby's best-known work is *The Secret Life of Saeed, the Ill-Fated Pessoptimist* (1985; *Al-Waqā'i' al-Gharībah fī Ikhtifā' Sa'īd Abī al-Naḥs al-Mutashā'il*, 1974).[71] The word *mutashā'il* (pessoptimist), Habiby's coinage from the combination of *mutashā'im* (pessimist) and *mutafā'il* (optimist), is immediately recognizable as such to a native speaker of Arabic, and is meant to indicate a type of razor's-edge ambivalence. Saeed, the luckless pessoptimist, is an informer for the Zionist state, who, despite his constant attempts, can never do enough to please his Israeli masters. A transformation occurs in Saeed's self-awareness, however, when during the upheaval of the 1967 June War he makes an idiotic blunder and is put in prison by the authorities, who hope that he will act as a spy for the state among the prisoners. There, Saeed is brutally beaten by the Israeli guards and put in a cell with his son and namesake, who mistakes him for a freedom fighter like himself.

After this, Saeed finds that he can no longer collaborate with the Israelis. His change of heart, however, cannot furnish him with a solution to his misery. While he rejects his former role of informer, he is still crippled by his natural cowardice. The dilemma in which he finds himself is symbolized in a scene at the end of the novel, in which he finds himself sitting on a tall, impaling stake, unable to move in any direction, a hapless Christ-figure. An extraterrestrial being comes to his aid, and safely transports him to outer space. An epilogue informs us that the entire narrative was contained in a letter sent from an insane asylum, and all trace of the inmate has disappeared.

Habiby gives us a narrative that functions on two levels—one of bantering humor, and one of grim reality. Like Eastern European novelists such as Milan Kundera, whose writing is steeped in the experience of political oppression in Eastern Europe, Habiby builds his narrative on paradoxical concepts that simultaneously mock the oppressive system and the passivity and complicity of its victims. This can be immediately seen in the chapter headings, such as "Saeed Claims to Have Met Creatures from Outer Space," "Saeed Changes into a Cat That Meows," and "An Event More Difficult to Believe Than Death Itself." These titles simultaneously recall such satiric classics of the Western Enlightenment as Voltaire's *Candide*[72] and *Gulliver's Travels*,[73] while even more importantly mocking the Arab literary heritage of *The Thousand and One Nights*.[74] The grandiosity and implausibility of the titles reflect Habiby's view of the legacy left by both these influences—an unrealistic expectation that political freedom could be magically handed to the Palestinians on a silver platter.

To emphasize the bankruptcy of such an attitude, Habiby uses references in *The Pessoptimist* to Arab history, folk tradition, and the geography of Palestine to evoke what is largely a vanished reality. The Palestine of Habiby's day now exists more in story, oral narration, memory, and rumor, than in the physical world. When Saeed crosses from Lebanon into Israel, the people who meet him offer a litany of the names of vanished villages from which they have come:

> "We are from Ruwais." "We are from al-Hadatha." "We are from el-Dumun."
>
> "We are from Mazraa." "We are from Shaab." We are from Miy'ār."
>
> "We are from Waarat el-Sarris." "We are from al-Zeeb." "We are from el-Bassa. . . . " (21–22)

This passage recalls the theme of exile as well as the indebtedness to Arabic literary tradition found in the following passage from Jabra Ibrahim Jabra's *The Ship:*

> Do you know that the ancient Arab poets used to fall in love with place names and that they repeated them in their poems as frequently as they repeated the names of women they loved . . .
>
> . . . And don't you remember these lines by Abeed Ibn al-Abras . . .
> Malhoub is desolate, all its people gone
> And Qutabīyah and Dhanub
> And Rakis and Thuaylibat . . .
> And Dhatu Firqayn and Qalib
> And Arda and Qafa Hibirrin
>
> And when he could not think of any more place-names to fill the second hemistich, he said, "No Arab soul is left of them there."[75]

Saeed comments that "We of Haifa used to know more about the villages of Scotland than we did about those of Galilee. Most of these villages I have never heard mentioned except for that one evening" (21–22). Thus, Arab Galilee has become an empty space, an ethnically cleansed field. Saeed's comment on the failure of memory has a hint of self-accusation in it. Similarly, in the opening of the book, when Saeed narrates the "history" of his family, he identifies himself as a member of "the family of Pessoptimist," an old and noble family that can trace its lineage to the time of Tamerlane and which occupied Beersheva, Acca, and Haifa. The obvious reason for recounting this history is to establish the claim of the Palestinians (the family of Pessoptimist) to their homeland.

Chapter 31, entitled "An Odd Piece of Research on the Many Virtues of the Oriental Imagination," is structured entirely on the ironic and paradoxical concept of the "Oriental imagination," which in fact is a tragic coping device:

> And how about that Arab youth who slammed into another car with his own on Lillinblum Street in Tel Abib? Wasn't it his Oriental imagination that saved him? By getting out of his car and screaming about the other driver, "He's an Arab—an Arab!" he so engaged everyone in attacking his victim that he himself was able to escape.
>
> And don't forget Shlomo in one of Tel Aviv's very best hotels. Isn't he really Sulaiman, son of Munirah, from our own quarter? And "Dudi," isn't he really Mahmud? "Moshe," too; isn't his proper name Musa, son of Abdel Massih? How could they earn a living in a hotel, restaurant, or filling station without help from their Oriental imagination, the same imagination that gave them the story of the golden fish, and the magnetic mountain deep in the raging sea? (101)

In another passage, the irony and black humor directed toward Israeli settlement and occupation is built on a paradoxical idea of holiness:

> "Oh no! These aren't Mamluks or Crusaders. These are people returning to their country after an absence of two thousand years."
>
> "My, what prodigious memories they have!"
>
> "Anyway, my son, people have been talking for two thousand years in terms of thousands—generals of a thousand men, men slain by the thousands, and so on.

> "There is nothing on earth more holy than human blood. That is why our country is called the Holy Land."
> "And is my city, Haifa, holy?"
> "Every spot of our land has been made holy by the blood of the slain and will go on being made holy, my son. (24)

Another ironic device used by Habiby is naming. Names are used both ironically and symbolically. Saeed, for instance, means "happy," his sister's name, Yuad, means "one who has returned," and his wife's name, Baqiyya, means "the girl who stayed":

> When Baqiyya gave birth to your son, she wanted to name him after her father, a refugee, whose name was Fathi, which means "victor." But the big man of small stature raised an eyebrow at that, and so we named him Walaa, which means "loyal." (97)

In this passage, "the big man of small stature" is the Israeli agent who controls Saeed's life down to the naming of his son. The name Walaa (loyal), of course, implies loyalty to the Israeli State, just as the name Fathi (victor) has, for the Israelis, a subversive overtone.

The most important ironic device that Habiby uses, however, is the character of Saeed himself. In an early study of *The Pessoptimist*, Trevor LeGassick compared the work to Jaroslav Hašek's *The Good Soldier Švejk.*[76] The comparison between Saeed and Švejk is an apt one in certain respects. The main characteristics that both *The Pessoptimist* and *The Good Soldier Švejk* share is the antiheroic nature of their protagonists and the use of this antiheroic stance as a means—in fact, a strategy—of resistance. Hašek created a character that is quintessentially paradoxical, who turns the notion of resistance on its head. *The Pessoptimist* also begins in a similar mode by casting its protagonist in the role of traitor-informer. It thus breaks fundamentally with the heroic conventions of Palestinian literature. Like Hašek, Habiby sees man fundamentally in an antiheroic position.

In *Jaroslav Hašek: A Study of Švejk and the Short Stories* (1982), Cecil Parrott writes: "Hašek makes it clear . . . that his hero is no mere idiot and that his innocence is only simulated." Švejk puts on the mask of a fool in order to mock the establishment and authority of the Austro-Hungarian regime. Parrot adds, "The battle that Švejk wages is thus a deadly serious and tense one—a struggle for bare existence."[77] Salma

Khadra Jayyusi notes in her introduction to *The Pessoptimist* that Saeed shares many of Švejk's qualities. Both characters are constantly preoccupied with the problem of defending their lives against an authoritarian system. They have evolved a system for doing so, one in which they "wear the mask of the subservient Fool, all too ready to demonstrate an ardent obedience and a willingness *ad absurdum* to serve those who control their destinies."[78]

There is an important difference between the two protagonists, however, which is obscured by comparisons that have, until now, been offered by LeGassick and other critics between *The Pessoptimist* and works such as *The Good Soldier Švejk* or Voltaire's *Candide*. This difference relates to the nature of the protagonists' antiheroism. Švejk is a fool with an "attitude." While everyone else is trying to dodge service in the Austrian army, he insists that he be examined in order to prove that he is fit to serve. He interprets his instructions literally, unflinchingly resolving to carry out to the letter the orders given him, no matter how idiotic they may be or how perversely he may interpret them. He is constantly punished for his over-zealousness. When the authorities decide to pension him off in order to get rid of him, Švejk will not accept it, and declares his intention to serve the emperor to the last bone in his body.

The power of Hašek's irony is in his consistency. There is never a time when Švejk reveals himself to be anything but the fool he appears to be, and yet the conviction is overwhelming that he is much more. Habiby's character, on the other hand is less consistent, and therefore more complex. Saeed is not just a fool; he is also a coward, and his cowardice makes him a conscious victim. His role as a fool seems to be a counterpoint to his desperate position, rather than the brilliant tactical strategy that Švejk's character seems to represent. As Jayyusi notes, "Saeed's exaggerated demonstrations of loyalty to the State are masked with innocence to appear true, but they convey the opposite meaning—the suggestion that a terrible punishment lies in wait for those who are not loyal."[79]

Of course, as Parrott notes, there is an underlying tragedy in Švejk, as well. The coexistence of the comic and tragic in the novel can, in itself, be considered a modernist characteristic. It is typical of modernism that comedy and tragedy are no longer regarded as antithetical gestures. Prominent writers such as Thomas Mann rejected the old classification, asserting that modern art views life as tragicomic. The most important characteristic that distinguishes *The Pessoptimist* from *The Good Soldier Švejk*, however, is that besides Saeed's position being compromised, he is aware of his compromised position. The first-person narration of Saeed also puts greater emphasis on his thinking, decisions, and motivations:

> I was so impressed by the Jewish worker's ignorance of Hebrew that I decided that this state was not fated to survive. Why should I not therefore protect my line of retreat? (50)

> I was therefore particularly subservient to my superiors all the next week, planing to slip over to Acre that Saturday, our day off. (53)

> "Now let this be a lesson to you. You should realize that we have the latest equipment with which to monitor your every movement, even including what you whisper in your dreams. With our modern apparatus we know all that happens, both within the state and outside it. Take care you don't ever behave this way again."
>
> Determined to be an ass no more, I refrained from giving the big man my opinion of all his ultramodern equipment. (52)

Thus, *The Pessoptimist* is more experimental in form, ambiguous in its conclusion, and multidirectional in its satire than is *Švejk*. Moreover, while *Švejk* depends on its consistently comic, antiheroic stance, *The Pessoptimist*, by virtue of its very instability, its vacillation between the comic and tragic, gives us a protagonist who presents both a mythic facade and an undercurrent of vulnerability and subjectivity. Saeed's narrative is informed by his own self-awareness, which alternates between denial and acknowledgment of his compromised position.

In this respect, *The Pessoptimist* has more in common with a confessional work such as Albert Camus's *La chute* (The fall)[80] than with *The Good Soldier Švejk*. In *Testimony: Crises of Witnessing in Literature, Psychoanalysis, and History* (1992), Shoshona Felman states that *The Fall* gives "a parodic picture of the contradictions of an entire generation of entrapped European intellectuals, unwittingly still struggling with the Second World War, in the grips of history . . . but hoping to erase it by a new beginning, falling for the rationalizations both of Marxism and of fascism."[81]

Felman notes that Clamence, the narrator of *The Fall*, gives "voice to the contradictions of an entire generation as well as to his own and to his own former delusions."[82] Clamence's ability to be a witness for truth, however, requires that he be among the guilty. "We cannot assert the innocence of anyone," Clamence philosophizes, "whereas we can state with certainty the guilt of all. Every man testifies to the crimes of all the others—that is my faith and my hope."[83] Saeed is a figure with more in common with Clamence than with Švejk, in this sense. He is a figure who bears witness to his own ambivalence:

> Is there, then, no place under the sun for me but this stake? Isn't there at least a lower stake where I can sit? A quarter stake, half a stake, a three-quarter stake?
>
> At first Yuad passed by. I stretched out my hand to her to pull her up, but she gripped me fast and began dragging me down . . .
>
> And Baqiyya arrived, calling to me to descend . . .
>
> Then I saw the young man with the newspaper again, now with an axe under his arm. I watched him swing his axe at the base of the stake as he cried, "I want to save you!" But I shouted down at him to stop, otherwise I would fall. And I held on to my stake all the tighter. (158–59)

Felman also sees Clamence, in the role of witness, as a Christ-like figure, in the sense that "Jesus, in Camus' atheological perspective, is himself not a man-God but an archetypal human witness . . . and in particular, witness to history as outrage."[84] Additionally, she connects this role of witnessing to a paradox that is geographical in nature. On the one hand, Clamence's narrative generates a sense of geographical isolation:

> They come from the four corners of Europe and stop facing the inner sea, on the drab strand. They listen to the foghorns, vainly try to make out the silhouettes of boats in the fog, then turn back over the canals and go home through the rain. (15)

At the same time, however, it generates a reciprocal feeling of location at the moral center of the universe. Felman notes that Clamence's complicity is reflected most clearly in the site that he has chosen to inhabit, the former Jewish quarter of Amsterdam. Felman explains that Camus uses "hell" as a metaphor for a historical reality. She suggests that the word *concentric* "connotes Camus' allusion to the historical fact of the concentration-camp and what it symbolizes in European history." Clamence himself elaborates on the symbolism of the place: "We are at the heart of things here. Have you noticed that Amsterdam's concentric canals resemble the circles of hell?" (14).

Similarly, the site from which Saeed composes his narrative—a room in an insane asylum (figuratively, somewhere in outer space)—constitutes him by location as an "underground man." This geographical symbolism is one in which the closeness to the center of a crucial historical outrage is juxtaposed with the anonymous physical placement in a tiny corner of the universe. The same placement, simultaneously on the fringe, and at the heart of civilization, is encountered in the work of a host of Western modernist writers such as Dostoyevsky, Conrad, André Gide, Thomas Mann, Ralph Ellison, Graham Greene, Paul Bowles, Gabriel García Márquez, and many others.

The Pessoptimist also has more of a literary orientation than does *The Good Soldier Švejk.* The use of the device of secondary narration is a typically modernist one, which tends to put a greater degree of concentration on the act of narration or writing. Saeed is a contrast to Švejk, who completely resembles a folk character, and whose history is given in a manner close to the tradition of oral narration. Saeed, on the other hand, represents more of a self-conscious writer, who leaves behind a text as an artifact that stands as a summation of his life or of his existential dilemma. None of this is to underestimate the extent to which *The Pessoptimist* is still a text of resistance. The narrative is laced with poetry, for instance, which strongly contrasts with the ironic tone in other parts of the narrative, expressing the "true feeling" of the Palestinians' displacement and loss.

Like Švejk (and Clamence) Saeed is an "anti-engagement" artist, whose nature is fundamentally subversive. He writes as a man apart, a minnow in the belly of a whale, a barely perceptible microbe whose presence nevertheless threatens to subvert the whole machine. Yet despite his insignificance, and the almost total awareness that the Israeli state apparatus has of his movements, there is the sense within the narrative of an immense energy being funneled to coerce and control this very tiny atom of potential destructiveness. Thus, although he is a bungler, a coward, and a buffoon, he is still a Palestinian, and this fact makes him feared and hated by the Zionist State.

Despite the sharp political critique concealed beneath its veiled narrative, Habiby's text, like Ghitani's *Zayni Barakat*, can be described as a defensive one, aiming to protect and defend a sense of integrity in the face of oppression. The sources of truth are distanced from the sources of power. The power of the artist is that of an underground man, subverting established authority from a tiny cell within the authoritarian structure. The underground man's text, like the narrative of the pessoptimist or even Ghitani's Venetian traveler, is a found object, like a note in a bottle, whose authenticity is convincing because of the indirect manner in which the reader receives it. This strategy is necessarily distant from that of Sonallah Ibrahim's, whose style is more the direct and reportorial one of a professional journalist, and who aims to challenge the reader by means of the text's complexity and ambiguity. In both cases, however, the writers aim to clothe the essential meaning they wish to convey in a form that is unconventional, new to the reader, and requires effort on the part of the reader to unwrap, decode, and understand.

Chapter 2

Recovering the Past: The "Arabization" of the Novel

The basis . . . of the establishment of Arab revolutionary thought is the analysis of Arab reality.

—Adonis

I am very much trying to work against literature that tries to build up a relationship between a character and the reader. What I am trying to do is to get the reader involved in drawing his own conclusions as to what is happening, rather than having preordained conclusions drawn for him. I would compare what I am trying to do with Brecht's theater, in which the onlooker is made aware that he is watching a play. Similarly, I want to make the reader aware that he is reading a work of fiction.

—Abdelrahman Munif

CULTURAL AND HISTORICAL COUNTER-NARRATIVE: ABDELRAHMAN MUNIF

As we have seen, both Gamal al-Ghitani and Emile Habiby used irony to comment in a veiled way on political subjects, as well as Arab history and folk tradition as a vehicle for that irony. At the same time, both of these novelists used their historical and cultural sources as a means of experimenting with narrative form. Ghitani's documentary style was a highly innovative method of constructing narrative, as was Habiby's use of the form of the fantastic fable. Written in the same year as Habiby's *Pessoptimist*, *Endings* (1988; *Al-Nihāyāt*, 1977),[1] by Abdelrahman Munif ('Abd al-Raḥmān Munīf), represents both a continuity with, and a departure from, these concerns. Munif is a prolific novelist, and presently among the most familiar contemporary Arab authors in the English-speaking world after Naguib Mahfouz, due largely to the translation by Peter Theroux of the first three volumes the "Cities of Salt" series. He defies classification in terms of his nationality. A Saudi by birth, he was deprived of his Saudi citizenship, and has lived in exile in Egypt, Yugoslavia, Iraq, France, and most recently Syria. He could be described an Arab cosmopolitan in the sense that, while his cosmopolitanism is sophisticated, it is not Western-centered.

The difference between Habiby's, and Munif's work is twofold. First of all, *Endings* is not a resistance narrative, but rather a counternarrative. That is, it does not use irony in order to combat a sense of oppression, victimization, or complicity, but rather simply asserts a cultural alternative. Secondly, Munif uses the form of oral narration in a much more directed and purposeful way as a means of experimenting with narrative form. Formal innovation is no longer subordinated to political engagement, but has rather become the very means of that engagement.

The environmental and historical settings of many of Munif's more recent novels are marked by a preoccupation with desert life and culture. He puts himself in the category of Arab writers who are primarily concerned with developing an innovative style that is not imitative of the West. Munif is extremely conscious of trying to fashion a novel that is uniquely "Arab" in its view of history as well as in its narrative style. In this sense he clearly allies himself with writers such as Ghitani, who are interested in working within the Arab cultural tradition. These writers tend to be particularly interested in Latin American and Japanese literature, because they are areas of the world that have developed innovative literary styles, while retaining an indigenous flavor. According to Munif, Arab writers such as himself are intent on scrutinizing these types of literature to see how they have managed to achieve this literary independence from the West.[2]

Endings is set is a small desert village called Al-Tiba. The events of the novel take place during a year of particular drought, and concern the sport of bird hunting, which infects some of the villagers and people from the surrounding area like a mania. The main character is a man named 'Assaf, an outsider in the village who is ridiculed for his nonconformity. 'Assaf, however, is in fact far wiser than the rest of the villagers. He is a master hunter, with an almost reverential attitude toward nature, and a strong awareness of the limits to the advantage man can take of it.

Although ‘Assaf feels himself to be an outsider, nevertheless he is loyal to the village, and during the drought, when hunger afflicts the villagers, he always leaves some game on peoples’ doorsteps, keeping little for himself. Gradually, as the villagers become aware of ‘Assaf’s hunting talent and his generosity, they begin to feel a gruff affection toward him. When people come from the city in order to hunt, ‘Assaf is always in demand to lead these veritable caravans, and is unable to refuse to serve as a guide. He tries to warn the people about the foolishness of hunting just for sport, maintaining that animals should only be shot in utmost dire necessity for food, but he is not rewarded with the sense that his words are heeded:

> “These birds belong to us,” he would say with some anxiety. “Either for today or tomorrow. If we’re careful about conserving them, they’ll be here for us to hunt. But if we kill them all or hunt them too much, they’ll make an end of it and look for somewhere else to live.”
>
> He pictured a land totally devoid of partridges to hunt. “Listen, you people,” he yelled testily. “If these birds disappear . . . you can be sure that the people of al-Tiba are going to die, the whole lot of them. I’m convinced of that.” (32)

Events accelerate one afternoon with the arrival of a party of four guests in two cars, a Jeep and a Volkswagen. Their arrival unnerves the villagers, most of whom have never seen such vehicles. For the occasion, they assemble for an evening meeting, during which the conversation centers on hunting. ‘Assaf is brought to the meeting, although he is known to dislike such gatherings. Although usually taciturn, on this occasion he is moved to speak:

> “I’ve told you a thousand times before. Only a short stretch separates us from death, and it consists of the game which we have to preserve till the rains come again. . . . I’ve told you all: don’t touch the female partridges; they’re needed for future years. They’re all we have left. I’ve told you: don’t waste ammunition, and don’t scare the birds. . . . But do you listen? No!” (46)

Despite his pleas, however, the villagers talk ‘Assaf into leading another hunting party, with the guests riding in the Jeep. During this expedition, ‘Assaf dies in a sandstorm. The community is stunned by this event, realizing that it has lost the individual who, despite his nonconformity, is most precious to them. The villagers and the guests gather to share their grief in an all-night vigil. During this meeting they talk amongst themselves, recite poetry, indulge in reminiscences and sorrows, and tell stories.

The text of *Endings* is thus divided into two parts. The first part concerns the "events" that revolve around 'Assaf and his relationship to the village community. The second part consists of fourteen "stories" that are told on the evening of 'Assaf's death. Munif is carrying out several simultaneous narrative experiments here. Not only is he experimenting with building the novel on the basis of the oral tradition of folk narrative, but he works at undermining the reliance on the main character or hero, as well as on the centrality of plot. With 'Assaf's death placed at the midpoint of the text, the immediate effect upon the reader is disorienting. To this point, Munif has built 'Assaf up as a heroic character by emphasizing his special qualities—his independence, his wisdom, his concern for the welfare of the villagers. At the point of the reader's greatest interest, however, Munif suddenly disposes of his main character. He wants to make the reader aware that he is reading a work of fiction, and therefore he interrupts the reader's identification with the character in an abrupt fashion.

From this point on, the text is held together on a thematic basis, rather than by a linear plot. The fourteen stories that follow all thematically reflect the character of 'Assaf, whose death they commemorate. The stories all involve animals, and all of them end in a sudden manner, with a death that seems abrupt and senseless. For instance, the Third Story tells of a pair of crows that develop a strange relationship with a bitch. The crows hound, attack, and dive-bomb the bitch in a game that becomes the spectacle of the village:

> Then one day the whole thing came to an end. The bitch disappeared. No one saw the crows any more either. (92)

In early summer, however, the bitch returns with a whole litter of pups. The crows also return, and the mock battles resume, much to the delight of the children in the village. Then, suddenly, one day, the town policeman shoots the bitch and all her pups. The crows are never seen again. Each one of the stories has a heartrending ending of this type. The

Fifth Story is about a dog with a unique personality, to which his owner, a *shaykh*, is devoted. One day the dog falls in a water hole and cannot be rescued. The Seventh Story is about a family of crows that live in a nest in a walnut tree in a garden. One day, the owner of the garden decides to get rid of them, climbs inexorably up the tree, and has his eye gouged out by one of the crows before he is able to smash the nest and kill all but the female. The Tenth Story is about a major's pampered little dog that wanders into a pack of village dogs and is torn to pieces.

The Eleventh Story is worthy of special note, because it is the only one told in first person. The narrator tells of lighting a fire in his fireplace on a cold winter's day, and being surprised by a piercing shriek. A cat had been up the chimney, hunting pigeons that nested there. It emerges, scared out of its wits, its body badly burned. But instead of going into a corner to lick its wounds and hide, it dashes back defiantly, into the fire. When his children ask him about the cat's behavior, the narrator tells them, "Cats aren't the only ones that behave that way." The story ends enigmatically, with the man voicing his own private thoughts. This brief expression of personal subjectivity is all the more striking for its isolation within the text as a whole:

> Once again there was silence. I raised my hand to scratch my head, hoping to get rid of both the dirt from the fire and the miserable thoughts I was contemplating. I wanted to behave in a way which would allow me to rid myself of a life in exile! (119)

Munif goes considerably beyond an interest in building the novel on the basis of the Arabic oral tradition in terms of his narrative innovation. It is important to note, however, that what he achieves is all done by means of a single experimental strategy. First of all, he is able to undermine the centrality of both the hero and linear plot. At the same time, he offers us an entirely new form of the Arabic novel, closer to that of a short story collection, and reminiscent of experimental modernist texts in the Western canon such as Jean Toomer's *Cane*,[3] Gertrude Stein's *Three Lives*,[4] and Ernest Hemingway's *In Our Time*.[5]

Also noteworthy is the sensitive concern the novel displays with local habitat and culture, and its privileging of a sense of community over individuality, which clearly reflect an ambivalence, if not outright criticism of modernity. Once again, these same characteristics—the retreat from modernity and the sensitive depiction of locale—are key characteristics of the same texts by Toomer, Stein, and Hemingway that experiment with building the novel on the form of the short story or vignette. Thus, paradoxically, Munif's move toward basing the novel on a more indigenous form of narrative makes it highly comparable to key texts in the Western modernist canon.

In his *Inkisār al-Aḥlām* (The shattering of dreams),[6] Muhammad Kamil al-Khatib (Muḥammad Kāmil al-Khaṭīb) makes the point that Munif was a member of a highly politicized generation that turned to literature as a form of alternative expression. When the political dreams they had nurtured failed to come to fruition, the writers of this generation used literature as a weapon trained against the power structure of their own society. Muhammad Siddiq, for instance, characterizes one of Munif's later novels, *The Trench* (1991; *Al-Ukhdūd*, 1985), as a work which challenges "the hegemonic master-narrative" of the "official Saudi account of the establishment of the Kingdom of Saudi Arabia."[7]

Munif may be among the most misunderstood and underrated Arab writers in terms of his formal experimentation. Western readers and critics are inclined to regard Munif's "Cities of Salt" series, of which three volumes have been translated and published in English, mainly as social critique of a highly elaborate and sophisticated nature. These works, in particular, have been the subject of proprietory claims on the part of self-styled "postcolonial" critics in the West. The claim is made on the basis of their preoccupation with broad historical or political themes, their rewriting of history from a distinctly "Arab" viewpoint, or simply their apparently unadorned, "realistic" style, qualities that endear them, respectively, to historicists, multiculturalists, and antimodernists.

At the same time, among Arab critics, Munif tends to be viewed as a novelist in the classical (realist) mode, the prose and structure of his texts unextraordinary, and their subject matter noncontroversial. There is a failure on the part of even highly sophisticated critics to grant Munif the status of an experimental writer. The "Cities of Salt" series is generally lumped in the category of the historical novel in the mode of Ghitani's *Zayni Barakat*. This is due partly to Munif's narrative style, which is unadorned, almost reportorial in tone. It is also due to the historical theme of these novels, as well as to the apparent absence of literary devices in these works, which either directly or obviously interferes with the sequentiality of narration. The latter technique is one that Arab critics, in particular, have come to associate with the experimental novel. Yumna al-'Eid, for instance, contrasts what she calls the "modern" novel from its antecedent in terms of its reliance not on storytelling, but on *discours*. According to this distinction, she asserts that Munif's *Cities of Salt* (1987; *Mudun al-Milh: Al-Tih*, 1984) is not a modern novel, since it is "preoccupied with the 'play' of composition, not with that which forms the elements of novelistic discourse" (125).

This type of distinction, however, tends to ignore the ways in which Munif's form of narrative is, in fact, innovative in comparison with that of early modernists such as Mahfouz or Kanafani. Eid provides a hint of such a distinction when she refers to "narrative techniques which are not employed without the specialized discourse of storytelling" (126), and concludes that

> The novel of 'Abd al-Rahmān Munīf departs from the form of the problem-solution novel, or the novel of the heroic personality, but, in terms of its orientation, it remains a novel which tells a story. (127)

In other words, Eid is acknowledging that Munif does away with narrative techniques that impose a "problem-solution" (as in *Miramar*) or a "heroic personality" (as in *All That's Left to You*), neither of which can be employed without the discourse of storytelling, without actually doing away with the storytelling discourse itself. For her, then, Munif occupies a transitional position with respect to modern narrative development. This analysis, however, ignores other ways in which Munif's writing is experimental. While his experimentation may be conservative in that it is not meant to overturn the discourse of storytelling, it nevertheless draws attention to the act of narration. It also highlights its own fictiveness in ways that are subtler, yet paradoxically bolder, than those of most of his contemporaries.

In some ways, Munif's work in the "Cities of Salt" series is written in a clearly more traditional mode. Like Sonallah Ibrahim in *Najmah Aghusṭus,* he offers a counternarrative instead of a resistance narrative. Unlike *Najmah Aghusṭus*, however, the "Cities of Salt" novels are not "negative" texts, in the sense that they do not aim at defamiliarizing—but rather with refamiliarizing—the reader with an alternative view of history. In this sense, Munif is working in a retrograde manner from the point of view of those critics whose only notion of experimentalism is as a defamiliarizing process. At the same time, this debate concerning the historical aspect of Munif's narrative obscures ways in which Munif is involved in an experimental project that specifically is meant to draw the reader's attention to the fictiveness of the text and, by implication, to the fictiveness of history itself.

The first of the volumes translated into English, *Cities of Salt*,[8] is the story of the arrival of Americans in the tiny desert village of Wadi al-Uyoun. It proceeds to relate the story of the destruction of the village, the dispersal of its inhabitants, and the monumental reconstruction of the port town of Harran, linked by pipeline to Wadi al-Uyoun. Munif plays with the reader's cultural perspective by writing from the viewpoint of the Arabs who have no inkling of the technology that the Americans bring with them:

> With the first light of dawn, huge iron machines began to move. Their deafening noise filled the whole wadi. So gigantic and strange were these iron machines that no one had ever imagined such things existed. . . .
>
> When the machines stopped, small windows and doors opened up in them and dusty men came out and looked around them. A bewildered silence reigned: Where had these men been? How had they entered and come out of these machines? Were they men or devils? . . . These yellow iron hulks—could a man approach them without injury? What were they for and how did they behave—did they eat like animals, or not? (98)

The narration is objective, yet at the same time it reflects a communal perspective, in order to give the reader an immediate feel of the shock that the Arabs are experiencing. Walid Hamarneh refers to this technique as the "dialectic of process and narration." He explains this term by noting that although Munif relies on using a narrative form with objective perspective, he combines it with an underlying voice that is "sympathetic, yet not completely submerged."[9] Such a perspective combines objectivity with an empathic voice that represents the shifting consciousness of the community.

The destruction of the village of Wadi al-Uyoun shows Munif's continued preoccupation with endings, as reflected in this shifting communal consciousness:

> This was the final, insane, accursed proclamation that everything had come to an end. For anyone who remembers those long-ago days, when a place called Wadi al-Uyoun used to exist, and a man named Miteb al-Hathal, and a brook, and trees, and a community of people used to exist . . . the . . . things that still break his heart in recalling those days are the tractors which attacked the orchards like ravenous wolves, tearing up the trees and throwing them to the earth. (106)

The collective ignorance of the villagers and townsfolk is particularly used in contrast with the presence of the Americans, creating a sense on the part of the reader that they are "absent," just as Western colonial texts tend to treat their native subjects:

> They were busy all day long. They went to places no one dreamed of going. They collected unthinkable things. They had a piece of iron—no one knew what it was or what they did with it—and when they returned in the evening they brought with them bags of sand and pieces of rock. Once they brought tamarisk and wormwood branches, and bunches of clover. They broke the branches in a strange way and attached pieces of paper on which they had written obscure things. That was not all: they placed wooden markers and iron poles everywhere they went, and wrote on them, and wrote things no one understood on the sheets of paper they carried with them everywhere. (30)

The Arabs' collective view of the Americans, who seem to accomplish things without exerting any visible power, confers on the foreigners an aura of mystery similar to that which orientalism conferred on the Arab world. In this case, however, the contrast is between an Arab culture that does not wish to know the causes of everything, and the fetishistic "scientific" attitude of the Americans, who constantly probe into every aspect of existence:

> "The bastards want to know everything," said Ibrahim al-Nasir. "Even why my father got divorced and remarried. They wanted to know if I was unclean, because I didn't pray all the time. They asked if I had a lot of wet dreams, and they laughed. The bastards want to know who has planted every seed and laid every egg in history." (329)

Irony is one of Munif's most essential narrative techniques, never more powerful than when he is depicting the Arabs' participation in their own downfall. One of the main characters is Ibn Rashed, a man who becomes a recruiter for the Americans, and rises to a powerful position in Harran. The Arabs succumb like sheep to the lure of the wealth he distributes, regardless of the cost to their previous way of life:

> In the first days a number of the workers thought of leaving Harran . . . but the first salary Ibn Rashed distributed changed their minds. No one had ever dreamed of getting that much money, and none had ever possessed that amount before. They received their pay in a silent, solemn, almost majestic rite. (185)

> Ibn Rashed . . . looked at their faces. "There's one more matter, my friends." He looked at them carefully. "The camels. From today onward they are of no use here."
>
> For the first time the men felt that they were confronting an agonizing situation and a decisive choice; they were being asked to give up the most precious things they owned.
>
> The next day they turned their camels over to Ibn Rashed with no discussion, and he gave them some money.
>
> No one said a word. They were all thinking of the safest way to store their money so that it would not get lost or stolen, and after long deliberation most of them decided that the best and surest way to safeguard it was to have Ibn Rashed keep it for them. (186–88)

Pitted against these overwhelming forces, Miteb al-Hathal resists the coming of the Americans from the moment that they first appear, and delivers dire prophecies of the consequences. When the destruction of the village is accomplished, he vanishes into the desert, yet he continues to exert an influence on the imagination of the people, and upon the reader. By means of this character, Munif plays with the paradox of presence and absence, and combines these qualities in the person of the prophetic, subversive character of Miteb al-Hathal:

> Long days of hard, uneasy waiting . . . but Miteb al-Hathal did not come.
>
> Miteb al-Hathal . . . No worker said it outright or pronounced his name out loud, but his specter filled the whole desert. . . . After the investigation they were all sure that Miteb al-Hathal, who had been gone for long years, no one knew where, was back, and that he would make the desert a hell for the Americans. (511)

In this passage, Munif connects the notion of disappearance or nonpresence with both the tradition of bedouin guerrilla warfare as well as Muslim messianic traditions such as that of the *Mahdī*. Munif is also playing here (and throughout the text) with the desert as symbol, in a way reminiscent of Kanafani's *All That's Left to You*. He uses this symbol, in part, to represent the Arabs, and he juxtaposes it with water, or the sea, which is associated with the Americans. The Americans arrive, via the sea, on great ships; they know how to swim; they are at home with water and on the water. The sea is the means by which they transport their men, their equipment, their technology, and even women who are brought for the pleasure of the colonists. In *Rich and Strange*, Marianne DeKoven argues that the symbolism of water, or the sea, is a uniquely modernist trope. In *Cities of Salt*, we can see how culturally specific such an observation is. Munif plays with this symbolism, echoed in earlier experimental Arabic novels such as *The Ship* and his own *Sharq al-Mutawassiṭ,* (East of the Mediterranean, 1975);[10] the desert symbolizes the native consciousness of the Arabs, while the sea represents the foreign consciousness of the Americans.

At one point, Miteb al-Hathal indeed makes an appearance, and here Munif borrows from the conventions of magical realism, all the more striking for its isolation within the lengthy text:

> Rain filled the earth and sky. The narrow *wadi* at the end of Rawdhat al-Mashti gushed crazily with water, and the people stood and watched in bewilderment.
>
> At that very moment, as a brilliant flash of lightning rent the sky, creating fear upon fear, Miteb al-Hathal appeared.
>
> He . . . seemed to stand squarely on the opposite bank of the wadi. He struck the earth with his staff, looked at them all sternly and shook his head three times. Before he turned away his voice rumbled . . . "Fear is from things to come."
>
> . . . "Didn't you see him? Where is he? He was there . . . he was there." (151–53)

Miteb al-Hathal is not a heroic figure, however, but rather an ambivalent one. He expresses his attitude toward the Americans in exaggerated, demonic terms:

> Watch their eyes, watch what they do and say. They're devils, no one can trust them. They're more accursed than the Jews. And the bastards memorized the Koran. Strange. (29)

> We should have done something a long time ago, when they first came. I knew they would return. I knew they would do things men and jinn never dreamed of. They came. I saw them myself. In the wink of an eye they unleashed hundreds of demons and devils. These devils catch fire and roar night and day like a flour mill that turns and turns without tiring out and without anyone turning it. What will happen in this world? How can we kill them before they kill us? (71)

The ambivalence in these passages comes from a tension between the truth that is expressed and the primitive terms in which it is articulated. Munif is here treading a thin line, suggesting a paradox. Miteb al-Hathal's anger and resentment is at once both visionary and based on ignorance. Munif's intention is to steer clear of a narrative that makes a particular historical or ideological point. Rather, he wants to present the reader with a broader, equivocal picture. His subject is the immense power brought to bear on one culture by another, the inexorable change this represents, and the subordination of everything else to this force of change, including personalities, ideology, traditional beliefs, and even culture itself.

Munif's subject is not so much the devastation caused to the traditional culture by colonial development, but rather the inexorable progress of that development. Within the framework of this progress, there are really no heroes or villains. The Americans who are so demonized by Miteb al-Hathal are similarly ambiguous figures, whose personalities are dwarfed by the historical process of which they are a part. In certain passages, Munif gives us a picture of the Americans as wide-eyed children, just as naive in the face of an alien culture as are the Arabs:

> The Americans, who looked and behaved like small children, showed endless, unimaginable surprise and admiration. They asked about everything, about words, clothing and food. (262)

> Every small thing excited the Americans' amazement. They took a great many photographs during the meal and tried to conquer their embarrassment at their inability to eat like the others. (263)

The subordination of character to history is also evident in the way in which Munif introduces and concludes his treatment of characters. They are introduced in an indirect manner. Often their actions have an effect on the narrative before they are formally introduced. The character of the American, Sinclair, for instance, crops up for the first time in the narrative as if he had already appeared previously. At the same time, characters are dispensed of or melt away without any formality. When the narrative moves to the port city of Harran, Miteb al-Hathal's prophetic role is taken over by another character, Ibn Naffeh, who similarly reviles every change that the coming of the Americans has brought. When Ibn Rashed becomes expendable, he too passes away without affecting the course of the narrative. In this sense, Munif has the instincts of a realist, interested in offering a panoramic view of society. He has said that the "Cities of Salt" series was an attempt to evoke a sense of both place and history.[11] But the laconic way in which he introduces and disposes of characters goes beyond realism, and, in fact, parodies realism's exaggerated dependence on character development. As in *Endings*, Munif is trying to heighten the awareness of the reader by defying his or her expectations in a way that contravenes the conventions of realism.

In *Variations on Night and Day* (1993; *Taqāsim al-Layl wa al-Nahār*, 1989)[12] Munif continues to follow his historiographic preoccupations. The narrative chronicles the creation and expansion of the fictional sultanate of Mooran. The jacket cover of the English translation advertises the novel as follows:

> Full of Machiavellian intrigue and searing political satire . . . *Variations on Night and Day* . . . chronicles the creation of a Persian Gulf nation by a corrupt Arab monarch and conniving British empire builders. . . . The novel depicts the rise to power of Sultan Khureybit and the emergence of Mooran as a modern nation. Khureybit expands his dominion, crushing rival clans by military force and internal opposition with bribes, guile, assassinations, and executions—all in the name of holy war, even as he is being sponsored by the British Empire, which is playing rival sultans off one another to secure its influence over the region. Against this setting we see as well the venality of the Sultan's polygamous household, in which his several wives vie for preeminence through gossip, chicanery, and murder.[13]

Such a description of the work could not be more misleading. Munif has said, "The point of the novel was not to write social criticism. There is far more corruption in Gulf society than is mirrored in the book. If anything, it treats the subject of social and political corruption with kid gloves."[14]

In this third volume of the "Cities of Salt" series, Munif experiments further with narrative point of view. This experimentation can be seen most clearly when he focuses on events of particular importance. At these points, he tends to stop and recount the event from numerous viewpoints. For instance, after describing the Battle of al-Samha, the narrator proceeds for two pages to give supplementary accounts of the battle:

> Before verdicts were given and the outcome weighed, there had to be an answer to the most basic question: what had happened?
>
> Even this question, which should not have caused any great dissension, gave rise to the wildest discrepancies.
>
> One of the Sultan's biographers, writing seven years after the Awali campaign, wrote. . . .
>
> One of Mooran's "historians" wrote of the Battle of al-Samha. . . .
>
> A more recent researcher who came to Mooran with a number of motives, one of which was the writing of history, wrote of the battle that. . . .
>
> Hamilton wrote about the Battle of al-Samha years later, working from his journals. . . .
>
> Much later a neutral historian recounting the battle wrote that. . . . (122–23)

At many other points in the narrative, the narrator is at pains to include various versions of an event, often conflicting. Sometimes versions are later even asserted to be plainly fictitious. The technique seems to aim at creating uncertainty in regard to history, or to make the point that the reconstruction or interpretation of any event depends on the viewpoint of the individual:

> The stories and tidbits, and even the rumors about their relationship, and the matter of Othman's money and other affairs, were full of contradictions and conflicting versions due to the numerous narrators and their varying motives, so that it was impossible to establish the truth, or even parts of it. (185)

> There were radically different accounts of what happened next, after the gold and jewels were handed over. According to one version, the Sultan sold all of the gold in the markets of Haifa and Jaffa; according to another, Olayan took it all to India and sold it there. The best-

> informed people said that no final sale took place: the gold had all been deposited or pawned with Jewish goldsmiths and money changers in Baghdad, against commercial loans at interest. (188)

> Why had the Sultan chosen this specific place? Was there any meaning in this?
>
> Historians were later perplexed by this detail, and found unnumbered interpretations for it. (195)

> As to how Ibn Bakhit knew, there were at least three different stories. (209)

At the same time, however, when Munif reports a given event from different perspectives or viewpoints, his purpose is to give the reader a more complete view of an event. It represents an ultimate attempt to "objectify," to write history in the form of fiction. The idea that material of dubious authenticity can help to construct a "true" historical picture is a modernist idea in Western literature, but a traditional one in Arabic literature. Specifically, it has a direct connection with the Arabic literary tradition of *hadith*, or the record of actions and sayings of the Prophet. In the earlier days of Islam, those people who had lived in the society of the Prophet were the best authority for this knowledge. Later, Islamic tradition was further built on the authority of the first generation after Muhammad, and then with that of following generations. Not all of these traditions can be regarded as reliable; in fact, numerous contradictory traditions arose, yet all still form a part of the total body of *hadith*.[15]

At the same time, the notion that an accumulation of viewpoints can heighten the sense of "reality" conveyed by a narrative is certainly a modernist technique, akin to that which we have discussed in relation to Faulkner, Mahfouz, and others. In view of Munif's connection with Jabra Ibrahim Jabra, it may also be worth quoting from *The Ship*, in which Jabra reveals indebtedness to Kafka with respect to this narrative technique:

> It was Kafka's habit in his *Memoirs* to describe an experience in one way, then again in another way, then again a third way, and so on for a fourth, or a fifth time in some cases . . . each time he would start differently, abbreviating some details in the previous version and expanding others. . . . It's like looking at a huge object and walking around

> it. . . . This is the closest thing to a kaleidoscope of words and ideas. Every time it is turned, a new shape appears, or new idea. . . . How many facets does truth have then?"[16]

Munif is intent on challenging both the Saudi view of history and the Western colonial view of history. He mimics the Western colonial and postcolonial literary tradition particularly in his depiction of Hamilton, a character who, in several instances, seems to be modeled on T. E. Lawrence:

> Hamilton . . . was loyal to the Empire but detested it. Money to him was a mere means of doing business, a means of entry, an autonomous power in itself. He wished he were a king people never tired of gazing upon, and yet longed to be an anonymous and unknown man. (50)

> When he was on camelback under the sun's burning blaze, with the desert sand below him rolling on like the leaves of a book, he felt that he was the only man capable of this mission; that an awesome power had been entrusted to him. (51)

> Hamilton . . . was addicted to Arab clothes; he could not give them up. When he was compelled to wear his own clothes, to board a plane or travel, he felt disguised. He smiled and laughed when he caught sight of himself in the mirror—this was the thing his friends did when they saw him in European clothes: they smiled. (54–55)

> With this exposure to nature and turbulence, he felt that his body would not obey him, that it had mutinied and would not revert to his control again, especially after such a long time without a woman, and that only by violent action, no less violent than war, could he restore strength and discipline to his body. (70)

Hamilton, in fact, is a composite character of the twentieth-century orientalist man of action. Munif has made the point that Hamilton is modeled more on Harry St. John Philby[17] than on Lawrence. Lawrence, he has noted, belonged to a generation associated with the end of an era—namely the Ottoman era, to whose destruction Lawrence was dedicated. Philby, on the other hand, belonged to a subsequent era, which was dedicated to building a new society rather than tearing an old one down.[18] The history of Mooran is a history of construction and consolidation, rather than dismantling and dismemberment. This is, indeed, a valid distinction, but one that relates more to the historiographical aspect of *Variations of Night and Day* than to the character construction. In choosing certain details needed for his portrait of Hamilton, Munif utilizes some characteristics associated more with Lawrence, than with Philby.

The point is that, by creating such an intertextual character as one of the focal points of his novel, Munif is at pains to counter orientalist history. Despite the detail that Munif lavishes on the character of Hamilton, he never allows him to dominate the narrative. Rather, he is subordinate to Arab history. In this sense, *Variations on Night and Day* responds directly to a work such as *Seven Pillars of Wisdom*, in which Arab history is subordinated to Lawrence's own personal psychological narrative. Here, the Western orientalist is a mote floating on the tide of history, rather than a maker of history.

Munif takes a posture that is the inverse of Lawrence's with respect to his intentions as a writer. While Lawrence sought to remake history into a personal fiction, Munif attempts to use fiction in order to rewrite history. While these twin impulses seem to be contradictory, in fact they spring from a similar modernist viewpoint that blurs distinctions between history or autobiography and fiction. Both produce metahistorical narratives, which look back to previous historical narrative traditions. Lawrence looks back to Doughty and the medievalists, revising their literary tradition, while Munif looks back and revises the Western orientalist tradition.

MAGICAL REALISM: SALIM BARAKAT

This same sensitivity to locale that we noted in Munif's *Endings* is the main feature of the early work of Salim Barakat (Salīm Barakāt), a Syrian-born Kurd, living in Cyprus. Unlike Munif, Barakat has yet to have a complete work translated into English, although he is also an Arabic novelist of top stature, and a prolific one. His first two works, *Al-Jundub al-Ḥadīdī* (The iron grasshopper, 1980) and *Fuqahā' al-Ẓalām* (Sages of darkness, 1985), are set in poor Kurdish villages near the Syrian-Turkish border. The former work is not a novel, but an autobiographical narrative, published in 1980, when the author still lived in Syria. *Fuqahā' al-Ẓalām* was published in 1985, after Barakat had moved to Cyprus.

Barakat's style is probably the closest of any Arab writer's to that of

Latin American magical realism. It not only represents reality by means of the mythic imagination, as does the work of Emile Habiby, but it also uses local culture as a means of conveying a more universal condition. In his article "From Realism to Magic Realism," Morton P. Levitt sees the work of Gabriel García Márquez, for instance, as an example of art in which "local political realities, the most pedestrian of sources, are transformed into universal truths."[19] We can see this latter tendency even in *Al-Jundub al-Ḥadīdī*,[20] Barakat's earliest work.

Although not a novel, *Al-Jundub al-Ḥadīdī* is a significant work. In it, Barakat is experimenting with narrative, although in what, by modernist standards, is still a tentative way. It is not innovative in terms of its form or structure, but rather in terms of its vocabulary, sentence construction, images, and narrative voice. The first part of its lengthy subtitle translates as "The unfinished memoir of a child who never saw anything but a fugitive land." The narrative focuses on the raw, violent nature of adolescent life set in an atmosphere of both extreme poverty and bucolic splendor, and is suffused with nostalgia for the Kurdish land and cultural heritage.

In this early work, Salīm Barakat's use of language differs from that in traditional narrative primarily through his metaphoric and metonymic use vocabulary. The result is a style that is so difficult that even Arabic readers will fail to understand it, and that is therefore very hard to render into English. This style is particularly evident in the lyrical introduction, which indulges heavily in mixed metaphors, a style of writing that is a traditional one in Arabic poetry. In essence, Barakat attempts to convert a traditional poetic style to prose. His technique is to deliberately strip a word of its original meaning, and press it into service in a new way, in effect substituting it for a more standard word. If we look simply at the opening paragraph, for instance, we immediately see several instances of this substitution technique:

> What do you see? Tell me, child, what do you see? Two hills on the horizon, a necklace of villages, soil staggering between an immature summer and dull winter. Your rendezvous, child, is with plants or birds. You close your eyes to the morning, while the veils fall from its baskets, and you grab hold of an ambiguous bridle as if you are preparing for middle age, or middle age is preparing for you, so that you can, together, distil that magic which pulsates only one time, while life will commit suicide yearning for another pulse. (7)

Such a text presents a multitude of problems for a translator. The awkward "necklace of villages," while true to the meaning of *'aqd* (necklace), might be rendered as a "chain of villages" without sacrificing much in meaning. Yet if Barakat had wanted to use the word "chain," he would have opted for the word *silsilah*. A more difficult problem is what to do with "soil staggering." The verb *yatarannahu*, used normally in connection with the gait of a drunkard, sounds incongruous when used in connection with *turāb* (soil, earth)—not just in English but also in the Arabic. Barakat is trying to suggest an additional meaning, as if the soil is somehow as unproductive as a drunkard. In essence, the choice of the verb provides the implicit metaphor.

The same is true with the use of the word *silal* (baskets) together with *aqni'ah* (veils, masks). A veil falling suggests the growing clarity of the day as it approaches noon (the time suggested by the word *ḍuḥa*), but the word *silal* adds a complexity to the image that seems hardly justified. (Veils in baskets do not perform the function of veils.) On the other hand, substituting the word "face" for baskets would result in too standard an image, while "fall from its baskets" gives the impression of a load being lightened by the progress of the day. Similarly, Barakat mixes two other metaphorical images to evoke the sense of intense participation in life: grabbing hold of a bridle, in which the implicit metaphor is of life as a horse, and distilling magic, in which the metaphor is of life as a potion. Roger Allen notes that this technique is reminiscent of the *maqāmah* tradition, where the major purpose of the compositional process was to play with the meanings of words (and, if possible, produce texts that would be virtually impossible to "understand").[21]

The other innovative aspect to the narrative is its dualism. The narrator repeatedly addresses a child: "O child!" or "We were children, my friend," yet it becomes clear that the child he addresses is himself because the narrator frequently shifts from first person to third person and back again in the course of his narration, as in the following example:

> I began to be aware of something new that didn't occur to me previously: You are a Kurd. The Kurds are dangerous. It's not allowed to speak Kurdish in school. This is new, because you know that three fourths of this city adjacent to the Taurus Mountains are Kurds. Here you're beginning to grasp the problem. (21)

This technique may be Barakat's adaptation to prose of conventions common in classical Arabic poetry, in which the narrative voice is conjoined to the addressee. As an example we can take a line from the poet Zuhayr Bin Abi Salma (Zuhayr Bin Abī Salmā):

> I was weary with the burdens of life, for whosoever lives for eighty years, [you] will certainly grow tired.[22]

The shift from first-person past tense to the neutral "man" (whosoever) is common in most languages, and can be found in prose as well as poetry. The second shift to second-person singular is really a stock expression. The form of the verb *yas'ami* remains in the third person. The example does, however, illustrate the tendency to slip from declaratory to rhetorical posture in classical Arabic, and this is mirrored in Barakat's prose: "I began to be aware of something new. . . . This is new, because you know that . . ."

A line from Al-Mutanabbi (Al-Mutanabbī) provides what is perhaps a clearer example:

> I loved you, my heart, before your love of the one who departed. He was treacherous; so remain loyal to me.[23]

Here there appears to be no shift at all. The writer addresses his heart. In fact, however, the writer and his heart are one. The object of their affection is the same. Barakat echoes this in the same passage: "I began to be aware of something new. . . . You are a Kurd."

Paradoxically, despite his Kurdish orientation, Barakat is perhaps the master prose stylist writing in Arabic today. Barakat's influence on the contemporary Arabic novel has almost been one of a "neoclassicist," due to his complex style and his application of techniques taken from traditional Arabic literature. While his style is a complete contrast to that of Abdelrahman Munif, both authors, via different paths, are producing literature that is distinctly Arabic. Munif accomplishes this via his use of historical perspective, Barakat via his use of language.

With his first novel, *Fuqahā' al-Ẓalām* (Sages of darkness, 1985), Barakat makes a large leap into a very pure form of magical realism. The tentative linguistic experimentation of *Al-Jundub al-Ḥadīdī* is largely left by the wayside. Here, Barakat emerges as a mature writer, whose experimentalism lies less in his use of language than in his use of images.

Within the framework of a realist narrative, he uses the techniques of magical realism to produce "mutations" in both time and space that upset the normal reality and play havoc with the characters and their situations.

In this novel, Salim Barakat uses the magical elements that play a supporting role in a novel such as Abdelrahman Munif's *Cities of Salt*, and elevates them to a dominant role. As Fakhri Salih observes:

> The narrative works of Salīm Barakāt are distinguished by . . . the use of the strange or the miraculous . . . but in *Fuqahā' al-Ẓalām* he uses this narrative principle in an exaggerated way, to the extent that the strange, the miraculous, or the fantastic becomes the focal point around which the novel is constructed. . . .[24]

In the Fall 1992 issue of *Michigan Quarterly Review*, Issa Boullata offers two tantalizingly brief excerpts from this novel. He accompanies these with a synopsis, as follows:

> *Sages of Darkness* is the story of two magical and snowy winters in the lives of some families in a small Kurdish Syrian village on the Turkish-Syrian border. Against the backdrop of the crude agricultural struggle, and the brutal life of tobacco smugglers, a child is born to Mulla Binav, on a freezing, snowy morning; a child who reaches the age of marriage by the waning of the winter day. From this day on, the village and the lives of its inhabitants take on a fantastic character. Bikas, the aging newborn, joins the violent, shadowy smugglers of the night, and the Sages of Darkness. Through the bewildered eyes of ten-year-old Kirzu, the Mulla's younger son, Barakat portrays the amazing events in the life of the beleaguered village: a grandfather confines himself to an old cupboard, while the cut fingers of a communist teacher grow in the garden, a eucalyptus tree turns into amber, scarecrows devour the cornfields, the village mosque slides away to the south, and some villagers develop gills under the ears. Then Bikas's child is born, and the time of the Sages of Darkness has come.[25]

The two brief sections translated by Boullata concern Bikas's "disappearance" after his marriage night. The Mulla sends Kirzu (one of his sons by a former wife) to inform his present father-in-law that Bikas is dead. On the way to deliver his message, Kirzu encounters Bikas, looking flabby and colorless. When the boy protests that his father asked him to lie about his stepbrother's death, Bikas tells him:

> "My father isn't lying, Kirzu, and in a little while you'll tell my grandfather Avdi Sari that. Don't forget." . . .
>
> So you're lying like my father," Kirzu said, his voice slightly angry.
>
> Bikas bent his head, then raised it again. He stared at his brother, then whispered: "Look."
>
> He opened his wool-lined cloak. . . . Simultaneously, the boy raised his hands to his face to protect it.
>
> From under Bikas's cloak, stormy flocks of starlings rushed out and bumped against the boy, who coiled himself up in surprise. When the noisy fluttering of wings had died, Kirzu slowly opened his eyes. Bikas was no longer there and all he could see was a black flock of starlings, flying high in the sky, heading north.[26]

Meanwhile, the Mulla has disguised a pillow as the baby, and organized a burial ceremony in order to cover up Bikas's disappearance. During the burial, however, he too encounters the ghostly form of Bikas:

> Sitting in the snow, naked up to the eyes which gazed at him with a heavy calm, a white face from which, on either side, hung two purple tufts of hair, two bright yellow eyes, a gray beard, and the head without form. . . .[27]

When the Mulla tries to get Bikas to come home with him, the aged son tells him he is presently preoccupied with the father's grain ledger. He holds the ledger out to the startled Mulla, and proceeds to show him certain discrepancies in the crop yields, which indicates that the distance between the two villages is decreasing, even though the villages themselves have not expanded due to any construction. The plot of the novel thus not only involves a "warp" in time, represented by the miraculous "aging" and "death" of Bikas, but also in space, represented by the mysterious discrepancies in the crop ledger.

At the same time, Barakat employs imagery that is offered as a contrast to the runaway nature of time and space:

> In the absence of the family, the little olive tree that will never grow became accustomed to specialize in beginning to become angry at the loneliness imposed on it. (177)

The image of time is slowed down, not only in the description of the tree as one that "will never grow," but also in the exaggerated length of time with which the tree exercises its "will" by becoming "accustomed to," "specialize in," "beginning to," "become angry." At the same time, in this passage, Barakat also adds another magical element to his narrative, namely an element of anthropomorphism extended to the natural world, in the form of the olive tree's subjectivity and intentionality.

When Sinam (Sīnam), Bikas's wife, gives birth, the baby grows into adulthood in a matter of hours, as did his father. Here, Barakat displays a humorous inventiveness in describing the interaction between the child, his mother, and his grandmother, Brina:

> Brina grabbed hold of the hand of her grandson, who was reclining with his back against a tall pillow, and asked him in a calm, heavy voice, "What are we going to name you?" The baby smiled, his vague features fragmented in the shadow of the lamps, as he gazed at his open-mouthed mother, as she tried to keep from bursting into laughter: "What are you going to name me, Mother?" (179)

The confusion over events soon erupts in a welter of questions on every side. Here the anthropomorphism is developed further, in an almost lyrical fashion akin to that found in the poetry of Longfellow, Whitman, or Lorca:

> Kirzu will ask the "second" Bikas what he meant by telling him "You have embarrassed me with your games." The embarrassed son of Sinam will ask Brina how tired she is from the burden that her father carried, and which he will now carry. The little olive tree that will never grow will ask the ghost, which is slowly advancing in its direction as it looks in the window of Sinam's room, about Mulla Binav. And the snow will ask the darkness about the problems it faces this night. (180)

The anthropomorphism is continued in Kirzu's attempted "dialogue" with the olive tree:

> Then he looked at the little tree with a wink. "Come on, let's catch up to Bikas." But the little tree didn't reply, of course, since, as a plant whose reality in this courtyard was determined by external forces, it was necessary for it to eschew conversation with the other life forms around it, of whom Kirzu was one, as well as the starlings, the snow, and the clouds. (190)

When the "second" Bikas slips away, Kirzu—the "eye" of the narrator, always on the heels of events—tries to follow him, and encounters a strange circle of men:

> The purple gleam was harsh on Kirzu's eyes as he opened the door: men in a circle, stern, motionless. . . . Due to his surprise, Kirzu did not think to ask himself about the source of the light. (184)

Bikas's son, meanwhile, is engaged in a similar ghostly encounter. The ghostly representative speaks to the second Bikas as if he were a child, or an acolyte, who knows nothing until he has joined them, on the other side of death:

> The ghost replied coldly, "Do you think you're prepared for what I asked you, when you go back there?"
>
> "Back where?" Bikas's son asked.
>
> "Back to what's passed you by, you idiot," the ghost muttered.
>
> Time was eating away at the body of Bikas's son just as, before, it had the body of his father. (191)

It is not only Bikas's son who joins the ghosts, but also the whole extended family, including the Mulla, Kirzu, and eventually the whole community. During the Mulla's encounter with Bikas in the graveyard, for instance, he asks Bikas to return the grain ledger to him. Bikas replies that he will only give it to him beyond the graveyard, a gesture symbolic of an afterlife:

> "Give me the ledger."
>
> The son, in turn, got up slowly: "Follow me. I'll give it to you on the other side of that hill over there." He pointed to the South, where the crest of the hill on which the graveyard was located dipped down. (108)

After this, the Mullah disappears from the narrative, except for in a passage in which his presence is perceived by the little olive tree:

> The movement of that hand, garbed in white . . . resembled a loving one with which the tree had once been familiar, one which used to carefully turn over some of its leaves, in order to examine its state of health. . . . It was surprised at the extent to which the movement re-

> sembled that of the hand of the Mulla Binav—fingertips rough from the purifying effects of cold—on its leaves. The little tree contemplated the fingertips of the dignified man, Brina's husband . . . summoning all its emotion to bend upon its stem: "Cover me with yourself before the darkness takes you." (178)

The whole community is now a ghostly one:

> The mass was advancing, a whispered sound throwing its net between the low hills. (198)

Finally, no one is left except the little tree:

> The little olive tree that will never grow because of its loneliness, surrendered to its fate as a plant . . . while the departing mass relinquished its hold on the place, until even the houses became uncertain, looking for an exit. (204)

In *Fuqahā' al-Ẓalām*, Barakat combines a fluid, effortless style, complete mastery of the language, striking imagery, and great sensitivity for the people and the land, which constitute his subjects. Especially impressive is the image with which he leaves the reader, of natural elements such as the snow, the wind, and the trees endowed with human-like awareness, yet deserted by the human inhabitants of the land, which have become a ghostly army, wandering without a home. Even the most casual reader will feel that there is something never explicitly stated behind this imagery.

The Kurds, it should be noted, are unrecognized as a nationality by the Syrian government. Not only are there no schools that teach the Kurdish language, but there are thousands of Kurds living in Syria who have never been given any passports or identity cards—that is, no official recognition that they are Syrians. Approximately half the Kurdish population lives in urban population centers such as Damascus, and is integrated with the rest of Syrian society. But the rural Kurds, who cling to their indigenous language and culture, are treated essentially as foreigners. They have no right to travel across borders, and can only do so illegally. Nor do they have the right to land or property ownership. Their official position in Syria is akin to that of ghosts.

This, however, does not quite explain the relationship that the "sages of darkness" have in relationship to the people. It is clear that they are in the position of having a superior knowledge. Bikas, as the first villager to be transformed, is in the position of a leader. The rest of the villagers are, in a sense, recruited, as if to a political movement. In the end, they have indeed become a movement. The story of Bikas, allegorically, is that of a transformation of the individual into an *engagé*.

In his article on *Fuqahā' al-Ẓalām*, Fakhri Salih points to chapter 2 as a key chapter in the novel, despite the fact that, in terms of plot, it has nothing to do with the main events involving Bikas, his son, or the "ghostly community." Rather, it narrates two other events, which serve as summaries, in parable form, of these twin themes. In this chapter, there are two stories being told. One involves an "animal" that is passing through a dark passage or tunnel, causing it to reflect on itself and its origins. The other story concerns a killing that leads to a massacre:

> The narrative of the animal's . . . journey is followed by a description of the killing. The story of the animal and its reflections paves the way for the massacre and its consequences: "All these bodies . . . these corpses entangled in one another in the darkness of the passage are like the tickling of death on my side." (65)[28]

Fakhri Salih interprets this intertwining of stories as follows:

> The summary of these two stories encompasses the vision of the entire work. . . . The story of the murder represents the changes and upheavals in the life of the tribe, while the story of the animal represents the strange nature of the person called Bikas.[29]

Salih concludes by stating the effect of this technique:

> In its narrative structure, *Fuqahā' al-Ẓalām* breaks the order . . . [of] the Arabic novel whose manner of expression is directly social or political. . . .[30]

In this respect, *Fuqahā' al-Ẓalām* is probably most comparable to Abdelrahman Munif's *Cities of Salt*. Both works are highly political, but subordinate the political element in their narratives in favor of creating a type of cultural panorama. Both attempt by this means to recapture or resurrect cultures that have been marginalized by political power and history. In a brief, understated passage in *Fuqahā' al-Ẓalām* that furnishes an important clue to the entire orientation of the novel, Barakat writes:

> The title "Ministry of Child Development and Education" remained prominent for a long time, from the time of Syrian independence until the '60s. After that, the word "Education" disappeared, as a result of the efforts of partisans for Egyptian-Syrian unity, who considered the most important thing for the country was simply to work on "child development" . . . which led to the utter neglect of "education." (79)

The implication of this passage is that Kurdish culture fell victim to Arab nationalism, particularly to the ideology of Arab unity, and that the public education system was used to enforce ethnic homogeneity. The passage offers a window into the Barakat's purpose, which is to find a means through literature to express what cannot be done for the Kurdish people politically. The irony of *Fuqahā' al-Ẓalām* is that the greatest work of its type in the Arab language asserts a cultural identity that is non-Arab.

FOLK NARRATIVE AND SUBJECTIVE EXPRESSION

The choice between political and artistic commitment has also affected the continuing trend toward building the novel on the basis of folk narrative. The interest in using the novel to draw a collective portrait of society has been particularly strong in Syria, where realism lingers as the primary mode of novelistic production. Syria can make claim to an extensive classical and modern literary tradition. Yet, apart from Palestine, preoccupied with political struggle, nowhere else in the Arab world has the novel been so resistant to experimentalism. It certainly cannot be said that Syrian novelists are unaware of the literary currents around them. They tend to be well read, and are familiar with contemporary world literature. Novels from around the world are the subjects of critical reviews in Syrian literary journals. Yet, aside from the work of exiles or diaspora novelists of Syrian origin, the dominant type of novel in Syria has been, and continues to be, overwhelmingly realist. Writers such as Hanna Mina (Ḥannā Mīnā), Faris Zarzur (Fāris Zarzūr), and Hani Rahib (Hānī al-Rāhib) are among its most prominent practitioners.

A large reason for the overwhelming prominence of realism in Syria is the (until recently) long-enduring historical and geopolitical fact of its alignment with the Soviet Union. Soviet influence in Syria was aided by Syria's alienation from the West, largely attributable to the persistence of the Arab-Israeli conflict. It was also aided by Syria's quest for rapid economic development and Soviet willingness to invest in major projects, as well as by the ideological affinity, on a broad platform of radicalism, between the Baath Party and the Soviet Union.[31]

In her study of Western influences on the Syrian short story, Souraya Botros[32] makes mention of the disproportionate translation of Russian works in the 1950s. These included Pushkin, Turgenev, Gogol, Chekhov, Dostoevsky, Tolstoy, Maxim Gorki, and Pasternak. She notes that this prominence was largely the result of the shift in strategic alliances after the partition of Palestine in 1948. Sabry Hafez also discusses the influence of Russian literature via translation in his book *The Genesis of Arabic Narrative Discourse*.[33] Although the Russians have virtually disappeared from the Syrian cultural scene today, the influence of Soviet-style control over the arts lingers on in Syria today. The preeminent Syrian novelist of the past thirty years is Hanna Mina, a writer whom Souraya Botros and Radwan Zaza[34] compare to Maxim Gorki.

Nabil Sulayman (Nabīl Sulaymān) has noted that, in Syria, literary movements have been intertwined with—in fact, have been inseparable from—political movements.[35] The three main political movements that have influenced literature in Syria have been the Arab nationalist movement—that is, the Nasserite movement, which espoused a pan-Arab philosophy, the Syrian nationalist movement, represented by the Baath Party, and the communist movement. Western notions of modernity influenced each one. Instead of exerting a complete hegemony over Syrian political life, the Baath party has tolerated the Nasserites and communists, and even claimed a fraternal relationship with them, as long as they remained on the fringes of power.

The fact that Sulayman connects literary production in Syria so completely with these political movements reflects the intense politicization of literature in the country. In a sense, the literary legacy of social realism has created its own momentum. In the absence of fundamental social change or upheaval, this tradition has simply been carried on by the succeeding generation. In addition, social criticism has been largely assimilated, controlled, kept in check, or co-opted by official sponsorship and approval of novelists who vent their frustration indirectly or at targets that are deemed harmless by the government.

A specialty of Syrian writers has been a subgenre of realism, the historical novel. The large majority of novels in the last ten years have been of this type. The most notable practitioners of the historical novel have included Nabil Sulayman, Fawwaz Haddad (Fawwāz Ḥaddād), Khayri al-Dhahabi (Khayrī al-Dhahabī), and Nihad Sirris (Nihād Sirrīs). While the fondness of Syrian writers for the historical novel seems to reflect a basic continuity with the realist tradition, to some extent it reflects disillusionment with the status quo. Due to the political influence to which they have been exposed in the past, there is an innate distrust of historians on the part of writers and other intellectuals. Since official history has been discredited in their minds, they have used the novel for the task of exploring historical issues. On the other hand, this phenomenon still reflects the meagerness of the channels that exist for expressing criticism or disillusionment. Since there is a fear of discussing present problems in Syria, novelists have tended to concentrate their critical attention on the problems of the past.

More recently, there has been a new literary movement is Syria, which has been characterized by some as a turning point in the Arab novel, more consciously "Arab" in its approach to the novel, and utilizing techniques based on folk narrative or the form of the orally transmitted tale. This trend is at least one area in which experimentalism in Syria makes some degree of contact with that in Lebanon, Jordan, and Palestine. In all these countries, interest continues to be generated in using folk narrative and oral tradition as a basis for the novel. Emile Habiby, as an Israeli Arab, made use of Arabic folk tradition in order to fill the political vacuum inhabited by the Palestinians. In Jordan and Syria, this same type of writing is being used as a means of filling other types of political and social vacuums. The phenomenon of migration to the city, for instance, is putting an end to traditional ways of life in these countries just as surely as Israeli occupation has been doing in Palestine.

Nihad Sirris is a young historical novelist from Aleppo, whose third work, *Al-Kūmidīyā al-Fallāḥīyah* (1990),[36] reflects this recent trend. Sirris's subject is the migration of people from the countryside to the city. While most of the narrative is set in the urban environment of Aleppo, the focus is entirely on the village characters. Instead of the urban culture supplanting the tribal culture, the tribal culture adapts to the urban environment. To some extent, Sirris experiments with narration on the model of the folk tradition or oral narration. The narration is introduced by a traditional storyteller, and is divided among several voices. This plethora of voices, however, is not aimed at exposing the reader to various subjective viewpoints, but rather at combining them to evoke the larger social reality. The storyteller has the dual role of speaking to the group, and at the same time representing the group. This is an experimental way of rendering the social or national consciousness in a way that attempts to be non-imitative of Western literary forms. The emphasis, however, is still wholly on that social or national consciousness, rather than on the individual; its aim is still that of social realism.

In the rest of the Levant, this collective viewpoint has waned, even while the interest in using folk tradition within the novel has continued. The result is that we find novels that invest deeply in the use of folk tradition, while at the same time displaying a greater interest in subjective expression. For instance, in recent years, before his death in 1996, Emile Habiby continued to work with themes taken from folk narrative in order to represent the vanished reality of Palestine. At the same time, he was moving away from overtly political resistance narrative and more toward a type of narrative in which the tone of self-reproach becomes more personal.

An example is his *Khurāfiyah: Sarāyā, Bint al-Ghūl* (Saraya, the demon's daughter, 1991),[37] in which the paradigm for Habiby's narrative is a Palestinian myth, legend, or fable *(usṭūrah)* whose pattern is reminiscent of fairy tales in the European tradition. The story is of a young, adventurous girl who is captured on one of her daily walks by a demon, goblin, or ogre *(ghūl),* who takes her to his castle at the top of a mountain. Her cousin eventually comes looking for her, and he calls out: "Sarāyā, yā bint al-ghūl / Dallīlī sha'rik li aṭūl," a piece of doggerel roughly equivalent to the familiar "Rapunzel, Rapunzel, let down your golden hair!" She hears him, lets down her hair, he climbs up on it, gives the *ghūl* a sleeping draught, escapes with Saraya, and takes her back to their village.

The narrative is written in the authorial voice, but one that is rendered in the style of a *khurāfiyah.* The term is a highly specialized one, derived from the more familiar Arabic word *khurāfah.* This refers to any fantastic element that is a part of myth. *Khurāfiyah* is strictly a literary term, used only in Palestine, referring to the literature of myth or legend, which employs *khurāfah. The Thousand and One Nights* would be an example of *khurāfiyah'* (except for the fact that it is used only for works indigenous to Palestine). In any other Arab country, this type of literature would be referred to as a form of *ḥikāyah* (story).

In his introduction, Habiby explains that Palestinians use the word *khurāfiyah*, generally, to signify anything strange:

> "The believer does not allow himself to get bitten twice at the same den." I have removed *Sarāyā, Bint al-Ghūl* from the class of the long novel from the beginning. What is it, then? I have called it a "khurāfiyah." I have found that we Palestinian Arabs, whether specialists or not, use the term "khurāfiyah" for every action that catches us by surprise. (6)

Habiby renders his narrative in the form of a *khurāfiyah'* by means of a traditional narrative technique known as "conveyed" narration. A fixture of Arab folk tales that have been converted into literature, it is accomplished by the use of the word *qāla* (he related). This phrase is interspersed at various points in the narration both to introduce a new section of the text and to bring the reader's attention back to the act of narration. There are thus two narrative voices, that of the narrator, and the voice that introduces or conveys his narration, and these two voices are one and the same. The technique, essentially, is the same as that employed by Salim Barakat in *Al-Jundub al-Ḥadīdī*. Both authors use the same traditional Arab narrative device for the modernist purpose of self-conscious narration.

As Habiby makes clear in the introduction, he (as the narrator) is an old man who lost his true love, Saraya, decades before. Although she once preoccupied his thoughts, he forgot about her until she "returned and appeared" to him:

> As for the hero of my novel, he had searched . . . for a girl that he had loved in his childhood. Then he became preoccupied with his daily concerns, and lost her. . . . So he neglected her, until she reappeared to him in his old age. (5)

This return, whether or not it is taken as a "real" event, is presented in a fashion that is somewhat dreamlike or magical:

> I let my thoughts go . . . when I was surprised by the agitated shadow on the troubled sea before me. On first impression, I thought it was the shadow of a shark . . . swimming in the water underneath it, telling me, "Take me!" But it is the one that has taken me. . . .
>
> Not until I heard a murmuring that came from the shadow that came from behind me.
>
> It was a feminine murmur.
>
> I turned my head. (27)

The novel concerns the narrator's (Habiby's) subsequent attempt to search his memory to "recover" her, and with her his lost youth. However, there are actually three narrative threads to the novel: a biographical narrative, a historical realist narrative, and the narrative of dream and hallucinatory memory, which occurs with each meeting with Saraya. Habiby interweaves these narratives very much like a braid. Each meeting with Saraya sparks, or is followed by, a new excursion into Habiby's biographical or historical narrative, which is followed by another reappearance of Saraya, which leads to another such excursion.

The parallel between the narrative and the paradigm of the legend becomes clear as Habiby, the narrator, recalls one of Saraya's appearances to him:

> I swore to her that if she would let down her braid, I would take hold of it and climb up, arm over arm, from the depth of the well of forgetfulness. (59)

This is clearly an allusion to both the processes of recovering his memory and writing (by pulling himself out by Saraya's braid) as the means of doing so. In addition, as we have seen, the braid is a curiously apt metaphor for the narrative method that Habiby employs. For Habiby, pulling himself out of the "well of forgetfulness" means a return to childhood. At the same time, these childhood reminiscences always bring him back to the present, and the present is very much concerned with the task of writing:

> He said:
>
> The transfer from the old school to the new school aroused apprehensive feelings in me. (71)
>
> And in the morning . . . I looked at my face in the mirror for the

first time in my life. It was my face. Those were my eyes, and it was me that was looking at me from those eyes for the first time.

I stood in front of the mirror . . . combing my hair in a style that would be appropriate for the move to the new school. The hairstyle didn't please me. I kept redoing it again and again, as I have done with my novel: I free my thoughts from times gone by. Then I arrange them, one by one, until the "hairstyle" satisfies me. (73)

Not only is there a surprising display of narrative introspection in this passage, there is also irony. At many points, such as this, Habiby uses the phrase "for the first time" or "for the first time in my life" in self-mockery, as a way of drawing attention to his slowness of realization or comprehension. In contrast to *The Pessoptimist*, in which Habiby created a character who was both mythic and ironic, in *Sarāyā*, he writes a much more personal narrative in which he conflates the tragic irony of his own life with the tragic irony in the life of his country:

My readers, male and female, do not ask me to spend the rest of my life searching in the houses of my city which have also disappeared from my sight. Or is it I who have disappeared from (my city's) sight? Even if I had found it, I would not have found myself reflected in its mirror, and I would not have seen with my own eyes, in that moment which occurred fifty-six years ago, a dark, negative vision of what would come, and yelled, Why?

Truthfully, I have said it to myself hundreds of times before I read it in Ibn al-Athīr: "I wish that my mother had not brought me into the world, and I wish that I had died before this, and was something that was completely forgotten." (77)

The reappearance of Saraya in his life is the spark that ignites these memories, and leads him to writing. Using the same technique we noted in Salim Barakat's *Al-Jundub al-Ḥadīdī*, Habiby switches between third and first person in order to express this:

Suddenly Saraya was shown to him from above her rock. She handed him her drink, and said, "Are you thirsty? Drink." He said that he drunk. And he said that now and only now had he found the secret for which he had been searching ever since he had been suffering, collecting the memories that had fallen from his old olive trees, piece by piece. Now he understood how Pythagoras had discovered the unity

> of the universe through mathematics. As for me, I find myself approaching my holy of holies through letters. (89)

Habiby thus constructs his *khurāfiyah* along three interconnecting lines of narrative: the personal, the mythic, and the political. Concerning *Sarāyā, Bint al-Ghūl*, Fakhri Salih asks:

> Is it a tale that the author enjoys recounting from time to time? Is it a search for the meaning of mythical names of existing things, of the meanings of words and their ancient historical significance? Is it a novel?[38]

The implication is that it is all of these things. Just as we have seen that he intertwines the political with the personal, and the personal with the mythic, Habiby connects the mythic with the political. He muses on the significance of the traditional story of "Sarāyā, Bint al-Ghūl" as he plays with the meanings and derivations of key words:

> Why doesn't *ghūl* (demon) come from *ighāl* (penetration)? And is there any *ighāl* more destructive than a lone baby's penetration of an inhabited prairie? (89)

Here it becomes obvious that Habiby is borrowing the myth of "Saraya" in order to write about a political issue. The *ghūl*'s capture of Saraya echoes the fate of the Palestinians in Israel. The paradox of a "lone" baby penetrating an "inhabited" prairie echoes the isolation of the Palestinians living among the Israeli population. As we have already seen, Habiby links the rescue of Saraya with his own attempt to retrieve the past through his writing, but at the same time, there is a clear political significance to both the myth and to his vocation as a writer. Habiby is drawing a connection between the myth of Saraya and both his own life and the fate of his country. He views his life and Palestinian history as a '*khurāfiyah*'—something strange, unbelievable, laughable, and absurd.

In *Woman's Body, Woman's Word: Gender and Discourse in Arabo-Islamic Writing* (1991),[39] Fedwa Malti-Douglas discusses the dichotomy between 'reality' and fiction in *The Thousand and One Nights*. She contrasts the impact of Shahrazad's stories with Shahrayar's concern with reality. "Shahrayar's search and desire for reality through what he can plainly see is illusory," she notes. "Rather it is through fiction that the proper uses of desire can best be learned."[40] This technique consists, in essence, of the interpretation of reality by means of the mythic imagination. In ancient times, men explained natural phenomena in such terms, because they had no scientific knowledge about them. For Emile Habiby, the Palestinian experience is such a phenomenon—one that cannot be explained in rational or scientific terms. Palestinian history is a "strange thing." The observation is both ironic and sentimental, based both on bitter experience and on hope.

There is a strong element of self-criticism in this text. Habiby, as both writer and narrator, was a seventy-year-old man looking back over a fifty-year period in which he was wedded to a particular ideological position. For many years, he belonged to the Israeli Communist Party (Rakah). The ideal of the Party was Arab and Jewish coexistence within Israel, that is, of a non-sectarian, heterodox Israeli state, of which Arabs would be full citizens. Arab communists living in Israel, unlike any other Arabs, recognized the existence of Israel and considered themselves Israeli citizens. Habiby, however, eventually became disillusioned in this ideal, and quit the Communist Party.

In *Sarāyā*, Habiby seems to be trying to deal with the realization that, for most of his life, he held on to a false ideal. Habiby went through a process of disillusionment with his previously held political ideals, similar to writers in other parts of the Arab world. But as an Israeli Arab, the nature of this disillusionment was quite different from that commonly experienced in the rest of the Arab world. As an Israeli communist, Habiby recognized the existence of Israel and believed in coexistence within Israel. Arabs outside of Israel, in opposite fashion, refused to recognize Israel, and did not believe coexistence with Israel was possible. Both previously held positions were undermined by the widespread disillusionment that set in among writers and intellectuals in the early '80s. This disillusionment was mirrored in the Oslo Accords and the Taba Agreement, which simultaneously represented a mutual recognition between Israel and the Palestinians and a type of divorce settlement. Coexistence was agreed upon, but this would not be within a single state, but within two separate entities.

It is, then, both Habiby's own life and Palestinian history, as a whole, that have been a *khurāfiyah*. Fakhri Salih writes that *Sarāyā, Bint al-Ghūl* is both a summation of Emile Habiby's personal feelings and a return to the story that is central to his work. The story is that of the

Palestinians who remained within Israel and their relations with those who fled and were dispersed throughout the region and the rest of the world.[41] Nevertheless, in this work, Habiby is less ironic and more sentimental toward Palestinian history than in *The Pessoptimist*. Saraya, for whom he pines and waits and searches, represents not only his childhood, but also the land, the Palestinian nation. His return to childhood with Saraya is the pretext, the motivating force for his return to history. If the quest for Saraya is a pursuit of memory and history, however, it is even more representative of a need for an emotional element that Habiby sees as having been previously lacking in his life. He gives us a picture of himself as a public, political, and intellectual man, far removed from his emotions. The return of Saraya sparks this interior exploration. Habiby's message to the reader is of the importance of the emotional element in life, symbolized by a feminine figure.

At the same time, this search has social and political implications. While the narrative represents a quest for the author's own identity, this personal identity is bound up with his identity as a Palestinian. Habiby's message to his readers is that they must make the same inventory of themselves. In this sense, *Sarāyā, Bint al-Ghūl* represents a sharp change in orientation from *The Pessoptimist*. In *The Pessoptimist*, Saeed is represented as a failure, a man caught in a contradiction. In *Sarāyā*, on the other hand, Habiby presents himself as someone who has had a profound experience that has changed him, and who is trying to convey this personal experience to the reader. The expression of yearning for emotion and sentimentality, represented by a feminine figure, is almost romantic in tone, while the focus on the retrieval of memory and its equation with "myth" harks back to the Western modernist canon. At the same time, all these characteristics still have their roots in Arabic oral and literary tradition.

In Jordan, a notable effort to make use of folk narrative within the novel form is represented by the first novel of a young author, Ramadan Rawashdeh (Ramaḍān al-Rawāshidah). The slender novel, *Al-Ḥamrāwī* (Al-Hamrawi, 1992),[42] won an important literary award in the Arab world—the Naguib Mahfouz prize as best Arab novel in 1994—although this may have been meant more as a means of encouragement to a young writer than as a seal of critical approval. The attention given to the work by Ibrahim al-Sa'afin (Ibrāhīm al-Sa'āfīn) in his study of the novel in Jordan can be explained in part by the desire to promote recognition of Jordanian writing. At the same time, despite its limitations from an artistic standpoint, it reflects certain characteristics that are truly innovative and that point to a possible new direction for the novel in Jordan.

Some critics have described *Al-Ḥamrāwī* as the first attempt to write a "Jordanian" novel, because it deals with folkloric elements of the indigenous Jordanian tribal culture. In this respect, it can be compared to a work like Nihad Sirris's *Al-Kūmidīyā al-Fallāḥīyah*. Both works are concerned with the folk traditions in their respective countries, and deal with the dislocation of this folk tradition in the context of an urban environment. Rawashdeh, however, goes beyond the social realist aims of Sirris. His story does not simply follow the rural culture into the city. Rather, it deals with the alienation of the individual caught between the two cultures.

The narrator suffers from a type of schizophrenia *(infiṣām),* malaise, or spiritual illness. Physically, he lives in Amman, but psychologically he lives in the world of his tribe, in the south of Jordan. This is one of the oldest modernist themes—the alienation of the individual within an urban environment. The only "event" in the narrative is one that is never fully described or explained. The narrator is frustrated in love, gets "sick," sees a doctor, and takes a prescription to a drug store. There, the people stare at him as if they see a monster. Something has happened to the narrator that marks him as different or apart from others. It may be a sickness, a change in his appearance, we never find out for sure:

> I told the druggist, "Give me the medicine and let me get out of this accursed city." A policeman entered the drugstore when he saw the crowd milling around so much to get a look at me that the main street was clogged.
>
> Everyone pointed at me. (The policeman) approached me. . . . He came closer and examined me for a long time. . . . Then he shouted at me: "You!"
>
> I told him, "Yes . . . Me?!"
>
> "But how did this happen," he said.
>
> I told him innocently . . . I just came to the drugstore to get medicine . . .
>
> He said, "That's not what I meant . . . You . . ." His hand was trembling as it came near my face. (17)

The narrator then glances at himself in a mirror, and becomes aware that something is wrong, the effect of which is similar to the opening of Kafka's *The Metamorphosis*:[43]

> I glanced around the whole place, saw a mirror nearby, and told myself, "Let me go see what might be strange in my personal appearance. And when I went to the mirror and looked into it, I was thunderstruck at the terrifying thing I saw. . . . (17)

At this point the narrator flees, and his narration becomes schizophrenic, as if he has been split or doubled:

> I wasn't the one who was seeing me. I got scared, and ran away from myself. I left myself alone, and joined the groups (of people) who were running away from me. . . . But I kept on following myself as the groups were running away in front of me, and as I was following myself, I looked back and I saw myself getting closer to me. . . . I was very afraid of myself, and wondered where to go. . . . (17)

Whatever the narrator's condition, it is certainly connected with a feeling of estrangement and alienation, which in turn is related to the urban environment of Amman in which he finds himself. Near the end of the short novel, the narrator revisits the doctor, who agrees that he is neither physically or psychologically ill, and suggests that the only cure would be for him to leave the city.

Tied to the narrator's "sickness" is his yearning for traditional tribal life. The bulk of the narrative consists of his reminiscences of this life, which he remembers in terms of its myth and folklore, and these reminiscences center on the character of Al-Hamrawi:

> Umran al-Hamrawi ['Umrān al-Ḥamrāwī] was a brave man who lived in our southern, far-away village. He was a father of ten, noble and stubborn. He helped others, and took part in people's sorrows and joys. He had a warm heart towards his relatives. . . . (10)

The narrator recalls an incident in which Hamrawi helped a woman from a neighboring village go to the hospital to have her first baby delivered. He looks around for a car, finds one, and takes the woman to the city. The baby was called Anud ('Anūd), which means "stubborn," because the birth was so labored. The narrator then comments: "The important thing was, Umran became the myth of the village" (11).

The narrator, however, inquires further into the matter, asking why the woman was called Anud. He is told there was a different reason:

> When I asked why she was called Anud, I was told that this legendary event occurred five centuries ago, when the bedouin came to the village and plundered everything. . . . (11)

The reason the legendary young woman is called Anud is because she had a different social personality from the other girls in the village. One day the *shaykh* of the bedouin, Shaykh Makazi (Shaykh Makāzī), fell in love with her. He asked for her hand from her father, but her father hesitated, and did not give a clear answer. Anud's answer was no, she would not marry the *shaykh,* because this was the man who had invaded their village and brought danger and fear to their people. According to narrators of this legend, Shaykh Makazi prepared an army to invade the village. The exaggeration of the legend is evident in the description of the *shaykh*'s army:

> Shaykh Makazi prepared an army as great as a typhoon. Leading it were a thousand commanders, and for each commander a thousand officers, and for each officer a thousand soldiers. (11–12)

Noteworthy is the fact that the village itself is called Al-'Anūd. In the end, the people of the village trap the invaders and take the *shaykh* into custody. The legend of the defense of the village, its female champion, and the identification of the village with this heroine is reminiscent of the sections of folkloric narrative in Maxine Hong Kingston's *The Woman Warrior*. There is a great identification on the part of the narrator with collective cultural memories of his tribe, and this collective memory is largely built upon exaggeration *(balāghah)*. Even ordinary people, such as the title character, Hamrawi, are made out to be great heroes.

Ibrahim al-Sa'afin incorrectly identifies the technique used by Rawashdeh as "intertextuality" *(al-tanāṣṣ),* when he really is referring to the interweaving of fictional and folkloric characters:

> It's not possible to neglect an important question in discussing this novel, namely the use it makes of the folk tradition in interweaving stories with the main plot of the novel. The heroes of these stories are intermingled with the heroes of folk tales, myths, and legends. . . .[44]

What *Al-Ḥamrāwi* lacks—and what *The Woman Warrior* possesses—is a consistent narrative thread that keeps the narrator's central conflict within the reader's view. A work such as Maxine Hong Kingston's, apart from its "postmodern" preoccupation with the connection between culture and identity, works precisely because it is built on a strong, preexisting tradition of subjective expression in the novel. The lack of such a novelistic tradition in the Arab world may be a factor contributing to Rawashdeh's difficulty in keeping his narrative focused.

The narrator's reflections turn from aspects of his country's folk tradition to its political history. A key historical event upon which the narrative centers was a rebellion that occurred in the southern part of Jordan (of which both the narrator and Rawashdeh are native), which occurred in April 1989. The people of this region, while instinctively loyal to the king, nevertheless were driven to rebellion by hunger and poverty. The inference made by the narrative is that this was a turning point in Jordanian history, since it led to the first parliamentary elections and thus to the first real steps toward democratization in the country. The intermingling of the mythic and the political would be an interesting narrative strategy if it were approached ironically. The effect produced by Rawashdeh's text, however, is one of romantic patriotism.

The narrator's obvious sympathy for political change, for democratization, is also somewhat at odds with his almost passionate yearning for the values of tribal life. This tension, conflict, or dialogue between traditional and modern viewpoints forms the core of the narrative. Ibrahim al-Sa'afin refers to this tension as "experimentalism based on the principle of duality," and notes that this principle is found in the work's very title:

> This novel, which carries the dualistic title *From the Life of a Man Who Lost His Memory, or Al-Ḥamrāwī,* is opposed to a structure that suggests its foundation in a direct manner. The first title suggests a Western type of experimentation, and, among its clearest manifestations, the use of a psychological (and particularly an analytical psychological) presentation. The second title suggests the tradition of storytelling. . . .[45]

The tension between these modernist and traditional viewpoints, however, is never resolved in the text. In a typical passage, the narrator is questioned by a foreign friend regarding his feelings toward traditional versus modern life. He refers to the fact that the narrator was denied marriage to his beloved because of her father's disapproval, and wonders whether this type of traditional custom is what the narrator really prefers. The narrator admits that this event is what probably caused his schizophrenia, his malaise, and his shell shock. Implicitly, there is a link between the patriarchy of the state, embodied by the king, and the patriarchy of the tribal society, embodied by the father of the narrator's lost love. Yet one patriarchal authority is challenged, the other is not.

The narrator thus shifts the weight of his emotional connection to the village or tribal community to the nation as a whole. In this sense, the novel still retains a political orientation. This political orientation is represented by the quotation that introduces the text. The quotation is taken from a work of the classical poet Al Hallaj (Al-Ḥallāj):

> Whom do I love
> Whom do I love
> If you've seen me . . . you've seen us.

The quotation, however, deletes part of the original poem. With the missing section, it reads as follows:

> Whom do I love
> Whom do I love
> Two souls transformed into one body.
> If you've seen him, you've seen me
> And if you've seen me . . . you've seen us.

The original poem is thus a love poem—actually a love poem to God disguised as a poem about an individual, which is a common trope in classical Arabic poetry. Rawashdeh, however, has deleted the spiritual references in the poem, and thus rendered it secular. The emotion is now directed neither to a lover, nor to God, but to the cultural community or nation. This sentiment is clear in the closing lines of the novel. The narrator is leaving the country, and records his emotions upon embarking, addressing himself:

> At the airport the officer looked at your passport, then at you. He gave you your passport back and wished you a good journey. You said, "OK?" He said, "Sure." But deep inside you wished that he'd prevent you from traveling like they used to.
>
> "Why this time are they allowing me to travel?" you said to your-

self. You reached the door of the airplane and looked back. You saw the country receding from you, little by little.

But at that point you tore up your passport, and ran back to hug this country, kiss it on the mouth, and cry beneath its hands. And it opened up its arms to you and hugged you back. And everyone was staring. (67–68)

Thus, although Rawashdeh's work possesses certain modernist traits in its theme of alienation and its brief burst of schizophrenic narrative, ultimately it reasserts themes that are more native to social realism and even romanticism. In its tension between traditional and modern culture, it bears a resemblance to classical Arabic novellas such as *The Saint's Lamp* (1973; *Qindīl Umm Hāshim*, 1948),[46] by Yahya Haqqi (Yaḥyā Haqqī) or Naguib Mahfouz's "Zaabalawi." The latter work, first published in the collection *God's World* (1973; *Dunyā Allāh*, 1962),[47] and also found in Denys Johnson Davies's *Modern Arabic Short Stories*,[48] is one in which the traditional values of the *rīf* (countryside) are contrasted with those of urban modernity. The first part of the title of Rawashdeh's work, *From the Life of a Man Who Lost His Memory,* suggests in particular a comparison to the plot of "Zaabalawi." In this story, the main character searches the streets of Cairo for a legendary character that represents the wisdom of the past, but is unable to recognize him when indeed he makes his appearance. In both texts, the faculty of memory, connected with traditional values, is threatened, jeopardized, or extinguished by modernity.

Al-Ḥamrāwī is interesting in that it illuminates the heterogeneity of influences at work in contemporary Arab writing, even in areas distant from the Arab world's cultural centers. The novel borrows from Faulkner in its reliance on interior monologue, its localism and regionalism, its use of dialect, and its nonchronological narration. Particularly striking is a last chapter consisting of a list of events, which forms a skeletal structure for the preceding narrative, imitating Faulkner's *The Sound and the Fury*. In a more general sense, however, Rawashdeh fits into the category of novelists who are aiming to produce writing that is local in its orientation (for which García Márquez is the model).

As Sa'afin suggests, *Al-Ḥamrāwī* is indeed a dualistic novel. To a certain extent it is modernist and psychological in tone, representing the individual in a state of crisis and alienation. At the same time, however, the narrative as a whole is weighted toward a collective viewpoint, with its emphasis on cultural and even national memory. This gives the novella what might appear to be a postmodern character. Such an impression would be deceptive, however. Rawashdeh is writing in a country with virtually no genuine modernist prose tradition. His use of modernist techniques such as the fragmentation of time and interior monologue only frustrate classification even more. The reality is that romantic, realist, modernist, and postmodern influences are all at work in *Al-Ḥamrāwī*. The Kafkaesque position of the narrator is superseded by a Proustian contemplative impulse, which in turn gives way to a Marquezian interest in folkloric tradition, which ultimately collapses in nationalistic sentiment.

Elias Khoury's *The Kingdom of Strangers* (1996; *Mamlakah al-Ghurabā'*, 1993) is a work written more in the style of a reflective essay than a novel, and also incorporates elements of folk tradition. Khoury interweaves several stories with one another, and intersperses these with his own thoughts and musings. One of these stories is a folk legend that the narrator pursues as part of his doctoral research, and which apparently had its origin in an actual event that was reported in the papers in 1946. The legend is of a Lebanese, Jurji Khayri, who left his village when he was eighteen in order to live in a monastery in Jerusalem. The monastery's administration and most of the clergy, however, were Greeks who hated Arabs. Jurji and three other Arab monks were persecuted, and given all the menial jobs to do.

After seven years of suffering, Jurji fled the monastery and became the leader of a gang in Galilee that robbed from smugglers operating between Lebanon and Palestine and distributed the loot to the poor. Eventually members of one of the Jewish settlements in the Galilee area ambushed the gang. Jurji and one other man were the only ones to escape. Finally, he returned to Jerusalem, where he rented a room in the Christian quarter. On Holy Thursday, he carried a huge cross and walked through the streets, shouting that this was the cross of the Arabs, which they would have to carry for a hundred more years. When he reached the Jewish quarter of the city, he was stoned to death.

Khoury interweaves this story with another one about a man named Iskandar Naffaa. Iskandar was married to a woman from a rich family in Beirut. His wife, Lody, felt that she had been shortchanged in her marriage, and her way of making up for this was to be arrogant toward her husband and tyrannical with her maids, who never lasted in the household more than a month. She would treat them like slaves, making them work day in and day out, even if there wasn't anything for them to do. Iskandar, for his part, had an ulterior motive in hiring the maids, whom he would typically approach on a whim—not to have sex, but merely to play around with, to touch, to kiss, or to squeeze. Finally, after the last maid attacked his wife and destroyed his house, he hit on what he thought was the solution by buying what he thought was a Circassian girl who had just arrived on a ship from Alexandria. The white girl knew no Arabic and didn't speak. She worked all day without a single complaint, expected nothing, and looked at things as though she didn't see.

One day, he approached this girl as he had the others. As he hugged her tighter and pulled her closer to him, he heard his wife's footsteps, but didn't let go. When his wife screamed, the sound of it had no effect on him. He took the girl, Widad, by the hand, left the house, converted to Islam, and married her. He turned her into a married woman and lived the rest of his life with her. She was docile and obedient, learned Arabic, but never spoke unless her husband asked her to. He lived his life as a lover, always fearing that this young white girl would abandon him. His former wife died twenty years before he did, full of spite. When he, too, died, Widad was left alone in the house. For three years, she spent her time at home and never went out. Finally, she got sick, and suddenly a strange thing occurred. She forgot her adopted language. All she could speak was a language similar to Turkish, and all she talked about was her childhood spent in a distant land before she had been kidnapped, sold in Beirut, and married Iskandar. The doctor explained to her stepson that this was a well-known condition in geriatric medicine. For victims of this illness, the brain blots out the present, and brings back the past. "Even acquired language goes," he states, "and nothing remains on the surface of the brain except the memory of childhood and the language of childhood" (76).

Khoury, in his narrative voice, wonders if the flaw in his story is "in the comparisons, and I'm not comparing" (91). The reader, in turn, must compare Khoury's tales in order to make sense of the narrative as a whole. Khoury's subject, as usual, is the vast tragedy of war-ravaged Lebanon, now extended to include the Palestinian tragedy as well. His interest in the folk tale is well expressed when he says: "Folk tales say things so they won't happen; they are a kind of psychological compensation" (24). In other words, they are psychologically true—truer than fact. For instance, one of the variations in the legend of Jurji is that he used to kidnap a Jew every Good Friday. Khoury as narrator allows that "Certainly, Jurji the monk did not kidnap Jews on Good Friday, because kidnapping a Jew, in the 1940's, in Jerusalem, was logistically impossible" (97). But the variation of the legend is psychologically true because the essence of the legend itself is that of Arab rebellion.

This is made clearer when the narrator tries to tell the story to his Jewish friend Emil, in New York. Emil loves the character of the monk, but suggests changing the part where he kidnaps the Jew because he thinks the monk, in this passage, seems anti-Semitic. Khoury as narrator objects that cutting this event out of the story would not only seem unfair in regard to the story, but is necessary for the sake of truth. As Khoury reiterates this idea: "[T]he very vitality of the monk's story is connected to an act he did not commit" (97). This is not a minor objection, but goes to the heart of the entire book. The myths and legends of Arab rebellion are cultural truths in the Arab world, just as the myths and legends of anti-Semitism are cultural truths for Jews. Thus, while the narrator might be able to have a friendship with a Jew in New York, as a writer he is waging a battle in which his culture and that of his friend are rivals and combatants. Significantly, he states, "Language is like land. . . . We can occupy other people's languages just as we can occupy their land. But the question is who are we?" (79).

This is where the story of Jurji interconnects with that of Widad. The narrator asks: "throughout her long life in this city, she was a stranger devoid of memory. . . . And when she forgot everything, she remembered everything. . . . Is the truth of white Widad her life as we tell it now? Or is it the life she did not live?" Then he explicitly draws the political connection, asking rhetorically, "weren't these wars exercises for the memory? They say war is an exercise in forgetting" (77). In other words, Khoury's task, and that of other Arab novelists still interested in working with the folk tale and oral narrative is not merely the resurrection of culture, but also of individual memory. The war in Beirut tore its memory apart, yet this process of forgetting engenders renewed memory. Khoury observes, "We find stories tossed in the streets of our memory and the alleys of our imagination. How can we bring them together, to impose order on a land in which all order has been smashed to pieces?" (84).

Chapter 3

Rediscovering the Present: The Lebanese Civil War

The playground of the poet is human weakness, not heroism.
—Murid Barghuthi

My stylistic innovations are simply attempts to express the present, to express what people are living now. What the people in Beirut are living is not particular to Beirut. It can be found anywhere. It is a universal experience. This is true of most Third World literature. Achebe's work, for instance, is not an African way of writing, but simply a way of writing only.
—Elias Khoury

FRAGMENTED REPORTAGE: GHADA SAMMAN

At the same time that writers such as Emile Habiby and Abdelrahman Munif were working toward an "Arabized" approach to the novel, a social and political disaster occurred in Lebanon from 1975 to 1990 that had the opposite effect on literature. Instead of engaging in a dialogue with Arabic culture and literary tradition, writers in Lebanon were forced to turn their attention to the present and driven to express the immediate moment in narrative. Elias Khoury, perhaps the most prominent writer and critic to emerge from this period, has gone out of his way to differentiate himself from writers such as Ghitani, Munif, and Habiby, claiming to place no value on the attempt to forge an indigenous Arab literature.

The effects of the Lebanese Civil War on the Arabic novel were threefold. First of all, it led to experiments on the part of some authors with a radical fragmentation of form, in an attempt to express the sense of complete dislocation caused by the conflict. Secondly, it caused women writers to emerge with their own perspective, based on the connection between war and sexuality. Thirdly, it led to an increasing introversion on the part of writers. Hemmed in by conflict and alienated from their surroundings, many writers were thrown back on themselves, contemplating their own lives, and combining memoir with fictional narration. At the same time, these writers shared with the Arabists similar formal concerns and experimented with many of the same narrative techniques. The objectives of both groups of writers have been to disrupt the relationship between reader and narrative voice in order to create a heightened level of awareness on the part of the reader toward the subject matter that they wish to convey.

The two most significant novelists to write about the early years of the war were Elias Khoury and Ghada Samman (Ghādah al-Sammān), and no writer documented the beginning of the war more strikingly and effectively than the Syrian-born Samman. Her most significant works, *Beirut '75* (1995; *Bayrūt 75*, 1975)[1] and *Beirut Nightmares* (1997; *Kawābīs Bayrūt;* 1976),[2] represent attempts to convey the brutality of the war using a full range of experimental narrative techniques in order to heighten the effect of this depiction. *Beirut '75* is notable for its prophetic quality. It did not go so far as to predict the actual event of the civil war, as did *Death in Beirut* (1976; *Ṭawāḥīn Bayrūt;* 1972),[3] by Tawfiq Yusuf Awwad (Tawfīq Yūsuf 'Awwād). Nevertheless, it described a psychological and moral condition that reflected all the elements of the social collapse to come.

The narrative of *Beirut '75* begins with five separate characters sharing a cab bound for Beirut, using the trope of a shared voyage utilized by Jabra Ibrahim Jabra in *The Ship*. After their arrival in the first chapter, however, the characters disperse and, with the exception of a brief encounter between two of the characters, are never reunited. From this point on, their stories are linked only thematically, exploiting the same technique used by Abdelrahman Munif in *Endings*, except without the emphasis on reproducing the pattern of oral narration. The theme that the characters' stories have in common is a brutal one. In each case, the characters are ground up by the merciless corruption of the city, exploited by other people, and betrayed by their own weakness. Their combined stories produce a portrait of a city that is on a course of self-destruction.

The societal self-criticism of *Beirut '75* is expressed more nakedly, perhaps, than that of any other work to come out of the Lebanese Civil

War. This is, perhaps, what the translator, Nancy Roberts, means when she speaks of "the overall realism of the novel," since it attempts to describe "the chaotic state in which Lebanese society found itself on the eve of its civil war."[4] The manner of the description, however, is far removed from the conventions of realism. What Ghada Samman evokes is not a social or political reality, but an inner truth, the state of the city's "soul":

> Cruelty—there was an atmosphere of cruelty that he became aware of whenever he tried to make a move in this strange city. He was constantly hearing the echoes of a long drawn-out wail wherever he went. Ever since the night of his arrival, the mysterious sound of mournful weeping had haunted him. It was as if it had taken up residence in his soul and refused to be dislodged. . . . Something about the climate of this city seemed to be slowly poisoning him, as if it were enveloped by a rare, venomous gas. (19-20)

Samman also uses symbolic events to create a sense of foreboding.

> Farah . . . picked up a bottle of catsup, shook it slightly, and opened it with some difficulty. . . . Its viscous liquid shot out in a semiexplosion, its wet, crimson contents spattering his face, hands, and clothes. After sitting there for a moment in a daze, he was suddenly overcome by a sense of horror from seeing himself covered with what looked like blood. (23)

Many of these events involve animals, since they are so often at the mercy of humans:

> When he returned to the hotel, he was surprised to find that the goldfish vendor had brought out a new display, the tiny fish for sale swimming about in their water-filled nylon bags . . . butting their heads against the sides of their translucent prisons. He suddenly noticed that one particular fish had facial features strikingly similar to his own. (23–24)

> As usual, Farah stood mesmerized in front of the colored fish, gazing at them as they swam around inside the clear nylon bags. . . . Then suddenly one of the bags burst, sending its contents splattering onto the pavement. (46)

These images, however, are only a preview of what becomes a horrific narrative, as the various characters compromise themselves morally, sink to depravity, and are killed, condemned, or go mad. Nancy Roberts is correct in stating that "both men and women are depicted in *Beirut '75* as being victimized by forces either partially or completely beyond their control."[5] At the same time that each of the characters is in the grip of powerful external forces, however, Samman also indicts the characters themselves, in each case illuminating some failure on their part to come to grips with their condition.

Ta'aan, for instance, is a young man who is the target of a family blood feud for no other reason than that he has obtained a university degree. His cousin had killed a member of another clan to avenge the death of Ta'aan's uncle. Since the slain member of the other clan held a university degree, his clan stipulated that the first young man of Ta'aan's clan to graduate from the university would be the next victim. He escapes to Beirut in a state of paranoia. One day, on the streets of the city, he hears the sound of footsteps behind him. He is certain that someone is pursuing him:

> Whoever it was came closer and put his hand on Ta'aan's shoulder. There was no more room for doubt now. Without knowing what he was doing, Ta'aan drew his gun, turned, and shot the man. Just like that, without a word. (66)

The man turns out to have been a foreign tourist who wanted to ask Ta'aan for directions. From Ta'aan's viewpoint, he has been driven to kill an innocent man; the rival clan has achieved its objective by sending him to the gallows. He has participated in his own dehumanization by succumbing to fear and paranoia. The end result is not only the killing of an innocent man, but also a killing that Ta'aan rationalizes away as having been instigated by others. His failure to take responsibility for his own actions in this respect is a veritable blueprint of the psychological engine that drove the civil war.

Another character is Abu'l-Malla, a poor, elderly, and pious man who works as an archaeologist's assistant. Put in charge of guarding a priceless statue that has been discovered and is waiting to be shipped to a museum, he decides to steal the relic. What is particularly brutal about Abu'l-Malla's story is the awful regression of his personality after a long life of having preserved his dignity and self-esteem despite his poverty:

> This was the first time in his life that he had broken a law, defied a system, or committed any forbidden act. He felt a tremendous rush of pleasure all over his body and the delirious ecstasy born of possessing infinite strength. . . . From now on he was going to acquaint himself with the path of pleasure and enjoyment. . . . He would steal again. He would try everything before it was too late. He would try his hand at murder as well. He'd never killed anyone before, but he'd give it a try. (74)

Samman uses a technique, familiar to us from Poe and Kafka, in which the statue "comes to life" to exact swift retribution upon its abductor:

> He saw the statue grow larger and larger. . . . With its now gigantic body, it approached him in a rage. Abu'l-Malla tried to scream but couldn't . . . get a single cry for help to come out of his mouth. He saw the statue's stony fingers encircle his neck. . . . He gasped and gasped, then . . . he gasped no more.
>
> Later Umm al-Malla came back to their hut to find that her husband had breathed his last. . . . As for his young children, they found on the floor beside their dead father a strange-looking stone doll. It smiled at them, so they picked it up, took it outside, and played with it until they got tired of it, after which it ended up in a mud puddle among the tinplate huts. (75)

To some extent, Samman's purpose here, like Poe's in "The Black Cat" or "The Telltale Heart," is a psychological one. At the same time, however, it anticipates the purposes of magical realism. The statue represents the traditions of the past, the power of the ancient gods, and Samman is suggesting that these gods must be respected, and that society, having ceased to venerate them, is inviting its own destruction.

Samman has a similar purpose in her story of another character, Abu Mustafa, a poor fisherman who has likewise lived a life of poverty. Mustafa is a dreamer who sees himself as a fisherman out of *The Thousand and One Nights*, who one day will pull a magic lamp from out of the sea. Here, Ghada Samman mocks one more aspect of Lebanese psychology—

a helpless passivity sustained by naiveté. She also a reveals sensitivity to the environment. For Samman, the sea is also a priceless aspect of Lebanon that, like the ancient gods, is misused and neglected:

> To the people of Beirut the sea had become nothing more than a lifeless painting nailed to the walls of the coffee shops overlooking it. It had become just a blue extension to the black asphalt of the city streets. (32)

Abu Mustafa, like Abu'l-Malla, is destroyed by his attempt to find a way out of his lifelong existence of poverty and deprivation. His destruction is not caused by greed, but simply by looking for salvation in the wrong place. His elder son, Mustafa, is a witness to his death:

> For thirty years he'd been running over the waves in search of the genie. For thirty years he had been casting his nets, then running his fingers through their contents in hopes of finding the lamp. . . .
>
> He cast his nets, then lit the fuse of the dynamite. He lit the entire bundle all at once, and before he could hear the protests of his son and the other men he had jumped with it into the water. Now his whole body was a bundle of dynamite whose purpose was to catch the lamp.
>
> The explosion rang out along with Mustafa's scream. . . . As the men brought the nets in, Abu Mustafa's body came up with them like a rare fish spattered with blood, mingled with bits and pieces of clothing and other unidentified, broken objects and remains. Among the debris Mustafa thought he saw the fragments of a very, very old lamp. . . . He also thought he saw a column of smoke and ashes slowly ascend from his father's remains, then vanish . . . like the smoke of a genie before its final disappearance. (86–87)

Ghada Samman followed up *Beirut '75* with the much more extensive *Beirut Nightmares*. While the former work was written before the war, *Beirut Nightmares* was written after the fighting began, and is a close-at-hand narration of the actual violence of the war. The remarkable feature of this work is the way in which Samman combines three different narrative aspects, which could be called the "experiential," the "creative," and the "reflective."

The "experiential" aspect refers to those parts of the narrative that represent the narrator's daily experiences, and which form the chronological thread of the narration. In the introduction to her manuscript translation, Nancy Roberts emphasizes this aspect of *Beirut Nightmares*. She describes it as "a diary-like account of events in the life of the narrator over a two-week period in which she is trapped in her house after street battles and sniper fire have turned her neighborhood into a virtual prison" (iv). In his book, *Arab Women Novelists*, Joseph Zeidan notes, however, that in this work, Samman was faced with a difficult artistic problem—a lack of action. The heroine, who is the focal point of the novel, is externally passive, because she is locked up at home the entire time. The two men trapped with her are passive as well. "To compensate for the lack of external events in the novel," Zeidan notes, Samman "resorts to devices that give the novel its internal unity."[6]

The chief of these devices is to structure the novel not by means of chapters, but by sections that she refers to as "nightmares." Some of these narrative sections relate to the overall narrative thread of the book, some are part of a distinct narrative series within the work, and others are single, self-contained vignettes. While the book is essentially written in diary form, with each "nightmare" representing a separate entry, only some of these entries relate to the external events. Others consist of the narrator's dreams or imaginings, while still others are merely stories whose only connection to the text as a whole is a thematic one.

The lengthy text, which even in the pared-down English translation approaches four hundred pages, is divided into 151 "nightmare" sections.[7] Of this bulk, the experiential portions of the text serve mainly to give unity and coherence to the work as a whole. One of the striking things about these, however, is the informal, self-reflective nature of the narrator's diary-like entries, with their references to the writing process:

> I sat down to write, to record what was to become *Beirut Nightmares*.
>
> I got up from where I lay, gathered my papers . . . which I carried with me into the corridor to resume my writing session. (131–32)

The alienating nature of the narrator's surroundings pulls her within herself, giving her a profound awareness of her own subjectivity:

> A string of familiar voices and faces went gliding through my consciousness. As I saw and heard them, I remembered, then forgot, remembered, then forgot . . . And as I did so, I found that at the bottom of it all there remained the "I." (375)

The "creative" aspect of the narrative refers to those parts that are in the form of inserted stories. These portions have an artistic self-referentiality; they implicitly represent the narrative voice as a creative voice, one capable of producing stories out of the rubble of the war experience. By producing such stories, the narrator is able to delve more deeply into the war than would be possible simply through her own personal narrative. An example will illustrate why this is so. Nightmare 81 concerns a seamstress turned fortune teller, a charlatan who has changed her profession just to make money, and has become highly successful, with people flocking to see her. Things turn peculiar, however, when she receives a visit from an influential bey who is rumored to have killed several people without batting an eyelid. A suffocating feeling comes over her whenever he visits, until she begins to suffer the symptoms she previously had been faking. The story concludes during one of his visits, as she looks into her crystal ball and for the first time really "sees" in it:

> Suddenly she found to her amazement that the ball was no longer empty. In it she saw the bey himself, his bloodied, bullet-riddled corpse flung onto the pavement. . . . The bullet wounds that dotted the corpse were bleeding profusely. As for the face . . . it was undergoing a kind of transformation. Instead of being just one face, it had become the faces of numerous other men. She couldn't make them out clearly and most of them she didn't recognize, although she'd seen pictures of some of them in the newspaper. (170)

What makes this story effective is the way in which it depicts a change in awareness on the part of the fortune teller. Like most of the other inhabitants of Beirut, she is blind to the extent of the dehumanizing process that is going on around and within her. She is intent on making money, that is all. Only in the presence of the abhorrent bey does she finally begin to "see." The story also illustrates why the first-person narration is less effective. The narrator already "sees" the horror of her surroundings, and has insight into the mentality of the people with whom she comes into contact. Because of this, her personal narrative lacks the drama of the stories. Each story encapsulates the process of becoming aware of this horror within itself, a process that the author repeats with many variations.

Many of the stories have supernatural or surreal plots. Nightmare 114 is a lengthy story that concerns a department store mannequin who comes to life after the store is shut down. Her only desire is that the business will reopen and everything will go back to the way it was before. After the place is looted, she finds herself out on the street. No one notices that she is a mannequin; they take her for a prostitute instead. Finally, several armed men who do indeed recognize her as a mannequin grab her. They transform her into a battlefield scarecrow, and she is eventually shot to bits and catches fire. The story ends with an expression of subjectivity on the part of the mannequin that is more "human" than the sentiments expressed by the "real" people around her:

> Even when she discovered that she'd caught fire, she didn't grieve over what had become of her once-spectacular body. Instead, she realized that inside her there was something precious that she'd never been aware of throughout her career as a "display-window girl." And it was something that couldn't go up in flames. (276)

The "reflective" aspect of the narrative refers to those passages in which the narrator relates various dreams and imaginings that belong neither to the diary narrative nor to the inserted stories. While they are part of the narrator's experience, they are, like the stories, more than this; they are reflective of a greater horror than can be summed up by a mere recounting of daily events that occur in her personal life. Some of these occur as dreams:

> I saw them lead a young man over to the pavement. . . . One of the armed men had a brother who'd been killed and he was on the lookout for any scapegoat he could find. . . . The armed man twisted the youth's neck until it was up against the fountain's marble rim, then in a flash his knife came down on the major artery in his neck. The youth gasped, and that was that. But the armed man continued to cut into the youth's neck even after his body had fallen limp, while blood came pouring out of the fountain. . . . The blood gushed forth, bursting out in copious torrents. . . . It flooded the streets, then rose higher and higher until it was lapping at people's windows and finally came pouring into the rooms of the houses. . . . As it rose, it immersed my knees, then my waist, then my chest, then my neck. . . . As I choked on the blood, I began to gasp and scream. . . . Then finally I woke up. (26, 29)

> It was a night of nightmares. . . .
>
> I couldn't feel a bed under me. Instead, it was as if I were suspended

> in midair, surrounded on all sides by the winds of the night and of the unknown. They picked me up and carried me across forests and jungles whose "trees" were human bodies—mangled, bloodied, screaming. Then they took me flying over charred grasslands where children were running along like rapacious kittens baring their tiny, sharp fangs. They transported me over seas whose black waters were bubbling with sulphur, salt and arsenic, and whose islands were inhabited by entire tribes afflicted with leprosy. . . . Then the tribespeople reached out with their leprosy-gnawed fingers and clutched at my hair. They pulled me to the ground and began devouring me. I screamed. But then I resumed my airborne journey, floating once more through the void of the night into the unknown. . . . (98)

At other times, the narrator is not dreaming, but imagining in the waking state, such as in the following passages:

> We were speeding along in the car through the streets of Beirut late last spring (the spring of 1975). . . . All of a sudden we were stopped by the strangest, most peculiar barrier. . . . A thin piece of string had been stretched from one side of the street to the other and in front of this extraordinary "checkpoint" there stood a group of children whose leader and oldest member was ten years old. . . .
>
> Then the ten-year-old said to us, "The woman should be kidnapped and murdered. She's of a different religion than ours."
>
> Then, addressing my boyfriend, he added: "As for you, though, you can pass through." His voice was fearsome and sharp, like the fangs of a wildcat.
>
> We sat there studying their faces. They looked like adult faces that had been mounted on children's bodies. Then they began to sprout beards, their fingernails grew out, their faces developed wrinkles and sweat came streaming down their foreheads. Suddenly they'd turned into a gang of pygmy highway robbers. . . .
>
> As my beloved pulled away, I screamed in terror.
>
> "What's got into you?" he asked. (31–32)

> I took the bullet in my hand and placed it beside my pen. Put a bullet beside a pen and you'll find that the pen is larger. But this bullet in particular looked to me at first as if it were the same length as my pen. Then it grew larger and larger until it became a pillar of fire. Meanwhile, my pen quaked before it, growing thinner and thinner until it had no more substance than the feather of a wounded bird, helpless in the face of a storm of fire. (60)

> I saw the city being transformed into a witch's cauldron. The cauldron and all it contained boiled and boiled and spun around and around in a whirlpool of bloody shrieks. Meanwhile, bullets pierced through every mouth that wished to utter anything contrary to the logic of the bullets themselves. I saw the poor dying, the innocent poor alone. As for their butchers, they had fled from the city of nightmares and madness to the cabarets of Paris, London, and Geneva. (64)
>
> Nightmares, nightmares. . . .
>
> Now I was seeing them constantly, even when I had my eyes wide open. (65)

Sometimes there is no clear dividing line between these dreams or imaginings and the diary narrative. For instance, as Nancy Roberts explains in her introduction, "a recurring theme in the novel is the narrator's preoccupation with the animals in the pet shop next to her house. The animals' suffering parallels those of the unarmed, defenseless civilians of Beirut."[8] As Roberts notes, the narrator makes repeated visits to the pet shop, where the abandoned animals are becoming increasingly hungry. But when she opens their cages, they don't even make any attempt to escape:

> I opened the door as far as it would go. But to my astonishment, they made no attempt even to move towards the door, much less to take off in search of the night, the winds, the open skies, and paths leading to other galaxies. Instead, they headed mechanically to the spot where their food was normally placed, as if they were either blind or hypnotized. . . . I was appalled to find that not a single sparrow came flying out. It was as if they'd forgotten what freedom was. (91)

Later on, however, the narrator finds herself writing about the pet shop from an imaginative perspective:

> I felt a painful twinge of hunger and, as it happened, it was as if the atmosphere had altered the frequency of my brain waves, transporting me to another plane of consciousness and causing my inner "radar" to begin picking up the sounds being made by the creatures in the pet shop.
>
> Their voices sounded to my ears like a symphony of rage that nearly drowned out the sounds of the thunder and the rain. (161)

Still later, she begins to imagine the animals freed from their cages, but still in the pet shop, fighting among each other:

> Now that they'd got a whiff of newly spilt blood, the dogs' appetites were reawakened. Soon the battle was on again, so the injured dog plucked up courage and began fighting for his life. . . .
>
> By the end of the second round, all the dogs were exhausted and a second one had been wounded. Too spent to go on, they lay down and went to sleep, at which point the other animals breathed a sigh of relief. After all, they had been looking on in consternation and horror as the dogs did battle, absorbing what seemed like death-charged ions that had been emanating from the bloody fray. (238)

Just as there is no clear dividing line between the narrator's waking experiences and her dreams or imaginings, there is also no firm dividing line between these and the separate stories she tells. For example, a sequence of narrated passages concerns her brother, Shadi. They begin as a dream narrative in which she is searching for him:

> I found myself stark naked in a freezing, empty room. Pacing around in tears, I wondered: Where's my brother? Where's my brother? Where's Shadi? I decided to try calling out to someone for help, so I went to open the window. But the "window" was nothing but colored lines drawn on to the wall. (238)

The brother appears in a subsequent section, which begins in a manner suggestive of another dream. Yet the narrative then takes on the tone of a "story":

> Shadi was seated at his desk in a room the shape of an immense tube. It looked something like an outsize sewer drainage pipe and emitted a stench like that of a sewer as well. The floor of the room was covered with black rubber and the walls with rust.
>
> Flanking Shadi on either side were hookers with obese, flaccid bodies and faces that looked as if they were made of colored wax.
>
> After leaving prison, Shadi had arrived at the conclusion that the war was really nothing but a great opportunity to make a fortune and he intended to do just that. . . .
>
> On this particular day he was expecting a visit from the leader of a Beirut weapons ring. . . .

> And as if these troubles weren't enough, all the whores left in Beirut were as unsightly as the war itself. . . .
>
> What he needed was someone who still had some of the freshness and youthfulness of women whose bodies haven't become common currency, so to speak.
>
> Then he remembered a woman who fulfilled his specifications perfectly. Without batting an eyelid, he gave his men a detailed description of her, adding: "She lives in a flat across the street from the Holiday Inn, and is alone at present. She's to be abducted without delay."
>
> And of course, he didn't bother to tell them that she was his sister! (296–98)

Suddenly, the narrator returns to her waking narrative:

> I woke up screaming: "Where's my brother? Where's Shadi?" (298)

THE PATCHWORK NOVEL: ELIAS KHOURY

In Elias Khoury's early works, *Little Mountain* (1989; *Al-Jabal al-Ṣaghīr*, 1977) and *Al-Wujūh al-Bayḍā'* (The white faces, 1981),[9] we find that his formal preoccupations do not differ essentially from those of writers such as Sonallah Ibrahim, Taysir Subul, Emile Habiby, Abdelrahman Munif, and Ghada Samman. These include the freeing of narrative from the hegemony of a hero, narrative introversion that focuses the reader's attention on the act of narration, and building the novel on the basis of the short story. What sets Khoury apart is his wholesale approach to experimentation. In *Little Mountain*, particularly, virtually every technique of defamiliarization is used to some extent, creating a very different effect from the controlled experimental style of Munif's *Endings* or the very personal and reportorial style of Samman's *Beirut Nightmares*. Khoury also expands into more complex experimental techniques, such as the insertion of the narrator into the text as a character. He assigns other characters roles of narrators. These techniques are among those associated with what John Fletcher and Malcolm Bradbury have called the "introverted novel," which they define as "concerned with the intricacies of its own form as well as with dramatizing the means by which narration itself is achieved."[10]

Like Samman's novels, all of Khoury's are an attempt to render the experience of the Lebanese Civil War in Beirut. His overwhelming problem in all these works is how to render the sheer horror, tragedy, and disillusionment of that experience. In this effort, he uses every technique he can in order to unsettle, dislocate, and fragment the narrative to the optimum degree. While taken individually, Khoury's narrative techniques do not go beyond what can be found in the works of Western canonical modernists, but Khoury's approach in this work has been to present the reader with a virtual grab bag of modernist devices. By piling one technique on top of another, affecting all facets of the prose—sentence construction, tense, person, time sequence, chapter division, and characterization—he creates a text that has a postmodern feel.

Khoury's preferred novelistic technique is to build the novel on the basis of a series of short stories that interweave and connect. This technique of building the novel on the short story form in order to undermine the classic structure of the novel is one that we find in the work of the early canonical modernists such as Hemingway, Toomer, Stein, Dos Passos, and Joyce. We also find it in the work of late modernists such as Lawrence Durrell and Samuel Beckett. *Little Mountain*, for instance, consists of five chapters, each of which shifts abruptly in terms of time and space. The first chapter describes the narrator's childhood in the Ashrafiyah quarter of Beirut, known as "Little Mountain," and depicts its gradual militarization. The narrative varies sometimes between the first person singular and plural, and between present and past tense, paragraphs are often introduced by equational sentences, and certain motifs are constantly repeated:

> A long line of small soundless cars. We'd sit on the edge of the hill and watch them go by. (6)

> Cars growing, closing in on me. Trees shrinking, disappearing. I was growing bigger and so were the cars. (7)

> Cars roaming the streets. The cars gnaw at the streets with their teeth. The big cars blast their sirens. . . . Black metal devouring me: roadblocks, they say. (14)

The repetition of the name of the quarter is also used to create a lyrical effect:

> They call it Little Mountain. And we called it Little Mountain. We'd carry pebbles, draw faces and look for a puddle of water to wash off the sand, or fill with sand, then cry. We'd run through the fields—or something like fields—pick up a tortoise and carry it to where green leaves littered the ground. We made up things we'd say or wouldn't say. They call it Little Mountain, we knew it wasn't a mountain and we called it Little Mountain. (15)

The description of a palm tree strongly suggests a symbolic representation of Lebanon's descent to a state of civil war:

> The palm tree in front of our house was bent under the weight of its own trunk. We were afraid it would brush the ground, crash down to it, so we suggested tying it with silken rope to the window of our house. But the house itself, with its thick sandstone and wooden ceilings, was caving in and we got frightened the palm tree would bring the house down with it. So we let it lean farther day by day. And every day I'd embrace its fissured trunk and draw pictures of my face in it. (4)

Particularly in this first chapter, which has the feel of autobiography, there is a strong nostalgic attachment to the land, displaying affinities to Proust, Hemingway, Jean Toomer, and García Márquez:

> One hill, several hills, I no longer remember and no one remembers anymore. A hill on Beirut's eastern flank which we called mountain because the mountains were far away. We sat on its slopes and stole the sea. The sun rose in the East and we'd come out of the wheatfields from the East. We'd pluck the ears of wheat, one by one, to amuse ourselves. The poor—or what might have been the poor—skipped through the fields on the hills, like children questioning Nature about Her things. What we called a 'eid was a day like any other, but it was laced with the smell of bargul and 'araq that we ate in Nature's world, telling it about our world which subsists in our memory like a dream. Little Mountain was just a tip of rock we'd steal into, wondrous and proud. We'd spin yarns about our miseries awaiting the moments of joy or death, dallying with our feelings to break the monotony of the days. (15)

Toomer's work is often analyzed both in terms of its lyricism as well as its nostalgia for a South that was soon to disappear. Similarly,

Khoury's nostalgia is for an innocent Lebanon that the Civil War was to relegate to the past forever.

The second chapter plunges the reader directly into the war. A group of *fedayeen*, of which the narrator is a member, capture a church and are confronted by two Capuchin priests. Unlike any other portion of the text, the narrative here is divided into scenes, as if to produce a cinematic effect. Although still rendered in the first person, there is nothing that necessarily connects the identity of the narrator in this chapter to that in the previous one. The tense also changes from the past to the present, and the tale is sometimes interrupted by an aside, as if to heighten the illusion of listening to an oral narrative:

> Boutros comes running from the church. Panting, he tells us: some of the pews have been taken. A whole lot of them came and covered the walls with their slogans. The two priests are very upset (by the way I forgot to mention that the two priests stayed in the church and struck up a firm friendship with Talal). (28)

The third chapter is perhaps the most fragmented, consisting of impressionistic fragments meant to give a picture of life during the war. Khoury uses terse, abbreviated sentences to evoke complex feelings, in a style reminiscent of Hemingway:

> We took the tank and colored it. We took off the 500mm. machine gun and fixed it down in the church. The neighborhood kids gathered around the tank. They drove it, then stopped. We tied a clothesline to the cannon from the window. The clothes hung out were of every color. Talal held the loaf. I don't know what we should do. The revolution should start. But it has started, Salem said. You don't understand what the revolution is. This is revolution. Revolutions are like this. Do you know why a loaf is round? Because it's a loaf. A loaf can't be any different, just like a cemetery. A cemetery is round but we can't see that from the inside. Everything's like that. We see only the surface of things. The smell of gunpowder was spreading. Carrying our guns, we were standing in the winter sun, relaxed. Scattered bursts of shooting. (63)

Sometimes the narrative becomes interiorized. The images spill out of the narrator so fast that they often are expressed in incomplete sentences. They become abstracted, lyrical:

> My foot was getting bigger, the snow lined my shoes. Look, said Talal. The colors of the rainbow spilling into one another. All the colors that I've ever seen and those I've never seen. The mountain opens its mouth and the sun tumbles out. A mountain rolling through the clouds. The colors resemble the sea but the sea is flat. Colors forming circular gaps. My hand reaching out, catching nothing. The perforated mountain moves. We run toward the valley. The valley embraces my body, cuts it into two halves, and the distant sea enters the clouds. I raise my hand to my face. My face is a big, wizened apple. And my hand rises toward the sun that falls into our eyes as it tumbles between the flames and the mouth of the whale that is about to swallow it. (70)

The fourth chapter, written in a mixture of first person and third person, focuses on a man who is not a fighter, but a married, middle-class individual, with a house, car, and children. At times, the prose in this chapter comes close to pure stream-of-consciousness, the flow of which is determined as much by the vagaries of the narrator's mind as by outside events:

> The glass was swaying in my hand as if it wanted to fall. The white liquid had a pungent smell and darkness was falling slowly. That's the way darkness comes. You think it's coming down slow, then suddenly without you feeling a thing you fall into darkness and turn on the lights. But in these black days, there's neither electricity nor anyone who turns lights on for that matter. Everything was quivering. Even the stars are only seen quivering in this cursed city called Beirut. The heat is stifling. The sound of gunfire coming over distantly. How can they fight in such heat? How can they not just sleep on top of the sandbags? It's impossible. The noise heats the air even further. And of course, the dust from the shells fills the air with clouds. So it's raining in summer. Yesterday there was rain. Hot air with rain. Like in miracles. The sky's sweating, my wife said, thinking she was being witty. But it's God's wrath. How can they? I don't know. These new shells that howl like wolves. The best of all is this yarn about Vietnam. They want a new Vietnam! There'll only be wars afterward. War means Vietnam and to have Vietnam you need a war. (84)

Another technique used by Khoury is the compression and extension of narrative in terms of time and space. He weaves in and out of specific events, suddenly closing in, in telescopic fashion, on a series of actions, then suddenly veering off into a reverie:

> Crazy Hani, what's he doing now in the grave? At least he's not asking questions and his eyes don't wander off when he's talking. His eyes were remote as two drops of water. The physics teacher always talked about the drop of water and I never understood what he meant until I looked at this man's eyes. Two, circular, depthless drops of water. He would disappear into his eyes when he talked and stay there, transformed by two drops of water, and curse the police and the state. I'd stand beside him and say nothing. What would I say? There's no police now, Hani's dead and the situation isn't any better. And this woman's dangling from the ceiling. Her leg is white and her thigh is white. No, not white. Something like white. And her foot's as big as a man stuck to the wall. I go up to the wall and press my body to it. But the man is moving, he's shaking. The whole room is shaking. My hand is shaking and the white liquid is spilling onto the ground. I put a bit of water in my mouth but don't swallow; I hold it, letting my right cheek swell. I go up to the chair and try to lean against it. But the shadows, the shadows are swaying as if we were inside a city made of thick cardboard. Colors dark and things receding. My hand drops but I try. I'm really trying. I stand in front of the woman who looks like a thick rope. I extend my hand toward the rope. I hear a scream, step back a little. I brace myself against the wall. The wall shakes. I feel the wall is about to fall on my face, it can't stand upright. I see the cupboard and smile. You can't but smile when you see the cupboard. My aunt loved that cupboard. When she died, the first thing I did was to go to the cupboard and weep in front of its doors. (82)

In this chapter, Khoury begins by distancing the sections of narrative that are in the first and third person from each other, giving the reader the sense that they involve different characters. But as the chapter progresses, the first and third person narratives come closer and closer together, until they alternate from sentence to sentence. It eventually becomes clear that the first person narrator is identical with the subject of the third person narration. This can be seen in the following passage, which recounts the central event in the chapter—the destruction of the main character's prize possession (his car) by a stray bomb. The passage is marked by recurring phrases, producing a pattern of cadenced repetition:

> Kamel Abu Mahdi stood alone. It was all alone in front of me. The street was full of shrapnel shards; the street was full of glass; the street was full of cars. But it had died. He went toward it. The front tire blew

> out. The rubber resembled chewing gum. The street was full of black rubber than looked like soldiers' boots. I told them we should move the car. The black rubber was spreading. I gripped the tires. Kamel Abu Mahdi kneeled. Everyone watched. He was gripping the rubber, trying to move it. He stood up, wiped his face. It was black. He knew he shouldn't cry. It can't be true, he said to his wife. The tears fell nevertheless. Tears are like nothing else. He sat down on the pavement, his head in his hands, and it rained. (103)

The fifth chapter is an exception in that it takes place in Paris, rather than in Beirut. The narrator is living in exile. Although no specific connections are drawn to any of the previous narrative voices, we once again feel that the narrative voice is the same as in the first chapter. By this means, Khoury creates an effect of impersonality, or ambiguity with respect to character. Similarly, Hemingway's *In Our Time*[11] presents the reader with a collection of fifteen stories and seventeen vignettes, which are all thematically linked with one another. Hemingway achieves the effect of impersonality by presenting Nick Adams as the central character in about half the stories, while playing with different protagonists and different methods of narration in the rest.

As with Khoury, Hemingway's most urgent theme is that of the disillusioning effects of war, although the war itself is rarely mentioned except in the vignettes. The violence of the vignettes contrasts with the stories, all of which occur far from the theater of the war. The vignettes unite the work thematically by forcing the reader to compare what happens in them to what happens in the stories. The effect is to further shift the reader's attention away from character and onto the thematics of the work. Hemingway uses the short-story form for two purposes: to create a larger, thematically unified work, and to undermine the conventional reliance on a single hero within that work, preoccupations that are evident in *Little Mountain*.

Moreover, it is important to stress that, like Abdelrahman Munif's *Endings* or Ghada Samman's *Beirut '75* and *Beirut Nightmares*, there is an overall thematic unity to *Little Mountain* with respect to time, place, and characterization. While each chapter represents a different moment in time, each takes place during the period of the civil war. While each chapter represents a different location, the focus is always on Beirut. And while each chapter presents different characters, together these characters form a composite portrait that is distinctly Lebanese. In this sense, Khoury's experimentalism in *Little Mountain* is not far removed from that of Taysir Subul, a generation earlier.

Like *Little Mountain*, Khoury's subsequent work, *Al-Wujūh al-Bayḍā'* is composed of a series of stories. What is surprising about it is that Khoury's narrative style is now more restrained. The various stories have different narrative voices, but now these narrative voices have a clear relationship to one another, as well as to a central character. Khoury's main preoccupation in this work is the strategy of allowing stories to emerge from other stories. While several narrators relate the stories, a single thread, namely the mental deterioration and death of Khalil Ahmad Jaber (Khalīl Aḥmad Jābir), connects all of them with one another.

The first chapter of *Al-Wujūh al-Bayḍā'* begins by relating this gradual deterioration, as narrated by Khalil's wife Nuha (Nuhā). Khalil's son Aḥmad has been killed in the war, and been dubbed a hero. For a while, after his son's death, life seems to return to normal for Khalil and his wife. Gradually, however, Khalil begins to change. When he tells his wife that he's going to work, she notices that he doesn't go. He stops eating and talking. He spends all day in bed and doesn't come out of his room except to go to the bathroom. Later he begins eating again, but then takes to erasing words and names from the family papers and newspaper clippings. He erases the name of his son, of family members, as well as his own name and words like "hero." He even erases them from clothing labels.

Following this, he begins taking the family pictures and painting the faces white, putting different faces on the heads, and telling his wife that they are the heads of different people or belong to "everybody." He also cuts out their hands and paints them white until everything is white. Then he stands in front of the mirror and starts cutting the edges of his beard; he washes the mirror with soap, and all the time he tells his wife that he is working. Later, he abandons the house entirely and roams the streets whitewashing the walls of the city. Khalil's neurotic response to his son's death is a powerful commentary on the war, perhaps more powerful than any overt description of it. This technique of indirectly evoking a feeling is a familiar one in modernism, particularly in the modernist short story. Examples can be found in the short stories of Chekhov, Flaubert, and D. H. Lawrence, as well as in Hemingway's *In Our Time*, and Joyce's *Dubliners*.[12]

The second chapter concerns the killing of an Armenian doctor and the killing and rape of his sixty-five-year-old wife by three youths. It has little connection with the story of Khalil Ahmad Jaber, except that someone who knew Khalil begins the narrative. The connections from story to story are made rapidly, by means of a few sentences or even a few words. For instance the transition from Khalil's story to that of the murdered doctor occurs when the initial narrator hears about the death of the doctor and his wife, and compares Khalil Jaber's death with this new event. He finds even greater horror in the latter crime. He can't believe how bestial it is, and is especially dumbfounded by the rape of the old woman:

> Is this believable? I read the news in the paper just as I read the news about Mr. Khalil. Is this believable? Three armed men invade the apartment, kill the doctor, rape his wife, and then kill her. . . . A woman sixty-five years old raped by a group of young men in their teens. Is it possible? (52)

The first narrator begins the story of the doctor and his wife, but soon hands off the narration to the doctor himself. The narration goes back and forth from a description of the doctor's actions, to his own internal dialogue:

> Doctor Harut [Hārūt] blinked his eyes. They're getting closer. They must not have seen anything in the living room. They're in the other room. He was able to distinguish their voices. But why are they talking so loudly? Thieves always talk in low voices. . . . But these guys don't seem to care. (47)

The first narrator intervenes again, briefly describing the investigation process after the youths have been apprehended, and then passes the narrative to the perpetrators themselves as the investigator interviews them:

> The investigator tries to understand why the killing and rape occurred.
>
> Asim ['Āṣim] relates: It's a simple matter, sirs. We wanted to steal. (55)

This technique has an alienating effect on the reader. The reader does not really want to hear the narrative of the youths themselves, yet

Khoury provides it. Their account of the grisly rape and murders is without emotion, without remorse, as if it had just been a common occurrence. Khoury's intention is clearly to unsettle the reader by giving voices to characters that committed such a heinous crime. The reader is forced to take a position to which Khoury himself does not commit, and to this extent the reader finds him- or herself at odds with the text itself, or at least in the position of having to do the work of judgment or interpretation.

Following this, we receive the reaction of the investigator to the youths' narrative, then the narrative is passed to the son of the murdered doctor, then back to the initial narrator, and so on. Thus, the narration is constantly shifting, in the fashion of reportage. Sami Suwaydan (Sāmī Suwaydān), notes that the technique of reportage utilized by Khoury does not merely inform us about the central events, which are the various deaths, murders, and disappearances, but also is a way of leading into the personal accounts of the various narrators: "Murder is the door through which language clamors in order to reveal more about itself than about the crime."[13]

A woman named Fatimah (Fāṭimah) narrates the third story. Forced to marry someone she does not love, she is raped by her husband, Mahmud (Maḥmūd), on her marriage night. Mahmud later goes mad, kills their son, and is later killed himself. The fourth story is about the discovery of a corpse, its examination, and the report of the autopsy. Suwaydan points out that killing is not merely the prevailing theme in *Al-Wujūh al-Bayḍā'*, but rather is part of the narrative's structure: "If we consider the murder to have a relationship to the account or story, observation confirms it as the general structure of the text as a whole."[14]

He goes on to note that each of the first three chapters is built on pairs of killings. In the first chapter, it is the killing of Khalil Ahmad Jaber's son, and then his own death. Khalil's death and that of the Armenian doctor and his wife frame the second chapter. The third chapter is built on the murder of Fatimah's son by her husband and, subsequently, her husband's death.

Throughout the text, each of the narrators possesses their own voice, and sometimes even an individual style of writing. Note, for instance, the way in which the uneducated Mme. Nuha writes "inshā' allāh" instead of "in shā' allāh" (28). This is more than just an attempt to portray her as uneducated. It is a type of narrative signature that is unique to her as a character. Khoury is one of the very first Arab novelists to be tentatively experimenting with giving characters such linguistic signatures.

Khoury also experiments with symbolism in this novel. For Khoury, white symbolizes both purity and decay, two qualities that are not mutually exclusive. Together, they represent a society that is seen as completely corrupt, and the response to that corruption. If what exists is corrupted; what does not exist is pure. In order to become pure again, the city must be destroyed, effaced; hence Khalil's whitewashing of the city walls. Thus, in the following passage, which describes Khalil's obsession with the whiteness of the sheets and bedcovers in his home, white is seemingly a symbol of purity, yet it is simultaneously evocative of decay and corruption:

> He told her about the white sheets. . . . He told her that the bed had to be painted white, and a white sheet and on it we put a white sheet, then we put a white cover over (it) and we went to sleep. We raised the cover to our eyes and we saw nothing except the light. It was scattered into white pieces strewn everywhere. . . .
>
> I am white. I want a white sheet to sleep on, and over the sheet a white cover. And a lamp in the middle of the room. I look from the white cover and see the light scattering. The light is points of whiteness. My teeth are white. And the walls. The white walls. . . . (101)

Khalil's obsession progresses to include the sheets, covers, and walls, as well as people's hands:

> The walls are becoming white. The hands. The important thing is the hands. Fatimah looks at her hands and at her fingers, as he looks into space. "The important thing is the hands. Everyone's hands are becoming white. The fingers. The fingernails. The walls." (103)

In the third story, Mahmud has a similar obsession with whiteness, linked now more clearly with the urge to annihilate the present. Everything, he says, will disappear, and then everything will be white:

> Nothing is left here. Everything is disappearing. You are disappearing, I am disappearing, the city is disappearing, and the walls are disappearing. Everything is disappearing and becoming white. . . . Everything is being effaced. . . . (115–16)

In the final chapter of *Al-Wujūh al-Bayḍā'*, Khoury inserts himself into the narration in order to speculate about his characters and philosophize on his role as author. In assuming the narrative voice, Khoury claims not to know the fate of his characters, and includes his authorial name among them:

> Truly, I feel at a great loss—the author of this story who feels lost, and doesn't know. He doesn't know anything. While usually the author knows all the details of the story, especially its ending, and offers it slowly and gradually. . . .
>
> But in this story, the author doesn't know . . . how to satisfy and amuse the reader. (244)

In an example of intertextuality, Khoury, writing like a literary critic, compares the experience of his characters with those of the characters in Ghassan Kanafani's *Men in the Sun:*

> It is clear that Mu'ayn Abbas [Mu'ayn 'Abbās] felt great pain. His pain was different from that of Ghassan Kanafani's heroes who were left to die from the sun inside the tanker truck. The heroes of *Men in the Sun* were a group, but Mu'ayn was alone, and death together with others is easier than an individual death. Most importantly, the heroes in *Men in the Sun* were symbolic heroes. But Abbas is neither a hero nor a symbol, but simply a young man who was killed in the toilet of the airport. (248)

Khoury claims, in this passage, that his characters are neither heroes nor symbols, and that the death of Mu'ayn Abbas is an individual, not a collective one. In this statement, Khoury is taking great pains to differentiate himself from the "collective" consciousness of writers like Abdelrahman Munif, Salim Barakat, and even Emile Habiby. Whether or not we can take entirely Khoury's word for this, however, is another question.

THE DYNAMICS OF WAR AND SEXUALITY

The Lebanese Civil War was a catalyst for women's writing, pushing it for the first time to a fundamental break with traditional viewpoints regarding both sexuality and power. This is not to say that the connection between these two issues had never previously been explored in the Arabic novel or by male writers. In Ghassan Kanafani's *All That's Left to You*, for instance, the oppressive power imbalance in male/female relations is brought out in the context of the Palestinian struggle, no longer merely seen obliquely via an ironized masculine position, as in Mahfouz's *Miramar*, but directly from the woman's point of view:

> Those sensitive folds of flesh that kept my eyes shut, burst open, and I felt the uninterrupted flow of tears stream down my cheeks. I tried to free my wrists from his iron grip, but he wouldn't relax his hold. The next instant a thin ray of sunlight entered through the window behind me, and falling on his face, split it in two, making his blazing anger appear still more violent.
>
> "Listen to me and remember tomorrow what I'm saying now: If you can't abort that little bastard. . . ."
>
> Without warning I began to scream at the top of my voice, trying to drown him out. . . . [15]

The legacy of colonialism also provided the context for one of the best-known modern Arabic novels in English translation, *Season of Migration to the North* (1969; *Mawsim al-Hijrah ilā al-Shimāl*; 1967), by the Sudanese émigré writer Tayeb Saleh (Ạl-Tayyib Ṣāliḥ).[16] The book is significant in many respects, but perhaps in no greater respect than the way in which it explores the intertwined relations between gender and power relations. The main character of the novel is a Sudanese intellectual named Mustafa who migrates to London and during his tenure there as a scholar wages a campaign of seduction whose victims, all Western women, either commit suicide or are otherwise ruined by their contact with him. Saleh dwells on Mustafa's allure for the Western women with whom he becomes involved. Theirs is an infatuated response laden with orientalist pity and sentimentalism. Mustafa sees in this pity a lie that is a hallmark of imperialism and colonialism. But Mustafa is not just a victim of Western attitudes. His relationships with these women are part of a campaign of revenge. He uses his intellectual abilities as a weapon, exploiting both consciously and unconsciously the history of British involvement in the Sudan to justify his behavior.

The actions of both Mustafa and his lovers can be seen as compensatory for imbalances in social, economic, and political power relations. Mustafa emulates the role of a colonizer in his London bedroom, while his lovers act out fantasies of colonial subservience. The violence and self-destructiveness of these relationships may be connected with the fact that they are ultimately belied by historical, political, and economic circumstances. Mustafa's lovers, despite their professed idolatry of him, are the more powerful in the sense that they represent the politically, economically, and culturally dominant West.

Finally, Mustafa marries a Western woman, Jean Morris, who, however, refuses to allow him to dominate her. This prompts him to kill her in the throes of their lovemaking. The dominance of the Arab male is revealed to be based on a deep insecurity, which cannot cope with the independence of Western women and the reciprocity that they expect in relationships with men. After seven years of imprisonment, Mustafa returns to the Sudan. He is able to rapidly integrate himself into his native society, and tries to reconcile Western values with traditional ones. He marries Hosna, a woman of the village in which he has settled down, and has a loving relationship with her. He meets the narrator of the story, also a Western-educated Sudanese, and reveals his entire history.

The climax of the narrative comes after Mustafa's disappearance and presumed death, however. Hosna is forced to marry Wad Rayyes, an aged man of the village. Having inherited Western attitudes about gender relations from the reformed Mustafa, Hosna is unable to tolerate the idea of an arranged marriage. At the climax of the novel, when Wad Rayyes attempts his sexual conquest of her, she brutally murders him and then chooses to commit suicide, rather than submit.

By telling two stories, one of Western, the other of native experience, Saleh forces the reader to recognize that the dynamic of gender relations in the Arab world are analogous to the political relations of imperialism. This reversal of awareness, in which the burden of guilt is shifted from an external source to the self, constitutes the confessional aspect of the text. In Joseph Conrad's *Heart of Darkness*,[17] the confessional voice is expressed by the narrator, Marlow, rather than by Kurtz. Similarly, in *Season of Migration to the North*, the narrator, rather than Mustafa, represents the confessional voice. It is the narrator who sees the position of the Western and Sudanese women as identical by virtue of the actions of the Arab male, who fantasizes himself as a conqueror:

> "I imagined Hosna . . . Mustafa Sa'eed's widow," he relates, "as being the same woman in both instances: two white, wide-open thighs in

London, and a woman groaning before dawn in an obscure village on a bend of the Nile under the weight of the aged Wad Rayyes." (86–87)

Among women writers, the Egyptian novelist Nawal el-Saadawi (Nawāl Al-Sa'dāwī) is notable for raising similar issues with respect to the lives of lower-class women in the Arab world. *Woman at Point Zero* (1983; *Imra'ah 'Inda Nuqtah al-Ṣifr*, 1975)[18] is a feminist narrative whose overwhelming focus is social protest. At the same time, however, it also contains a subtle confessional element that reflects the author's own conflict as a member of the upper class and the intelligentsia, wishing to represent the voice of the disenfranchised in Egyptian society. The story is that of a former prostitute who killed her former pimp and, indirectly, of the woman psychologist who interviews her as she waits to be executed. Even before they meet, the former prostitute, Firdaus, is invested with a charismatic aura in the eyes of the psychologist. When the prisoner initially refuses to be talk to her, the would-be interviewer senses her almost imperial aloofness, her complete disdain for society or company. This gives the condemned woman the air of a majestic, morally powerful figure.

Finally consenting to the interview, Firdaus tells her painful story of victimization and realization. As a prostitute, Firdaus presents herself to men as a commodity, and in so doing she obtains a degree of control both over herself and over the volatile power of money. Her power to charge more money, and handle money in greater quantities gives her a greater feeling of her own self-worth. When she finally abandons prostitution, she substitutes a series of values—respectability, personal freedom, love, independence, and courage—as ideals in place of the power of money. But her final epiphany is a rediscovery and emphatic rejection of money as a source of freedom and even power. This rejection of money is based on her recognition that money underlies the entire oppressive, male-dominated system. More importantly, in her utter rejection of money as power, she rejects power itself. In a sense, she removes herself utterly from the material realm, and looks forward only to death.

After listening to Firdaus's entire story, the psychologist feels guilty and indecisive:

> I got into my little car, my eyes on the ground. Inside of me was a feeling of shame. I felt ashamed of myself, of my life, of my fears, and

> my lies. . . . I rammed my foot down on the accelerator as though in a hurry to run over the world, to stamp it out. But the next moment I quickly lifted my foot and braked hard, and the car came to a halt. (108)

By Firdaus's impeccable moral example, the psychologist has discovered that she is implicated in the system, yet because she is a member of the privileged class, and has so much to lose, at the last minute she steps on the brake. In this sense, she is akin to many characters in Western confessional fiction who come to an awareness of their own guilt, yet are ambivalent as to what to do about it. While the confessional element in the text consists of a mere brief paragraph, it nevertheless comes at the very end of the text, which emphasizes its significance. Moreover, as Georges Tarabishi points out in his critique of this work, the narrator evinces an "overwhelming desire to identify with her subject," and both the preface and the last chapter of the book "betray an intensely personal tone."[19]

The dynamics of gender and power inequality in the Arab world has been explored most powerfully, however, in the work of women writers in the wake of the Lebanese Civil War, as they began to question the ideological assumptions underlying the conflict. At the outset of this period, many women writers perceived the issue of national identity as consonant with feminist issues. The struggle for national liberation was seen as compatible with the feminist struggle, the "soul" of the Arab nation with the "eternal feminine." By the '80s, however, women novelists began to distance themselves from the nationalist struggle and to view all types of politically motivated conflict as aspects of patriarchy. Femininity was held up as something contrary to the process of armed conflict, regardless of its ideological motivation. The issues of war and sexuality were not only juxtaposed, but the connections between the two were also exposed and analyzed. This subject is treated at length in Miriam Cooke's *War's Other Voices: Women Writers on the Lebanese Civil War.*[20]

In *Sexuality and War: Literary Masks of the Middle East*, Evelyne Accad discusses the work of three female novelists (Hanan al-Shaykh, Etel Adnan, and Andrée Chedid) and three male novelists (Tawfiq Yusuf Awwad, Halim Barakat [Ḥalīm Barakāt], and Elias Khoury). The main focus of her book is a discussion of the ways in which the issues of war and sexuality are juxtaposed, and the differences between male and female writers in this respect. She says,

> In this study, my hypothesis has been that although both female and male novelists make the connection between sexuality and war, their ways of expressing it and most of all the solutions implied are quite different. Women writers paint the war and the relationships of women, men, and their families in the darkest terms. . . . Men writers also paint the war and relationships among men and women in the bleakest terms, and they emphasize the connection between the two. But their depression does not lead them to search for alternatives different from the historically accepted ones: heroism, revenge, and violence as catharsis.[21]

This observation reflects the huge fault line between the sexes in the Arab world, which was exposed by the civil conflict in Lebanon. Ghassan Kanafani's *All That's Left to You* is one of the few novels by a male writer that succeeds in juxtaposing sexual oppression and war. At the same time that Hamid is in a death struggle with the Israeli soldier, his sister Maryam struggles under the oppression of her husband Zakaria. Here, the parallel is inescapable, and anticipates the juxtaposition of these themes by women writers during the Lebanese Civil War. Significantly, however, the armed conflict depicted in Kanafani's work was not a civil conflict, but one that involved an outside aggressor. In relation to the sectarian conflict in Lebanon, there was little such insight on the part of male writers. Accad fixes on a quote from Elias Khoury's *Little Mountain* as an example:

> And this city, what is it? A whore. Who could imagine a whore sleeping with a thousand men and continuing to live? The city receives a thousand bombs and continues its existence nonetheless. . . . When we had destroyed Beirut, we thought we had destroyed it. . . . But when the war was declared finished . . . we discovered we had not destroyed it. We had only opened a few breaches in its walls, without destroying it. For that, other wars would be necessary.[22]

Clearly the comparison of the war-damaged city to a whore is offensive to Accad, and for good reason, since it expresses only the most thinly concealed male rage against a feminine Other that somehow retains its individuality despite repeated assaults of the most ferocious kind. Such a metaphor clearly allows any notion of victimization to escape. The city itself appears as an evil that must be extirpated.

Beirut '75 already contains certain sections in which the themes of sexuality and violence are interconnected. One of the main characters in the novel, for instance, is Yasmeena, a young woman from Damascus, who has escaped the stifling atmosphere of a nun's convent, where she has taught for the past ten years. She falls under the sway of Nimr, a handsome and wealthy young man who has no respect for her whatsoever, and simply uses her for sex, leading her on with the word "love." Yasmeena becomes addicted to sex because of her very deprivation, and sees her experience as representative of all Arab women who, in her view, have suffered this deprivation for a thousand years:

> His body . . . I'd become accustomed to it, addicted to it. . . . For all of twenty-seven years I'd been forbidden to partake of this amazing pleasure, and here I was now, ill on account of it, a deviant who . . . devoted her life to the bed. In my blood ran the passionate desires of all Arab women who had been held prisoners for more than a thousand years. It was no longer possible for me to experience sex as merely one part of my life. Instead . . . it had become my entire existence. (41)

> It isn't because I'm a whore, but simply because my hunger for his body is more than a thousand years old. (42)

At the same time, Yasmeena ponders whether or not there isn't some way in which she could have avoided this fate:

> She wondered to herself, if I'd known another man before Nimr—if they had allowed my body to experience wholesome, sound relationships in Damascus—would I have lost my way to this extent? (95)

Yasmeena's fate is more gruesome than that of any of the other characters in the narrative. Once Nimr stops showering her with money as part of his plan to get rid of her and shunt her onto someone else, she returns to her brother's apartment. The brother, enraged that she has given herself to Nimr and come to him without any money, attacks her:

> He lunged at her and grabbed her handbag. Finding nothing in it, he flew into a rage. He began striking her repeatedly on the face, the blows coming in rapid succession along with his curses and insults.

> "Where's the money, you slut?" he demanded. "Where? Where?"
>
> "You filthy whore . . . I'll slit your throat!"
>
> Her mouth was full of blood, and before she could say a word, the knife sank into her chest. She didn't feel anything but astonishment.
>
> Half an hour later, her brother entered the nearest police station carrying a pail covered with a newspaper. He sat down in front of the officer on duty, removed the newspaper from the pail, and took out his sister's severed head, which was still dripping with blood.
>
> In a manly voice he said, "I killed my sister in defense of my honor, and I want to make a complete confession."
>
> A look of admiration flashed in the officer's eyes. . . . The brother then began making his confession while the clerk wrote it down, in his eyes, also, a look of appreciation and respect. (95–96)

The most prominent character in the novel is Farah, a young man from a small village near Damascus who is seduced by the prospect of fame. He finds a sponsor in Nishan, a wealthy movie mogul. In doing so, he discovers that he has made a pact with the Devil. Nishan promotes him as an icon of virility, when this is in fact far from his true nature:

> He lit a cigarette and didn't say anything. . . . Seven women in one week . . . and he hadn't been able to "come" with a single one of them. . . .
>
> With the kind of phony sensitivity and tenderness that women put on in such situations, she said, ". . . Come, my love, you 'singer of manliness'!"
>
> When Farah heard her address him by his title, "singer of manliness," he nearly burst out laughing and crying at the same time. It was with this image that Nishan had launched him to stardom. (67)

His patron, Nishan, turns out to be a homosexual, and Farah's seduction part of the "bargain":

> Under "orders" from Nishan, I lay down for a while on the balcony of the chalet, since he'd said that a bronze-like tan was a "must" . . . and that, consequently, sunbathing was part of my job . . .
>
> Every once in a while he would come along and rub me with suntan oil. . . .
>
> At first his fingers moved gently and delicately back and forth over my skin. . . . But then his touch became rough and violent, like a plow going down into the soil. And then I understood. (68–69)

Samman's portrait of Nishan is that of a highly stereotypical homosexual, as is his depiction of Farah's deteriorating character in response to his seduction:

> Nishan's thick, flabby flesh quivered with amorous passion as he said, "Women aren't able to give me this kind of pleasure, you magnificent man!" (69)

> When Nishan came to take me to the party, he got really angry. He shouted at me, "Farah, look at yourself in the mirror!"
>
> He told me I was wearing women's clothing and that I had makeup on my face. I hadn't exactly noticed, but in any case, I don't know what made him mad. (99)

> What's happening to me? Let me get up and put on my dress and my silk underwear. And let me try on that bra . . . I just adore those partly see-through lace brassieres. (100)

Despite this stereotyping, however, Samman's frank description of homosexuality represents a sharp break with conventions in Arabic literature. This is another area that, in the West, has been a vanguard in the process of the "feminization" of the novel form. Western modernism is inconceivable without the contribution of homoerotic texts, which steadily eroded a patriarchal legacy in literature in terms of form, as well as in terms of themes, underlying values, and preoccupations. In the Arab world, there are few known writers with a homoerotic orientation, and the subject hardly comes up in the work of male novelists. For the most part, the only writers who have dealt with the subject have been women.

Ghadah Samman's text is also innovative in terms of form. Most of the narrative is in the third person, but switches to first person in a few select passages, once in the case of Yasmeena, and the rest in the case of Farah. There is no pattern to these changes, no concern for symmetry, and in this respect *Beirut '75* (1975) anticipates Khoury's *Little Mountain* (1977) and Munif's *Endings* (1978). Most striking of all is the way in which Samman brings the novel to a conclusion, with twelve nightmares appended to the penultimate chapter, and a single nightmare that concludes the text. These nightmare vignettes are all in the first person, and represent Farah's deteriorating mental condition. At the same time, however, they stand as allegorical fragments that reflect the societal insanity of Lebanon:

> Nishan decided that I should go to a toupee shop to pick out a suitable hairpiece for my new film. . . .
>
> I was calm and, as usual, complied with all of Nishan's orders so that I could become rich and famous like him. . . .
>
> In the toupee shop, the sales attendant brought me a collection of severed human heads that were still dripping with blood and said to me, "Pick out the hair that you like the most!" (106)

> I woke up and found myself trapped inside a glass jar. It walls were clear, but I couldn't pass through them.
>
> Nishan picked me up in the jar and put me in his pocket. . . . He took me to a warehouse. . . . But everyone there, like me, was a prisoner inside a jar. . . .
>
> The actress, who was beautiful and only half-clad, was hitting the walls of the jar that enclosed her. She was beating on them with both fists and screaming. (109)

> It was the night of my big singing concert. . . .
>
> I began to sing with all my heart, and the crowd began to laugh. I kept singing, and the crowd kept laughing.
>
> The band left the stage, while Nishan beat his head with both hands. They said I'd howled like a wounded dog, that I hadn't sung a single word. All I did was howl and howl at the crowd.
>
> I swore I'd been singing. (113)

In the final chapter, Farah has escaped from a mental institution, and is hiding out from the authorities. He has become an underground man reminiscent of Habiby's main character. The closing vignette also displays a form of black humor reminiscent of *The Pessoptimist:*

> When I ran away from the hospital, the first thing I did was to steal the sign at the entrance that said "Hospital for the Mentally Ill."
>
> I took it to the city entrance, removed the sign saying "Beirut," and planted the other one in its place.
>
> I burst out laughing as I read the sign saying "Hospital for the Mentally Ill," with Beirut looming up behind it in dawn's light like an infernal beast preparing to pounce. And I ran away, fleeing to the safety of my lair. (115)

Although *Beirut '75* is clearly a novel of social protest and makes connections between war and sexuality, it does not concentrate on the situation of women, but rather represents men and women in the position of common victims. In her subsequent *Beirut Nightmares*, there is a degree of change in this respect. For instance, Samman narrates the story of an impotent man, contrasting his violent nature with that of his passive wife, yet paradoxically hinting simultaneously at his weakness and her strength:

> The woman hadn't said a thing to her husband. However, when he got up at dawn, his heart was weighted down with a feeling of deep distress. His powerful muscles, his towering height, a mustache that could stop a falcon in midair, his copious chest hair—none of these outward signs of manliness did him a bit of good in his battle with . . . her body.
>
> He still hadn't been able to occupy the tender-skinned fortresses of this soft, mild young woman whom he'd taken as his third wife. It had been fifteen days now and this hand of his which could slaughter a sheep with a single stroke still fell limp when it came up against her body. In fact, his entire body would droop and sag when it encountered hers. . . .
>
> And as if to make his suffering all the more unbearable, this poor young thing . . . remained utterly silent. She didn't say a word—she didn't object, she didn't explain, she didn't complain. Yet in her eyes he glimpsed a womanly look of frightful hardness and scorn. (67–68)

The man's sexual frustration leads to a truly shocking expression of violence, in which his feelings of injured manhood dwarf any concern for his wife. She becomes little more than an animal in his eyes. Samman's narrative ties the barbarity of his sentiments both to his male pride as well as to the chaotic environment of the war, thus clearly connecting these two social conditions with one another:

> Early one morning, his bitterness was turning into such a volcano of physical violence that he thought of cutting off her head instead of the sheep's, accusing her of immorality and unfaithfulness. But he couldn't do that yet, since she was still a virgin. With all of Beirut in chaos on account of the civil war, there wouldn't be any qualified medical experts around to examine her corpse. So . . . why not just shoot her on her way home from the market some day? Then, of course, suspicion

would fall on a sniper. Yes, that was it. It would be better to kill her in the street, because then she'd just die like so many thousands of others in the city, without anyone taking the least notice. (68)

Sitt Marie Rose (1978),[23] by Etel Adnan, differentiates radically between the roles played by men and women against the backdrop of the Lebanese Civil War. It focuses on a young Christian Lebanese schoolteacher who has fallen in love with a Palestinian Muslim. Held hostage in her school by four young Christian guerrillas along with her young pupils, she is eventually executed. But the true theme of the novel is not the fate of Sitt Marie Rose, but the divisions of Lebanon—Muslim versus Christian. Sitt Marie Rose defends a pluralistic society:

> I am the mother of three children. I left my husband. I live with a young Palestinian who is, at this moment, in danger. I was defending the Palestinian cause before I even knew him. I'm defending a common culture, a common history, theirs and ours. I don't see any difference. (56)

More significantly in this novel, however, is the depiction of men as in love with war, not merely as a substitute for sexuality, but in preference to it:

> Fouad hunts as though obsessed. He prefers killing to kissing. He hates the expression "to make love" because you don't make anything, as he says. He prefers jeep-speed-desert-bird-bullet to girl-in-a-bed-and-fuck. (2)

> These young boys were exalted by the Crusades. Mounir identified with Frederick Barbarossa because he was himself slightly red-haired. He bitterly regretted, as though it has happened recently, that Saladin had conquered Jerusalem. It caused him actual pain. The Crusades excited all of them. (47)

> Marie Rose frightens them. They have all the means in the world to crush her in a second, to subject her to all forms of disgrace; to throw her, cut into pieces, onto the sidewalk. . . . But . . . the more she spoke to them of love, the more they are afraid. . . . Mounir, Tony, Fouad . . . finding themselves before a woman who can stand up to them, are terrified. . . . To them, love is a kind of cannibalism. Feminine symbols tear at them with their claws. (69)

The *Story of Zahra* (1986; *Hikāyah Zahrah*, 1980),[24] by Hanan al-Shaykh (Ḥanān al-Shaykh) makes a similar point by means of an opposite strategy. Instead of a bold female protagonist who is not afraid to challenge the male ethic of violence, Zahra enacts a pattern of passive complicity with that violence. Zahra is a plain young woman, considered of marginal suitability for marriage, who has suffered the almost characteristic experiences of rape, abortion, and marriage of convenience.

Returning to her native Beirut during the period of civil war to live with her parents after the failure of her marriage, she visits a sniper on the roof of an apartment building for mute sexual encounters. For the first time she experiences sexual arousal and climax. Her descriptions of these sexual encounters form the most arresting part of the narrative, for they combine the motif of dominance and submission with that of sexual awakening:

> My back aches from lying on the ground. I want to rise, but the sniper never seems to have his fill of me. He drops down on me like a bat out of the air. Yet I like him weighing down on me. I clutch his back so that he weighs as much as possible. It is a weight that transforms itself into lightness until the sniper seems weightless, bodiless. (138)

The contradictory imagery of weight and weightlessness reinforces the central paradox of pain and pleasure. The rooftop where Zahra meets the sniper is situated virtually in the calm eye of the storm of the civil conflict. The initiation into pleasure is experienced within the eye of this painful storm. By ironic comparison, we can compare this with the Deraa scene in T. E. Lawrence's *Seven Pillars of Wisdom*, which similarly exposes the connection between war and sexuality, mocking and disrupting the discourse of war:

> I remember the corporal kicking with his nailed boot to get me up . . . I remembered smiling idly at him, for a delicious warmth, probably sexual, was welling through me.[25]

Zahra's response to war, like Lawrence's in the Deraa chapter, is passive, even masochistic:

> Oh, you sniper! You weigh on me like a vast but weightless mountain! Oh, you who dig these deep craters in my body, can't you dig deeper

> and deeper. . . . Oh, sniper, let me cry out in pleasure so that my father hears me and comes to find me sprawled out so. I am one with the dust in this building of death. Let my father see my legs spread wide in submission. (137)

Nevertheless, Zahra's response represents a type of rebellion that is perhaps even more effective than that of Sitt Marie Rose. Although Marie Rose represents a feminine ideology, it is nevertheless an ideology. Moreover, through her purity and resistance she becomes a martyr, and thus a symbol. Zahra, on the other hand, is more than a symbol. She is a living, breathing person, with human weaknesses. Through her very human rebellion, she achieves a much more lasting and satisfying liberation:

> It begins to occur to me that the war, with its miseries and destructiveness, has been necessary for me to return to being normal and human. The war, which makes one expect the worst at any moment, has led me into accepting this new element in my life. Let it happen, let us witness it, let us open ourselves to accept the unknown, no matter what it may bring, disasters or surprises. The war has been essential. It has swept away the hollowness concealed by routines. It has made me ever more alive, ever more tranquil. (138)

It does not matter that, at the end of the narrative, Zahra is betrayed by the sniper, that he guns her down after she confides to him that she suspects who and what he is. In the apotheosis of her death, the concluding sentence—"I see rainbows proceeding towards me across the white skies with their promises only of menace"—does not erase the impression that there was something liberating in her experience. The ambivalence of the narrative—its paradoxical quality, in which victory is defeat and defeat victory—is the quality that it has most in common with Western modernist texts.

In *The Stone of Laughter* (1994; *Ḥajar al-Ḍaḥik*, 1990),[26] Hoda Barakat (Hūdā Barakāt) simultaneously utilizes the alternative techniques of Etel Adnan and Hanan al-Shaykh, challenging the male ethic of violence on the one hand, and exposing its ambiguities and contradictions on the other. She achieves this by combining feminine and masculine qualities in a single character—a feminized male named Khalil. In her introduction to *The Stone of Laughter*, Fadia Faqir writes that "because Khalil is feminized, he is excluded and alienated from his own society.

Khalil objects to the cyclical violence around him and tries to keep the personal and public spheres of his life separate. While the country is engaged in a most atrocious civil war, he spends his time shopping, cooking, cleaning the house, day-dreaming about male loved ones, replacing broken window panes and reading."[27] In comparison to the other young men in Beirut, Khalil is a virtual female:

> A young armed man came out . . . and looked scornfully at pale Khalil and his bag, which looked like a housewife's shopping bag. Khalil held onto the bag and kept walking, trying to take firm strides, knowing the young man was looking at him . . . and he did not forget to pass by the cleaners. (37)

When his friend Naji is killed, Khalil's response is to try to putter around in the kitchen. The description here conveys a desperate contrast between a calm, even reverential attitude toward life, with a violent fear and loathing close under the surface:

> He crushed two cloves of garlic, squeezed a bitter lemon over them then opened a tin of brown beans; he warmed them up and poured them onto the plate . . . he beheaded the red tomato and sprinkled on some salt. He opened the last jar of pickled cucumbers . . . he took one out and put it on the little plate. . . . Khalil sat down to eat, watching the window . . . he switched on the radio and listened to the news . . . he put the dishes in the sink and filled the copper coffee pot with water . . . he turned off the tap and began to throw up violently as if he wanted to bring his guts up out of his mouth. (58)

After he gets over Naji's death, he befriends another young man, Youssef. When Youssef asks Khalil if he should join one of the paramilitary groups, Khalil does nothing to dissuade him:

> He's right, thought Khalil . . . he might as well take the opportunity to be like people his own age and make his own bad memories, he might as well enjoy their company as long as he likes and then disown them later, he'll get tired of them and grow up, there's no escaping that . . . if not, what do I have to offer him? (115)

> I am a wife of the wrong sex as if, in my stupidity, I wait for Youssef to come one day and ask for my hand. To knock at the door in his most

splendid raiment and ask me . . . while I blush, shyly, hesitating a little before nodding my head in agreement. (128)

After Youssef, too, is killed, Khalil feels guilty for not having dissuaded him from joining the militia:

Well, said Khalil, sitting on his bed . . . I'm the one who dug every trap for him. . . . I threw him into it, I made a mistake and I sat down half expecting him to come back. . . . I'm the one who killed Youssef and got away, free, from the poisonous magnetism of his body. I'm the one who's free of him now, I'll say I'm the one who killed him. I'll make my confession like a big watermelon. I'll eat his death, morsel by morsel, until the watermelon is finished. . . . I will weep with regret, for my great sin, for my passion that was snapped in two. I will weep long for him and sob deeply and bitterly as he deserves.

But the tears did not come. (147)

The turning point in the narrative occurs when Khalil falls ill, undergoes an operation, and has a near-death experience. As a result, he undergoes a transformation remarkably akin to that of Michel, the protagonist in André Gide's *The Immoralist*. He falls in love with the body consciousness:

Nothing is pure save love of the body. No one who has not lost it can love his body. Who loses it, cannot. He dies. (185)

I came back from there . . . my chest rises, to breathe in the air and spread oxygen through every cell of my body, then falls, to expel what it does not need.

My living body is the blessing.

My living body is wisdom, all wisdom.

And nothing in this world is happier than I am. Nothing, as I hear the rush of blood roaring just by putting my head, my ear on my hand. (186)

Just that you are alive. Just that you are alive. What wicked ingratitude . . . what denial . . . what misunderstanding. Understanding.

How happy I am. How happy I am. Khalil repeated, his eyes bathed with tears of gratitude for the blessing as he looked at the street from the window of the taxi on his way to his room. He loved his wound which hurt him and loved his body which was stretched out comfortably

> on the back seat. He looked upon his body as if it were a beautiful and beloved prodigal son. I love my beautiful body. (189)
>
> I'm so sorry. I didn't know. I didn't know how much I loved you. How much I loved life. He who hates himself doesn't love life. He who hates himself doesn't love life, Khalil my lovely. (191)

As in *The Immoralist*, however, there is something wrong, or partial, about this realization:

> Khalil is filled with childish delight with his new body. (195)
>
> But . . . despite the deep sense of jubilation which his knowledge gave him, felt apprehensive that he may lose a little link in this chain, a link which he has never known, he had a faint, distant suspicion that his great knowledge of this was lacking in some way . . . a pale and frail and small and distant lack . . . but a lack all the same. (197)

Gradually, Khalil begins to discover the nature of this lack:

> Oh, Khalil who came back to praise life, to love yourself. . . .
>
> This is the missing link that you were afraid of, the thing you did not know, this is the thing that was lacking. It's time for your confusion to end, for your delight with the arteries of your hand which pulse with life to flower and open and lean over the lush branches.
>
> It's not enough . . . it's not enough . . . it's not enough for you to love yourself Khalil. (219)

Eventually, Khalil becomes susceptible to the advances of a sinister homosexual gangster, called the Brother. He is torn by doubt as to what to do:

> He knew how intensely the Brother desired him. Desire so strong that it began to be reproduced in its object, that is, Khalil, for to ignore it was no longer possible. People desire and lust for those who realize the extent of their desire for them.
>
> Khalil thought: we certainly become like the people we have sex with and I do not want to be like this man. (216)

This passage is another of the rare occurrences in which the subject of homosexuality is broached, and once again by a woman writer. As in

Ghada Samman's *Beirut '75*, the practice is seen as an evil, insidious influence, which threatens the protagonists' very sanity. Khalil's confusion and guilt is reflected in an internal dialogue with his "feminine" self:

> Khalil's self tried to control herself.
>
> Well, what are you doing? Work as a prophet, work as a messenger, start a war, set up a party? Have you found a comrade for yourself, a brother, a soldier?
>
> You haven't found one because they don't exist. They are the way they are, you ass. Sorry. Khalil's self apologized . . . she drew a deep breath, crossed her legs and straightened her skirt . . .
>
> Sit down, Khalil . . . Khalil's self put her hand on his hand. She said in a last, desperate attempt: let's spell out every word in the sentence and lay it on the table:
>
> we know now that there is no choice. . . .
>
> Khalil's self slammed the door behind her and stood, panting heavily, in the entrance to the building. (220–21)

Khalil's innocence is shattered by the choice he is about to make:

> Khalil walks in the city now and hears his regular footfall on the soaking tarmac.
>
> He walks as if he were walking over it, above it.
>
> This hideous city.
>
> this uniquely hideous city.
>
> How can the poets sing of its beauty. This depravity. (22)

By falling prey to the Brother's seduction, Khalil has willingly chosen the life of a slave. He becomes alienated from himself and closed off from the world around him:

> He starts with a smile from the master's eyes or with a kind word from him. He begins to sway backwards and forwards until the movement becomes smooth and his breathing becomes even. Backwards and forwards with a regular tempo, to make the talisman move in a straight line. The talisman which protects him from the smile, from the kind voice, which blocks up the cracks through which the master might seep in. So that he stays bolted shut on himself, so that what is his remains his.

> Only after that does the slave take his eyes off his master's door and come out of the master's siesta cloaked in hatred. And, free, the slave begins to rhyme and sing as he prepares the bath water and a glass of wine for his master who will awake shortly. The city will not reach me because I will rise, I will ascend. I will be the hymn that rises from it. (224)
>
> My real, burning fear is that I might come to look like the flocks of people down there. That I will wrap myself in a thick casing and I will not hear them nor get wind of their smells.
>
> Khalil feels disgusted because a shoulder bumped into his shoulder on the street. He feels disgusted, his stomach shrinks, nauseated, don't touch me don't touch my purity . . . don't touch me. (225)

By the conclusion of *The Stone of Laughter,* the unthinkable has occurred. Khalil assumes a brutal male identity in the service of the Brother:

> She opened the door and waited in the entrance. Khalil closed the door behind him and went up to her. He saw a still hidden fear shining in her eyes. Fear or was it desire.
>
> He took her head in his hands and kissed her. She tried to slip away . . . she put her hand on his arms and began to pull at his arms to free her head. Khalil bit her lips. She lifted her head: you bastard, she said, as if she were crying. Khalil held onto her hair and slapped her hard.
>
> She won't scream, her son is asleep inside.
>
> He threw her onto the floor and ripped her nightshirt from the bottom. She began to kick and writhe and crawl until they reached the middle of the sitting room. He pinned down her thighs with his knees, on top of her, and she started to hit him. He hit her hard across the face over and over again and her hands fell . . . then she fell still . . . she went limp like a corpse.
>
> That won't do you any good, he said, and slapped her again. Kiss my hand. Kiss my hand. Then he moved down on to her chest. Kiss me . . . kiss me . . . kiss my neck . . . my neck . . . lift your head up . . . take off . . . this dressing gown. Take your nightshirt off.
>
> Spread out here. (230)

In the end, the authorial voice takes up the narrative in the first person, and mourns the disappearance of the Khalil she once knew:

> Khalil's henchman opened the back door of the car. . . .
> The henchman got in and turned over the engine.
> I went up to the rear window . . . Khalil had a mustache and a pair of sunglasses. Where are you going, I asked, and he did not hear me.
> It's me, I told him, and he did not turn around.
> The car moved off and, from the back window, Khalil seemed broad-shouldered in his brown leather jacket. . . .
> Khalil is gone, he has become a man who laughs. (231)

The text, which exerts a great deal of power on the reader by virtue of the loving intimacy with which the portrait of Khalil is drawn, magnifies that power immensely with this plot twist. The horrific nature of his transformation is far greater than if Khalil had simply been murdered. He is still alive, but his humanity has been effaced, extinguished. Fadia Faqir writes that Hoda Barakat wrote this novel in order "to enter into a debate with the dominant culture of war, a debate in which writing is the only source of power available to her."[28] But this characterization of *The Stone of Laughter* understates the work. In fact, Hoda Barakat atomizes the masculine war culture, and at the same time renders it highly complex—a matter not only of perverted masculinity, but also of the repression of femininity, which is seen as a quality not exclusive to women.

THE NOVEL OF INTERIOR SITUATIONS

Ghada Samman's most important innovation in *Beirut Nightmares* is the interweaving of chronological narrative, fable, and dreamlike situations. In some of the narrative sections, regardless of type, there is a clear symbolism. For instance, in the pet shop sequences, the animals have an obvious reference to the human inhabitants of Beirut, and this is true of both the sequences that are part of the narrator's waking life, as well as of those that are part of her dream life. Many of the stories, such as that of the little boy who dies during his conversation with Death, have a similar symbolic quality. Other sequences, however, are not intended to be directly symbolic. They exist simply to evoke the situation of war, communicating a sense of horror and emotional fatigue. The story of the mannequin, for instance, is symbolic in the general sense that she represents the viewpoint of a war victim, particularly a female victim.

But more important than this symbolism is simply the heightened feeling that her story generates.

Elias Khoury has referred to this type of writing as the "narrative of interior situations,"[29] and he uses this technique to remarkable effect in a novel which is a great departure from his other works. *Gates of the City* (1993; *Abwāb al-Madīnah*, 1981),[30] is arguably Khoury's most powerful novel. According to Khoury, *Gates of the City* was an attempt to express situations related to the war symbolically, to re-understand the civil war by putting the reader inside the experience from the interior situation of men, rather than from the point of view of ideas, ideologies, or political positions. The result is different from *Beirut Nightmares,* which mixes the experiential, creative, and reflective aspects of narrative, but in a way in which they can still be differentiated from one another.

In Khoury's text, this is impossible. The novel is clearly symbolic, but it is not a concrete symbolism that can be interpreted. An anonymous stranger arrives at a nameless city with high, bare walls and seven iron gates, guarded by seven women. The city is a maze, with streets leading to more streets, and alleys leading to more alleys. The entire city is white. In its center is a square, and in the middle of the square is a coffin with a corpse turned to stone which was the body of a king. All the characters are nameless and fantastic. They include a virgin with three daughters, and another whose words come from her belly instead of her mouth.

Khoury's techniques in *Gates of the City* are similar to those of Kahlil Gibran (Jubrān Khalīl Jubrān), whose continuing influence on Arabic literature should not be underestimated. Gibran's work is generally considered in the category of romanticism. Its religious and philosophical ideas express a transcendent unity similar to that found in Blake, Emerson, and Whitman. Much of his work in both English and Arabic, however, is also marked by a Nietzschean sense of the absurdity of the social condition. Khalil S. Hawi notes, for instance, that Gibran's *The Madman, His Parables and Poems* (1918),[31] "is concerned with the annihilation of the accepted values of civilization and of the normal conscious life of society."[32] Hawi explains that Gibran attacks social values in two ways: (a) by reducing them to the subconscious motives behind them, which contradict their overt assumptions, and (b) by showing them in the most extreme and extravagant forms, thus reducing them to absurdity. The first method is essentially that of the "interior situation," while the second is a symbolic technique.

As an example of the first method of subconscious revelation, Hawi cites the parable of "The Woman and Her Daughter." Both the woman and daughter of the title walk in their sleep. One night they meet each other and, in doing so, their subconscious hatred to each other is nakedly revealed. The mother believes that her daughter's life has been built on the ruins of her own, while the girl in turn hates her mother because she stands between her and her "freer self." In the morning they return to their normal behavior, addressing one another as "Darling" and replying "Yes, dear." In this story, the nocturnal behavior of the mother and daughter simply serves to expose the emotions hidden under the surface of their lives.

To illustrate the second method of reduction to the point of absurdity, Hawi cites, among others, the parable of "The Blessed City," in which the so-called wisdom of reading and writing has brought everyone in the city of the title to live according to Scripture. In their conformity to this, all the inhabitants have plucked out their right eyes and cut off their right hands, for according to Scripture, "it is more profitable for one member to perish than for the whole body to be cast into hell fire." The narrator dryly comments that in the city "there is none whole save such as are yet too young to read the Scripture and understand its commandment."[33] In this parable, we see an example of what is essentially a symbolic technique. The inhabitants' plucking out their eyes and cutting off their hands represents their conformity.

The text of Gibran's "The Madman" shows a particularly close connection to Elias Khoury's *Gates of the City*. It begins as follows:

> You want to know how I became a madman? It happened thus: Long ago, before the birth of many gods, I awoke from a deep sleep and found that all my masks were stolen—the seven masks that I had fashioned and worn in seven lives. And I ran through the crowded streets shouting: "Thieves! Thieves! The cursed thieves!" And men stared at me and women ran away in fear of me.
>
> And when I reached the city square someone shouted: "He is a madman!" And when I lifted up my head to look at him, the sun kissed my naked face for the first time. And as if in a dream I shouted: "Blessed, blessed are the thieves who stole my masks." Thus I became a madman.[34]

Gates of the City contains a number of recurring symbols, themes, and motifs that are similar to those in Gibran's "The Madman." Khoury's central figure is an anonymous stranger, wandering through a nameless city. As in the introduction to *The Madman*, the number seven has significance in Khoury's text. The madman has fashioned seven masks in seven lives, while in *Gates of the City* the stranger encounters seven women at the city gates. The madman comes at last to the city's main square, and this is also the destination of the stranger in *Gates of the City*. Gibran's madman has lost his masks, while Khoury's stranger has lost his suitcase with its pencils and papers and is constantly in search for them. The narrative is expressive of the sense of loss, the attempt at recovery, the futility of the search, and related themes of sight, memory, and nakedness:

> The man decided to walk around the walls. He carried his suitcase and his exhausted body and walked. The walls were naked and high. (9)

> The man saw and shut his eyes, he tried to shut his eyes, he stood, he tried to stand, he bent down, he tried to bend down. He said things he doesn't remember well. He told stories about eyes that don't close and the city whose seven gates he came to and whose square he didn't find. And when he did find its square he lost its gates and when he found his suitcase he lost the woman, and when the woman, the woman said, then he found himself standing all alone in the middle of the white square that had a white stone coffin in its center, and the man goes back to the square and searches for a suitcase he lost. (20)

There is the suggestion of symbolic meaning, as well. The very vagueness and ambiguity of the text gives it the power of suggestion in this respect. The suggestion has been made, for instance, that the women represent political parties, the suitcase political ideas, and the king the social conscience of the nation. Nevertheless, the effect of the novel is, on the whole, diminished by such attempts at allegorical interpretation. Muhammad al-Baridi (Muḥammad al-Bāridī) notes that the very element of the fantastic serves to heighten this ambiguity.[35] The strength of the text is exactly that the events are vague and unable to be deciphered. Thus, the ambiguity of the text is twofold, serving both to suggest interpretation and defeat it, a quintessentially modernist characteristic.

We can find similar use of ambiguous symbolism in the work of contemporary Arabic short story writers. The short stories of the Jordanian writer Suhayr al-Tall, for instance, are often devoid of characters or plot. They are more like internal dialogues, often with only two "characters"—that of the narrator and an anonymous person whom the narrator addresses. In her story, "Al-Mishnaqah" (The gallows)[36] from a collection of the same title published in 1987, we are plunged into a monologue delivered by an anonymous voice to an anonymous hearer. The voice describes the hearer's experience, commenting on what the hearer is experiencing, giving directions, advice, warnings, and predictions. The experience of the hearer is rendered in abstract fashion. The narrator is swimming in a dark, gelatinous sea, part of an immense mass flowing in all directions. Once again, there is no clear connection between signifier and signified, nor is there the clear gap between the two that gives a clue as to the real meaning:

> You're leaving now. . . . Come closer. . . . Don't be afraid of that terrible, dark, compact mass. . . . You are a small part that has not yet attached itself. . . . Come closer. . . . You are now clinging to it, and are disappearing in its crowdedness. . . . The noise is deafening to your ears. . . . It's not a noise; it is the echo of your scream. . . . You are now . . . a tiny part of an immense jellylike mass, flowing in all directions. . . . (76)

Like the anonymous stranger in *Gates of the City*, the hearer then arrives at a place that the narrator describes as "the square." The square exists within what the narrator calls "the city," although the narrator remarks that "it is not really a city." The square is a place of neutrality, which divides the city in two, and where individuals like the hearer rapaciously contend with one another.

> Good. You've arrived. You're now in the square. The square? Yes. A place where a mass is accidentally created like the next one that you are a part of. There has to be a square. And around what is called the square is what is called the city. But the city is not a city. The squares exist in order to separate the one into two, a city into two cities. (78)

Suhayr al-Tall was put on trial in Jordan because *Al-Mishnaqah* was considered offensive. The charge stemmed largely from the title story, which makes very sparing use of certain sexually charged expressions in ways designed to puzzle, provoke, or mystify the reader. The perceived tone of prurience and salaciousness did not originate from the expressions themselves, which are in no way pornographic. Rather, they stem from their insertion at points in the narrative that did not seem to require any reference to sexuality, thus giving the impression that the whole text had a sexual overtone. The ambiguous way in which these references are made undoubtedly contributed to this impression. Even fellow writers who supported Suhayr al-Tall questioned the purpose of such imagery and how it related to the story as a whole.

For instance, while the narrator always addresses the hearer as a male, at one point he suddenly likens him to a woman whose breasts are about to explode:

> Do you see that thing in tattered rags? That is you. . . . Or that thing which resembles a woman whose chest is exploding like a bomb speeding towards its destination? That is you also. (76)

The startling combination of feminine and masculine imagery is provocative, intended to prick the reader, perhaps even to shock. At the end of the text, the narrator predicts that the hearer will surrender his body to a huge gallows, whose rope, to be wound around the hearer's neck, is described as male genitalia:

> You climb up to it wrapped in your comfortable stupor and, anaesthetized, surrender your body, without knowing that that to which you have surrendered it is nothing but a huge gallows, whose rope, which in a few moments will be wrapped around your neck, is nothing other than a large reproductive organ. (80)

The story could be interpreted in many different ways, as an allegory of the biological process of human development from birth to death, as a philosophical meditation on human existence in general, as a critique of society, or even as a veiled reference to political issues. But whatever the interpretation, it is unlikely that Suhayr al-Tall uses sexual imagery without reason or without relation to the monologue as a whole. If the monologue has a social validity, and the conflict it describes can be seen as social in nature, then the type of power to which the hearer will be made to surrender possesses a sexual character. Thus, the text is making, although ambiguously, a connection between gender and problems in the deep structure of society, a connection that is not readily accepted in the Arab world, even by members of the intellectual elite.

The stranger in *Gates of the City*, like Gibran's madman, could be seen as maskless in the sense that he experiences everything in a uniquely personal and painful way. On the other hand, it might be more accurate to say that, along with all the other inhabitants in the city, Khoury's stranger wears a mask, but instead of taking it off, he is distinguished from the others only in that he is painfully aware of this fact. Thus, *Gates of the City* differs from Gibran's parable of alienation followed by transcendent vision in that it is a narrative that only grows deeper in its pain, doubt, indecision, and feeling of powerlessness.

Gibran's madman, of course, is not mad, but rather alienated from society. The stranger in *Gates of the City,* however, is living not merely in a narrow, constricted society, but in a truly mad society, a society that is being completely destroyed. This is the difference in the position of Khoury and Gibran. While Gibran contemplates his own alienation, Khoury contemplates the destruction of an entire city:

> Then the sea came. The sea ate up the fire and spread over the city. The sea ate up the walls and spread over the gates, and the gates collapsed, and the remains of corpses floated over a blue rooftop and dark domes. Everything was floating, and nothing remained of the city except weeping voices coming from the entrails of the fish and rising to where no one can listen to them. (97)

As usual, Khoury's experimentalism in *Gates of the City* is not limited to one aspect of the narrative. Khoury not only plays with the *ḥikāyah* form of oral narration, but with the sentences themselves, often failing to complete them, achieving an effect of prose-poetry very unique in Arabic literature:

> The storyteller said that it faded away. The city that faded away.
>
> The storyteller said:
>
> "And the story doesn't end here, because stories don't end this way, women running in every direction and a stranger who doesn't know, and small white rocks in the shape of small animals buzzing in the ears and white dust spreading on the square and a city whose name we don't know but we tell its story that doesn't end."
>
> And the storyteller said:
>
> And it was told that the man slept a long time. He would try to get up, he would open one eye and not see and think he was still asleep. (80)

> The storyteller said that the man saw everything. He saw the bodies stacked on top of one another, he saw the sea with its black color and its black waves, he saw the women weeping over bloated corpses. (83)

> The storyteller said that the stranger saw bodies running in every direction and voices rising up. (84)

Also, once again, Khoury plays with changes of tense:

> And the stranger was sitting all alone. The voices no longer were the same voices. He sits in the square and waits and doesn't look at the women. He listens to the faint weeping and doesn't feel at all curious, but he stays. (85)

The narrative is more repetitive than that of *Little Mountain*, and its cadences are strongly reminiscent of the prose experimentalism of Gertrude Stein. Occasionally Khoury ends his sentences without an object, and at other times he mixes metaphors in a disturbing way:

> He was a man and he was a stranger,
>
> There he walks and walks, he asks and asks, and I'm the one who saw him. I didn't see him there and I didn't see him here, I spotted him and I approached him, and he was walking and walking, the roads were an extension of his emaciated body, but he went further away. He didn't know more than a few useless words, but they were his words. What does a man do with his words if they aren't useful for anything? He didn't ask that question, because he was walking, and his words were walking along with him, and breaking down with him and falling as if they were leaves falling from the branches of an old tree.
>
> He was a man and he walked,
>
> Like a man he walked to his death, he saw his death close at hand, but he walked. He was walking and asking and no one answered, then he stopped and started answering, he didn't know the answer but he answered anyway.
>
> It was said that he burned, and it was said that he melted on the grave and it was said. But the city he came to from faraway places vanished. It was said that it had sunk in the eyes, and it was said that it had gone to the sea and it was said that it had caught fire in the forest and it was said. But it vanished and the search for it was no longer possible, the city was no longer possible and the man was no longer.
>
> He was a man and like a man he walked. (3–4)

Most of all, Khoury seems to be trying to give words equal weight, which is also similar to the intention behind Gertrude Stein's prose:

> And I say, I am the one who says, I am the one who.
>
> But I no longer remember, and this square doesn't remember, and I am here. My back bends over an odorless ground, and I see the whiteness. This whiteness that plunges into my eyes, this whiteness and this square. (89)

The response to this type of writing on the part of most Arab readers is also similar to the response of Western readers to the work of Gertrude Stein. First there is a shock at the fragmented, yet measured and cadenced nature of the prose. Then the reader begins to question the purpose of this style of writing. The prose experiments of both Stein and Khoury are imbued with a similar purpose. Both writers attempt to describe the world in an oblique manner that causes readers to reassess their assumptions about reality.

The difference between Stein and Khoury is the utterly contrasting nature of the social situations they attempt to describe. If one reads Stein's "Miss Furr and Miss Skein,"[37] for instance, one encounters a satirical treatment of a way of life that is indolent and self-indulgent. Typical of Western modernists, Stein is attempting to expose a reality that is hidden beneath a veneer of manners. Khoury is also trying to describe a reality that is inescapable and omnipresent, but it is a reality of utter horror and devastation, exposed on the surface of life like bones sticking through flesh. Both narrative situations require an oblique approach in order to shatter a type of complacency. In the case of Stein, the complacency is reflective of material comfort and purposelessness. In Khoury's case, it is caused by numbness in the face of terror. Khoury's writing is thus a modernist response to a postmodern reality.

What is striking about *Gates of the City* is that it sustains the use of this symbolic technique throughout length of an entire novel, albeit a very short novel in comparison to *Beirut Nightmares*, for example. When we consider the ambiguity of *Gates of the City*, however, this is understandable. Samman is able to sustain her narrative for considerable length precisely because of her interweaving of several different techniques. Khoury's choice of concentrating purely on interior situations, by contrast, is very difficult to sustain over the narrative distance required of the novel form. After a certain point, not knowing where he is and what meaning to associate with the test, the reader's attention simply gives out.

The simple problem of sustaining such narrative over distance is perhaps the most fundamental reason why Khoury did not continue to write in this vein. Another possible reason is that Khoury, like Munif, is a methodical experimentalist who sets himself different problems with each work he produces. If we can think of Ghada Samman's *Beirut Nightmares* as made up of three narrative components—experiential, creative, and reflective—we might similarly think of Khoury's first three novels as concentrating, in turn, on one of these narrative aspects. His experimentation with radical narrative displacement and fragmentation in *Little Mountain*, for instance, represents essentially a creative approach to narrative, one that is designed to highlight the authorial voice as self-referential artisan, molding the narrative in whatever shape he pleases. The frank and even gruesome reportage of *Al-Wujūh al-Bayḍā'*, is more of a retreat to a more direct, experiential style of narration.

Gates of the City, finally, is written mainly in a reflective manner, using interior situations to symbolically represent a horrendous exterior reality. Ghada Samman's narrative in *Kawābis Bayrūt* is most effective in the emotionally heightened passages of her dreams and imaginings. Similarly, Khoury succeeds in *Gates of the City* at depicting the horror of the civil war in a way his other novels had not, and have not since, approached. But perhaps only by shrouding his subject in ambiguously symbolic images and situations could the horror and magnitude of the experience be fully conveyed to the reader. The interior situations described are ones of intense pain, and the painfulness is made more intense by the mystery and ambiguity that surrounds them.

This same reliance on ambiguous imagery, something between waking experience and dream, is reflected in the very title of the novel *Fusḥah Mustahdafah Bayna al-Nu'ās wa al-Nawm* (An exposed space between drowsiness and sleep, 1986),[38] by Rashid al-Da'if (Rashīd al-Ḍa'īf). Dream and physical reality are interwoven in this text. The author also uses gaps and jumps in the narration to create ambiguities that are not elucidated or resolved, giving the text a hallucinatory quality, and frustrating the reader's attempt to establish a an idea of the narrative's chronology. At the same time, as Mona Amyuni observes, he "reproduces the same succession of events with variation, with obsessive repetitiveness."[39]

In Da'if's novel, the narrator, a young Christian, returns to his apartment in Beirut during the civil war period after an indeterminate absence. The concierge informs him of the general state of the building. In the midst of the concierge's monologue, the narrator fixes on certain words and comments that trigger suppressed fears within him. As Samira Aghacy notes, the concierge's words "remind the narrator not necessarily of what has happened but rather of what is bound to happen."[40] His abstract fears are then concretized and visualized in the form of hallucinatory actions and images. He picks up a *service,* or shared taxi, sits near a pregnant woman, quickly reaches home, carefully enters the building when nobody is around, avoids stopping at the concierge's but asks him to come up and see him an hour later. He goes up to his apartment, and a little later hears knocks at the door, opens it, and is shot by a gang of militiamen. In three rapidly successive sequences, the narrator is killed three consecutive times, yet continues to narrate. These incidents clearly represent the workings of his imagination, kindled by his feelings of apprehension. The reader, however, is given little idea of where the "real" leaves off and the imaginary begins.

As in a recurring daydream, these sequences are repetitive, yet at the same time, their details vary. In the first sequence, the narrator has no sooner arrived in his apartment, and been received by the concierge, when he hears a knock on the door, opens, and is killed:

> I went towards the door. I opened it with my left hand. I took a step outside, and in a loud voice:
>
> "Yes?"
>
> After that I can't remember a thing.
>
> I was killed at once. (7)

The narrator notices the concierge among the group that fires on him. In the second sequence, which is much longer, he is given time to settle into the apartment. The concierge is with him in the apartment when there is another knock on the door. This time the concierge insists on getting it himself:

> I went towards the door to open it, as I heard knocking, and he stopped me by saying.
>
> No, no, don't go, don't show yourself, let me open for them.

> He went down the ladder and went towards the door, opened it, and took a step outside, stayed there for a minute, maybe two, maybe more, maybe less, who knows? Then he came in alone, and shut the door behind him, and climbed the ladder again, and continued bringing the curtain down, which I couldn't lift after that.
>
> Six people.
>
> I went towards the door, opened it with my left hand . . . took one step outside, and said, in a loud voice;
>
> "Yes?"
>
> After than I can't remember a thing.
>
> I was killed at once. (15)

Once again, the narrator sees the concierge among the group that fires on him. He sees the concierge firing, but is aware of an inconsistency in his account, for the concierge is unarmed:

> The concierge was with them, among them. . . . All of them shot at me, and the watchman, as well. How could that be, when the concierge was unarmed? This is a weak point in my statement, I do admit.
>
> But I saw him with both of my eyes.
>
> I saw him. He was unarmed, shooting at me, and his bullets went through me, as did the others' bullets. (15)

The third sequence is much longer, and ends in a different manner. He does not open the door, but they enter. They do not find him anywhere, yet suddenly he is lying on the floor dead. As in the other two sequences, the narrator's death does not interrupt his narration. But in this third sequence, the narrator goes on to describe how they put his body in a sack and take it away:

> Then I heard a knock on the door made by a sharp instrument. Then they came in. . . . They didn't find a trace of me. . . . Not on the bed, not underneath it, not in the closet, not on the balcony, not on the sidewalk, not in any place. But when they turned me over on my back, my features became visible, there was nothing left of me, except my (front) features, a face without thickness, like a drawing on paper.
>
> "He is dead."
>
> That's what they said.
>
> Then they put me in a small nylon bag, and took me to the area control center. (36)

The central event in the novel is one in which the narrator loses his arm up to the shoulder as he crosses from East to West Beirut. Amyuni describes this as follows:

> A bomb falls on the fateful avenue, kills dozens of people, wounds many others, and he is directly hit. He throws himself down on the pavement. He feels his arm racing away from him and tries to run after it; then it comes back to him, and he presses it hard against his other arm. He will not part with it for the rest of the novel. . . . He falls down on the black . . . asphalt, and his blood runs into the public sewers. Camus' rats . . . come out and start licking the blood with disgusting relish. Such provocatively realistic imagery recurs in many episodes of the novel, as the protagonist tries to remain conscious. He drags himself to the other side of the avenue and is finally taken to the hospital. He will later describe his accident, creating one scenario after the other, similar but with variations, as if . . . recalling a bad dream.[41]

Aghacy notes that, in an attempt to tell how he lost his arm, the narrator comes up with three different versions or scenarios. The narrator swears he is telling the truth, but at the same time he tells at least three different stories of how he died, going so far as to say that his remains were put in a plastic bag and delivered to his family who decided to take revenge. She asserts that the narrator's own awareness of guilt plays a large part in the creating the major tensions of the narrative. As a young man, he admits to have joined other men from his village in the attack on a neighboring Muslim village. "They poisoned the wells, ravaged, burnt and exterminated village and villagers in retaliation for the sacrilege of their own religious symbols and their dead."[42]

When the narrator starts on his journey from East to West Beirut, he leaves the apartment and looks for a *service*. He is careful to look for one with women passengers, since he does not want to be recognized as a Christian. This is a lesser possibility in a taxi with women, since they are not as involved in the fighting, and, even if he were recognized, they are weaker and less apt to harm him. He finds a taxi with a woman passenger, gets in beside her, and is later squeezed closer to her by the addition of other passengers. The woman is in mourning for her husband. Suddenly the narrator recognizes her as the widow of a man whom his brother had killed. He becomes afraid that she will recognize him.

Finally she gives him a long look, recognizes his features as similar to those of her husband's killer, and gets out of the cab, cursing him.

The woman reappears when he is taken to the hospital, after the bomb blast has severed his arm. In a dreamlike sequence, the narrator finds himself in a tent—apparently part of the hospital, since it contains fifty beds—yet he is the only one there. The entrance to the tent leads to a cemetery, where the widow comes every day to cry at her husband's grave:

> The tent was very big. It held no less than fifty beds, and I was in it alone.
>
> The door of the tent was across from her husband's grave. She used to come every morning to the cemetery and kneel at her husband's grave. (59)

The narrator/dreamer cannot stand this situation, and attempts to put a stop to it by force. This leads to his attempted rape of the widow:

> I approached her intending to rape her. It had been a long time since I had touched a woman. . . . I put her underneath me. She refused. I put my hand on her mouth, so she wouldn't scream. After a great effort I was able to lift her dress. (60)

At this point, he is aware of what his left hand is doing, but when he turns his attention to his right hand, he in unable to complete the sentence:

> My left hand was on her mouth, and my right hand was. (60)

The woman escapes from his grasp and curses him just as she did when getting out of the taxi. A pair of guards then questions him. They beat him, and when he tries to resist, they shoot him. Finally, the narrator/dreamer asserts that he "intentionally" lost consciousness, and awoke to find himself in the hospital:

> After I had tried to slap back. And after the guard had shot me with one bullet, and I was laying on the ground . . . and the stump of my hand was bleeding . . . I felt an unbearable pain, I tried my best not to scream, so she wouldn't enjoy my pains, the way the murderer of her

> husband did. And at the same time, I was cautious not to be silent, and grit my teeth. She might have thought that I didn't feel pain. She might order the guard to shoot again. Or she would leave me, then come back to me the next morning. Then I would remain like this the whole night bleeding with pain. I was in a tough situation. . . . I decided to become unconscious. So I became unconscious. After a few moments . . . I became conscious again. I remained like that . . . until I found myself in the hospital's emergency room. (64)

In the hospital, the narrator adopts the attitude of a victim, unable to accept the loss of his right arm, and demands that the arm be reattached, even though it is lifeless:

> No one can imagine the extent of my anger. When they wanted to take it away from me, and bury it in the ground. But they returned it to me, so I laid it by my right side, in its exact place, and I tied it to the side of my body, and it became the way she was before. It would stay with me anywhere I went, wherever I settled, and however I moved, and I've taken an oath to protect it the way I protect the pupil of the eye. (66)

What Da'if achieves through techniques of fragmentation and interiorization of narrative is to lay bare the psychological and existential conflict of the war, and the powerlessness of the individual caught between complicity and victimization, confession and protest. Samira Aghacy notes that the narrator "sees himself simultaneously as victim and oppressor, executioner and executed, and realizes that he cannot extricate himself from what he represents at the public level." She quotes a passage from Da'if's text written in a marked confessional tone, which depends upon the narrator's identification with the victims of his past actions:

> We left no male survivor without annihilating him, no female without wiping her out, no life without extinguishing it. We left no hen, no beast or tree standing on its trunk. We burnt their crops and then we moved into the graveyard and devastated it. We set fire to it and turned it into hell, and the flames went up until they reached the sky. At night, I went back to the village alone, sneaked into the water reservoir where I emptied a tank full of gas-oil. I awaited the news. It was decisive, casualties by the dozens: nausea, vomiting, abdominal pain, diarrhea, dizziness.
>
> I gloated over it.[43]

Aghacy further notes that

> The act of crossing the boundaries between the East and West sides of the city [is] an act of blurring differences [and] at the same time . . . an act of defiance.[44]

Chapter 4

Redefining the Future: Questions of Artistic Choice

Poetry can be divided into two types. One is concerned with the "the mirage of language" *(sarāb al-lughah),* the other with the "dust of life" *(turāb al-ḥayāt).* The mirage of language is really a matter of playing with something that is nonexistent. In essence, it is doing nothing. Poetry should be concerned with concrete scenes, with reactions. It should be a psychological mosaic of the human body and soul. To write about a tyrant, should I call him names, or should I describe him?

—Murid Barghuthi

The modernist novel has now become the classical novel of our time. Yet it is still not outdated. People are still writing modernist novels. This shows the depth of modernism, and particularly the strength of modernist values. To say that a work is skeptical is not enough to place it outside the sphere of modernism. There is no such thing as absolute skepticism. There are no absolutes. Even Kafka is not necessarily an absolute skeptic. The humanism that I feel is so important is present in the works of the classical modernists (Joyce, Proust, Faulkner, Woolf), in the work of present-day modernists (Marquez, Kundera, Rushdie), and in the work of the great Arab novelists (Mahfouz, Habiby, Kanafani).

—Ibrahim Nasrallah

THE "MIRAGE OF LANGUAGE" AND THE "DUST OF LIFE"

With the waning and ultimate end of the Lebanese Civil War, experimental novelists in the region have been faced with the problem of emerging from a mentality of trauma to one of relative normalcy. In the process of recovery, the past trauma can still seem like a palpable presence, warping one's perspective. Writers have to address fundamental literary questions that were safely ignored in the past, and have to make artistic choices on their merits alone, rather than on how they might serve the purpose of dramatizing a particular social or political situation.

Writers who have distanced themselves from ideology face a choice with respect to techniques. Can the best effects be produced by means of interior or objectified narration? This, once again, is a choice that Arab writers have been making all the time, but never free of other determining factors. Never has the choice been purely an aesthetic one. Some Arab novelists have staked out radical narrative positions, others have alternately chosen one approach, then another, but for still others it has been a question of finding a suitable balance. Behind this choice, however, the conflict between social and artistic commitment still hovers, if only faintly. Objectified narration has the aura, the patina of social engagement; interior narration carries the taint of subjectivity, of bourgeois concerns, of retreat from the life of society. The most satisfactory results have been obtained by seeking a balance between these extreme narrative viewpoints or by seeking a dialectical solution that embraces dichotomy and paradox.

In distinguishing between poetry that is concerned with "the mirage of language" *(sarāb al-lughah)* and poetry that is concerned with the "dust of life" *(turāb al-ḥayāt),* the Palestinian poet Murid Barghuthi (Murīd Barghūthi) is speaking both as a modernist and as an *engagé.* The object of his scorn is the modernist of the type more familiar to Westerners, the modernist afflicted with ennui *(dajar),* who has retreated into isolation *('uzlah).* To better understand Barghuthi's point, it will help to look at an example of Ibrahim Nasrallah's poetry, taken from *An Anthology of Palestinian Literature*, edited by Salma Khadra Jayyusi:

> It is the hand
> day's beautiful branch
> blossoming with fingers,
> soft as the dove's cooing,
> that neither catches the wind,
> nor arrests the water . . .
> columns of light
> or a handful of embers
> that quicken or subside.
> It is the hand

a field, and a posy of children's songs,
and a planet . . .
It is the hand
do not read it
read what it will write
read what it will do
and raise it
raise it
till it becomes a sky.[1]

Nasrallah's poetry is often composed in this way—as a chain of equivalencies. The hand is "a beautiful branch." It is "columns of light." It is "a handful of embers." It is "a field." It is "a posy of children's songs." It is "a planet." It is "the sky." Nasrallah changes one object into another. What he is trying to do, as he explains, is to look at things through feelings.[2] To the logical mind, such equivalencies make no sense. A hand is not a field, nor a planet, nor a sky. The only thing that makes these things equivalent is feeling, and this feeling ultimately conveys a sense of the underlying unity of life.[3]

For comparison's sake, we can juxtapose this poem with one by Murid Barghuthi himself, also included in Jayyusi's anthology, and also focusing on the image of a hand:

His hand toys with the soap suds and their scent rises
his hand trims the mustache before an elegant mirror
his hand smoothes the silk necktie over the starched white shirt
the triangle sits in the middle, not leaning to right or left
and he stretches out his hand to the sugar bowl,
two and a half pieces
he stirs the fragrant tea, drinks it down
kisses the little girl, and the boy,
embraces his wife, she hands him the briefcase
and says: "and the handkerchief"
in the blink of an eye the folded white square was there in his hand
and he's off to work . . .
A handsome well-groomed man sitting in the back seat
one of his duties
is to conduct lovers
from happy clouds
to the hangman's noose.[4]

There is, of course, a very different mood to Barghuthi's poetry, compared with Nasrallah's. While Nasrallah's poetry is transcendental, ethereal, Barghuthi's poetry is like a surgical operation, cutting into the diseased portion of reality. Nasrallah's poem ends triumphantly, while Barghuthi's ends on a jaundiced note. Barghuthi's poem is concrete, concerned with daily scenes, with the apparently insignificant details of life, which add up to something greater than the sum of their parts.

In Barghuthi's poem, the hand belongs to a specific individual and, unlike the hand in Nasrallah's poem, it is not symbolic of anything. By concretizing, Barghuthi works in a completely different spirit from the transcendental tendency of Nasrallah's poetry. According to Barghuthi, the danger with Nasrallah's type of poetry is that the whole world can be made into a transcendental unity, and ultimately into a cliché. To quote Barghuthi, such a text is "not a dangerous text. Anything that does not name things as they are is a benign contribution. And this 'finds an *autostrada*' [a broad avenue] in terms of acceptance."[5] In many ways, Barghuthi's criticism of Nasrallah's type of poetry mirrors the discourse of Western critics of modernism—that it is benign, that it is apolitical, that it is hackneyed, clichéd, or commercial. He sees Nasrallah's poetic techniques as fraught with danger. Everyone sees a bird "as a sign of freedom," Barghuthi notes. "No one stops to think if a bird can be a sign of something else."[6]

The choice between the "mirage of language" and the "dust of life"—between aestheticism and social concern, transcendentalism and irony, the expression of subjectivity and objectification—has increasingly become an artistic issue in the Arabic novel in recent years. An eminent example of experimentation in the application of aesthetic principles to the novel is Ibrahim Nasrallah's *Prairies of Fever* (1993; *Barāri al-Ḥummā*, 1985),[7] in which the author experiments with applying specific techniques commonly found in symbolist poetry to narrative. His text combines the lyricism of Salim Barakat's *Al-Jundub al-Ḥadīdī* with the fragmented, interiorized quality of Khoury's *Gates of the City*.

The central character of the novel is a young teacher hired to teach in a remote part of the Arabian Peninsula. The novel opens as the narrator is confronted by five featureless men who appear late one night at his doorstep and demand that, since he is dead, he pay them the expenses of his own funeral. Desperately, Muhammad Hammad tries to convince them—and himself—that he is still alive. Although he refuses to pay, they leave him racked by doubt, unsure whether he is alive or dead. The second chapter is written in second person, a technique that we previously encountered in Barakat's *Al-Jundub al-Ḥadīdī*, and for which sources were found in traditional Arabic poetry. The narrator addresses his missing double. This double shares his life and answers to the same name. Later, the double is found and accused of murdering the narrator. The five men eventually accost him again, and demand payment for his funeral.

At this point, the distinction between first- and second-person narration breaks down entirely. The narrative voice is conjoined to that of the addressee, just as was the case in Barakat's *Al-Jundub al-Ḥadīdī:*

> Five faces without any features surrounded you.
> "Yes, what is it you want?"
> "Have you changed your mind about the thousand riyals?"
> "What thousand riyals?"
> "Those we asked you to pay towards the cost of your burial." I laughed out loud—it was a way of convincing myself I was still alive and functioning. (49)

In the translator's foreword, Jeremy Reed refers to Nasrallah's theme of the divided self as one that "surfaces in the European novel from Dostoevsky to Hermann Hesse's *Steppenwolf*,[8] and from Thomas Mann's *Death in Venice*[9] to Jean-Paul Sartre's *Nausea*."[10] We can even go further back, of course, to Edgar Allan Poe's stories "A Premature Burial" and "William Wilson,"[11] whose combined themes would furnish the essential plot of *Prairies of Fever*. The condition of being two is something that marks the protagonist off from other people and identifies him as someone who is at odds with society and especially with the authorities who, when dealing with individuals, tend only to count up to one.

The narrator describes how he looks for his double in his apartment, and how he reports his disappearance to the police, describing him as his "roommate." When asked to give both his name and that of the roommate, he answers with the same name, Muhammad Hammad. Later in the narrative, the police return and ask him to describe his roommate. Muhammad can only describe him as someone who looks like himself. Nor can he say when he met him for the first time, other than to say he believes he has known him since childhood. Following this, Muhammad searches among his roommate's clothes, tries them on for size, and finds that they fit perfectly. He trembles at the thought that he himself might be his double.

Along with his application of a dualistic scheme in terms of imagery and narrative voice, Nasrallah uses another symbolist technique—that of partiality. In other words, he suggests a whole by means of metonymy; avoiding a description of the world as a whole, he furnishes one in parts. This technique is applied both to objects and to events. Nasrallah rarely, if ever, describes the whole of an event. The reader is given suggestions, pieces of an event, but never the complete picture. Although the cover of the book refers to the narrative's "negation of chronology and sequence," there is a chronological sequence to the narrative. It is simply given to the reader in fragmentary fashion, without ever supplying a description of a scene as a whole:

> "He'll only find me when I'm dead," you told yourself.
>
> But everything now had changed. You'd hardly reached the western end of Sabt Shimran when you discovered you weren't the only person running. There were women in flight, children screaming, and men grinding the stones with their bare feet.
>
> It was as if the southern hill had exploded, throwing everything to the sky—houses, people, the sun and the crows. A spontaneous combustion. You wondered:
>
> "Do the police want to arrest us all?"
>
> When the crowd stopped running your instinct was to hide among them.
>
> The old man said, "Make way, make way."
>
> And you saw a well. You hadn't forgotten it.
>
> "But tell us what's happening. What's going on?"
>
> "Abdullah fell into that well. He was filling the water tank with gas and the tank plummeted down. He climbed down to get it, and he's still there."
>
> Motors were installed in the middle of wells, and the connecting pipes fed into cement reservoirs. Hanash the baker volunteered to go down. (32)

In this passage, it is barely clear what is happening. The protagonist is running, along with a crowd. Suddenly, there is a new event involving someone who has fallen down a well. The second event, which has already begun, intrudes abruptly on the first, which has not been completed. The reader is thrown, metaphorically, like Abdullah into a well of narrative subjectivity, in the manner found in the works of such modernists as James, Proust, Joyce, Faulkner, Woolf, Mann, and Beckett, in which time is not expressed as a linear sequence of events.

Nasrallah also adapts the same symbolist technique of equivalence that he uses in his poetry to prose narrative. This technique is related to what both Reed refers to as the process of "transformation" or "metamorphosis." He notes that

> All of Nasrallah's characters are one character for they are all interchangeable. The desert, he says, eliminates gender: they are somehow neither man nor woman, they are inchoate, on the "edge of becoming."[12]

In her introduction to *Prairies of Fever*, Fedwa Malti-Douglas recognizes this technique as applied to the relationship between human and nonhuman. In this connection, she refers to Nasrallah's use of anthropomorphism. "The very environment and objects surrounding the central character come alive. The road being built becomes a giant black being, the village a fever-infested 'lung of the desert.'"[13]

Reed states that the application of the transformational process in prose causes "inner and outer worlds [to] lose their distinction."[14] This process, by definition, applies as well to the expression of subjectivity as it does to the representation of the outer world. The very dualism of Muhammad Hammad's coexistence with his double is the product of this type of transformation. Muhammad becomes his double. In this context, Franz Kafka, whose theme of transformation underlies *The Metamorphosis*,[15] must clearly be seen as an influence. Kafka's narrative in *The Trial*[16] offers even closer similarities. The men who come to demand Muhammad Hammad's payment are faceless, anonymous, and represent a type of undefined yet powerful authority. *The Trial* offers a clear parallel in this context. Nasrallah also achieves an equivalency between life and death that is close to the mood Kafka achieves when K. is led to the gallows. When Nasrallah's narrator tries to prove to his interlocutors that he is alive, he feels for his pulse:

> I thought quickly, trying for the easiest way to regain my composure. Without letting them see, I felt my pulse, then let my fingers travel up to my chest. Everything appeared normal, my heart was regular and my veins echoed its beats. . . .

> This rhythmic coursing of my blood was the one proof I needed. I waved my arms joyfully in their faces.
>
> "My heart is still beating," I said.
>
> With one voice they replied: "That's no proof you're alive." (12–13)

Another related type of equivalency or lack of distinction that the text achieves is related to the sense of direction:

> "Ali, where's Thuraiban?"
>
> He pointed to the north and said, "There . . ."
>
> You turned your head. The young boy was staring at you with mischievous eyes. You said:
>
> "But I came from the east, Ali, from this direction."
>
> "Ustadh! I'm a native of this section. I know it well . . ."
>
> You said, "Tell me, Abu Ali, from where we're standing, in what direction does Thuraiban lie?"
>
> He pointed to the south.
>
> "There, at the bottom of the mountain, Ustadh."
>
> You said, "But Ali pointed to the north!"
>
> "What ignorance, Ustadh. Ali is very young, but we are natives of these parts, and couldn't mislead you . . ."
>
> You questioned an old man coming out of the mosque as to the whereabouts of Thuraiban.
>
> He said, "Over there, son," and pointed to the west. No matter how you juggled north, south and west in your mind, they wouldn't form a composite picture. You waited for two hours not daring to ask further directions to Thuraiban. You feared the next person you questioned would say it lay to the east, near those palm trees. And the trees were of course an illusion. (27–28)

The protagonist's inability to distinguish direction is another clear manifestation of the protagonist's feeling of alienation. The heightened awareness of the physical surroundings of the desert contributes to this alienation in much the same way as one finds in many Western colonial and postcolonial texts. The depiction of such alienation in the midst of desert imagery, in particular, is reminiscent of the work of such late colonial and early postcolonial Western texts as T. E. Lawrence's *Seven Pillars of Wisdom,* Albert Camus's *The Stranger*, and Paul Bowles's *The Sheltering Sky*:[17]

> Sabt Shimran resembles stones strewn between two hills of black rock. On entering it you face its east side, perched on the heights of a hill fortified with old castles, studded with stones that shine like knives, deflecting birds into collision courses, magnifying the blueness of the sky and the sun's apogee remorselessly beating down on exposed houses. (24)

The main problem with *Prairies of Fever* is that it lacks a certain development that we expect in a novel. Fakhri Salih, for instance, takes issue with the well-known Arab critic, Kamal Abu Dib (Kamāl Abū Dīb), who referred to it as a novel, noting that Ibrahim Nasrallah himself calls it simply a "text."[18] Salih then goes on to criticize Nasrallah for providing essentially only a single narrative voice in the text, despite the apparent division of narrative voices. He notes that

> The language [of the text] is not divided into dialogue and monologue but is rather a monologue hung on a skeleton frame of characters and events. . . . This cannot be a novelistic text because the language of a novel . . . must be a differentiated one. . . . The character that narrates it is a split personality, and the language of the text must reflect this.[19]

Salih is making a very good point from a critic's perspective. It is true that *Prairies of Fever* is unsatisfying as a novel, largely because of the failure of the author to differentiate the narrative voices in the text. At the same time, by pointing out that *Prairies of Fever* should not be considered a novel, Salih is being somewhat contradictory. If it is taken as an experimental text, rather than a novel, then one cannot necessarily apply the standards of a novel to it. It may be argued that Nasrallah set out to write a "narcissistic" text in order to create exactly these types of feelings of dissatisfaction in the reader. In any case, regardless of the author's intent, *Prairies of Fever* is representative of a marked trend toward highly interiorized narrative that exhibits little of the social consciousness typical of most Arabic literature.

Sonallah Ibrahim, in *Najmah Aghusṭus*, pioneered the narrative equivalent of Murid Barghuthi's poetic technique. Ceza Draz, as we have already seen, noted that Ibrahim's narrative technique is to present objects without mediation. On the first page of the novel, for instance, the narrator boards the train that is to take him from Cairo to Aswan. She notes:

> Sitting behind a closed window he sees people standing on a platform; he cannot hear what they say. He does not try to guess what they are saying or to understand what they are doing; he remains at the surface of the physical world and does not try to penetrate beyond this surface. (143)

The narrator presents to the reader only what can be apprehended by his or her senses. Moreover,

> The narrator himself is dehumanized, his subjectivity is suspended. He presents himself to the reader as he presents the other characters. He describes his actions from the outside as though he were an automaton. In the train, the narrator . . . describes his minutest gestures in closing the door of the compartment: "I got up and went to the door, turned the metal handle; it turned in my hand. The door opened towards me. I closed it again and secured it with the hanging metal chain. I returned to my place by the window." (144)

Examples of this spare style of writing can be found at almost any point in the first and third parts that comprise the bulk of the text:

> I went to the bathroom, rubbed the shaving brush in the bathtub soap and shaved. Then I took off my clothes, stood under the shower, and showered with water that was almost boiling hot. Then I stood wavering, not know how to dry myself. Finally, I took out a handkerchief from my clothes and rubbed my body with it. I remained for a while in the middle of the bathroom and presently my body was completely dry. I put on my clothes and went out into the living room. I drank a cup of tea . . . and then left the house.
>
> I looked for the Russian Club according to the description . . . given to me, and found it to be an elegant old house with a kiosk at the entrance filled with Russian books and magazines. The restaurant was in the rear portion of the building, and was spacious, clean, and filled with people eating, most of them Egyptians. It turned out that Salīm was the manager of the restaurant. He told me to be patient and he would order me some breakfast.
>
> I sat down at the table, and the food came right away. It consisted of a quarter of a chicken with vegetables and rice, followed by a plate of iced watermelon. I polished off everything on the table, left the restaurant, and went to Sabri's [Ṣabrī's] house.[20]

One other example offered by Draz is the following:

> There was a small rack next to the window on which there was a tumbler; below was a faucet of water and a metal panel that I pulled down out of the wall. It was converted into a basin. I filled the glass and raised it to my mouth. The water was warm, and I contented myself with only one sip. I let the water from the faucet collect in the bottom of the basin until it became full. Then I pushed it back into its place in the wall. I listened to the sound of the water as it drained toward the outside. (145)

Draz points out that this type of narrative represents a subject devoid of subjectivity, and that it is diametrically opposed to the technique of interior monologue. The nature of the actions and gestures described are mainly of the minute actions and gestures that make up the core of one's daily life. Seemingly unimportant events are given exaggerated importance, or space in the text (144–45). The point of this is to attempt to present a "clean" text, free of the techniques of fictionalization and mystification. Draz also describes this type of writing as both resistant and transparent—resistant in the sense that the reader is not allowed to penetrate the surface of the physical world, yet transparent in that its discourse is neutral. The language effaces itself to allow the referent to emerge in "objectivity" (143).

This style of writing has become increasingly imitated by the new generation of Arab writers, particularly in Lebanon, who have come under the dual influence of the French *nouveau roman* and of pioneers of modern Arabic narrative, such as Ibrahim. In *Taḥta Shurfah Ānjī* (Under Anji's balcony, 1984),[21] a collection of short stories by Hassan Daoud (Ḥasan Dāwūd), the title story provides a series of vignettes that focus mainly on the description of women, often nameless and designated only by certain distinguishing physical features. For instance, in the title vignette, Daoud introduces us to three women, referred to respectively as "the tall, thin one," "the one with the slightly curved back," and "the one with permed hair." They are never referred to by anything but these appellations throughout the narrative, and their actions are rendered collectively throughout:

> They wait by the sidewalk. [You hear] their feet step along the road. One foot stepping after the other. They scatter in the wide road. They gather and then they scatter. They enter side-by-side into the wide aristocratic

> hall. They walk a few steps, and then each of them goes in a different direction. In the aristocratic hall, there is a dancing party, but it's empty except for them. (11)

The women's actions are then implicitly compared to those of animals, in this case a turtle, by using the same descriptive pattern:

> A foot steps on the road. Another foot follows. Three turtles separate from each other in the open road. The three turtles sit on the cafe chairs. They poke their heads out a little, and then retract them into their domed house. The three turtles poke their heads out, retract them, and on top of the table their cold intimacy spreads. (12)

The women are also pictured as neither feminine nor masculine, but a third sex, a sex apart, as if independent, without relation to the male:

> Within the young women, there is no male or female, but the sex of an angel. The tall slim one does not hide anything under her body. If there is anything to be hidden, it has no color. The young women are a spectacle, and there is nothing behind the spectacle. They are [made] just for intimacy and [to produce] a natural spectacle. (13)

The rigid forms with which Daoud has endowed these "creatures" is enforced by the text, which insists that they do not change, that they remain the same:

> But, after a period of this discovery, the one with the permed hair became the one with the permed hair, just as the one with the slightly curved back became the one with the slightly curved back, and as the tall, thin one became the tall, thin one. (15)

The vignette ends by describing the women's actions from a very distanced perspective:

> The young women gather and scatter, disagree and reconcile. They fill chairs at a distance from each other but they meet at one table. (15)

Taḥta Shurfah Ānji shares with Jean Toomer's *Cane* an interest in describing the life of women, as well as the tendency to give women a certain archetypal quality, or to treat them as representative of certain types. Still another common quality is the lyrical nature of the prose, its incantatory nature, and the tendency to incorporate paradoxes within descriptive prose. Toomer was clearly more interested in women as flesh-and-blood characters, while it could be charged that Daoud's women are little more than societal fixtures. Yet Daoud is also interested in the life of these women, although not in their lives as individuals. In modernist fashion, he attempts to evoke a vitality underlying their social habits, which is bound up with, rather than contradicted by, appearances.

It is important to understand that, while *Taḥta Shurfah Ānjī* focuses entirely on descriptive narrative, it cannot be considered realist. On the contrary, instead of attempting to render a panoramic or objective description of society, both works play with reality by imposing certain limits or patterns on the narrative. The descriptive narrative is tightly focused, and reflects a particular narrative interest or bias, upsetting the reader's expectations by means of his staged series of thematically arranged vignettes and his incantatory phrasing.

Another novelist who has invested heavily in this style is Rashid al-Da'if. In *Tiqnīyāt al-Bu's* (The techniques of misery, 1989),[22] Da'if extends Sonallah Ibrahim's pioneering effort, developing an entire novel that is based on this type of minute recording of reality. This results in a radically objectified descriptive style. The main character, Hashim (Hāshim), is a man of symbolically short stature, who has to deal with everyday reality and objects in a very deliberate manner. When he turns on a light switch or a faucet, for instance, these are at eye- rather than waist-level. Much of the action of the text focuses on Hashim's life within the confines of his apartment, and whole pages are devoted to the way Hashim, the antiheroic protagonist, smokes a cigarette, or cooks a meal, or flushes the toilet, or reads the paper. More importantly, however, Hashim represents an attitude. Always looking down, rather than up, he is a character without feelings or self-awareness. No emotions are expressed in the novel, except in regard to the character's vague, dream-like ambitions.

The attention of the text is on all the little things of life with which Hashim must contend in the context of the Lebanese Civil War. Mona Amyuni mentions "inflation, electricity cuts, water shortages, disruption of telephone lines, bombs, and explosions" as among the "many preoccupations that reduce men and women to the level of low animal existence."[23] Moreover, when he ventures outside, Hashim must contend with the discourtesy of the cab drivers and shopkeepers. Hashim's response is a passive one. He has adapted to this way of life. He has not turned away from the world. He is a part of the world, but an object in it—a thing, an automaton. His desires are suppressed. Nothing moves him to tears, laughter, anger, or rebellion. The resulting dehumanization of the individual is narrated through the use of "objectified" prose. There are no words in the narrative for feelings. Absent are such words as "memory," "feelings," "I feel," "He was afraid," and so forth.

An interesting comparison can be made between *Tiqnīyāt al-Bu's* and William Kotzwinkle's *The Fan Man* (1974),[24] an American satire that lampoons the hippie lifestyle. Two points of comparison are narrative style and characterization. Kotzwinkle's antihero is a stereotypical hippie who is constantly high and lives in a trash-filled apartment. Kotzwinkle writes in a stream-of-consciousness mode that mimics the purely physical consciousness of his main character. Thus, he piles description on description, delighting particularly in the lingering detail of his protagonist's grungy lifestyle. Similarly, Mona Amyuni notes of Da'if's text that

> Important matters do not exist or are absolutely ironed out, while daily actions such as taking a shower and checking one's bowel movement when there is no water, are put into focus extremely slowly. The derision of it all is skillfully rendered, too, as when garbage bags piling up in the streets of Beirut are poetically described as if they formed a "festival of bright colors." (12)[25]

Another common characteristic between the two works is the passivity of their characters. The attention of Kotzwinkle's main character is on a very basic level. Stoned most of the time, it takes all his concentration simply to tie his shoelaces; he has not attention or energy for any more complex task. Rashid al-Da'if's character has developed a similar numbness toward his surroundings. He expresses no outrage when a taxi driver drives too close, splashing him all over with muddy water from the street, or when the grocer mockingly fires a gun at him in order to make him purchase something. And when his girlfriend, Maryam, refuses to have sex with him out of concern for her virginity, he doesn't protest. He tries to force himself on her briefly, and when that doesn't work, he gives up, without thinking of challenging her way of thinking.

In a recent interview, the author explained that the idea of the book is that misery is something "learned."[26]

Da'if, like Kotzwinkle, is essentially criticizing an entire attitude or way of thinking. Of course, the most obvious difference between the two works is that *Tiqnīyāt al-Bu's* is not a broad satire. Hashim's way of life does not come across as funny, but as dull, pathetic, and finally, irritating. There is a deeper parallel, however, that could be suggested between the two texts. Both war and drugs have the effect of desensitizing the individual, rendering him an object, directing his attention down to the lowest level of reality, and encouraging a passive acceptance of all experience. Hashim's life is lived in a kind of shell shock, and Rashid al-Da'if mercilessly exposes the absurdity of such an existence.

Da'if's triumph in this work, like Kotzwinkle's, is to match his writing technique with the state of consciousness that he wishes to capture. Da'if stressed, significantly, in his recent interview, that the narrative in *Tiqnīyāt al-Bu's* "adopts an adversarial stance toward traditional rhetorical form, making the Arabic language itself one of the subjects of the text."[27] His obsession with descriptive detail mirrors Hashim's own state of consciousness, which is riveted on a multiplicity of things. Moreover, Hashim is also a writer, and his concern with trying to capture this multiplicity in his writing is frustrated simply by the day-to-day need to attend to these irritating details of daily life. There is thus a writerly theme to the text, as well:

> There were seven million thoughts in Hashim's head that he wanted to record instead of being occupied in cleaning the toilet. (47)

There are three types or aspects of "misery" in the text. The first is simply the failure of appliances, utilities, vehicles, and other aspects of urban life in the face of the reality of war, or simply the reality of underdeveloped life in the Arab world. The second level is that of human adaptation to this phenomenon. In the face of electricity, water, and telephone cutoffs, and all the other inconveniences of this abnormal life, Hashim simply adjusts, as if he were Adam put down in an absurd Eden in which nothing works, the child of a dysfunctional urban environment. The title, *The Techniques of Misery,* refers particularly to this second aspect of misery—the adaptation of the individual to a life of slavery to his environment. The third aspect of misery is related to the reader's response to the text. Da'if has succeeded in developing a type of prose style that is a "misery" to read. It goes on in such stultifying detail that the reader feels that he is being led around like a dog on a leash. In a sense, the author forces the reader to experience the distress he writes about in two ways—through the writing itself, and through the act of reading. Thus, Da'if does not simply resort to innovative language, narrative devices, or experiments in perspective in order to create a particular effect on the reader. In addition, he adjusts his narrative technique to fit the object of its description. This marks him as a modernist of greater sophistication than most of his predecessors and contemporaries. To give an idea of the misery involved in the act of reading the text, it is necessary to quote a fairly lengthy passage:

> The basin was in the middle of the bathroom floor, between the washstand in front and the toilet behind. The bathtub was to the right and the door to the left. The heater was between the door and the wall. His underclothes were hanging on the long handle of the squeegee used for cleaning the floor, and the sponge was hanging on the wall. To the left, the mirror hung above the washstand.
>
> Everything was now ready.
>
> After a few minutes, the water would be well heated. Hashim was in the kitchen, his hand on the handle that turned on the gas, his eyes closely watching the bubbles that were starting to dance in the water in the pot.
>
> The water was now hot. Hashim put his finger in it, felt it, and withdrew the finger quickly. Then he turned on the light. He carried the pot by its two handles and transported it to the bathroom, where he put it on top of the washstand, underneath the two faucets—the hot water faucet and the cold water faucet—as if he were going to fill it from both of them. . . .
>
> Hashim took hold of the small vessel that was filled with a quarter liter of water, which was sitting on the edge of the bathtub. He put it on the edge of the washstand. As if by a miracle, the edge of the washstand was wide enough for that. He took two bottles from a box of bottles stored in the space between the bathtub and the wall, which was about one square meter in area. He put them on the edge of the washstand, too, but in front of the mirror.
>
> He took off his slippers and put them in the narrow space located between the squeegee and the wall, where spraying water could not reach during his bath. He stood in the basin, where he took off his sock with his left hand while leaning his right hand against the washstand. . . .

Then he took off his briefs, and threw them on top of the socks. He buried his hand where a corner was formed with the interior of his thigh, opened his fingers a little, and inserted them in his pubic hair, running them through it like the teeth of a comb, their tips touching the roots of the hairs. . . .

Hashim took off his undershirt, and before throwing it in its designated place, he tilted his head and raised his arms, in order to smell under one of his armpits and then the other.

Hashim toyed with the hairs on his chest with his right palm that was stretched over it, covering as much of its area as possible.

He picked up the little container from the edge of the washstand, filled it half full with hot water, and poured cold water in it from one of the bottles, until it was an acceptable temperature.

He poured it slowly down his body in a continuous stream, starting from the left shoulder near the neck all the way to the right shoulder. The water streamed down his chest, reaching to below his belly. Its rivulets reached to his thighs. When Hashim looked at the point below his belly, to the meeting-point of his thighs, he saw how the water flowed on to his penis, as if it were flowing away from him. . . .

He took a bar of soap in his right hand, first rubbing it on the damp hair on his chest, and then. . . .

With his left hand, he rubbed his whole chest, his belly, his shoulders, and his neck, but he wasn't able to reach his back. . . .

With his left arm, he moistened the hair of his right armpit.

He put away the container after he had emptied it completely three times, and rubbed his underarms vigorously with the bar of soap for a long time until both places were thoroughly lathered. He then returned to his back and his chest. The lather had started to dry a little. He filled the container for the fourth time, and poured part of it on his back, part of it on his chest, feeling the warmth, and part of it under his armpits.

He filled the other container, poured it on his head, and rubbed his head with the soap. He poured the final container; its water ran down his whole body. After that he wiped the hair on his head and his face with his hands, and opened his eyes after having closed both of them while rubbing his head with the soap, and used them to examine his whole body. Finally, he began to pour a little water just on the places where the soap remained. (50–52)

The minute description of Hashim's bathing procedure might be unremarkable if it was a matter of particular focus in the text, but it is not. Virtually every aspect of his life and routine is described in this way, depicting Hashim as an individual inextricably bound to the most mundane aspects of urban existence.

The climax of the narrative comes in a scene between Hashim and his girlfriend Maryam in which Hashim's failure to conquer Maryam's virginity, and his passive acceptance of his failure, is the one event in the whole text that captures and involves the reader. Similarly, in Kotzwinkle's highly satiric book, the main character sits chanting a mantra all day long, while a friend of his steals a girl who is crashing at his pad from under his nose, without his even noticing what is going on.

Yumna al-Eid[28] characterizes the style of Rashid al-Da'if as one that is purely descriptive:

> In Da'if's narration, we fall into a cold, isolated language, without feeling or poetic fire. We find ourselves before a narrative language that kills the warmth of expression and feeling, a language that is independent of its meaning, as if it does not belong to the author or the narrator. It leaves the writing to bear witness on its own. (63)

She considers this narrative style as a reaction to Beirut's reversion to a more primitive state, in which it loses its modernity:

> In *Tiqnīyāt al-Bu's*, the story of the war appears as a variation on the story of the city that has lost its modernity, or its urban culture, [in which] the individual has lost the structure of his time, in which he—the cultural being and cultured individual who narrates the story—has been plunged into a search for alternative techniques that will ensure him the primary means of existence. The search for alternative techniques takes, in the novel, the place of first importance. . . .
>
> A person (involved in) war is busy. In Da'if's novel, in the concerns of daily life . . . it is as if by this means he reminds us of the importance of this luxury. . . . He finds himself cut off from thinking about the bigger issues: the issues of liberty and the dreams of change. (61)

Eid points out the paradox that with the de-modernization of society and its reversion to a more primitive state comes an increasing modernist tendency in literature:

> The object of satire that is drawn by the novel has to do with the relationship between modernism and modernity. It is as if the novel is speaking about the cultural depth of daily life, and it creates a lan-

guage along the lines of the concerns of life; it creates what it sees as its modernity. (62)

If we compare this type of a text with Western texts of the late colonial period, we can see a shift in the dynamic of ambivalence toward modernity. The Western works portray the shell shock of the colonial in the face of cultures outside his own sphere. In each case, the motivation to escape from modernity leads to a cul-de-sac, as the individual reaches the limit of endurance, resulting in a passivity, depression, and even suicide. The characters in these works are modern creatures; their desire is to escape from themselves, from their own natures.

The Western escape from modernity, however, was largely a matter of choice and conscience, while the situation represented by Rashid al-Da'if and other postwar Lebanese novelists is one that has been forced on the society. In the environment of postwar Lebanon, there is no chance for escape, because modernity and antimodernity coexist within the same space. The inhabitants of this world, like Kotzwinkle's Fan Man, are anachronisms. Irony, satire, the techniques of the "dust of life," are more appropriate to this condition than the introspective approach that was the luxury of Western modernists.

Despite this marked difference, there is a potential for comparative study between late Western colonial literature and the literature produced in the wake of the Lebanese Civil War. The significance of such a comparison in terms of the Arabic novel is that, for the first time, 'modernity' is no longer seen as an objective on the part of the writer or his characters. Like the old socialist ideal, it no longer seems achievable. In Sonallah Ibrahim's *The Smell of It*, as in existential works like Camus's *The Stranger*, the emptiness of the main character's existence nevertheless spurs him to a paradoxical sense of purpose, if only as a means of sheer survival. But in a work like *Tiqnīyāt al-Bu's*, there is no groundswell of motivation in the main character. In this sense, the 'modernism' of the contemporary Arabic novel reflects a postmodern sensibility.

THE CONFLICT BETWEEN POLITICAL AND ARTISTIC COMMITMENT

The waning of the power of ideology over literature in the Levant presents a problem for writers who still cling to strong ideological viewpoints.

Old political biases and loyalties have become tangled with new artistic values. These new values declare that the novel should be "polyphonic," "decentered," "impersonal," and "ambiguous." But no matter how heavily a writer invests in formal techniques designed to democratize narrative, this cannot paper over strongly held viewpoints if they exist. Jordan, at the moment, is a unique place to observe this artistic struggle. Long considered a cultural backwater, it has recently been developing rapidly in a short space of time, due largely to the influx of refugees and political exiles from Palestine, as well as from Iraq.

While political pressures are far less in Jordan today than in neighbors such as Iraq, Syria, and Palestine, this is not to minimize the extent to which life in the country has been politicized by national, ethnic, religious, and factional strains. What we find in Jordan at this point, then, is a nation with little literary tradition and a history of twenty years of political suppression finding itself with a greater degree of freedom of political and cultural expression than it imagined possible only six years ago. At the same time, this political freedom has its limits, as those who opposed the recent peace agreement with Israel quickly found out.

Writers in Jordan, particularly those of the '60s and '70s generation, can generally be categorized in terms of the extent to which their writing is politicized. Some have distanced themselves from politics altogether and have devoted themselves to a strictly artistic ethic. These writers tend to be the most clearly modernist in the conventional sense of the term—devoted to the craft of writing, to artistic innovation, to style, to aesthetics, to abstraction, and are accused by their more activist peers of being escapist. On the other side of the spectrum are writers who remain preoccupied with historical, political, and social issues and are attempting to bridge the gap between political and artistic commitment by applying modernist literary techniques to these themes.

Mu'nis al-Razzaz (Mu'nis al-Razzāz) is perhaps the foremost Jordanian novelist today, and among the most activist writers in the country. His father, Munif al-Razzaz, was a prominent member of the Baath Party in Syria who authored a book, *Al-Tajribah al-Murrah* (The bitter experience, 1966), severely critical of the Baath regime. He was subsequently purged and fled to Iraq. Conditions in Iraq were no more hospitable to him, and he died there under house arrest. Razzaz considers himself an activist as well as a writer; at the same time, he insists that he is a modernist. He differentiates between two types of writers in Jordan today—those who are oriented toward seclusion and the contemplative life, on the one hand, and those who are oriented toward action and political involvement, on the other.

Razzaz disparages the work of the former as marked by what he calls the "language of masturbation."[29] This refers to an overweening concern with the intricacies of language at the expense of personal or political expression. Razzaz sees the work of such writers as an abdication of the social responsibility that has traditionally been felt to be part of the very definition of a writer in the Arab world. For Razzaz, the artist is not an absent prophet, at the margins of political conflict, but rather an activist, who is in the center of it. He does not recognize a contradiction between his self-identity as a modernist and his political activism. Thus, Razzaz walks a tightrope between political and artistic commitment, a balancing act that reflects the continuity of artistic struggle between his generation and that of Sonallah Ibrahim, Gamal al-Ghitani, Ghassan Kanafani, and Emile Habiby.

This connection is illustrated in Razzaz's best-known and most highly regarded work, *I'tirāfāt Kātim Ṣawt* (Confessions of a hit man, 1986).[30] The events in the novel are loosely based on his father's house arrest in Iraq and the effects that this had on the other members of his family. The main characters in the novel are Dr. Murad (Dr. Murād), his son Ahmad (Aḥmad), and Yusuf (Yūsuf), a political assassin who poses as their bodyguard and protector. Dr. Murad is a Marxist political thinker and writer whose dedication to political principles has resulted in his purge from the reigning political party of an unnamed Arab state, whose politics has turned nationalistic. Razzaz's novel has an Orwellian tone throughout. Dr. Murad's house is bugged, and his watchers know his every move and almost his every thought. To cite Orwell as a comparison, it must be said, does not imply a lack of realism, since Razzaz is writing in an age in which Orwell's visions have come only too true.

The writer and the writing process are of central importance in the novel. Throughout the narrative, there is a contrast between the father's principles and values, which are those of a thinker and writer, and the values of those controlled by the regime, which are those of people who deal in power. Implicit, therefore, in the novel is a rejection and repudiation of power, and an idealization of the higher intellectual and creative faculties. The products of these faculties are seen as having a lasting value, while power is ephemerally wielded by one personality after another.

Artistic endeavor bestows immortality, while the busts of dictators and monarchs crumble into dust. This theme is personified in Dr. Murad who, obsessed with his writing, sees it as the only thing that can stave off death:

> It is a mistake that I don't end my life. It is a bigger mistake that I don't write. It is necessary for me to persevere in writing the book that will be banned. (22)

The figure of Dr. Murad is that of the committed and engaged intellectual at the very epicenter of politics. The suspicion that his narrative is really just a substitute for that of the author is substantiated in the last chapter, when the authorial voice finally intrudes without the disguise of the personality of any of the characters, and reflects on his own artistic ambitions:

> The author assumed the guise of seriousness, preparedness, and sobriety in order to discuss all these questions. But—deep inside—he was laughing with happiness (slyly and wickedly) because he finally saw ten readers reading his novel. (224)

The narrative viewpoint that Razzaz creates is very close to that found in Emile Habiby's *The Pessoptimist*. The intellectual, the artist, the *engagé*, is operating outside the power structure. Like Habiby, Razzaz puts his characters in the center of politics, even while, at the same time, he places them on the margins of existence, similar to the situations of Dostoevsky's underground man,[31] Ellison's invisible man,[32] or Camus's Clamence. His authorial stance, which is one of resistance to a pervasively oppressive power structure, mirrors that of his characters. If even only a few people read his book, he claims to have won a sly victory.[33]

Razzaz sees his modernist critique of power as harmonious with Marxist theory. He uses dialectical materialism as Marx himself did—as a critique of an existing system of power, rather than as a basis for setting up and justifying a new power structure. In particular, the narrative is bent on exposing the dangers of nationalism. Nationalism is seen as a posture, rather than an idea. Ideas are universal, while nationalism is particular. Thus, for Razzaz, Marxism has something in common with writerly values, in that both are universal in their appeal, and therefore both are opposed to fascism, Baathism, and other manifestations of particularist nationalistic socialism.

Much of the action in the novel involves the relationship between Ahmad and Yusuf, the hit man who, as Ahmad's professed friend, shadows him day and night, contemplating his murder, the political purpose of which is to permanently weaken and disable Ahmad's father. Yusuf's philosophy of power, by which people are mere objects to be manipulated, is identical with the philosophy of the anonymous regime of which he is a tool. The most original aspect of the novel is Yusuf's narration, given in the form of a confession. Fakhri Salih considers this the most important part of the novel:

> The special section of Yusuf the hit man's confessions comprises the essential material of the work. The other parts of the text are nothing but a clarification and completion of the internal pattern of the work and an illumination of the moment of the confessions itself.[34]

Yusuf's narrative opens with his attempting to convince his audience that he is an ordinary person:

> I know, ladies and gentlemen, that you will never believe that I am fashioned from the same clay as you. I am a human being. An ordinary person. Who loves and hates. I know, I know. I know that you will frown and raise your eyebrows in surprise and comment: A paid, professional killer . . . and a human being! Impossible. . . .
>
> But I assure you that I am a human being like you. (51)

Yusuf goes on to argue that he is a sensitive individual, that he was not always an assassin, that he went to school, and that he eventually realized the necessity of confessing and confided everything to a woman whom he met in France. We then hear his direct confession to her, in which he details his feelings of insecurity and resulting desire for power:

> Life is not logical, and its contradiction is as bright as shame. And the proof of that is that I feel impotent, sterile, weak, and dead. Yet I have power over others and control over their lives, and even their deaths. (55)

Yusuf envies Dr. Murad precisely because he senses that he does not have an investment in power. He has no need of it because he is a man of inner strength:

> He is not a man of power. He is a man of opposition. . . . He has a strong backbone and doesn't break. . . . I detest his toughness. I begrudge him it. I'd like to see him in a position of weakness, even just one time. (60)

Yusuf's attitude toward Ahmad is different. He views the son as weak, naive, and sees his casual attitude to life and to his own fate as tantamount to a death wish. When he encounters Ahmad in Beirut, he warns him of the dangers of living in the Hamra area. Ahmad's reaction is one of indifference, and Yusuf's view of this is one of scorn. There is an almost comic irony in the fact that Yusuf is intent on killing Ahmad, yet warns him of the "dangers" of his lifestyle. He has less respect for the unworldly son than he has for the principled father, yet both inspire him with hate, because both live contrary to his own ethic.

Yusuf's entire philosophy is a corrupt one. The reader's expectation is that somehow, through the process of confession, he will change. But this never occurs. The reader follows Yusuf's actions as he inveigles himself first into Dr. Murad's confidence, then into Ahmad's. Even with Yusuf's purpose finally known to Ahmad, the hit man remains obsessed with killing his "friend." His motive is now a complex matter—a mixture of frustration with Ahmad's attitudes, and his own search for a way out of a persistent feeling of guilt for which he has no explanation and no cure.

A revealing and comical episode occurs when, troubled by sleeplessness, nightmares, and headaches, Yusuf consents to visit a psychiatrist in Paris, with Ahmad going along as translator. When Ahmad explains to the doctor that Yusuf wants a cure, but without having to go into any details about his life, the psychiatrist throws them out. The incident reveals the extent to which Yusuf's profession has created a suspicious mind-set within him, and to which his paranoia is at odds with the need to get at the root of a problem within himself.

When Yusuf confronts Ahmad with the truth of who he is and what his intention is towards him, Ahmad breaks down and cries. At this point, the hit man revels in his power over his victim, yet it is not enough for him just to kill Ahmad. He wants to do so in an almost ritual way, explaining to Ahmad the reasons for his actions:

> Ahmad's tears produced strange feelings within me. I felt pleasure similar to the sweetness of sensual perfume. I felt his weakness

> and fragility. And that I was strong and dominant. I handed him a handkerchief to dry his tears. And I told him that his father was strong, but that you are his weak spot, his fatal weakness. Your fragility is the secret center of weakness within him. Your death will destroy him. . . .
>
> I'm not joking. But I have to pass judgment on you first. Like any judge. . . . Then I'll judge you by executing you. You know why? Because I don't want you to die without knowing the reason. I want to give you the justification. I'll give you a perspective that will assure you that your death will not have been free of charge. (154–55)

The reason for Yusuf's insistence that Ahmad die with the knowledge of the reason that he is being killed is connected with Yusuf's own feelings of guilt. He wants to justify himself to his victim. Ahmad, on the other hand, feels that the destruction of his illusions has liberated him. Life has become a theater of the absurd, and he laughs in the face of the power that Yusuf wields so seriously and with such determination:

> [Yusuf] spoke in a murderous voice: "Ahmad . . . You are not free. You are not the master of your self. You are a symbol." Ahmad broke out in a hysterical death laugh, and said that he was exactly the opposite. He said that disillusionment had made him completely free, shorn of the weight of an oppressive dream. (215)

While Ahmad's change of attitude is significant, the emphasis of the narrative is squarely on Yusuf's limited self-awareness. Although Yusuf's self-understanding is minimal, he does comprehend that the code of power by which he has lived, by which people are merely objects to be manipulated, has rendered him an object as well. Yusuf's narrative stops short, however, of displaying any new awareness of his own self.

Razzaz is working here along the lines of Italo Svevo's *Confessions of Zeno*,[35] in which the confessional figure is unable to be completely candid either with himself or with the reader. The modern confession rarely consists of a successful self-diagnosis. The success of the narrative hinges on the extent to which the diagnosis is apparent to the reader, rather than to the confessional character. Confessional narrative is thus a mixture of intentionality and unintentionality, a device that the author uses in order to involve the reader in the ethical process.

The main problem with Razzaz's novel is that Yusuf is only too adept at diagnosing himself. He presents us with a detailed account of his childhood, in the process of which he claims to have a full understanding of the causes of his inferiority complex (64). It strains the credulity of the reader, however, that someone like Yusuf should have this degree of understanding about his own character, and this detracts from the confessional nature of the text.

The resulting impression made on the reader is that the voices of the characters in the novel are only thinly disguised vehicles for the author's own viewpoint and sentiments. We can see this in certain oversights in the text, particularly in the language of the characters. Yusuf frequently speaks in a formal manner that does not succeed in giving the reader an idea of his personality, much less of the nature of his profession, but sounds rather more like the carefully reasoned and planned expositional prose of an authorial voice. Fakhri Salih compares Razzaz's narrative technique unfavorably with that of Virginia Woolf. He sees the problem as one in which Razzaz uses the characters' monologues less in order to reveal their character than so that he, the author, can reflect on those characters:

> The essential point of difference between the style of Virginia Woolf and the use of stream of consciousness and interior narration in *I'tirāfāt Kātim Ṣawt* is that in the latter novel we stumble over logical connections that dominate the description of feelings and exterior events.
>
> Logical connections dominate the narration of the characters. In other words, I consider the description of feelings and events to be a kind of contemplation on the events and characters.[36]

Similarly, in his *Al-Riwāyah fī al-Urdunn* (The novel in Jordan, 1995), Ibrahim al-Sa'afin notes that the persistent mistake that Razzaz makes in this novel is his attempt to differentiate characters, but without giving them voices appropriate to their natures. Referring to another work by Razzaz, *Al-Dhākirah al-Mustabāḥah* (Permissible memory, 1991),[37] he remarks that all the characters use the same type of speech and interact with one another in the same way.[38] The key to this phenomenon is the ambivalent relation between Razzaz's political and social commitment and his choice of authorial position. He wishes to distance himself from his authorial voice by substituting Dr. Murad's voice, Ahmad's voice, and even Yusuf's voice for his own. The motivation for this is quite simply to turn what would otherwise be a polemic into something artistic. The problem, however, is that a polemical impulse still dominates the text, and for this reason the author fails to give the various voices qualities of their own.

The conflict between political and artistic commitment is also at the root of tensions in the work of Elias Khoury. Khoury is a writer who experiments with narrative techniques that create a feeling of depersonalization or distance between the reader and his subject. He engages in wholesale manipulation of his texts in order to present as fragmented a narrative as possible. It is legitimate to ask, however, whether or not the "democratization" and depersonalization of narrative are just pretexts and whether ultimately, as in the case of Razzaz's work, they are devices used to conceal the authority of his own authorial voice. Critics such as Samira Aghacy have claimed to detect subtexts in Khoury's work that contain hidden biases.

In *The Journey of Little Gandhi* (1994; *Riḥlah Ghāndī al-Ṣaghīr*, 1989),[39] Khoury continues to experiment with narration built on a chain of stories, focusing the text on a central character, Abd al-Karim Husn (also known as "Little Gandhi"). Little Gandhi is a simple man who works as a shoeshine, gets married, has two children, and dies during the Israeli invasion of Beirut. There are two main narrators: a first-person narrator and a prostitute named Alice. Khoury's narration is built on a chain of stories, which are integrated into a single continuous narrative in a manner that is both delicate and spontaneous. The stories are held together by a chain of memory and association, and the smallest thing—a single word, for instance—can act as a tripwire to set the narration off on a different course. Frequently, stories begin in the middle, and then get around to the beginning. In the following passage, for instance, intimate details of the affair between Gandhi's son Ralph (also called Husn), and a woman called Madame Nuha are first told, and then the narrative jumps to their initial meeting in the hair salon where Ralph was working:

> He'd come and make passionate love to her. She'd take him in, into her insides. Ralph would shake violently inside this white woman. She had a blinding whiteness about her. Ralph would always ask her to turn off the light, but she always left it on.
>
> "I like to see your face, how handsome it becomes. I like to see you."
>
> It all began. Madame Nuha sank down with her hair under the water while Husn was pouring on the apple-scented shampoo and delving his fingers into her long blond hair. (72)

Often the stories are introduced with their main features or events mentioned at the outset, and often they are mentioned in a casual fashion, introducing characters or situations as if they had already been introduced before, similar to Munif's technique in *Variations on Night and Day:*

> Umm Amin was the one who told Eugenie about his grandmother Umm Tanios. . . . Umm Amin told Eugenie the story of Umm Tanios and how she became a Muslim Saint. (100)

In this example, the stress on Umm Amin is deceptive, since the character actually being introduced is Umm Tanios; Umm Tanios, on the other hand, is mentioned as if she had been already introduced to the reader. This technique imitates the informality of storytelling, yet, like the work of the canonical modernists in the West who experimented with "informal" prose styles, it is actually an extremely calculated technique that makes great demands on the reader.

The narrator's third-person account of Little Gandhi, as well as other characters, is so interiorized that it often comes close to stream-of-consciousness narration. Not only is the narrative extremely dense, jumping from one scene to another, but it also tends to blur the boundaries between the narrator's persona and that of his subject:

> The Reverend forgot everything, even Madame Sabbagha, whom he wished would fly. He used to tell her she was incapable of flying, because she was a worthless woman, and that he'd loved her because, he'd discovered, he was no good with women. He forgot everything, and he'd been cast aside, alone, in front of the church of the Virgin, with no one to care for him, in the middle of the bombs of war that fly and transform the city into a desert of lost faces. When Alice took him to the nursing home in Ashrafiyyeh, he couldn't speak. He was standing in front of the church, with some militia men around him who were making fun of him. He was like a stray animal, smelling dirty, unshaven, his hands clinging to the church banister so he wouldn't fall down. (40)

The narrative further blurs the boundaries between the persona of the narrator and that of the author. In a conversation with the prostitute Alice, the narrator tells her that he is a writer and wants to write about her, a metafictional strategy traceable in the Western modernist novel back to André Gide's insertion of himself, in his writerly role, into *Les faux-monnayeurs* (The counterfeiters).[40] In an introduction to the English translation of the book, Sabah Ghandour notes that by situating himself inside his narrative, the narrator-author accomplishes two goals. "The first is to dismiss the idea of a god-like author who knows everything; second, to invite us, the readers, to participate in the act of reading" (xi).

Samira Aghacy, on the other had, raises questions about Khoury's authorial voice and its relationship to the text as a whole. In an article entitled "Elias Khoury's *The Journey of Little Gandhi*: Fiction and Ideology."[41] Aghacy begins by noting that Khoury's own comments about this work reflect

> Two contradictory views: an open and declared political and ideological stance and a marginalized, noncommittal, pluralistic perspective. The first sees society in terms of class struggle and economic factors and sanctions a dominant and privileged ideology. The other perceives society as a diversified unit, with a variety of voices . . . and does not give one subject or ideology privilege over others. (163)

Aghacy maintains that Khoury's use of narrative techniques associated with "polyphonic" discourse is paper-thin, and that he actually imposes a monologic discourse on his narrative. She notes that "at a gathering held to discuss the book shortly after it was published, Khoury referred to the narrator and himself interchangeably" (168). At the same time, the narrator clearly identifies with the main character, and particularly with his death, which seems to be a very personal one for Khoury himself:

> She didn't ask him where he was going. She let him go and die. She knew, she said to me, she knew he was going to die. "He was afraid of death, and so he went to it." (14)

> They found him lying on the road with the shoe-shine box next to him. They said he'd gotten scared. He heard the Israelis were arresting everyone, he was afraid of going to jail. . . . He was scared. he carried his shoe-shine box, hung it around his neck, letting it swing by its old leather strap, and he walked. And they were everywhere. They shouted

> at him to stop, or they didn't shout, no one knows. But they fired. They left him to fall on top of the box. (18)

Yet, at the same time, according to Aghacy, Khoury makes the death of Little Gandhi an important event:

> He dies in the first chapter, and the remaining five chapters begin with a sort of lament for that death. It is obvious that the narrator wishes to magnify the role of the little man and make a hero or martyr out of him (the name "Gandhi" obviously aligns him with the Indian leader). (166–67)

Little Gandhi is thus a martyr, a victim, and a hero, yet, as Aghacy points out, "this undermines the claims made by Khoury himself . . . in which he rejected the concept of the hero out of hand." Moreover, she notes that while "the narrator presents Little Gandhi as a decent, harmless little man . . . the text . . . provides evidence enough for a counter-interpretation of his character" (167). Above all, she comments:

> The narrator laments the death or disappearance of Alice, Gandhi, Husn . . . after the Israeli invasion of Beirut, and attributes their misfortunes to the occupation, although the text reveals that a great deal of their misery and squalor is self-inflicted or directly related to the long-raging civil war. This society has lost its emotional and moral bearings long before the occupation. (167–68)

Little Gandhi's death is announced at the beginning of the text, and at the beginning of each chapter.

> Alice said he died.
>
> "I came and saw him, I covered him with newspapers, no one was around, his wife disappeared, they all disappeared, and I was all alone." (7, 19, 43, 83, 185)

Parallels in Western literature include Gabriel García Márquez's *The Autumn of the Patriarch*[42] and Vladimir Nabokov's *Laughter in the Dark*. The latter opens as follows:

> Once upon a time there lived in Berlin, Germany, a man called Albinus. He was rich, respectable, happy; one day he abandoned his wife for

> the sake of a youthful mistress; he loved; was not loved; and his life ended in disaster.
>
> This is the whole of the story and we might have left it at that had there not been profit and pleasure in the telling . . . [43]

The constant insertion of the fact of Little Gandhi's death injects a note of ultimate futility into the act of narration as life-extending process. The narrative constantly reminds us that the process has, in fact, already come to an end:

> All of that was over. Time passed by all of them like the blinking of an eye. (127)

> "Everything that was, was a long time ago," Alice says. "You think I'm Alice, but it's not true, my son. Alice was, now means what was, and what was means a long time ago. And everything was a long time ago. There's no such thing as now." (18)

The act of narration is thus constantly shadowed by death. Death, disappearance, and absence provide the impetus for narration. At various points in the text the narrator steps in once again to remind us of the inevitable:

> It had become impossible for him to go back to his old line of work, and he didn't decide to go back to it until the morning of September 15, 1982, when the Israelis entered Beirut and the city was filled with their black boots, their beards, and their stench. This was the day Gandhi would die, on top of his shoe-shine box, and the story would end. And when all trace of Alice would be lost, in 1984, after the war broke out anew in the city, we would lose track of all the characters in this novel. (61–62)

Thus, the narrative is built from a chain of events consisting of deaths or disappearances, all of which eventually lead specifically to the act of writing:

> If Kamal al-Askary hadn't died, then Alice wouldn't have met up with Gandhi, and if she hadn't met Gandhi, then he wouldn't have told her his story. And if Gandhi hadn't died, Alice wouldn't have told me the story. And if Alice hadn't disappeared, or died, then I wouldn't be writing what I'm writing now. (14)

As in *The Thousand and One Nights*, the act of narration itself represents a willful attempt to stave off death, or to extend life. The self-referentiality of the narrative seeks to make the reader aware of the text as a narrative act, as does the technique of introducing the death of Little Gandhi at beginning of the text and reminding the reader regularly of it. The main interest is no longer in the history of Little Gandhi in a chronological sense, since we know what happens to him from the beginning. The reader's interest thus shifts from the illusion of realism that chronological narratives create to an awareness that the narrative is sustained only by the writer's desire to sustain it. Thus, within the narrative there is a continual tension between a present from which it seeks escape, and a past that it seeks to lengthen and extend.

One of the most puzzling aspects of *Little Gandhi* is Khoury's preoccupation with names and naming. At the beginning, the narrator states:

> The story is nothing but names. When I found out their names, I found out the story. (1)

He goes on to list the names of over thirty characters. The narrative ends with a similar statement:

> The story is a game of names. "And he taught Adam all the names." When we knew the names, the story began, and when the names were extinguished, the story began. (194)

The narrator also plays with names, by giving more than one name to many characters. As Aghacy notes, in addition to Abd al-Karim, the shoeshine is given the name Gandhi (by Mr. Davis, the American professor), while his wife calls him "man." His son Husn changes his name to Ralph when he works at a beauty salon, and when the war begins he changes it again to Ghassan. Sometimes the name of the character changes in the middle of narration:

> Everyone said Husn was the murderer, but comrade Abu Karim put his mind at ease. He said don't worry about it, "She has no relatives, and no one's going to ask about her." But Rima became fearful of Ralph. He told her not to call him Ralph ever again, that his name was now Ghassan, and she should call him Ghassan, and so she did. (48)

Here, Gandhi's son is referred to by all three of his names. The use of Ralph and Ghassan together is explained by the context. The use of Husn interchangeably with Ralph is not. Aghacy notes that this use of more than one name for characters shows that "the name as an index to personality has been undermined." It is, she explains, the little men who dominate the scene. "These are men who murder and are murdered, men who take up violence or flee from it, men who are alienated from themselves and the world around them and who lack any sense of personal or national identity" (166). At the same time, however, Khoury seems to be striving to retrieve some shred of identity from these same characters. Shortly before the end of the narrative, the list of names is given again, introduced as follows:

> The water that is swallowing him sweeps me away to the abyss, where I walk, and see all their faces. (190)

Clearly, for Khoury, this is more than just a game. Names are connected with faces. Ambivalence is thus being expressed with respect to character. There is an urge to give the characters faces, but at the same time an urge to resist this at the same time, and keep their identities to some extent fluid or interchangeable with one another. Following the listing of the names, the faces of the named characters are contrasted with those of the Israeli soldiers: "I see them and I see the faces of the soldiers, from where did the city get filled up with soldiers?" (190). Later the Israeli soldiers are reduced to black shoes: "Gandhi died. He died when Beirut fell beneath the black shoes" (193). Here there is a clear political viewpoint being expressed. The named individuals have a greater degree of humanity and individuality than the unnamed individuals, and the unnamed individuals are the Israeli soldiers who invade the city, and whose black shoes are more prominent than their faces.

Aghacy notes that "All these names are supposed to reveal unstable identity" but that "Khoury understands his characters' names—particularly Gandhi's—in the context of power relations and imperialistic and oppressive measure taken against the people." She quotes Khoury from an interview given to the newspaper *Al-Safir* in 1989: "The American professor is the one who gave him the name Gandhi, and this shows that the Americans were and still are giving us names, which means that they possess the knowledge and the power." At the same time, she notes that this statement subverts another claim of Khoury's, made in the same year in an interview with another newspaper, *Al-Nidā'*. In this statement, Khoury rejected the concept of the hero out of hand. Thus, the "game" of naming stems from an ambivalence toward rendering characters as dehumanized, depersonalized, and alienated from themselves and the world around them, on the one hand, and humanizing them, indeed glorifying them, on the other. This ambivalence, in turn, stems from a deeper ambivalence toward the war itself, in which, as Aghacy notes, Khoury participated, and in relation to which he affirmed his political and ideological stance. She further quotes from his interview in *Al-Safir:*

> "I am not one of those who preach against violence, nor do I claim I am against the war. I have participated in the war, and I remain true to my original choice, and loyal to my comrades who died the death of martyrs. I refuse to go along with the popular 'anti-war' fad." (163)

Similarly, she notes that

> The language used by Alice is shaped to reflect male values and male narrative hegemony. Her discourse is male-centered, and all of the stories she relates are about the "real men" before the war, as opposed to the general effeminacy that prevails in the present. (170)

Sabah Ghandour states that "Elias Khoury does not offer any definitive answers for the dilemmas of life, war, and invasion. The novel's structure with its embedded stories parallels the 'Lebanese war' with its seemingly unresolved events. Although the 'journey' is tragic for most of the characters . . . writing . . . provides life and continuation to the act of creativity in the midst of war and destruction" (xix). Aghacy, however, sees Khoury's narrative very differently, as one on which the author wants very much to impose a particular viewpoint or ideology onto these events. She writes that, despite his claims to the contrary,

> The narrator's ideology is everywhere. From the very beginning, he calls his own authority into question by assuming no control over his characters. . . . He assumes an "I don't know" attitude to give readers the freedom to draw their own conclusions. However, despite such claims, the narrator dominates the narrative and dictates. His imprint is everywhere: his vulgarity, his moral indignation, and his lack of imagination. . . .

> The apparent disruption of the story line and the narrator's self-effacement do not undermine the narrator's authority. On the contrary, the text reveals that the chronological order is only scrambled. Incorporating the *ḥakawātī* (storytelling) style into modernist multiple narrational technique and metafictional devices, the narrative reveals the tension between the two. Despite its claims to free and independent discourse, the novel drifts toward the narrator's point of reference, highlighting the strong alliance between discourse and power. . . . In his attempt to recount Gandhi's story, the narrator, who consciously tries to distance himself from the information, ends up expounding and dictating his own subjective views. (172–73)

If we compare *The Journey of Little Gandhi* and *Al-Wujūh al-Bayḍā'*, we immediately note that the themes of violence, madness, and murder are much more pronounced in the former work. The whole novel is a testament to a city that has completely lost its humanity, very much in the spirit of Ghada Samman's *Beirut Nightmares*. In *The Journey of Little Gandhi*, however, there is an attempt at distancing the reader from these "banal" facts of war, a retreat into a storytelling mode that, as Aghacy points out, seems designed to advertise the narrator's self-effacement. As in Razzaz's *I'tirāfāt Kātim Ṣawt*, however, the novelist's characterization betrays him, and the novel no longer reflects the reality of the war. Rather, as Aghacy points out, paraphrasing Peter Currie, the novel is preoccupied only with its "own genesis and growth," "its own condition of artifice," and its own "devices and strategies" (171).

THE LIMITS OF MASCULINE PERSPECTIVE

The choice between transcendental and objectified narration impacts directly on the way in which male writers approach the question of gender and sexuality. Formal experimentation is always an attempt on the part of a writer to solve some type of artistic problem, conflict, or paradox. There is no puzzle more profound for male Arab writers than that posed by the opposite sex. Like politics, gender is a subject that tends to reveal hidden biases and assumptions. Freed from the constraints of other determining factors, the opposite sex looms as a subject of existential magnitude. Those male writers bold enough to tackle this theme head-on have chosen radical narrative strategies, from the heights of lyrical, transcendental prose to the most "concrete" or "reified" style of narrative, in an attempt to deal with it in an artistically satisfying way. But radical narrative strategies do not necessarily lead to breakthroughs in the face of such an intractable subject.

Girls of Alexandria (1993; *Yā Banāt Iskandariyah*, 1990),[44] by the Egyptian novelist Edwar al-Kharrat (Idwār al-Kharrāṭ), is an example of experimentation with the lyrical form of the novel. A practitioner of the so-called new novel in Egypt, Kharrat writes in a style reminiscent of Proust. *Girls of Alexandria* is set in the Alexandria of the thirties and forties. In her introduction to the novel, Frances Liardet deals particularly with the thematic framework of the text, namely "the girls of Alexandria" who "inhabit every corner of his beloved city." The text is "saturated with the presence, not of any particular one of the Alexandrian girls, but of the one woman who is all of them. However many she is, she is one: however fleeting, she is eternal."[45]

According to Liardet, the thematic structure, essentialism and resulting feeling of unity and transcendence are typical of high modernism. She also notes that the text portrays Alexandria as "at once fleeting and eternal," and "illustrates the tension between transient surface experience and the unending dream of life which underpins it,"[46] a quality also typical of European high modernist texts. Kharrat, in other words, is a master of the "mirage of language" approach to narrative in Arabic. What is of interest to us at this point is how this narrative approach affects the viewpoint conveyed with respect to the opposite sex. In the following passages, for instance, Kharrat's descriptions of women are lovingly sensual, yet they also border on obsessional:

> Mona . . . had changed. Her summer housedress had ridden up to show her graceful thighs. The material was soaked around the neckline and clung to her bare skin, outlining the bumps of little breasts snuggled solidly in wetness. I could not tear my gaze away from the depth of the coveted obscurity between her thighs. (2)

> Nefisa could be seen from the waist up. Her small bosom, finely formed and perfectly round, was gathered up so that it almost spilled out as she leaned out of her window. (5)

> Her tight dress rode up a little to reveal her dark thighs with their strong, glistening muscles. (7)

> Her breasts were firm and pert, her muslin blouse no longer white; it had become transparent and molded her body, running tightly over her rounded breasts to outline them damply. It was clear to my eyes that they had no support; they were rising freely on their own, unhindered and unsheltered. Her two small nipples were round hardened fruits. Her waist was very slim. (29)

> In the morning she came to breakfast with her bosom almost bare beneath a thin billowing blouse which, as it drooped down over her full breasts, echoed the soft thick fall of her hair tumbling loose over the jut of her shoulders (61)

Kharrat's narrative is robust, emotive, expansive, spontaneous, and lyrical. He paints a panorama. In his memory, he roams throughout Alexandria, and the women he remembers represent a connective thread of experience that unifies and distils for him the essence of the city, and of his own existence. Sometimes the narrative passages are written in a stream of consciousness in which memories and associations spill out almost faster than the reader's ability to absorb them. As Frances Liardet notes, "they are not so much streams of consciousness as torrents of the subconscious":[47]

> The scent of roses wafts from cheeks oh maidens of poetry and magic bring me a flower who has also lost her way for she has grown to spread perfume and poison amidst the skulls and in the twinkling of an eye I heard a voice from within me. (42)

> I shouted in a godlike and tyrannical grief My God, my God, my God, why hast Thou abandoned me, *Eli, Eli, lama sabachtani* have I been given this grace only to grieve over it lips braided with crimson in a sea of blackness the sparkle of your eyes in the shackle's harshness and now I return loaded with my harvest of brittle chaff my bliss lies in my dreams in my ivory tower in my seventy-seven heavens in my seven hundred darknesses and not in that filthy tunnel they call life. (43)

One of the most striking aspects of the prose, despite its effusiveness and near overabundance, is the sense it conveys of being rooted in a strong realist tradition. In the following passage, for instance, there is nothing that does not add to the descriptive quality of the image:

> The belt tightens bounding the fragile waist the gold chain swings over the peaked domes of her breasts in the cling of the shiny brassiere encumbered with its compliant load the earring dangling from the delicate lobe to tremble a drop of musk from the liver of a slaughtered gazelle the wide bracelets clasp her thin upper arm or her slender waist or both together the shiny strap of the brassiere held by fine hooks binds her upper back to grip it to press the spare flesh under her armpits so that it looks soft and blooming and the kohl which serves to emphasize the merciless craving in her eyes, the dark depth, the rapacious glitter the black beauty spot on her taut cheek. (82)

Gradually, the author moves away from purely visual description to a type of prose that is more blindly sensual; then he interweaves the two together:

> The shackle of burning thirst close rigorous sharp clutch of long gripping nails hands with featherfine stroke with gentle skill the lotus incensed with passion a kiss withheld a drop of saliva still barred still forbidden the top of her slender thighs ringed by a garter sprinkled with golden sequins loosely clasp the sheer black stocking the accoutrements of sensual desire soft and slithering beneath the fingers at her neck a scarf tied in a big knot on one side and the scarf drifts unhindered across her naked back falling with deceptive gentleness the narrow buttocks pressed firmly over the locked-in embellishment and wrapped in the taker of the embrace the walls liquefy as if they are open to receive the tumultuous wave of ecstasy with the sound of a crash of waters softly-desiring fountain cleaving the earth of a pliant smooth body a single body merged in the gown of braided darkness a heavy flow atremble a warm distant wave hotly athirst for imminent consummation. (83)

The narrative progressively becomes more fragmented, more impressionistic, until passages merge into a series of vignettes:

> Yellow strips of silk run between her legs to tighten over the small hot mound and trace the line between the tender twin firmness cloven and gleaming and then to dangle in noiseless play over her thighs.
>
> When my mother said Wipe the glass of the No. 5 kerosene lamp I felt the lightness of the hollow belly of the glass, the soft rag introduced by my fingers through the narrow round nether aperture; my

cloth-covered hand wiped the glass which became warm from my wiping and my gentle attentive grasp in a slow and orderly revolution, and I was immersed in silent tenderness.

White cloud-formations in the night sky behind them the hidden soaring lamp casting a diffused light and the tarmac wet with sea-moisture reflects their image and locks it within my breast. (109)

Fragmented and impressionistic as this may seem, the narrative as a whole conveys a feeling of unity and transcendence, its lyricism comparable to the work of Proust, Joyce, and Virginia Woolf. The contrast with the carefully plotted, formalistic modernism of Mahfouz is considerable. What is striking, however, despite the highly developed expression of subjectivity, is the extent to which such lyricism is still used strictly for the purpose of masculine self-representation.

If Kharrat's transcendental approach to narrative fails to bridge the gap between the masculine subjectivity and feminine object, the objectified approach to narrative suffers from the same problems. An example is *Ḥadīqah al-Ḥawāss* (Garden of the senses, 1993),[48] by Abduh Wazin (ʻAbduh Wāzin). From a narrative perspective, this text makes use of the same spare, objectified style which we have seen in Sonallah Ibrahim's *Najmah Aghusṭus*, Rashid al-Da'if's *Tiqnīyāt al-Bu's*, and Hassan Daoud's *Taḥta Shurfah Ānjī*. Abduh Wazin subtitles *Ḥadīqah al-Ḥawāss* as a "text" *(naṣṣ)*, rather than a novel. There is no dialogue, no division into chapters, and no character except that of the narrator. The objects of the narrator's attention are simply his room with its writing desk, an open door and window, with a glimpse of the sea beyond, and his reminiscences of a woman, her body, and the act of lovemaking.

Wazin builds his text on a description of bare reality—the table, the paper, the body of the woman. He divides the narrative into stages that traverse the woman's body like a landscape. The primary focus of the text is on exerting a control, albeit tenuous, over objective reality. This quality is far removed from the transcendent, Joycean, Proustian style of *Girls of Alexandria*, with its exuberance and sense of unity underlying life. Wazin is clearly influenced by the French *nouveau romanciers*, such as Alain Robbe-Grillet. In an introductory essay to two novels by Robbe-Grillet, Bruce Morrissette observes that the characteristics of Robbe-Grillet's special universe include "repetitions, minute descriptions, studies of gestures and movements of objects." He also mentions the "absence of any attempt at psychological *notes* or any use of the vocabulary of psychology, total rejection of introspection, interior monologues, 'thoughts,' or descriptions of states of mind."[49]

At the same time, however, the text is an exercise in memory, and as such is concerned with control over its own subjectivity, which is as circumscribed as the world that is the object of its attention. In his study on French literature in the twentieth century, Christopher Robinson argues that the *nouveau roman* is essentially an extension of the "self-conscious" novel of James, Conrad, Proust, Joyce, Mann, and Gide. The worlds that novels such as Nathalie Sarraute's *Tropismes* (Tropisms)[50] or Robbe-Grillet's *La Jalousie* (Jealousy)[51] create are self-referential. They do not reflect the external world at all. Memory is an act of imagination. The time scale of these novels is the psychological time of the narrator's mind. Like the plays of Beckett and Ionesco, Robinson observes, these works embody the existential position of Camus instead of merely propounding it. "In *Jealousy*," he notes, "Robbe-Grillet places the entire perception of events within the consciousness of a single character, but without giving that character an 'I' voice or the distance from self that accompanies such a voice."[52]

Ḥadīqah al-Ḥawāss does not go quite this far, since it retains the "I" of first-person narrative. His prose is more akin to that of Samuel Beckett's novels,[53] which represent the ultimate refinement of impersonality in narrative. Wazin's narrator is just a voice. We know nothing about him. Yet the narrative is ultimately concerned with subjectivity, through the act of writing. The act of writing becomes the action of the narrative, and this reinforces an impression of narrative self-consciousness. *Ḥadiqah al-Ḥawāss* thus locates itself squarely within the tradition of the introverted novel, in which writing becomes the object of importance, overshadowing the subject about which it is being written:

> I write in order to be alone and in order to realize that I am alone, and also in order to realize that writing is nothing but what it is, and that there is nothing else greater than what it is. (57–58)

Mona Amyuni describes *Ḥadiqah al-Ḥawāss* as a text that "seems, at first, to be an escape from the world."[54] The anonymous male narrator is "seated on a chair before a desk, reminiscing as he gazes out a window or stares at a blank sheet of paper in front of him."[55] Through the narrator's eyes, Amyuni writes, "We see . . . a blue patch of sky and the sea outside, a bed with a white blanket behind him, a mirror facing the bed, and a door left open through which a woman disappeared one day at dawn."[56] Through the narrator's reminiscence, we learn that he and the woman met by chance, and went to the extreme limits of lovemaking. When they had exhausted their sexual relationship, they formed a suicide pact, but when they failed to kill themselves the woman "slipped away silently at dawn, mysterious and enigmatic as she had always been."[57]

The world outside the room and apart from himself and his memories of his lover does not exist. His world has shrunk radically. It ends at the open door. Moreover, this isolation is clearly a result of the narrator's own choice:

> I chose to seek my isolation when I felt that the world no longer engaged me, that the world was no longer the world, when I felt that I no longer desired anything and that I had lost everything. (8)

> I truly failed to understand the world not because it was incomprehensible . . . but because I myself was enigmatic. I concealed myself from the world. I wasn't able to justify my existence in it, or to explain it, either. (15)

At the same time, there are no events as such; whatever events can be discussed are those that have already occurred. There is no time in the novel except the present, or rather, there is only the time of the act of writing. Fictive time is stationary. The text moves along only with the act of writing, which in turn is moved along by shifts in the narrator's attention. The woman who is the object of his remembered contemplation is little more than a collection of body parts. The narrator's attention wanders from one feature of her body to another. He considers her hair, the wounds on her body, her perspiration, the whiteness of her skin, her breasts, her genitals, and so forth. This fragmentation of the body relates to authorial time. The inner world of the writer's attention and contemplation, which is a world of movement, is contrasted with the static quality of the outside world, normally considered the world of "events."

In a significant passage, however, the author distinguishes between three distinct periods of time:

At that time I was in a void that followed the body, a void that preceded writing, in a desolate wasteland without boundaries, without depth, and without color. (55–56)

The three periods of time, then, encompass the period in which the body (of the woman) was present, a period in which the body was absent but before he began to write, and the period of writing. He describes the middle period as a period of emptiness. In fact, he devotes only a page to describing this period, yet the reader, putting himself in the narrator's position, senses that this empty period has provided much of the motivation for the act of writing:

I forgot everything and locked myself up, not in order to write, nor in order to fast, but to spend a long time staring at the walls without stirring even to move my hand or my face. I lost the habit of writing, remained a complete stranger to it, and no longer ventured to sit in front of a blank piece of paper. The whiteness of the paper frightened me, as did the dark ink clotted like the thoughts that plagued me and would not be extinguished. (55)

The narrator's isolation involves a fundamental paradox. The outside world no longer exists for him. Anything beyond his room is of no importance. The world has shrunk to the dimensions of the woman, yet the woman has left via the open door. The narrator wants the world to return to him in the form of the woman, but this is not to be. The world has fled from the narrator. On the other hand, he has rejected the world, fled from it, and closed himself off from it. The impulse toward engagement with the world, normally so fundamental to the Arabic novel, is entirely missing here. A new note has crept into the Arab novel, expressive of withdrawal and abandonment.

If, however, the narrator has closed himself off from the world, what is the significance of the wounds and scars on the woman's body? Mona Amyuni, in her review, offers an interpretation that is perhaps precipitous: "Is there any possible release, one wonders, from the savagery outside? We have just witnessed blood splashing over the lovers' faces and bodies. The scars are Beirut's own scars; the wounds that of a city which has been compared to a woman by many contemporary Arab poets. Beirut disappears from Wazin's external landscape only to live intimately within him, and to be identified with this archetypal woman."[58]

To what extent is this conclusion justified? If, indeed, the wounds on the woman are intended to be symbolic of the war or of Beirut, there is nothing in the text itself that specifically points to this conclusion. The wounds certainly represent traces left over from past experience in the outside world. But is the narrator interested in them in terms of their connection to the world, or is he interested in them solely as an aspect of the present moment?

> The wound possesses me. I try in vain to forget it. She did not desire to speak about the injury. She was afraid to talk about it, so as not to reveal old secrets. (46)

If we consider where the wounds are located on the body of the woman, we find that they are located in very suggestive places—the stomach, under the breasts, on the wrists. The wounds on the wrists could be taken as a sign of attempted suicide, and the wound in the stomach could be taken as a sign of an abortion. We may recall that in *Gates of the City*, Elias Khoury eliminated all specific references to the civil war. His "interior situations" could represent virtually any type of horrific experience. Yet no Arab reader would think that his narrative depicts anything other than the Lebanese Civil War.

In *Ḥadiqah al-Ḥawāss*, however, there are no "interior situations" other than the narrator's isolation. There is simply the symbol—or fact—of the woman's body itself. The narrative must be primarily evaluated in terms of what it sets before the reader, and the overwhelming preoccupation of the text is with femininity. The wounds may be a result of war or of a personal desire for suicide, but symbolically their impact is felt in their congruence with the processes of the female body, such as menstruation, birth, and feminine sexuality. At the same time, we must also be aware that there is a strong strain in Arabic literature of highly refined symbolism, traceable to the Sufi tradition. Just as for the Sufis the reality of the spiritual experience was at the core of all artistic expression, for Lebanese writers between 1975 and 1990, there was no escape from the central theme of the war occurring around them.

If Abduh Wazin is indeed writing about the war and its effect on the city of Beirut, he has chosen to do so with a kind of mystical irony, by removing the narrator entirely from any environment of conflict. Alone in his room, the narrator's fixation with the body of the woman is linked to his abandonment of the world and its abandonment of him. This dual theme is expressed in terms of a static, existential condition, rather than in terms of movement or psychological development, and reinforced through the repeated allusion to both the presence and absence of the woman:

> Thus, there remained nothing except her body in front of my eyes. I open them to it; I close them to it. It is absent within me; it is present within me. It is absent and present. (90)

The world has shrunk down to the dimensions of the body. Just as the world has fled and he has retreated from the world, so the woman's body is no longer there, except in the form of memory. The writer thus renews the presence of the body in the act of writing, and at the same time confirms its absence.

In *Ḥadīqah al-Ḥawāss*, the objects of the narrator's attention are so few that they take on an almost fetishistic quality in relation to the narrator: the mirror, the paper, the woman's body, the whiteness of the paper, the whiteness of the woman's body. Each time the narrator focuses on one of these qualities, he calls attention to it via a considerable amount of word repetition. In the following brief paragraph, for instance, the words *al-bayḍā'* (white) and *bayāḍ* (whiteness) occur with great frequency, as do their opposite, *sawdā'* or *al-sawdā'* (black) and *sawād* (blackness). The words for body *(jasad* or *jism)* and skin *(jild)* also occur onomatopoetically with great frequency:

> When she would emerge from the water, she would wrap her body with the white towel; presently she gently rubbed herself with it. The whiteness blended with that whiteness, the whiteness of her skin, and that blackness, the black of her hair. And every once in a while the features of her body would be revealed and I would look at her. . . . And when she threw the white towel on the bed, her body would impress itself on the whiteness, the traces of a body would impress themselves on the whiteness. (95)

The sensuality of Abduh Wazin's text clearly owes a great deal to the influence of Western writers such as Marguerite Duras,[59] yet it is even more primarily an expression of revolt against the conventions of the Arabic novel. Wazin's provocative sensuality contrasts sharply with his conservative use of language. He writes in an almost classical style, with extreme attention to the most refined use of the Arabic language for the purpose of prose. His is a poet's attention to language. He paradoxically uses the traditional authority of the Arabic language as a weapon against the conservative and even fundamentalist strain in Arab culture. Such prose is as near to eroticism as can be found in modern Arabic literature, and it is this that sufficed to have *Ḥadīqah al-Ḥawāss* banned in Lebanon, and its distribution effectively cut off throughout the Arab world:

> Her body was restless, cramped, bleeding and trembling, screaming with desires, yet pure and calm. Her body was strange between my hands. It was my body. It was her body. Her strange body. I held it and became it. Looking at it. Hurt by its wounds. I smelled the deep odor that emanated from it. I sucked it in. It had a soft heat, a fragrance that I don't remember ever smelling before. Her sweat had the odor of sandalwood. I don't remember. Her sweat had the scent of the fields, the aroma of the earth wet from the season's first rain. Her sweat was sweeter than water. Its beads glistened in the glow of her skin, and sometimes it flowed like tears in rivulets. Often she oozed with sweat that covered her face, her chest, her warm thighs, and wetted her fine skin, more delicate than a flower. The moisture that filtered out of her was nothing other than the water of her soul, a fluid that burst from her interior, the water of hot desires that ebbed and flowed. It was the water of her dependence on the body, on the spirit, distilled and unadulterated and pure, springing from the radiant feelings of her body, from my body which was her body, wounded by softness, wounded by sweetness, by goodness, wallowing in its unity. . . .
>
> The inner fluid of her vagina did not differ from her sweat. It possessed a fragrance rare in its own way. It was like sticky sap. It sometimes foamed like butter. Every time her desire blazed, the fluid flowed and became buttery, until her black pubic region became white with the sticky substance. Then her whole body was swept away by a burning feeling. It shook, trembling, and contracted. It wasn't easy for me to enter her. Her vagina was moist as a blossom, and the first entry was always painful. She moaned and sighed the first time, as if she was still not used to that which had repeatedly occurred since we had first known each other. It was as if she lost her virginity over and over again, a virginity that she surrendered without losing it. . . . And when she had taken the member into herself wholly, she was afflicted with

strange tremors. She was filled and flowed and overflowed . . . with sweat and fluid, a sticky fluid redolent with lewd ecstasy. And when we became still, we felt our sticky fluids intermingled with the nectar of our bodies and the aroma of our desires. Our obscure, secret fluids discharged in the fullness of hidden pleasure, in the repletion of that euphoria which was like the intoxication of death. How delicious it was for me to moisten my hand in her fluid, in the moistness of labia and vagina, in the dew of her flesh opened like a shy flower. I moistened my hand, my hand and my face, in order to imprint her fluid on my memory, a memory of our absence, of our presence, of our death which we did not experience.

I penetrated her sometimes with a delicacy appropriate to the fragility of her small body, and sometimes with the force needed to take possession of it—an external force appropriate to her internal force, which did not reveal itself. Her body was a mixture of warmth and fluid, of light and sweat. And when it flared up suddenly, it died out like a storm becoming gentle as a breeze. It was pleasant for her to surrender to the warmth and the fluid, to burst forth in flame and be extinguished, insensible to herself, staring at my eyes, at my hands, at my body, immersed in me, isolated from me. When we interlocked, she flowed like a candle gently melting, her senses opened like a flower, her eyes closed, her eyes opened. We were carried away as one, wet and burning, alone in the most complete unity.

She rose up and overflowed, remained, receded, and overflowed. My face remained joined to her chest, my eyes hidden, while her body resisted its own motion. She twisted, writhed, clung to me at times, and pushed me away at others, hot, delirious, and trembling. Her moans increased slightly and were muffled by her convulsions. Her eyes were furtive, her hands on intimate terms with the motion of her body, her feet rising and descending. When she rolled with me, her body was converted into a single piece of sweat and fire, expressing its defiance from one end of the bed to the other. She filled the bed. We filled the bed. We filled it and would not leave it.

In the violence of our union, our bodies became one body—a body that began with the complete spiritual demolition of two separate bodies. From our destruction arose a body of many desires and pains and wounds.

In the violence of our union, blood and spirit mixed like wine and water. When the body touched the fire, it touched its light, the fire of its hell and the light of its sun. And when it burst out greedily, it wafted and became serene like the daybreak. . . .

> I saw her as most beautiful when she opened her eyes after coming, her face open, and her gaze reflective and calm, as if she had suddenly awakened from a deep sleep; from a deep death. As if a sun had blinded her eyes, and she proceeded to open them, blinking them shyly. At that moment, it seemed that her face was strange, tender, and completely pure. Her smile was as complex as a flower, as diffident and fresh as cotton. The traces of the desires that had preoccupied her were evident on the blemishes of her face. Those desires in which her body had been immersed and which had flooded it. At that moment, her face was like a mirror directed towards her interior, revealing hidden feelings that she felt but could not express, which she could barely distinguish. Those fine pure feelings of pleasure were not easy to distinguish from the intoxication of death. When she opened her eyes, she became lost in contemplation without thought, her glances unstable, her body limp, letting go of desire and what followed it. This state was, in its way, a part of her desire, the beginning or end or which she had no knowledge. (90–93)

Wazin uses metaphors of "liquid," "water," and "melting" to describe genital secretions, and metaphors such as "mouth" and "wound" to describe the female sex organs themselves. He also employs little-used words to describe the female genitalia and the sexual act, such as *hayā'*, a rare word for the female genitals, which has the related connotation of "modesty":

> She appeared most beautiful when she stretched out on her back, parting her thighs, shortening [the length of] her body, and exposing her genitals. The button of her sex hung down like a blossom with moist petals. (100)

Wazin's stated preoccupation in this text was to research the Arab erotic traditions and revive them in a modern work. He claims to have sought out erotic terms in the *Lisān al-'Arab*, the classical Arabic lexical encyclopedia, in search of precise words to describe women's genitalia and the sexual act. He discovered a wide range of expressions, which impressed him as representing irrefutable evidence of the importance of eroticism in Arabic literature. In effect, he argues that if this vocabulary was part of Arab culture, there can be no objection from traditionalists to their use today. He is thus challenging the hypocrisy of moral standards that claim to be based on Arab custom, but in fact are based on only more recent cultural practice. These artistic aims are largely obscured by translation. Indeed, to a reader of English, Wazin's text may appear hackneyed in relation to the well-established Western literary tradition of eroticism in modern narrative. It is hard for Western readers to appreciate what a striking departure this text represents in the context of modern Arabic literature.

While the text is a pioneering one in terms of style, use of language, and erotic expression in Arabic, however, we also must examine it critically with respect to its limited masculine perspective. The second and third paragraphs of the extended quote offer some examples. When the narrator states, "It wasn't easy for me to enter her," or, "I penetrated her . . . sometimes with the force needed to take possession of [it]," he celebrates, even romanticizes, the power discrepancies he perceives in the sexual act. Whether this discrepancy is in any way perceived by the woman, or is simply a masculine fantasy, cannot be divined from the text, because it is written entirely from the narrator's male perspective.

Other passages reflect typical male fantasies associated with this perceived power discrepancy. "I imagined that blood was flowing" links the image in a confessional manner with the narrator's imagination. No blood is flowing, but the imagined image is important to the narrator, fulfilling some need on his part, perhaps associated with breaking the hymen. "It was as if she lost her virginity over and over again" represents a similar fantasy. Obviously, the woman does not repeatedly lose her virginity. Yet the idea seems to have a delusional appeal to the narrator. There is no attempt on his part to divine what meaning losing her virginity might have for the woman, nor if there is really any feeling on her part that engaging in sex reenacts this event. Thus, we find that in both *Girls of Alexandria* and *Ḥadīqah al-Ḥawāss*, the narratives are entirely focused on an "I" whose attention is completely absorbed in the contemplation of the feminine Other. Both texts are dominated by the subjective consciousness of the narrative voice, yet in neither of these texts does the narrative voice interrogate itself. It merely leaves a record of its impressions and its own self-awareness.

More successful as a self-interrogating text is Rashid al-Da'if's *Fusḥah Mustahdafah Bayna al-Nu'ās wa al-Nawm*. Samira Aghacy notes that when the concierge tells the narrator of his relatives who have escaped the violence in a southern suburb of Beirut, and are temporarily staying with his family, the narrator begins to envisage them sharing his own flat. The intruders who knock on the door of his apartment are visualized in the menacing figure of the concierge's brother-in-law, who is seen as harassing and tyrannizing everybody, particularly his sister-in-law, her child, and the narrator. He views the woman in the house as a stereotype of the Shi'ite woman, and the concierge and his brother-in-law as mere stereotypes of violence. The concierge is vexed because he himself is seen by the narrator as a mere stereotype of the dishonest Shi'ite concierge, yet he views the narrator as a mere Christian living on the West Side of Beirut. The problem, as Aghacy notes, is that the narrator's reaction to these intruders represents as stereotyped and abstracted a view of them as they have of him.[60]

> Bogged down by such restrictions, the narrator attempts to break the deadlock, if not at the general public level, at least, at the private personal level. Since he cannot handle the hard, impenetrable world of male hegemony, he tries to do it through the softer, more accessible world of the female. . . . He contemplates marrying a Muslim woman to protect himself physically, but dismisses the idea. His family, background and religion render the act inconceivable . . . however, he still sees his salvation as through the female in general.[61]

The pregnant woman in his flat begins to infiltrate his thoughts. Aghacy notes that he sees her as the "stereotypical peacemaker," the only creative force within a destructive atmosphere, and a redemptive model of love. She becomes a signifier of his desire for peace and security, as well as his desire to reach out for the other.[62] Plunging into this contemplation of the feminine, he goes as far as transgressing gender boundaries, seeing himself as a woman in the mirror:

> An urge came to me, and I went to the bathroom, feeling my way cautiously in the midst of this darkness. I sat down on the bathroom seat, a beautiful woman sitting down on the bathroom seat, and I urinated, and I got up lifting up what I had brought down to my knees, and my dress was hanging down after it was drawn up, and went back to the kitchen without washing, waiting for it to end, and I was beautiful. (109)

Radical and startling as this move is, Aghacy points out that "the narrator's desire for a world free of differences and violence is constantly subverted and violated by the aggressive phallic impulse, reminding him that he is a Christian at war with Muslim Beirut. . . ."[63]

In *The Kingdom of Strangers*, Elias Khoury also takes up the contemplation of the feminine, with decidedly mixed results. Writing in a style that is very spare, somewhat abstract, yet rhythmical and lyrical, Khoury celebrates women less as objects of attention, attraction, or fascination and more as true partners in relationships:

> I laughed, too, and we danced. She danced in front of me, her body held together by a thousand invisible threads. She was moving right and left in a single motion. . . . I took her to the sea. We went out in a sailboat, drifted from the shore out into the deep water. . . . She laughed. I haven't forgotten that laugh. How can I forget? She was dancing, and I was dancing; then she went to sleep. She didn't sleep. She went to the balcony and lay down on a hammock. I walked toward her. Her eyes were closed, but she saw me. She saw me with her eyes without opening her eyes. She saw me coming, and so she moved over a little as if to leave me a small space to lie down next to her. I held onto the edge of the hammock and then gave it a push. . . .
>
> Her face was covered with water, with what looked like water. Then I went closer and lay down beside her. She didn't say a word. I shut my eyes the way she had shut hers, and I saw her the way she had seen me, and the hammock cradled us like a ship rocking in the middle of a calm sea. (4–5)

> It wasn't sex, and it wasn't love. I didn't take her the way you take a woman. I used to think a woman is taken from the outside in, and when you make love to a woman, you enter her. But with her, it wasn't . . . we were together; I entered her, and I didn't enter her. It was as though I didn't enter her. I was beside her and with her and in her. Sex came like flowing water, as if it were an extension of my body and hers, as if without any entrance or exit, like a dream, like the dreams we don't remember but that leave traces on our eyes. That's how I was. As though I were in a boat, rocking, as though I were in the sea, watching a seagull skim over the water and the water doesn't cover him. As though I were the water. (6)

At the same time, the reader gets a sense that this prose comes too easily, as if Khoury is more interested in women simply as subjects for writing:

> I knew that Ali loved a woman named Samia (of course, that's not her real name. I change women's names when I see they are in love because I think love changes everything about a woman, even her name). (100)

The meat and bones of interpersonal relations between men and women is not discussed. The characters act toward members of the opposite sex as if they are living in a dream:

> Iskandar told his wife he was going to marry the Circassian when his wife saw him embracing her in the kitchen and the young girl sighing in his arms. That was what drove the man crazy. That sigh that came from her eyes. Those eyes whose color Iskandar never could quite define. (33)

The passivity of Iskandar's initial encounter with Widad leads to a sense of separation once they are married:

> Now she is mine. But I don't know her. When I took her to the Sofar Grand Hotel and married her, I thought she had become mine, and she had become mine in every sense of the word. But love, my son, means that the other never really becomes yours. In love, the abyss remains forever open. Widad remained an open abyss. I tried to wipe out love with marriage, to tame passion with lovemaking, but I discovered instead the abyss. (40)

It doesn't matter that in this passage Iskandar has lied to his son, and the son knew that his father was lying to him. The thought has been expressed, and, like the variations on the folk legend of Jurji the monk, it is all the more potent for not being true. The upshot is that in Khoury's text, as in those of Edwar al-Kharrat and Abduh Wazin, women remain the great imponderable for male Arab novelists. Yet there is a greater ambiguity to the text as a whole. There is no implied criticism of Iskandar's relationship with Widad. The reader gropes futilely for the narrator's viewpoint. The only tool left to the reader is comparison with other stories.

For instance, when Khoury interweaves the stories of Jurji the monk and Widad, he clearly is interested in the importance of memory. But there is another link that one can find between the stories, and this is the link between male-female relationships and religion. Jurji is married to the church; Iskandar marries the white Circassian girl. Both "marriages" take place as if in an instant. Events unfold in the manner of a fantasy or fable. Yet white, if we remember *Al-Wujūh al-Bayḍā'*, is for Khoury a symbol both of purity and of decay. Perhaps also of forgetfulness. Perhaps also of religion. Perhaps also of death. When we consider this, what is striking in both stories is the passivity of these relationships. The entire text possesses this feeling of passivity, as if events unfold effortlessly. We don't know if this is something that Khoury, in his narrative voice, participates in, or that he is seeking to expose. It may be that he is trying to link this passivity with the entire panorama of tragedy in the region. Or it may be that he is a victim of this very passivity.

THE DIALECTICAL SOLUTION

The works of Ibrahim Nasrallah in *Prairies of Fever* and Rashid al-Da'if in *Tiqnīyāt al-Bu's*, or that of Abduh Wazin in *Ḥadīqah al-Ḥawāss* and Edwar al-Kharrat in *Girls of Alexandria*, represent extreme choices in terms of technique. Other contemporary Arab writers have been more concerned with striking a balance in this respect. *Ayyām Zā'idah* (Excess days, 1990),[64] by Hassan Daoud, is a work that threads a thin line between an objectified, distanced viewpoint of its subject, and an interior, psychological view. This dichotomy still indirectly reflects the dual commitment to artistic expression and social engagement that animates the work of most contemporary Arab writers.

Daoud's style of writing is more conventional than that of Elias Khoury. His narrative follows a linear pattern, rather than a patchwork approach. The main character in *Ayyām Zā'idah* is an old man who gradually becomes more and more infirm. He has only the house that he lives in. As his infirmity increases, he is forced to relinquish his claim to virtually everything that he possesses, and the space that he inhabits becomes more and more restricted, as if it were constantly shrinking. The narrative is in the first person, told from the viewpoint of the old man. The opening line sets an important tone. The old man wants to introduce himself by telling the reader his age, yet he does not actually have a clear idea of exactly how old he is:

> According to picture that's pasted on my I.D. when I was forty, I am now ninety-four. For years I imagined saying that I was three years younger than my I.D. (7)

In the narrative, the old man's ambiguous sense of time is replaced by a heightened awareness of place. He is attached to everything in the house, and as his claim on and connection with these things is gradually reduced, he continues to hold on in obsessive fashion. His "place" is whittled down from his house to his single room, to his bed, and finally just a spot on the floor, where they unceremoniously dump him. Even at this point, while he does not fear death, he is obsessed by the idea that, when he dies, at least the spot of ground in which he lies will belong to him.

Yumna al-Eid elaborates on this idea:

> And by this means, the concept of the place opens up to the concept of time. And time is an extended period that awakens in the mind the grandfather the picture of the repetitiveness of life or its stability as non-action, as if the place absorbed time.[65]

An important aspect of the space that this old man inhabits is its filthiness. We are not given an indication when this first became a condition of the house, but it is a condition now. It is a condition for which he is clearly responsible to a great degree. As he relates his history, he tells us of his habit of urinating from the balcony of the house. When his state becomes that of an invalid, he gives off an odor that contributes to the foul stench of the environment in which he lives. He understands the extent to which he is responsible for this, but even more, he understands that the squalor of his environment is not due to his living in the place, but rather in his *lack* of connection with it:

> The house was cleaner than what it was after we lived in it alone together and did a little cooking. I thought that the house would not get dirty from living in it, but rather from leaving things lying around and from the slowness of the occupants and the small amount of their activity.
>
> It's not dirtier than it was before she died, even though I went back to the habit of pissing on the cement courtyard underneath the balcony. (25)

The paradox of the old man's existential condition is that he hangs on to his consciousness of place even as his contact and connection with that place is constantly diminishing. Thus, by the conclusion of the novel, he himself has become a physical object. Yumna al-Eid sees the filthiness of his environment as emblematic of Lebanon:

> The house stricken with collapse and destruction is given greater prominence than the home of the individual or the family. It is the refuge or the place to which the citizens escape. Or maybe it is the homeland.[66]

As in Elias Khoury's *Gates of the City*, there are never any direct references to the war in *Ayyām Zā'idah*. There are references to the social environment of Beirut, which reflect the typical effects of migration to an urban environment. As Eid points out, this is illustrated by the old man's own commentary on the effects of the city on urban immigrants like himself:

> Coming to Beirut was not coming to a place in whose building they took part and which would have participated in creating them. Each one of them spent their time Beirut without changing anything in it. They "remained the same." (37–38)

> The city was just a place for work, for laying down the body and dying for money.[67]

At the same time, there is a conflict, a resistance to this process, on the part of the old man, and this is seen through his interior narrative perspective. The social environment reflects the alienation and isolation of the old man, just as much as he represents the society as a whole. In *Ayyām Zā'idah*, the old man faces the pressures of being old, and these pressures come less from his physical infirmities than from the people around him, who are, in a sense "pushing" him to be weak. His age is something offensive to them. In other words, Daoud is criticizing the tendency to dehumanize the elderly in a society that essentially caters to the young.

One of the main themes of the book, then, is the paradoxical observation that age and weakness are seen as a threat by society. Strength at such an age is considered an aberration, and there is the tendency on the part of other people to attempt to control a person who resists the natural forces of aging. This theme regarding age and illness, combined with the themes of urbanity and isolation make *Ayyām Zā'idah* powerfully reminiscent of canonical modernist texts such as André Gide's *The Immoralist*,[68] or Thomas Mann's *Death in Venice* and *The Magic Mountain*.[69] Moreover, these themes are not common ones in modern or contemporary Arabic literature, which has, by and large, been preoccupied with larger social issues such as those of war and occupation.

An even greater parallel with Western canonical modernist texts whose theme is old age and illness is the heightened awareness of the old man as a result of his condition. This awareness seems to increase as his physical condition deteriorates. He is aware that he has become an object and a part of the filth around him. When the old man asks his family for a doctor, the request is refused. Yumna al-Eid comments on his reaction:

> So we see that the grandfather searches for something that will assure him that that was when he was asleep, only in his dream, and not a truth on the battlefield, as if what he saw in his dream became reality. . . . There he is looking at himself in order to assure himself that he is still wearing his pajamas. . . . Nothing has changed. It is as if the battlefield that he saw was just a picture. The fight did not change anything. And his body is still the same.
>
> Thus is emphasized in the novel, and through the words of the grandfather, the necessity of knowing the "I" or the self.[70]

Eid thus stresses a process that occurs in the novel, which begins with a picture of an objectified, dehumanized individual and ends with a heroic attempt at self-understanding in the face of death:

> *Ayyām Zā'idah* sees the deficiency in the "I" and speaks of knowledge before action. The deficiency is in the body, in the grandfather's body. His body was ill, declining, but now, with his awakened voice, he wants to know the reason for his illness. . . .
>
> The grandfather demands from his son and grandson, then from Mr. Mahdī, to get the doctor so he can find out about his illness and his deficiency, but they do not grasp the depth of the request and let him die.[71]

The last three chapters gradually develop dramatic interest in this process. In chapter 10, the old man is present at a gathering in the apartment of a neighbor who lives in the same building, during which he urinates in full sight of the guests. This is the beginning of his increasing senility, failing powers, and loss of control over his body. At one point, he is depicted as practically immobile, unable to signal to a friend when he wants to greet him:

> Seated, I am unable to move, to the extent that I cannot raise my hand to wave to Muhammad Habib (Muḥammad Ḥabīb) to come to me. (105)

Here, the old man's passivity is reminiscent of the death scene in Thomas Mann's *Death in Venice*, in which Aschenbach's gaze follows Tadzio as he walks out in the sea:

> The observer sat there as he had sat once before. . . . His head, resting on the back of the chair, had slowly followed the movements of the one who was striding about out there; now his head rose as if returning the gaze, then sank on his chest. . . . His face took on the slack, intimately absorbed expression of deep sleep.[72]

In the penultimate chapter, the old man has a dream of his own grandfather awakening from his bier as he is about to be buried, and this dream reflects an underlying emotional crisis that accompanies his physical deterioration:

> My grandfather Shaykh Ahmad (Shaykh Aḥmad) raised himself from the upraised coffin that was being lowered into the grave. (165)

As Eid points out, in this section, we are presented two images—an image of the old man and that of his grandfather—that nevertheless meld together into the image we have of the old man himself. Thus, the dream conveys the old man's apprehension about his own death. A very significant aspect of this is that it brings the text into the realm of the psychological novel. This scene is also reminiscent of Thomas Mann's use of a dream sequence for an entire chapter ("Snow") in *The Magic Mountain*, which similarly represents a turning point in the awareness of the main character, as well as in the momentum of the narrative. In the last chapter, the members of his family who look after the old man treat him like an object, yet he is still an alert and active narrator. Remaining silent when people are present, he pretends that he doesn't hear or can't speak. Aware that his age is felt as a transgression by society, and that no one knows how to deal with him, he theatrically plays down to people's expectations. Yet his outer passivity masks a heightened self-awareness.

Hoda Barakat achieves a similar effect in *The Stone of Laughter*. Khalil's femininity alienates him from the rest of society, and this alienation, in turn, gives him a critical perception of that society:

> Laughter . . . thought Khalil as he made tea in his room. . . .
>
> This is the place where people laugh more than anywhere else in the world. When the bombing is in full swing the children laugh and the government employees laugh because it's a holiday. . . .
>
> The women laugh amongst themselves because they will have more opportunity to meet their neighbors and more opportunity to talk endlessly about their health. . . .
>
> The shopkeeper will laugh because people will be so busy buying so many provisions that they will virtually empty his shelves.
>
> The man who owns the restaurant will laugh because people will resist the feeling of being hemmed in and having to be stuck at home by going out more and they will be more extravagant, because they love life and because death knocks at the door every day.
>
> The moneychanger will laugh because the currency conversions will pour in from outside, in sympathy for family and close relations. . . .
>
> The poet will laugh because . . . someone in his family or sect will be martyred, which will lend him the microphone of the crowds which come . . . begging him to lament and warble. . . .
>
> The foreign correspondents will laugh because it gives them juicy stories to work on. . . .
>
> The landlord will laugh because the bombing will make hosts of people move to the city. . . .
>
> And you, Khalil, drinking your tea coldly, why are you not laughing? (134–37)

After Youssef's death, however, Khalil's physical symptoms become more prominent. Like the old man in *Ayyām Zā'idah*, he closely resembles those "sensitive souls" that inhabit Western modernist novels such as André Gide's *The Immoralist*, Thomas Mann's *The Magic Mountain*, or Gabriel García Márquez's *Love in the Time of Cholera*.[73] In these works, illness becomes a major theme, and is seen as akin to a process of feminization, involving increasing passivity, a retreat from the world, and a deeper awareness of the processes of life and death:

> This is what Khalil saw in the exhibition in the glass hall of the Ministry of Tourism, a pool with many tiers at the top of which was a foun-

> tain which sent out a red liquid which flowed over the lower tiers and gushed out. He did not understand . . . he came closer to have a better look. Blood. A pool with a fountain that overflows and makes a sound like blood. He fainted.
>
> What's the matter with him, asked the people who gathered around . . . give him some water to drink. Water. He fainted again. He will not drink. The blood flew from his body as if drained by thousands of powerful suckers and his body did not want to come round. (121)

> Khalil was very ill. He kept vomiting up water mixed with short, red threads. (157)

> He feels that excitement which goes directly from his lungs to his loins whenever he sees a corpse with its chest and waist and hip and throat and arms laid bare in the newspaper, for those firm, naked bodies of theirs confirm to him beyond all doubt that they are men, that the sharp flame of their masculinity is what led them to kill. They are so masculine that they make Khalil's pale, pale, still body nothing. (158)

When Khalil finally enters the hospital for an operation on his ulcer, he finds joy in its neat, antiseptic quality, its removal from the rest of the world, and the kindness of the doctors, nurses, and attendants. Here, one is reminded particularly of Hans Castorp's sanitarium existence in Thomas Mann's *The Magic Mountain:*

> Khalil had not known that the city's real paradise was in its hospitals.
>
> Everything inside was prepared with amazing precision. The hospital was one of the places most isolated from the outside, even the lighting did not acknowledge the light of day outside. . . .
>
> They are so concerned to isolate us that they thought to provide Thai or Filipino nurses who speak no Arabic except for the short, functional phrases which they coo. What they say is so broken that they manage to make the patients forget their own language. (174)
>
> Here is total recognition, without language, total compliance to an illness they could treat, which they could not ignore, or refuse to recognize or impose order on it to conceal it. Here, there is primitive time, time which is for your body, not against it.
>
> On this white, floating island Khalil feels he is above the city. That he looks over it from afar and so he only sees, if he stares, what a

> passenger in an aeroplane sees of a city over which he passes on a long journey. (175)

It is important to understand that Khalil is not simply a weakling. Like the old man in *Ayyām Zā'idah*, he is, in his own way, a strong character. The strength of Khalil's self-awareness is reflected in the heightened subjectivity of his near-death experience as a result of the operation. This near-death experience is told by means of a fragmented combination of third-person narration, dialogue, and interior monologue:

> —Breathe. Take a deep breath. Breathe. It's no.
>
> —Breathe. Take a deep breath. Breathe.
>
> Khalil heard the sound of a slap. He was completely awake but he knew that his body was outside him. In front of him. He did not see his body.
>
> Khalil saw utter darkness, in which a few exquisite, radiant, phosphorescent blue haloes hovered around him. The haloes were them.
>
> —Breathe.
>
> Khalil's soul clings onto his mouth, lashes out and falls in its place. In it. Khalil's soul clings . . . to the lung. To the lung . . . it lashes out. It falls. You. You for me to breathe.
>
> You do it.
>
> I hear. I can't. Say that I can't hear. Hear. Hear. Here. I
>
> —Breathe.
>
> You c. Please.
>
> Mouth . . . mouth. Hand. Hand. Eyelid eyelid. For a sign. To. . . .
>
> —Press press harder. He's not responding doctor. He's not. . . .
>
> Here. Don't go away.
>
> I don't think it's my body. I don't know. I can get to me without it. And hear. Do it with him. You.
>
> Now he slips backwards. Quickly. Fearfully. It isn't quick. It's not called quick. It doesn't have a name because anyone who isn't dying doesn't know it. The total darkness is a tunnel now. Not a tunnel.
>
> The tunnel of a dying man.
>
> It's gray. Horizontally backwards. The phosphorescent haloes are still close.
>
> —He's not . . . no.
>
> He knew.
>
> They will not hear me.
>
> I'm alone.
>
> Very.

The "very alone" of a dying man.
Shame.
Khalil.
Alone.
Quick. Backwards he's leaning. Under.
The haloes suddenly shrink.
Quick.
His soul pulls away from his fingers.
All of them.
He finds not.
It's sucked up backwards and downwards.
They've gone away.
They've gone out.
Black.
A white dot ahead. Ahead.
Very small.
Backwards and downwards and towards it.
That's it.
I die.
Shame.
Shame. (182–83)

Throughout *Ayyām Zā'idah*, the grandfather's narrative remains completely lucid. Yumna al-Eid points out that Hassan Daoud has created a dual voice in the narration. There is only one narrator, the old man, yet he has two personalities—a silent, withdrawn personality that he reserves for use with those around him, and an active, alert personality that is reflected in his role as narrator:

> By this dual voice, the narration is built upon two harmonious, melodious rhythms, welded together in one character—the character of the grandfather, silent in his relationship to his surroundings, expressed in his relationship to himself.[74]

Thus, on one level, the old man presents the reader with an example of a "disappearing subject." The paradox that Hassan Daoud establishes, however, is that this does not apply to the narrative voice, which remains the same throughout. The awareness represented by the narrative voice actually increases in strength as the novel progresses. Hassan Daoud has stressed that his main character is not an ordinary man or an everyman.

Rather, he wished to write about an extraordinary person who remains extraordinary despite his age.[75] This interest sets Daoud somewhat apart from writers such as Elias Khoury, who claim to be consciously aiming to undermine the position of the hero in narrative.

Daoud can also be distinguished from many of his contemporaries by the apparent lack of self-reflexivity in his novels. His work is not concerned with the lives and thinking of intellectual elite, nor is it preoccupied with the place of the authorial voice in narrative, nor with other questions of narrative introspection. According to Daoud, he is specifically reacting against these tendencies, which he regards as a legacy of French influence on the Lebanese novel. He traces this influence most directly via the work of canonical novelists such as Proust and Gide. Daoud claims that his writing is more socially conscious, closer, in fact, to the realism of Mahfouz or Victor Hugo. In this sense, he sees his work primarily as a reaction against ideologically generated narrative. He illustrates this with the example of Fu'ad Kin'an (Fu'ād Kin'ān), a Lebanese writer of the mid-1940s. Daoud notes that, when Kin'an describes a monk, the character is drawn as an example of the author's hatred of the church. He maintains that he does not fit his characters to an idea, but rather selects a personality, and then tries to get inside that personality as fully as possible, much the way a portrait artist does.[76]

While Daoud avoids injecting an authorial voice into his narrative in the fashion of Elias Khoury, this does not mean that he does not manipulate the text to reflect his own voice or his own ideas. Yumna al-Eid, for instance, questions Daoud's claim not to put himself in his narrative. She cites the apparent inappropriateness of the old man's speech patterns as evidence that, like Mu'nis al-Razzaz in *I'tirāfāt Kātim Ṣawt* and Elias Khoury in *The Journey of Little Gandhi*, Daoud is simply using his character as a mouthpiece for his own ideas.[77]

It is true that many readers of *Ayyām Zā'idah* view the way in which the old man expresses himself as unconvincing. Like virtually all novels in Arabic, the text is written in the literary *(fuṣḥah),* rather than the colloquial, language. Yet the old man is supposed to be illiterate. Hassan Daoud claims that this is a problem that he took very seriously in writing the book, asking himself with virtually every sentence if the old man's language was suitable to his illiteracy. Classical speech, he claims, was a necessary choice in order to give the character sufficient gravity to convey the strength of his personality. Thus, he thus chose a manner of speaking for the old man appropriate to an individual of the Abbasid period.

Underlying this is the common assumption on the part of native Arabic speakers that the colloquial is a corruption of the classical language, and that the latter is thus useless in rendering a "strong" character. This shows the extent to which even the most self-consciously experimental Arabic writers today are still restricted by very conventional assumptions about language. In Western literature, it has been possible since the early modernist period for writers to create strong characters with culturally weak linguistic signatures, as in Gertrude Stein's "Melanctha"[78] or Faulkner's *The Sound and the Fury*. Because of the perceived inappropriateness of colloquial language to the novel form, however, experimenting with this type of narrative innovation is still highly problematic in Arabic.

In addition, we normally expect the writer to give us a sense of the old man's deterioration through a change in the narrative. This does not occur in *Ayyām Zā'idah*. Daoud does not tailor the style of narration to his subject, as we find, for instance, in the work of Faulkner or Joyce. On the other hand, Yumna al-Eid's own analysis suggests that this may be intentional, with Daoud trying to go against the expectations of the reader, creating a paradoxical tension in the narrative. The reader is given a sense that the old man's awareness is unconnected with his bodily state, or, even more accurately, that there is even an inverse relationship between the two. Through this inverse relationship, *Ayyām Zā'idah* achieves a certain tension between the objective and the psychological, between exterior and interior narration. There is a contrast not only between the way in which the old man is objectified and the power of his individual subjectivity, but also between the language with which this subjectivity is rendered and the expectations of the reader, based on the old man's objective condition.

A similar tension is achieved from a more personal point of view in Rashid al-Da'if's work of autobiography-as-fiction, entitled *'Azīzī al-Sayyid Kāwābātā* (Dear Mr. Kawabata, 1995).[79] In this text, the author uses the *Doppelgänger* technique to create a feeling of ambivalence toward his own self. The narrator, whose name, Rashid (Rashīd), gives the reader an indication of the autobiographical nature of the text, addresses the late Japanese novelist Yasunari Kawabata with great affection, like a type of comrade in whom he can confide. Much of Da'if's story is overtly political, beginning with his engagement in the Communist Party in the 1960s, and involving his sympathy for the Palestinian struggle, his military training, and the tribal politics of Lebanon. The choice of a real-life novelist for the role of confessor indicates, however, the extent to which Da'if is intent on approaching the task of autobiography from a literary standpoint. Indeed, Mona Amyuni notes that "'style as politics' is striking in this autobiography."[80]

Like Mu'nis al-Razzaz and Elias Khoury, Rashid al-Da'if could be described as a Marxist who is nevertheless aware of many of the conflicts and contradictions inherent in his political viewpoint. While his narrative is comparable, in this sense, to works such as *I'tirāfāt Kātim Ṣawt* or *The Journey of Little Gandhi*, instead of splitting his authorial voice into multiple characters, Da'if incorporates these conflicts and contradiction into a single narrative voice. Rashid tells of his life growing up in Lebanon, and of his love for his family and native environment. He also talks about his gradual intellectual awakening as a young man. There is a change in the narrator over time, however. As he grows older, his intellectual nature becomes stronger, and his emotional nature weaker. When he adopts the Marxist philosophy, his connections with his roots—his home, family, and culture—are weakened. In his mind, his native village becomes a symbol of backwardness, ignorance, and religious conservatism. One of the values he clings to, however, is the beauty of the Arabic language. He is in love with Arabic culture and with the Arabic language. He constantly interrupts his narrative to point out to Mr. Kawabata some expression he has used, invariably remarking on its beauty, its aptness, or its uniquely Arab quality:

> Notice this expression, Mr. Kawabata: "The war has laid down its burdens [come to an end]." (10)
>
> As quick as lightning! (Notice this eternally beautiful expression.) (13)

The narrator gives several reasons for writing to Mr. Kawabata. He says that he liked the sound of his name, that he was attracted to a novel Kawabata had written, that he himself is an aspiring novelist (18). As an aspiring writer, Rashid clearly identifies with Kawabata, the novelist. But there is more to his choice than this. He is attracted to Kawabata not merely because he is a novelist, but because he is a foreigner, an alien:

> I used to love the innocence of the stranger, and maybe I still do. The emptiness in the mind of the stranger signifies isolation to me. (17)

The Arab world, traditionally, has looked to Europe for its civilizational model, while contacts with the Far East are much weaker. Da'if, the novelist, is interested in going against tradition and convention in this sense. At the same time, Rashid feels that he is an outsider in Arab society. In a way, he feels more of a kinship with a foreigner than with his own countrymen. The "emptiness in the mind of the stranger" is a freedom from cultural baggage. The alien's position of cultural isolation is also a position of freedom. This sentiment echoes once more that of the alienated man in Western literature from Dostoevsky to Rilke to Camus, as well as its facsimile in the work of Jabra Ibrahim Jabra and other Arab novelists of the early modernist period. Rashid criticizes conformity and emphasizes his uniqueness as an individual by asking, "Why do the Arabs tend to accept similarity and not uniqueness?" (31).

Rashid tells a number of stories that illustrate the contradictions inherent in Lebanese society. One story is a traditional one concerning the mother of the classical poet Umar Ibn Abi Rabi'ah ('Umar Ibn Abī Rabī'ah). The traditional story is that after she died, she was being buried, and that after her casket was lowered into the ground, a voice was heard from inside the casket, muttering that she had always been a Christian. She had never told anyone her religion. Even her son did not know. The story is meant to illustrate the extent to which people hid their religious affiliations during the war. Rashid comments, "Why this isolation, and why is the individual put in [this] coercive situation!?" (202). He tells another story about a young woman whose father was a communist. His behavior toward her was patriarchal in the extreme. The paradox between his "idealistic" political philosophy and his "traditional" attitudes illustrates the difficulty that Marxists in Lebanon had in practicing what they preached. The confessional aspect of *'Azīzī al-Sayyid Kāwābātā* resides in the fact that Rashid feels contradictions such as these not merely in the society around him, but also within himself.

Finally, this contradictory pressure becomes too great for Da'if to express in a straightforward memoir. This is where the author's narrative enters into a fictional mode. Da'if turns to a familiar motif as a means of expressing his self-critical viewpoint, one that we have seen in Ibrahim Nasrallah's *Prairies of Fever*, namely that of the *Doppelgänger*, or "double." The narrator, Rashid, is walking along Hamra, the main street of Beirut, when he sees a man who looks exactly like him, who is, in fact, himself:

> I was going down Hamra Street in Beirut when I suddenly saw him and thought that I was seeing myself.
>
> First I believed that I was seeing someone who bore a strong resemblance to me, but quickly it was clear to me that the situation was more than one of resemblance. I told myself that I was in front of a mirror image in which my portrait was reflected with a suspicious clarity. But the image was walking in another direction, and in a different manner, and in clothes other than mine. This was not an image of me, but it was me, myself. (7)

As the narrator considers this figure, it becomes clear that it represents a side of himself that he does not wish to see:

> When I met him in Hamra Street, I saw my life pass rapidly and briefly, but clearly, before my eyes. . . .
>
> I hate him, Mr. Kawabata. (9)

Rashid indicates that what bothers him about the sight of the double has to do with a lack of awareness on the double's part:

> He didn't see me.
>
> Not because I wasn't in his field of vision, but because he didn't see except what he chose to see.
>
> He didn't choose to see me.
>
> He didn't choose to see except what pleased him. And I didn't please him. (11)

He also chafes at what he perceives as the double's sense of superiority or conceit:

> He's three centimeters taller than me, but that doesn't give him the right to feel superior. (11)

This sense of the double's superiority is combined with an impression of his innocence:

> There wasn't a wrinkle or fold on his face or neck. His face was smooth as a baby's. . . .
>
> A face radiated purity, with the smile of a virgin. . . .
>
> The face of someone who falls asleep as soon as he closes his eyes, who had kept his conscience clear, white as the driven snow. (148–49)

Rashid's double is a former Party member, who has not only given up the cause, but boasts that he hasn't killed:

> The insolence took him to boasting, after he had resigned from his activities with the Party. His palm was clean from any drop of blood. But rather, he had increased his invitations not to participate in the struggle. Then he became a "marginal" activist, someone who spent most of his time on gambling . . . in the belief that everything is acceptable except murder. . . .
>
> He boasted . . . that he had never fired at anyone in a war that killed thousands. (187–88)

While Rashid remains more faithful to the Party ideology than his double, his anger at the double is not really a matter of ideology, but rather in the double's assertion of distance and detachment from the situation:

> The clothes he wore before were never as fine as those he wore now. They were more suited to his middle-class status. . . .
>
> What caused him to dress in such finery? And where did he get that pride that allowed him to walk with his head up . . . gazing ahead. . . .
>
> What, then, did he see in the distance, almost making people conclude that the war was over. . . .
>
> Was he trying to discern the coming peace?
>
> Then I saw him smile ever so slightly, and look in the distance over the heads of the people, as if he were afraid of being surprised by a historical camera, while he was in a non-historical state.
>
> He smiled!
>
> And how this smile angered me! (149–50)

The image of the double looking "in the distance over the heads of the people" refers to what was a common phenomenon in Lebanon in the late '80s. People were saying that the war was over, or was about to end, because they all wanted peace. Yet the war continued. What Rashid is criticizing both in himself and others is this unrealistic tendency. Rashid is not an ideologue. He does not want the war to continue any more than his double does. But he is a realist. He objects to people who have a false sense of security based on wishful thinking. Mona Amyuni notes that

> During his engagement with the Marxists, he saw himself and his friends as "makers" of history. They fought and believed they would change the world. His autobiography closes with a very old Arabic saying to the effect that "life goes thus whether we like it or not." Life is the actor, and human beings forbear. Al-Da'if [Da'if] accepts this with great simplicity.[81]

MIMICKING POSTMODERNITY

The same theme of the loss or erosion of modernity found in Rashid al-Da'if's *Tiqnīyāt al-Bu's* can be observed in a recent work by Sonallah Ibrahim, entitled *Dhāt* (Dhat, 1993).[82] Although written twenty years after *Najmah Aghusṭus*, *Dhāt* continues many of Ibrahim's characteristic methods of narrative experimentation, and his style is still easily identifiable. What has changed, however, are the conditions in Egypt that are the subject of Ibrahim's social and political criticism. Relatively free of the political upheavals that have occurred in the Levant in recent years, Egypt divested itself of the socialist system and began to acquire some of the characteristics of a consumer culture. The period with which *Dhāt* deals is that of the Sadat years, a period in which the country had shaken off the control of a military clique only to fall under the power of an oligarchy with ties to the mercantile elite, as well as to the religious establishment. The exposure of this relationship is the essential subject of the novel.

As in *Najmah Aghusṭus*, Ibrahim casts around for a fitting symbol to represent the political situation he aims to criticize, and he finds one in a female character, Dhat (Dhāt). In Arabic, *dhāt* means simply a being, person, or individual in the most generalized sense. Like Rashid al-Da'if's Hashim, Dhat is devoid of subjectivity. She is an everywoman, nothing more. A young, recently married woman, without a university degree, forced by economic circumstances into the workplace, she finds a job as an office functionary in a newspaper. The setting of the newspaper allows Ibrahim to construct a bridge between the world of politics and national events and the world of the ordinary person.

The narrative of Dhat's life is rendered in an extremely simple, unadorned prose. There is no pretense that Dhat is a heroine, or that her life is remarkable in any way. Indeed, the author from the outset conveys to the reader his impatience with the classical pattern of narrative, which attempts to build up the reader's interest in the main character. He adopts a candid authorial tone with the reader, which reflects his attitude toward the writing process, as well as his ironic stance toward contemporary culture:

> We can begin the story of Dhat from its natural beginning, that is, from the moment that she burst forth into our world stained with blood, followed by the first kick that she gave when she was hoisted up in the air, her head immediately turned upside down, and a slap applied to her behind (whose later increase in size by virtue of the frequency of its trips to sit on the toilet will not henceforth be mentioned). A beginning such as this, however, won't win over the critics. The straight path, both in literature and in ethics, doesn't lead to anything of importance, and doesn't produce anything in this situation of ours except a waste of time on the part of both reader and writer. This is time that they can spend with the television, for instance. (9)

Ibrahim has no interest in Dhat apart from her status as representative of the most average class of Egyptians, struggling at the margins of poverty. Her life, and the decisions she makes that affect it, is told in the simplest possible fashion. At the same time, there are certain fundamental conflicts introduced with respect to Dhat's life. For instance, she is at odds with the employees at the newspaper office where she works, particularly the female employees, because she initially comes to work in a miniskirt, while they all wear the *ḥijāb*, the traditional covering of a Muslim woman. Eventually, Dhat succumbs to peer pressure and adopts the *ḥijāb* herself.

The narration of Dhat's life is interspersed with chapters made up simply of what appear to be newspaper clippings, including articles, headlines, and editorials, a technique reminiscent of the work of John Dos Passos.[83] As in *Najmah Aghusṭus*, Ibrahim has chosen a form that mirrors the content of the work. Just as the High Dam symbolized the

Egypt of grand socialist projects, the newspaper, with its shrieking headlines, and Dhat's life of bare-bones consumerism, symbolize the capitulation to capitalist culture. The alternate sections mirror each other in two ways, both in content and in form. From the point of view of form, there is a similarity in the style of writing between the narrative sections and the sections made up of newspaper clippings, in the sense that both are direct, reportorial. The narrative sections have one aim only, and that is to show how Dhat, her family, and their neighbors live.

The chapters of clippings similarly exhibit the bare bones of contemporary Egyptian politics, stripped of all but the "facts." In terms of content, we see at the end of the book that Dhat is a victim of the very forces that are reported in the paper. For instance, the newspaper reports of the conspiracy of government to protect business interests over that of consumers in the following sequence of clippings:

> Workers in the public sector and the government in Alexandria refuse the delivery of their quotas of dried meat because of a horrible smell emanating from it.
>
> A tabloid paper: "The spoiled dried meat was imported with the knowledge of controlling interests. An import permit had been rejected by the health inspection department, but a high official put pressure on the Minister for Food Supplies until he lifted the ban on the pretext of making up for apparently nonexistent losses."
>
> A group of workers at the Mirco Refrigeration Company, belonging to the Minister for Food Supplies, discovered the existence of huge amounts of spoiled imported meat in a burned-out refrigerator.
>
> Seven merchants control the import monopoly of perishable goods required by the Ministry of Food Supplies.
>
> Report to the Department of Trade in Cairo: The importers forge inspection certificates designating the contents as good commodities when the safety of these goods is in doubt, obscuring the dates marking the limit of their fitness for human consumption.
>
> The son of a prominent authority was importing a load of meat which, after being weighted in the market, was found to be unfit for human consumption. An inspector from the Ministry of Food Supplies subsequently collected it from merchants and government cooperatives. (222)

> The German press reported on a deal involving milk spoiled by radiation sold to an Egyptian import company owned by the son of a prominent

authority for approximately only a hundred thousand marks, even though its original value was three million marks. The German press confirmed that the shipment had entered Egypt.

Eight hundred tons of spoiled dry milk received a certificate of good quality from the Port of Alexandria without its inspection having been completed.

A responsible source in the Council of Ministers: "There isn't any milk spoiled by radiation in the whole of Egypt or its ports." (227)

In the last scene of the book, Dhat is portrayed as a victim of the conspiracy documented in the press clippings:

She returned to the kitchen and put the glass tumblers in the hot water, scrubbing them with a plastic sponge. Then she took them out, placed them on the marble slab by the sink, and moved on to the dishes and pots. A feeling of relaxation returned to her, despite the pain that had spread to her lower back.

When she finally could see down to the bottom of the sink, she collected the submerged refuse and put it in the waste container. Then she did a thorough cleaning, enjoying a moment of clear daylight before being drawn back to the glasses and pots covered with soap. She turned on the water and began to rinse (a process that could have been shortened if she had a sink free from corrosion).

When she was finished, she rewarded herself with a glass of tea that she sipped in the hall. Then she returned to the kitchen and untied the package of fish. She saw that it contained two large pieces, one a head with the bones sticking out, the other a bony piece of the tail. She felt for anything on them that would be edible, didn't find anything, and put them to the side (planning to given them to the cats on the staircase). After reproaching herself for not examining the contents of the package before leaving the shop, she moved on to the piece of herring.

She slit open one of the plastic packages with the knife, and pulled out the dried fish. She was astounded to find that it crumbled in her hand. She stripped it meticulously of its skin and pulled out its bones, exposing its desiccated interior. She put a piece to her mouth, chewed it, and found that it had a sharp taste. She pulled out another fish from its wrapping, slit open its belly, and saw that it had a similar crumbling consistency and a taste that resembled that of vinegar. It was the same story with the remaining two fishes.

She broke open the plastic wrappers and looked at the little seal

> that was stamped both the date it was produced and the period for which it was guaranteed. The production date was the present month, and the guarantee was for the entire year. It was not difficult to imagine what had happened: the herring had spoiled, and they put it in vinegar to cover up the change in taste, then put it in a new package. And for that reason it was displayed for sale at a lower price.
>
> She bent over the sink, filled with despair. What was she going to do now? Go to the shop under the burning sun and try to get her money back? And if they refused, go to the adjacent office to demand her rights and from there to the police station . . . ? She imagined the comment of the Chief of Police: "Spoiled fish? So don't eat it already!" He was right. The matter was trivial. Very trivial. She felt the tears welling up in her eyes. She threw the fish and the herring in the waste container. Then she took control of herself. She left the kitchen and went with heavy steps toward the place of tears: the toilet. (351–52)

In this work, Ibrahim is making a connection between two phenomena that are difficult to understand from a Western perspective as being allied: materialism, largely imported from the West, and traditionalism, particularly religious traditionalism. Westerners might consider Dhat's miniskirt as more reflective of Western materialism than her *ḥijāb*, given what is seen as the abstemiousness of Islam and the self-indulgence of Western culture. The traditional *ḥijāb* seems deliberately nonmaterialistic, unadorned, like the Amish dress in America. But this is not the main issue, from Ibrahim's point of view. It is not that a miniskirt is any better than the *ḥijāb*, but that the wearing of the latter is something that is forced on people. For Ibrahim, it is a matter of freedom, rather than fashion. Moreover, the *ḥijāb* can be a veil in more respects than one, its outer, abstemious appearance concealing a materialistic appetite.

Ibrahim is criticizing Arab society on two levels. Economically, it is dependent on imported goods. In other words, it is not a productive society. Ibrahim equates this lack of productive capacity to the type of traditionalism that insists on women wearing the *ḥijāb*. In cultural terms, the society is also not productive. It doesn't encourage independent thought. Rather, it encourages passivity in the same way that consumerism does. Ibrahim also focuses on what he sees as a collusion or conspiracy between two oligarchies: the capitalist interests and the religious interests. Separation of church and state does not exist in the Arab world, nor is there the necessary separation between the state and capitalist interests.

In *Tiqnīyāt al-Bu's*, there is a sense that the present modernity in the Arab world is actually less "modern" than it was in the past, that society has gone backward. There is the same notion underlying the text of *Dhāt*. Ibrahim focuses on the retrenchment and reaction of the society—the grasping at traditionalism reflected in the wearing of the *ḥijāb*. Ibrahim's point is the paradoxical one that openness to material things leads to backwardness, that it is antithetical to openness and freedom of thought. This is a case in which the Arab mentality differs from the Western. In the West, one cannot separate materialism from freedom of thought and expression. The two go hand in hand. The dichotomy is a necessary one for Ibrahim, however, since the failure to separate the two is perceived as a mechanism of control by the power structure.

As in *Najmah Aghusṭus*, the field of journalism is a counterpoint to the text. In *Najmah Aghusṭus*, there was an implicit reaction in Ibrahim's narrative to journalistic writing, which used hype, exaggeration, and the technique of familiarization for ideological purposes. In *Dhāt*, the press has become an entirely different phenomenon, more commercial, and more competitive; instead of a model to avoid, Ibrahim uses it as a reflection of reality. The little snippets, or excerpts, from press clippings function as competing voices, some of them even contradicting one another, like the intelligence reports of Zakariyya Ibn Radi in Ghitani's *Zayni Barakat*, or the conflicting versions of events in Munif's *Variations on Night and Day*. One could say that in *Najmah Aghusṭus*, journalistic writing represents an implicit antithesis of the text, whereas in *Dhāt*, it supports the text, in fact becomes part of the fabric of the text. Muhammad al-Baridi (Muḥammad al-Bāridī) notes that the newspaper clippings have nothing to do with the novel, except to create a thematic unity,[84] a technique we have already observed not only in Ibrahim's *Najmah Aghustus*, but also in Munif's *Endings* and Samman's *Beirut Nightmares*.

The lack of plot mirrors the documentary aspects of the text. There is no story here. It is merely a panorama of how people live. Nor is there any clue, any message, as to how these problems can be changed. There is no ideology, no socialist vision any more. There is implicit criticism of the corruption at the highest levels, and there is also implicit criticism of what has happened to ordinary people, now caught up in the consumer culture, and only thinking of how to get rich. Life has lost its values and principles, and Sonallah Ibrahim presents this by simply presenting the bare bones of life, that to which it has been reduced. If we were to understand the contemporary Egypt that is the subject of *Dhāt* as a "modern" society, then it would be possible to say that we are dealing with a "postmodern" text. What Ibrahim is criticizing, however, is a social system with the outer trappings of a modern society, yet which in fact is still ruled by principles of coercion and mass submission. It still lacks the quality of civic loyalty that Arab cultural critics such as Adonis ('Alī Aḥmad Sa'īd) has seen as a prerequisite of true modernity. As such, *Dhāt* only mimics the tone and style of postmodernism, or rather, uses these to modernist ends.

More recently, Arab writers, particularly in Lebanon, have been working to combine elements of "objectified" narration, cinematic technique, *pastiche*, and intertextuality to produce works that invite comparison with contemporary Western texts. *Rālf Rizq Allāh fī al-Mir'āh* (Ralf Rizqallah in the mirror, 1997)[85] by Rabi' Jaber (Rabī' Jābir) is such a text. Yumna al-Eid describes the narrative as beginning with the suicide of Ralf Rizqallah (Rālf Rizq Allāh), just as Elias Khoury's *The Journey of Little Gandhi* begins with the death of Little Gandhi and Jabra's *Al-Baḥth 'an Walīd Mas'ūd* begins with the death of Walīd. Reading the newspaper, one day, the narrator reads about a professor of psychology who just killed himself. He becomes interested in the man, wondering why a successful professor such as he would commit such an act. Eventually, his interest becomes something of an obsession, and he sets out to investigate his life. He visits Ralf's family, but finds no clues. The man's relationship with his family turns out not to have been out of the ordinary at all.[86]

The narrator's search into Ralf's identity is, of course, a search for his own. He becomes lost in the contemplation of Ralf's picture, and of his own image in mirrors or any reflecting surface. He examines reflecting surfaces, such as the surface of the sea and, in his imagination, the surface of a polar ice cap that he reads about in an encyclopedia. He sees his own face, the face of Ralf, of Ralf's father in the mirrors, the image of Narcissus in the water, that of a polar bear in the imagined ice cap. And he even sees the face of the author, Rabi' Jaber. At the end of the novel, Ralf comes out of the picture that the narrator has borrowed from Ralf's father, and says to the narrator:

> Sometimes I watch you from the mirror, when you're asleep. I look at your face as if it's the face of my father, and sometimes as if it's my face.[87]

In her review of *Rālf Rizq Allāh fī al Mir'āh*, Yumna al-Eid begins by comparing the book to Paul Auster's *The New York Trilogy* (1990),[88] an influential work among Lebanese writers ever since it was translated into Arabic in 1993. Eid finds that the principal characteristic the two works have in common is the use of multiple characters to represent different aspects of a single narrative voice. She then poses the question whether or not *Rālf Rizq Allāh fī al-Mir'āh* is imitative of Auster's work. She states her conclusion as follows:

> "No. Rabī' Jābir's novel is not imitative. At least, not necessarily. . . . The multiplicity of characters representing the narrative voice is not itself necessarily a sign of imitativeness. . . .[89]

Nevertheless, *Rālf Rizq Allāh* does mimic a number of the narrative features found in *The New York Trilogy*. First of all, both works are highly intertextual. *The New York Trilogy* is full of references to Cervantes in "City of Glass," for instance, and to Walt Whitman and Thoreau's *Walden* in "Ghosts." Another example of intertextuality in "City of Glass" involves Lewis Carroll's *Through the Looking Glass*:[90]

> "The initials H.D. in the name Henry Dark refer to Humpty Dumpty."
> "Who?"
> "Humpty Dumpty. You know who I mean. The egg."
> "As in 'Humpty Dumpty sat on a wall'?"
> "Exactly."
> "I don't understand."
> "Humpty Dumpty: the purest embodiment of the human condition." (97)

Similarly, the narrator in *Rālf Rizq Allāh* invokes the names of many authors and literary texts. He discusses Lewis Carroll at great length, reciting the adventures of Alice, and even inserting the Humpty Dumpty verse into the text. His own image in the mirror, and his reflections on this in the context of *Alice in Wonderland* and *Through the Looking Glass,* is the starting point for his investigation of Ralf, who is closer to a referent for his own self-awareness than his *Doppelgänger:*

> I decided to begin an investigation about him. Just like that . . . in a moment. I looked at myself staring at my reflection in the mirror, try-

> ing to ignore the black space that appeared behind my ears, and said that I would investigate him. (37)

Like Auster, Jaber also uses a combination of spare, objectified description, as well as the mention of actual locations to give a cinematic feel to the text. The latter technique involves the use of what Roland Barthes terms *les embreyeures*, that is, the signs or indicators that connect the narrative with reality. Elias Khoury makes use of this technique to some extent in *Little Mountain* in order to help give the reader a feeling of the Ashrafiyah quarter in Beirut. Auster and Jaber use the cities of New York and Beirut, respectively, as backdrops to events that really could occur anywhere. By anchoring his text in geographical minutiae, Auster saves it from being too abstract, even surrealistic:

> They traveled to the West Side on the shuttle, walked through the dank corridors of the 42nd Street station, and went down another set of stairs to the IRT trains. Seven or eight minutes later they boarded the Broadway express, careened uptown for two long stops, and got off at 96th Street.
>
> Stillman stopped at the corner of 99th Street, waited for the light to change from red to green, and crossed over to the other side of Broadway. Halfway up the block there was a small fleabag for down-and-outs, the Hotel Harmony. (69)

In *Rālf Rizq Allāh*, Jaber similarly uses geographical details to impart to the reader a sense of intimacy with the locale, despite its unfamiliarity:

> I crossed the square to the other side and went up to 'Abd Allāh Mashnūq Street in the direction of Police Circle. To my right was a tall building, behind it was where the old United Nations Center used to be. I ran my hand along it as I walked. Then I took a taxi to the American University. There I sat on a bench among the trees and let the wind into my lungs. (11)

Auster's place-name dropping recalls Joyce's use of Dublin geography in *Ulysses*.[91] Some of the locations in his stories have historical and intertextual significance, such as Orange Street in Brooklyn Heights, where Walt Whitman published his first edition of *Leaves of Grass*, which serves as Blue's base of observation in "Ghosts." Auster even inserts a diagram of a section of the city at one point. He also makes use of "reality" as fictional material, referring, for instance, to real-life players on the New York Mets baseball team in "City of Glass." Jaber's text uses similar techniques. At one point, a map of the portion of the city is included.

While Eid compares *Rālf Rizq Allāh* to Tayeb Saleh's *Season of Migration to the North* on the basis of their polyphonic narrative, this comparison is very forced. Saleh's indebtedness is mainly to Conrad's *Heart of Darkness;* Auster's inspiration begins with Poe. The motif for the first novella in the trilogy, "City of Glass," closely resembles that of Poe's "The Man of the Crowd," in which the narrator follows an anonymous man through the streets of a city until he becomes exhausted with the pointlessness of the task. The pseudonym of Auster's narrator in this story is William Wilson, the eponymous title of another story by Poe, notable for its pioneering use of the *Doppelgänger* motif.

To this basic structure, Auster adds a metafictional motif, which creates not merely a doubling, but a tripling, even quadrupling of characters. Thus, Quinn is a writer of mystery novels. He uses the pseudonym William Wilson. Max Work is Quinn's private-eye narrator in the novels. And in the story, Quinn meets another writer by the name of Paul Auster. All this is, in a sense, nothing more than an accurate representation of the existential situation of a writer. A writer, by the dictates of his craft, is parceled into these various parts: private self, persona as writer, narrator or main character, and subsidiary characters.

In *The New York Trilogy*, the three stories combine elements of a detective novel with narration that reflects both on man's existential condition and on the process of writing, which are seen as intimately connected. The detectives in these stories are invariably writers, as their method of detective work involves writing. They react to the attempt to make sense of apparently fathomless situations by writing. For instance, in "Ghosts" the detective, Blue, has been hired by an anonymous man, White, to watch another man named Black. Asked to turn in "reports" on his investigations by White, he finds that he has nothing to do, and plays with the notion of recording his subjective impressions. In Auster's work, the role of a detective is a cover for that of a writer, and his text is specifically concerned with a writer's existential self-consciousness.

Yumna al-Eid points out that unlike the stories in *The New York Trilogy*, *Rālf Rizq Allāh* does not imitate the form of a detective novel. Yet, like Auster's writer-detective, Blue, Rabi' Jaber's narrator is motivated to look for something elusive in his own nature by scrutinizing the fate of another man. According to Eid, the narrator delves into Ralf's suicide to find the meaning of life. In the suicide itself, all he sees is failure. Yet, at the same time, it is this failure that prompts him to write, and in typical modernist fashion, writing provides him with a sense of purpose.

Nevertheless, there are important differences in the two texts. *Rālf Rizq Allāh* is much closer to the classic existentialist texts, like Sartre's *Nausea*,[94] in which the focus is on the existentiality of life itself, while *The New York Trilogy* deals more with the existentiality of human relationships. At the end of the narrative in "Ghosts," for instance, we find out that White and Black are the same man, that Blue has been hired by Black to spy on himself, and the emphasis of the story shifts from Blue's efforts at detection to Black's manipulation. The existential situation of man, from Auster's point of view, is that we are all in the web of other people's devices and stratagems.

In *Rālf Rizq Allāh*, the mirror symbolizes the multiple aspects of the self, or the endlessness of the self. Sometimes the narrator looks in the mirror and sees himself, sometimes he sees other people, and sometimes he sees another world entirely. In this sense, the text is really much more similar to Jabra's *Al-Baḥth 'an Walīd Mas'ūd*, in which the absent Walīd reflected, and was reflected in, the other characters. The main difference between the two texts is the greater degree of narrative fragmentation in *Rālf Rizq Allāh*. In *Walīd Mas'ūd*, events are clearly expressed, realistic. They have a beginning and an ending. In *Rālf Rizq Allāh,* the events are cut off, incomplete.

In *Majma' al-Asrār* (Collection of secrets, 1994),[95] Elias Khoury experiments both with narrative fragmentation and with metafictional narrative. This time, however, the connecting links in the text are not spatial, but chronological. Most of the events in the novel take place in Beirut between 1946 and 1948. A few of the events take place during a period of eight days just shortly after the beginning of the civil war, in 1976. The period from 1948 and 1976 is left unaccounted for, yet there is continuity in the relationships between the primary characters during this period. This continuity contributes to the prevailing sense of the city as located in time, rather than space. The technique is the converse of that used by Abdelrahman Munif in his "Cities of Salt" series. Instead of fiction being used as a means of reinterpreting history, historical reality is used to underpin fiction. The narrative is full of dates and references to historical events, as well as intertextual references to the works of Kafka, Camus, and Gabriel García Márquez.

The nucleus of the novel concerns a triangle relationship between three characters—Ibrahim (Ibrahīm), Hanna (Ḥannā), and Norma. Ibrahim and Hanna have a friendship that dates from their youth. They are of the same age, and came from the same quarter of the city. Norma has a sexual relationship with them both. She is in love with Ibrahim, but he hesitates to marry her (influenced by his aunt, who does not consider Norma good enough for him because she is not of his social class). Norma's relationship with Hanna is based on similarities in their social class, but a love bond is lacking between them. The lack of stability inherent in this triangular relationship, as well as its continuity over a span of thirty years, is ultimately meant to represent the lack of stability in Lebanese society as a whole. Perhaps the biggest unanswered question of the novel is exactly how such an unstable relationship does, in fact, continue for thirty years. This suggestion on Khoury's part, and his silence about it within the narrative, can be seen as a parody of Lebanese history.

At the same time, the title, *Collection of Secrets,* refers most obviously to Khoury's manner of interrogating events as they unfold. The narrative is constantly peppered with questions that remind us of the narrative presence. As in *Rālf Rizq Allāh* and *The New York Trilogy*, the effect is parodic of the mystery genre. The narrator is in the position of a sleuth, piecing together the fragments of the characters' personal history, wondering aloud as to their meaning, and sometimes taking advantage of his position to ask philosophically rhetorical questions:

> Was Norma lying? Do we know the secret when we listen to the words? Do the words reveal or conceal? (84)

> How did Ibrahim die . . . did he suffocate or was he stricken with heart failure? (203)

> What is the secret of the friendship between Ibrahim . . . and Hanna . . . ? (125)

> Where is the story? And where is the truth? (151)

Another narrative technique that Khoury uses is to begin most chapters with the formulaic phrase: "The story began thus." This is another method of making the reader aware of the narrative presence and the process of telling a story. The reader shares the narrator's own viewpoint that the story can be begun at any point. Each chapter is like a repeated attempt on the part of the narrator to get back into the thread of his narration. Khoury expands on this metafictional technique in *The Kingdom of Strangers*, beginning each section of the book with the question, "What am I writing?" At first glance, this question is perturbing, giving the reader the feeling that the author is wandering aimlessly, unaware of what he is writing or the reason for which he is writing. But eventually, the question becomes provoking, as does the narrator's claim that "I'm not writing a story. I just let things come to me" (16).

Conclusion

The Experimental Arabic Novel and Postmodern Discourse

Scholars of western literatures tend to be assiduous in their worship of theory gods more impenetrable and certainly less applicable to our work than our local deities.

—Beth Holmgren

Khoury has forged (in the Joycean sense) a national and novel, unconventional, fundamentally post-modern literary career. This is in stark contrast to Mahfouz, whose Flaubertian dedication to letters has followed a more or less modernist trajectory. Khoury's ideas about literature and society are of a piece with the often bewilderingly fragmented realities of Lebanon in which, he says in one of his essays, the past is discredited, the future completely uncertain, the present unknowable. For him perhaps the most symptomatic and yet the finest strand of modern Arabic writing derives not from the stable and highly replicable forms native to the Arabic tradition (the *qaṣidah*) or imported from the West (the novel) but those works he calls formless—e.g. Tawfik al-Hakim's *Diaries of a Country Lawyer*, Taha Hussein's *Stream of Days*, Gibran's and Nuaimah's writings. . . . What Khoury finds in these formless works is precisely what Western theorists have called post-modern: the combinatorial amalgam of different elements, principally autobiography, story, fable, pastiche, and self-parody, the whole highlighted by an insistent and eerie nostalgia.

—Edward Said

In his introduction to Elias Khoury's *Little Mountain*, Edward Said argues essentially that Khoury is a postmodern novelist. He draws a distinction between the work of the early Arab experimental novelists in the 1960s and 1970s, represented by Naguib Mahfouz, and the practitioners of the so-called new novel, such as Khoury, that emerged in the wake of the Lebanese Civil War. Furthermore, he suggests that the experience of the civil conflict in Lebanon created an utterly fragmented social environment that, uniquely in the Arab world, fosters a postmodern outlook and mentality. Said implies that the reason Mahfouz deserves to be classified as a modernist is that his writing derives from "stable and replicable forms." Khoury's status as a postmodernist, according to Said, stems from his reliance on a more diverse, heterodox assortment of models. Said clearly privileges Khoury over Mahfouz and allies his writing with what he sees as an emerging postcolonial perspective, declaring that Khoury's "work embodies the very actuality of Lebanon's predicament, so unlike Egypt's majestic stability as delivered in Mahfouz's fiction." I suspect," he writes, "that Khoury's is actually a more typical version of reality, at least as far as the present course in the Middle East is concerned."[1]

There are, however, a number of objections that can be raised regarding the way in which Said constructs his typology. Foremost among these is the arbitrary and ambiguous way in which he associates specific literary qualities with either modernist or postmodern forms of the novel. Is "an insistent and eerie nostalgia," for instance, a postmodern quality? What about "comedy and irreverence," "lyricism," "informality," or "disorientation"? How is a career that is "national," "novel," or "unconventional" fundamentally a postmodern one? In what way can a "Flaubertian dedication to letters" be considered to constitute a "modernist trajectory"? Is the "amalgam of different elements," moreover, really the salient characteristic of the postmodern novel? Is this a sufficient criterion to make a distinction between modernism and postmodernism? When, for that matter, has the novel ever been a "stable and replicable" form? Hasn't one of the major characteristics of the novel throughout its history been its elasticity, its ability constantly to assimilate new forms? Isn't the distinction between the formal stability and heterogeneity of the novel simply a relative matter? And of what intrinsic significance is such a distinction?

When linked with so many disparate qualities, the very concept of postmodernism resembles what it purports to describe—a formless pastiche of literary notions. And the more formless the concept, the more easily it can be applied to any object. In addition, there are objections that can be raised concerning the way in which Said applies these criteria specifically to the Arabic novel. Arab and Western writers, for instance, are compared and contrasted in terms of their relatively "stately" or "carnivalesque" qualities. Thus, "Habibi's [Habiby's] world is Rabelais and even Joyce to [Mahfouz's] Balzac and Galsworthy,"[2] while Khoury is identified with a "postmodern" Joyce and Mahfouz with a "modernist" Flaubert. What Said is doing here is using the dichotomy between form and formlessness as a cutting tool to slice and splice the thread of literary history in whatever way he chooses. This does violence to both Arabic and Western literature, for which reasonable typologies are necessary to understand their respective histories of development. It also implicitly promotes the perception of modernist canonical narratives as somehow musty and stodgy, while the extent to which they were radically innovative is neglected.

What we are dealing with here is the convergence of two viewpoints—one political and the other aesthetic—both united in their vague bias toward "fragmentation." Said's brand of aesthetic postmodernism is biased towards the fragmentation of form, while his postcolonial perspective is allied with a multiculturalism that, from the Western perspective, possesses the allure of a fragmented social reality. By transposing this viewpoint, which professes hostility to stable elements in Western culture, onto the Arab world, Said is able to characterize the least stable regions of the latter as representing "a more typical version of reality."

Said's theoretical practice in this case seems to have been carried out on the implicit assumption that the relationship between form and content in the Arabic novel is the same as in the Western novel. This relationship, however, cannot be nearly so simply formulated. Complexity and fragmentation of form are not, in themselves, a sign of postmodernity. Stylistic devices can be borrowed or imitated. Instead of judging contemporary Arabic narrative by formal criteria alone, it is crucial also to inquire into the purpose to which formal innovation is employed and the literary precedent to which the writer is responding. A work such as Khoury's *Little Mountain* may represent a great leap in terms of formal complexity. On the other hand, it is fair to question whether, in looking at the "new" form of the novel being pioneered by Khoury, we are dealing not with postmodernism, but rather simply with modernism at a later stage and in a stylistically more complex form.

Said also allows this same perspective to distort his social and cultural picture of the Arab world. His contrast of Khoury and Mahfouz, for instance, is linked to a differentiation between their respective societies.

He characterizes Egypt as a country that is "fundamentally settled and integrated" and "has a stability and an identity that in this century have not disappeared," while he sees Lebanon as an "eccentric and resistant society."[3] He concludes that the "disintegrating effects" of the civil war have been so powerful "that readers of Lebanese writing need an occasional reminder that this after all is (or was) an Arabic country, whose language and heritage shared a great deal with writers like Mahfouz."[4] At the same time, however, Said's cross-referencing of Khoury with Mahfouz reinforces the very notion of a cultural continuum between Egypt and the Levant. When he states that "Khoury's work bids Mahfouz an inevitable and yet profoundly respectful farewell,"[5] he implies that Khoury has superseded Mahfouz within this cultural continuum.

At the root of this apparent contradiction is a lack of specificity with respect to the social or context of Arabic literature and its cultural context. In social and historical terms, Egypt and the Levant indeed present a strong contrast. Egypt has provided a more stable social environment for novelistic development than has Lebanon. In cultural terms, however, there is less of a difference. Both regions share a common literary heritage, a cultural permeability, which has always produced a reciprocal exchange of literary influences. Writers in the Levant are as steeped in Egyptian literature as they are in their own. By conflating these two contexts, Said creates the impression that, as the Arabic novel has shifted from modern to postmodern, the locus of innovation in the Arab world has shifted from Egypt to Lebanon. What is omitted from this comparison, however, is any mention of the new novel in Egypt, such as the recent work of Sonallah Ibrahim, which can be seen as equally significant as that emerging in the Levant, and differing, in its own way, as greatly from the style of Mahfouz. At the same time, Said fails to consider the extent to which the emergence of the new novel in Lebanon may be a phenomenon associated with the end of the civil war and a return to a measure of stability, rather than a reflection of endemic social fragmentation.

The positive aspect of Said's analysis is that, by focusing on the resurgence of experimentalism in Lebanon in the wake of the civil war, it forces a reconsideration of the novel in both Egypt and the Levant within the framework of a shared cultural context. Within this context, the work of Naguib Mahfouz is undeniably of key significance, since it represents the apogee of the imported and domesticated realist tradition, as well as the starting point of experimentalism in the Arabic novel. Fakhri Salih recognizes Mahfouz as having a dual importance in modern Arabic literature, since he reacted against his own work and superseded his own style:

> If [the new generation] in Egypt superseded the Mahfouzian form represented in the Trilogy, in the work that followed it Naguib Mahfouz himself superseded the realist narrative structure that had become his chief trademark.[6]

Nevertheless, there are lingering aspects of realism in Mahfouz's later work. The "new generation" in Egypt referred to by Salih, including writers such as Sonallah Ibrahim, Gamal al-Ghitani, and Edwar al-Kharrat, were clearly reacting in a more radical way to realism than Mahfouz was, and to Mahfouz's style as well. The present practitioners of the new novel are both continuing and extending this type of experimentation. Said's introduction not only raises the question of what relationship the new novel in Lebanon bears to its counterpart in Egypt, but also of the position of both in relation to modernism and postmodernism, as these words are used in Western literary theory and criticism.

To properly evaluate this, however, we also need to develop a more specific set of characteristics that we can identify with postmodernism. Certainly, both the terms "modernism" and "postmodernism" have for the most part been identified with Western literature, and postmodernism has specifically been associated with Western literature that represents both a continuation of, and a reaction to, certain specific features of modernism. In her book *A Poetics of Postmodernism*, Linda Hutcheon severely delimits literary postmodernism to narrative, particularly the novel genre. She confines it more specifically to what she calls "historiographic metafiction," by which she refers to novels that incorporate a "theoretical self-awareness of both fiction and history as human constructs." In postmodernism, this self-awareness, she maintains, "is made the ground for its rethinking and reworking of the forms and contents of the past." According to this definition, postmodernism directs itself with subversive intent toward modernist conventions, which are seen as emblematic of the inherited discourse and ideological structures of liberal humanism.

If the expression of artistic self-consciousness in Western modernism was allied with the expression of individual self-consciousness, postmodernism has been seen primarily as a reaction against this. "What, precisely, is being challenged by post-modernism?" Linda Hutcheon asks rhetorically in *A Poetics of Postmodernism*. More than anything, it turns out, it is "liberal humanist discourse and its assumption that subjectivity is produced by or based in somehow eternal values . . . the whole, integrated ideal of subjectivity."[7] As an example, she turns to E. L. Doctorow's *The Book of Daniel*, in which "the narrator comes to see his subjectivity not in terms of any humanist notion of uniqueness and individuality, but as the result of processes which appear to be outside him [politics]."[8] Hutcheon's definition of postmodernism as a critique of liberal humanism also implicitly involves a critique of Western power vis-à-vis the Third World. This reflects a tendency on the part of Western and particularly Anglo-American literary critics in recent years to discuss contemporary literature in developing nations from a prevailing viewpoint that privileges postmodernism over modernism and allies it with postcolonial theory.

In their book, *Colonial Discourse and Post-Colonial Theory*, Patrick Williams and Laura Chrisman go further in this direction. They define postmodernism in postcolonial terms—as "European culture's awareness that it is no longer the unquestioned and dominant centre of the world."[9] The very emphasis on "European culture's awareness" in this definition, however, betrays its Eurocentric orientation. Just as Chrisman and Williams's definition of postmodernism could not possibly apply to areas outside of the European center, Hutcheon's definition of postmodernism could not possibly apply to a culture that was not founded on liberal humanist principles. The question, then, is at what point can we begin to speak of postmodernism in Arabic literature, and what would be the characteristics of Arabic postmodernism?

For one thing, it is reasonable to theorize that we could not expect to see an emerging Arabic postmodernism until the modernist impulse had reached some degree of maturity. In an article entitled "Is Post-modernism Possible Outside the 'West'?" Gregory Jusdanis reflects this viewpoint, suggesting that literature in many areas of the developing world has been conservative in nature, due to the lack of the condition of art as an autonomous institution requisite for the appearance of an avant-garde. Jusdanis elaborates on this argument in his book, *Belated Modernity and Aesthetic Culture*, theorizing that "belated" societies exhibit an uneasy fit between traditional and modern constructs.[10] He challenges the idea that postmodernism can arise under cultural conditions in which modernism has not yet become legitimized. "Central to the appearance of post-modernism," he states, "is the prior existence of high modernism, not only in art and literature itself, but in its institutions.[11] Jusdanis notes that postmodernism is seen either as a continuation of modernism's radical sensibility or as an assault on its aestheticism, and argues that it would be meaningless for a movement to emerge in order to negate what did not exist or is not complete.

Jusdanis's point is to criticize the Eurocentric tendency to extrapolate the European historical experience onto non-Western countries and, in particular, the belief that the history of the West can be repeated and that non-Western countries are fated to pass through comparable stages of development.[12] His choice of the term "belated society" seems unfortunate, however, since it implies the use of Western cultural development as a yardstick for the non-Western world. In any case, it cannot be denied that Jusdanis's model is highly suggestive of the Arab world today. Indeed, the sheer politicization of life in the Arab world has presented even further obstacles to modernist development by focusing the attention of writers on explicitly political issues, and this has tended to work against the development of a humanistic or universal sensibility. This has been nowhere more true than in the Levant, where the dominance of political discourse has continued longer than in many other parts of the Arab world due to the lingering conflict in the region. As Roger Allen notes in *The Arabic Novel*, Arab novelists for the past fifty years have been preoccupied with political events and social transformation, attempting to fill a role as reflector and even advocate of political and social change. "It is hardly surprising," Allen writes, "that the majority of Arabic novelists chose to engage these social and political realities in the most obviously available fictional mode, that of realism."[13]

Prairies of Fever, by Ibrahim Nasrallah, is another example of an Arabic novel which, having been translated into English, has been presented to readers as a postmodern work. In her introduction to the book, Fedwa Malti-Douglas claims that Nasrallah is among "the growing ranks of post-modern Arabic authors." In attempting to define the postmodern impulse in Arabic fiction, Malti-Douglas refers to its exploitation of "metafiction, or self-conscious narrative." She adds that this "involves a heightened awareness of the narrative process, involving (among other techniques) the intrusions of a self-conscious narrator or making the act of writing (or its absence) the center of the text itself."[14] Anyone familiar with the writings of Proust, Gide, or even Henry James, however, will recognize self-conscious narration of this type as a technique pioneered by these canonical modernists. A review of the same book in *World Literature Today* refers to the lack of unified character, coherent plot, and temporal frame of reference in Nasrallah's novel, and comments that this "breaks with several of the narrative conventions of formal realism."[15] Such a comment would seem to place Nasrallah's work in the category of modernism. Even the jacket cover of the book, in contradiction to Malti-Douglas's own introduction, refers to it as a "modernist" novel. Clearly, if nothing else, there is a great deal of confusion among Anglo-American critics, theorists, and marketers of literature regarding the application of the terms "modernist" and "postmodern" to the Arabic novel.

Malti-Douglas uses three criteria to place Nasrallah's text within the sphere of postmodernism. First of all, she describes the novel's "postmodern sensibility" as one "marked by a sense of rupture, of loss, or of absolute unredeemable exile."[16] Secondly, she characterizes the environment of Nasrallah's narrative as "conducive to the creation of ambiguities, to the elimination of individuality," and comments that his vision "questions the identity, even the existence, of the individual as social reality and conscious subject."[17] These observations, however, are both hyperbolic and contradictory. Certainly, the protagonist's feeling of loss reflects a condition of alienation, and this state of awareness marks him off from the rest of society. Yet as in innumerable Western modernist texts, such an alienated condition can ultimately be seen as an affirmation of individuality amid a distorted and demeaning social reality rather than a negation of it. At the same time, a text that would aim to express such an absolute negation of individuality would seem to have little in common with one that seeks to create the ambiguity that Malti-Douglas identifies as characteristic of Nasrallah's writing.

A similar point can be made with respect to Samira Aghacy's analysis of Rashid al-Da'if's *Fusḥah Mustahdafah Bayna al-Nu'ās wa al-Nawm*. Aghacy, a professor of English at the Lebanese American University in Beirut, writing in the *Journal of Arabic Literature*, discusses what she refers to as the author's "undermining of the reality, coherence, and unity of the individual."

> The narrator swears he is telling the truth, but at the same time he tells at least three different stories of how he died. . . . The narrative here dispels the illusion of reality and uncovers its own artificial nature, sliding into metafiction. In this context, the narrator's unreliability is highlighted and the view of the individual as unified and coherent entity is challenged, producing a diminished image of a man marginalized and simplified by the war.[18]

Aghacy is certainly correct in characterizing the narrator in Dai'if's novel as unreliable, but his unreliability is not a function of his feelings of guilt alone, but stems from an awareness of both his guilt and innocence. The text reflects the narrator's conflict and compromised position. What Da'if achieves is to lay bare the psychological and existential conflict of the war and the powerless position of the individual caught between complicity and victimization, confession and protest. As in the case of Ibrahim Nasrallah's *Prairies of Fever*, however, this does not necessarily affect the status of the narrator as "a unified and coherent entity." One could argue that, by this means, the subjectivity of the narrator is intensified, and that Da'if's narrative method provides a way of negotiating, recouping, or salvaging some integrity from the nightmare of the war.

Fakhri Salih takes a far different approach, criticizing the text for the lack of differentiation in its narrative voices. He notes that

> It's not possible for the characters to multiply while retaining a single voice, except in a novel with a narcissistic hero who views the world only from his point of view, and sees his personality mirrored in the world.[19]

In other words, the very qualities in *Prairies of Fever* that appear to Malti-Douglas to erase or call into question the nature of individuality are seen by Salih as reflective of an almost unhealthy obsession with subjectivity.

Salih also effectively addresses Malti-Douglas's third assertion, that Nasrallah's novel partakes in a particular trend of "Arabic post-modernism" characterized by "the process of writing through (or rewriting) the distinctive discourse of classical Arabic literature, effectively redefining that literature and the traditional culture which nurtured it."[20] Using the word "hybrid" to describe Nasrallah's text as one constructed of different types of narrative forms—that is, by means of pastiche—he connects the technique itself not with classical Arabic literature, but rather with the literary work of Borges[21] and the critical work of Barthes and Kristeva. He further traces the technique back to its earliest practitioners, who included poets such as Rimbaud, Mallarmé, and Lautréamont. At a loss to identify Arabic writers who represent a similar precedent, he remarks:

> This question does not produce a firm answer, especially since the small amount of experimentation in this field does not offer a basis for comparison with this type of writing, despite some experimentation that benefited from the grafting of the classical Arabic tradition (the writings of Emile Habiby and Gamal al-Ghiṭani). These, however, are scattered texts that do not resemble the experimentation with which we are faced.[22]

Salih's clear implication is that while Habiby and Ghitani experimented with a type of pastiche using sources from the classical Arabic literary tradition, Nasrallah belongs to a different generation, whose inspiration comes from a different source. Here it becomes clear on what shaky ground Said stands when, in his introduction to *Little Mountain*, he groups Elias Khoury with Ghassan Kanafani and Emile Habiby, and contrasts their work with that of Mahfouz on the slender basis of the "disintegrating" or "unpredictable" quality of their prose. Not only are these descriptive terms virtually meaningless, but they simply do not stand up to an analysis of these authors' works. Kanafani, for instance, belonged to a distinctly earlier literary generation than Habiby, and his writing is generally as meticulously constructed as that of Mahfouz.

Emile Habiby belongs to the generation that most successfully challenged Western narrative influence by attempting to forge a distinctly Arabic novel. We have seen that he, as well as Abdelrahman Munif and Salim Barakat, sought to reconcile artistic innovation and political engagement by engaging in a dialogue with Arabic history, culture, and literary tradition. These authors looked essentially to the past in order to recover a feeling of stability, sanity, and meaning from the Arab historical, cultural, and political predicament. Habiby experimented with pastiche within this context. His literary materials have a wide and diverse provenance, but from these materials Habiby fashions an aesthetic unity, which is far removed from the fragmented reality that Khoury's use of pastiche is intended to convey.

With the consideration of the work of Elias Khoury, we thus reach another distinct point in the history of narrative experimentation in the Arabic novel. There is no doubt that the so-called new novel that has emerged particularly in Lebanon in the wake of the civil war, of which Khoury is representative, is distinct from the postrealist novel of Mahfouz. The novelists who emerged from the Lebanese Civil War are clearly more cosmopolitan and less culturally specific or pan-Arab in their orientation and agenda than their predecessors were.

To a great extent, however, this simply reflects Lebanon's location at the eastern end of the Mediterranean and, in particular, the continuity of French cultural influence. A recent article in *Magazine littéraire* on contemporary Lebanese novelists writing in Arabic suggests by its title, "L'émergence du moi,"[23] that the thrust of recent developments in the contemporary Lebanese novel reflects a return to, or rediscovery of, the French tradition of the self-conscious novel. The supplement devotes a great deal of attention to the work of Lebanese francophone writers such as Amin Maalouf, Georges Schéhadé, Alexandre Najjar, Andrée Chedid, and Rashid Boujadra, implicitly linking their work to that of writers living and working in Lebanon, who write in Arabic rather than in French.

Clearly, the point of view expressed by the supplement reflects the vested interest on the part of the French cultural establishment in promoting the view of French and Lebanese literature as part of a unified cultural tradition. There is, however, substantial foundation for such a perspective. As an example, Hassan Daoud sees the influence of the French *nouveau roman* on the Lebanese novel today as a matter of French cultural influence in Lebanon in a general sense. This clearly affects some writers more than others, depending on the depth of their francophone backgrounds. Daoud traces the source of reigning French literary influence on the contemporary Lebanese novel farther back, to the self-conscious novel of Proust and Gide. More importantly, he identifies the main artistic problem in the Lebanese novel today as one of a choice between this self-absorbed literary tradition and a more socially oriented approach to the novel.[24]

The work of Khoury and other contemporary Lebanese writers has been distinguished further from that of their predecessors by their investment in a vocabulary of skepticism. Fakhri Salih states that the skeptical worldview reflected by this use of language is similar to, though not necessarily related to or derived from, the French *nouveau roman.*

However, he sees it as particularly indebted to the positivist philosophy that is the basis of the novels of Alain Robbe-Grillet, the best known of the practitioners of the *nouveau roman* in the Arab world.[25] Salih further describes this worldview as one of uncertainty *(al-lāyaqīnīyah)* and, in this context, he emphasizes the cultural continuum between Egypt and the Levant, citing novelists from both regions as having this same worldview in common:

> Various texts by Edwar al-Kharrat, Haydar Haydar (Ḥaydar Ḥaydar), Abd al-Hakim Qasim ('Abd al-Ḥakīm Qāsim), Elias Khoury, Salim Barakat, Ibrahim Abd al-Majid (Ibrāhīm 'Abd al-Majīd), Mu'nis al-Razzaz, and Emile Ḥabiby give the forceful impression of a world that is no longer capable of being comprehended and whose essence cannot be grasped.[26]

This change in worldview parallels that which occurred during the transition from modernism to postmodernism in the West, in which an entire tradition of rebellion came to be seen as too restrained and ultimately futile. In an article comparing George Orwell's *Nineteen Eighty-Four* and Herbert Marcuse's *One Dimensional Man* in terms of their political theories of pessimism, Alfred Meyer has made the following observation:

> Both Orwell and Marcuse write in praise of the heretic who will not allow himself to be brainwashed. But Orwell's heretic is a man whose anchor of sanity is knowledge of the past, whereas Marcuse's heretic is the person who dreams of a different future; and while Orwell wants us to return to good old plain English, Marcuse advocates a philosophy and vocabulary of negativism, arguing that it is necessary to break through the boundaries of the established vocabulary. One must call things by their wrong names. "Critical analysis must dissociate itself from that which it strives to comprehend. . . . " This philosophy requires using language in a way which would make Orwell shudder with disgust.[27]

Orwell and Marcuse are united in their pessimism, as well as in the importance they place on gestures of rebellion. Orwell's heretic, whose "anchor of sanity is knowledge of the past," is clearly a modernist by instinct, however, while Marcuse's heretic, who "advocates a philosophy and vocabulary of negativism," adopts a postmodern strategy. This, in itself, however, does not suffice to put the practitioners of the new novel in the Levant in the category of postmodernists. As Ibrahim Nasrallah has commented:

> The modernist novel has now become the classical novel of our time. Yet it is still not outdated. People are still writing modernist novels. This shows the depth of modernism, and particularly the strength of modernist values. To say that a work is skeptical is not enough to place it outside the sphere of modernism. There is no such thing as absolute skepticism. There are no absolutes. Even Kafka is not necessarily an absolute skeptic. The humanism that I feel is so important is present in the works of the classical modernists (Joyce, Proust, Faulkner, Woolf), in the work of present-day modernists (Márquez, Kundera, Rushdie), and in the work of the great Arabic novelists (Mahfouz, Habiby, Kanafani).[28]

In this context, the comparison with Latin America is very instructive. In the introduction to a special issue of *boundary 2* entitled *The Postmodernism Debate in Latin America,* John Beverly and José Oviedo note that "postmodern" seems a particularly inappropriate term for nation-states and social formations that are usually thought of as not yet having gone through the stage of modernity. They argue that the term may be appropriate, however, if we understand that the engagement with postmodernism in Latin America does not take place around the theme of the end of modernity that is so prominent in its Anglo-European manifestations. The nature of this engagement, Beverly and Oviedo argue, has to do, above all, with its relation to the crisis of the project of the Latin American Left in the wake of its defeat and/or demobilization in the period that extends from 1973 to the present. They note that

> The Cuban Revolution in 1959 inaugurated a new historical dynamic in Latin America—the possibility of an "alternative," non-capitalist Latin American modernity—which, however, it was unable to sustain. . . . A number of interrelated developments indicate the containment and eventual exhaustion of this dynamic. These include the failure, at the end of the 1960s, of both the armed struggle strategy . . . and . . . the eventual problematization of Cuba itself as a model for an achieved socialist society.[29]

These developments, they conclude, led to a pervasive climate of "disenchantment" and a demand for a new "political realism." Unquestionably, as in Latin America, the mood in the contemporary Arab world is dominated by disillusionment in the face of a similar failure of revolutionary strategies and rhetoric to provide a sustainable sociopolitical alternative. This disillusionment has marked a decisive change in literature.

In formal terms, Fakhri Salih sees the lack of central focus, or the reliance on *qawl* (discourse) over *ḥikāyah* (storytelling) as the crucial distinction between the modernist Arabic novel of the '60s and the Arabic new novel. Yumna al-Eid seems to be making the same distinction in discussing what she refers to as the "modern," rather than the "new," novel. This modern novel, according to Eid, is characterized by the play of composition, founded on *discours*, in contrast to the structure of storytelling.[30] While Mahfouz was highly innovative in his later works, Eid points out that this innovation is still always contained within a clearly discernible structure. Works such as Mahfouz's *Miramar* or Ghassan Kanafani's *All That's Left to You*, no matter how radically innovative, retain a formal cohesiveness. They always hold to the rule of story or plot. This cannot generally be said of the works of the so-called new novelists, whether in Egypt or the Levant.

A greater looseness of form, as well as abandonment of many of the rules of writing and composition distinguishes Elias Khoury's major works. The characteristics and preoccupations of these works include fragmented chronology, as well as the freeing of narrative from the hegemony of a hero and narrative introversion that focuses the reader's attention on the act of narration. In several of these works, Khoury plays with building the novel on the basis of the short story and experiments with the insertion of the narrator into the text as a character. He also experiments with assigning other characters the role of narrators. These techniques are all associated with what Malcolm Bradbury calls the "introverted novel," exemplified in Western modernism, and concerned with the intricacies of its own form as well as with dramatizing the means by which narration itself is achieved.

Khoury's technique in building the novel on the basis of a series of interwoven and interconnecting short stories is discussed in an article on *Little Mountain* by Fakhri Salih. Salih poses the question as to what extent this work can be classified as a novel, rather than a collection of short stories. His conclusion—that it is a novel built on the short story form—is less significant than his observation that Khoury uses this technique to undermine the old "classical," or realist model of the novel:

> *Little Mountain* is a novel integrated by means of technique, rather than thematic purpose . . . This "sequential" arrangement constitutes a substantive technique in *Little Mountain* . . . [and] we find this technique . . . [to be for the purposes of] the disintegration of the character of the hero and the destruction of the classical structure of the novel.[31]

Yumna al-Eid focuses particularly on Khoury's experimentalism in terms of his undermining of the position of the hero, main character, or protagonist in narrative. She refers to his attempt to free the other characters in a narrative from the supremacy or hegemony of the hero, as well as the creation of ambiguity in terms of the relationship between the hero and the author or narrator in his works.[32] The term *al-lāmawqi'*, used by Eid in this context, refers to a lack of situatedness in narrative. She explains that in most narratives there are two basic sites—the story and the act of narration itself. The hero is associated with the site of the story, while the narrator is associated with the act of narration. Khoury attempts to break up and disrupt this basic pattern. Thus, in *Little Mountain*, there is no longer a fixed relationship between the narrator and narration or between the characters and the story, because the characters share the act of narration with the narrator, and the narrator takes part as a character in the action along with the characters. Via this approach, Khoury is able to build the novel on the basis of different narrative voices and perspectives, as well as on the interconnection of these voices and perspectives in terms of their situatedness in different times, locations, and situations.

According to Eid, the modern Arabic novel is overwhelmingly based on either a bias, partiality, or some other type of attitude *(inḥiyāz)* on the part of the narrator toward the hero, either direct or implied. In the romantic novel, exemplified by the works of Kahlil Gibran or *Zainab* (1989; *Zaynab*, 1914),[33] by Mohammed Hussein Haikal (Muḥammad Ḥusayn Haykal), there is a direct partiality. In the realist works of Mahfouz, such as his Trilogy, there is an implied attitude. In *Palace Walk* (1990; *Bayna al-Qasrayn*, 1956),[34] for instance, there is a negative or critical attitude toward the main character projected by the narrative. Even in a work such as Abdelrahman Munif's *Cities of Salt*, where there is no main character in terms of a single personality, the village or city functions as a main character whose attitudes the narrative represents. In the case of *al-lāmawqi'*, however, the narrator no longer knows everything about the hero or other characters. Khoury's attempt to free the narrative from the domination of the narrator reaches the point where the narrator is reduced to a spectator. The relationship between the narrator and main characters becomes ambiguous; their viewpoints are neither identical, nor strictly separate. Nor is the viewpoint of the narrator toward the main characters either sympathetic or unsympathetic.

This attempt to free the narrator from any position regarding the characters, or to free the characters from any connection with a single narrative viewpoint is, of course, a narrative technique that has been associated with the earliest forms of Western modernism. In his concept of "polyphony," for instance, Mikhail Bakhtin expressed his concern with the notion of granting the voices of the main characters in a novel as much authority as the narrator's voice, and even of the narrator engaging in active dialogue with the characters. He claimed that "the chief characteristic of Dostoevsky's novels [is] a plurality of independent and unmerged voices and consciousnesses."[35] Simon Dentith observes that this concern on the part of Bakhtin is further reflected in the work of later canonical modernists such as Joyce, Brecht, and Gide. Dentith comments that this "addresses the fundamental question of narrative authority, the view that realist novels are made up of a hierarchy of discourse, with the narrator's discourse at the top speaking the language of unproblematic truth."[36]

Khoury's primary innovation is that, instead of simply reporting the same event from different viewpoints, he takes a central event as a point of departure only. While Mahfouz and Kanafani report the same event from different viewpoints, for Khoury the idea is not to tell a story by means of different witnesses, but to get away from any central event altogether. There is no main problem by which the novel can be summarized. It might even be said that Khoury is trying very hard *not* to tell a story, or that whatever story he tells escapes from beyond his control, or from beyond his attempt to contain the storytelling aspect of his narration. Khoury's technique can also be contrasted with that of Munif. In *Variations on Night and Day*, when Munif reports a given event from different perspectives or viewpoints, his purpose is to give the reader a more complete view of an event. It represents, in fact, a deeper attempt to be objective than what could be offered via the conventions of realism. Khoury is attempting to do almost the opposite—to question, put in doubt, or even erase such objectivity.

Moreover, Khoury's very purpose in fragmenting the text can be seen as lending a unifying element to his work. In her introduction to Gertrude Stein's *Three Lives*, Ann Charters refers to the idea at the root of Stein's experimentation by quoting Stein's explanation of it: "Cézanne conceived the idea that in composition one thing was as important as any other thing. Each part is as important as the whole, and that impressed me enormously. . . . I was obsessed by this idea of composition."[37] In Khoury's work there is no single idea at the root of his composition, but a number of ideas or techniques. Yet the multiplicity of techniques used to convey fragmented experience could be seen, in itself, to be an organizing technique.

In sum, *Little Mountain* is a novel in which the urge to express the experience of war has sparked a wholesale turn toward narrative experimentalism. None of Khoury's narrative techniques are new; they can all be found in the canonical works of Western modernism. What sets Khoury apart from Western modernism and gives his work a postmodern feel is simply his wholesale investment in so many of these narrative techniques in a single text. This conclusion is admittedly not far removed from that of Edward Said. Said based his argument in his introduction to *Little Mountain* on the relative degree of fragmentation evinced by the text. And it is true that the fragmentation of narrative is so total that it is both bewildering and impressive. Moreover, it is a fact that the Arabic novel already went through a modernist phase with the later work of Mahfouz and his contemporaries. It is also true that Mahfouz's experimentalism is staid compared to Khoury's. It would therefore seem reasonable to conclude that the "new" Arabic novel, represented by Khoury and other novelists writing today, is postmodern.

But how complete was the modernism forged by Mahfouz? Mahfouz employed certain narrative devices found in Faulkner—most prominently polyphony. But did that constitute a complete shift to modernism? For a Westerner to read the realist Mahfouz in translation, the effect is something like reading Balzac. But for the same individual to read the modernist Mahfouz does not really produce the effect of reading Faulkner. It is more like reading a Balzac *influenced* by Faulkner. Thus, modernist experimentalism in the Arabic novel began without the wholesale revolution in form and language that was fundamental to the development of literary modernism in the West.

Modernism in Arabic literature began from a radicalized political viewpoint and a conservative approach to experimentation with language. Modernism in the West, on the other hand, presented a radical experimentation with language, but with a much more conservative political agenda. At the point at which the latter caught up with the former, Western literature made the transition to postmodernism. And presumably, at the point that Arabic literature begins to revolutionize language, it will make a similar transition. For now, the effect that a Westerner tends to experience in reading contemporary Arabic novels is of reading texts that have a postmodern form, yet there is something unreal, artificial, about this impression.

Here the comparison with Latin American literature is once again of relevance. In his book *Journeys through the Labyrinth: Latin American Fiction in the Twentieth Century,* Gerald Martin makes some points concerning the career of Jorge Luis Borges that are very pertinent to the study of contemporary Arabic literature. Martin writes, "The extension of this sense, stronger in Borges than almost any other writer (it is a motivating force) is that just as all human beings are no one (Shakespeare being the paradigm), so Latin America is nowhere, a place cursed to be empty of history, culture, and even people, mere shadows or echoes of other places and other times; or if there is a Latin America, it is just a hybrid chaos of imperfect copies, incoherent fragments, second-rate gestures."[38]

Martin continues, still referring to Borges: "Far from being a straightforward, all-encompassing view of reality, then, this is the ideological construction of a middle-class member of a Third World community who is ashamed of his background, humiliated by his nation—and still more his continental culture—and who has reacted against this existential predicament by emphasizing the futility and emptiness of all human existence in a world without God or meaning."[39] This comes very close to describing the impression that much of Elias Khoury's work makes on many Western readers, and yet most Arab readers who comment on Khoury express the impression that he is the best Arab novelist writing today. So there are really two stories that one can tell about Elias Khoury. In one story, Khoury is little more than a Western imitator, in the other he is a brilliant and distinctly Arab innovator.

It is similar with Borges. Borges is accused of a kind of cosmopolitan inauthenticity. His is a splendid case of the colonized writer writing back with a complete mastery of the colonizer's experience. He is so cosmopolitan in his writing that his Argentinian-ness disappears. In his essay "The Argentine Writer and Tradition," he defends this tendency, citing Gibbon's observation in *The Decline and Fall of the Roman Empire* that "in the Arabian book *par excellence,* in the Koran, there are no camels; I believe," he writes, "that if there were any doubt as to the authenticity of the Koran, this absence of camels would be sufficient to prove it is an Arabic work. . . Mohammad, as an Arab, had no reason to know that camels were especially Arabian . . . he had no need to emphasize them; on the other hand, the first thing a falsifier, a tourist, an Arab nationalist, would do is to have a surfeit of camels, caravans of camels on every page."[40]

Thus, the fact that Borges is not in search of his Argentinian identity could be taken as proof of his Argentinian-ness. And the same could be said of Khoury with respect to his identity as an Arabic writer. Westerners may be looking for something in Khoury that is not there, whereas the very lack of those elements that they expect is what gives his work inauthenticity in the eyes of native Arab readers and critics. After reading *Little Mountain,* they feel that they have read something new, something that hasn't been attempted before in Arabic literature.

Clearly, the Middle East is not untouched by contemporary literary trends. Elias Khoury travels to England the United States, he lectures abroad, and he writes under the conscious influence of Western postmodern literature and criticism. In this context, Khoury's experimentalism in *Little Mountain* can legitimately be seen to be a reaction to modernist, rather than realist, conventions. His use of so many of the narrative techniques of Western modernism into one work could be seen as an attempt to finally be done with them, or to get beyond them.

Literary criticism in the Arab world is still overwhelmingly modernist in orientation, but postmodern criticism is making some inroads, particularly in academic circles. It is important, in this context, to understand that literary criticism in the Arab world differs from that in the West. The majority of Arab critics work in the field of journalism, and write in less theoretical terms for audiences in their own societies. The relatively small minority of Arab critics that has adopted the vocabulary of postmodernism, on the other hand, tends to be made up of members of an academic establishment writing primarily for a Western audience in European and American journals. Samira Aghacy's discussion of Rashid al-Da'if's *Fusḥah Mustahdafah Bayna al-Nu 'ās wa al-Nawm,* cited previously, is an example of the relatively rare discourse of postmodernism used by an Arab critic living and working in the Arab world. It is to be noted, however, that Aghacy teaches at an English-language institution and that her article was published in an English-language journal.

More representative of Arab critical opinion is the Syrian Faysal Darraj (Fayṣal Darrāj). Darraj emphasizes the particularity of both Arab and European literary development. In an article entitled "Mā Ba'da al-Ḥadāthah fī 'Ālam bilā Ḥadāthah" (Postmodernism in a world without modernism), he comments that "Postmodernism is a European phenomenon which is not separated, and cannot be separated, from the historical context in which it is situated, and this is something that non-Europeans do not have the capacity to repeat."[41] Specifically, he notes that while prevailing Arabic literary and cultural discourse focuses on modernism, the reality in which it lives actually resembles premodernity. He argues that, as a result, while one can define modernism in the Western sense as the awareness of living in a modern era, modernism in a non-Western sense can be defined, conversely, as the awareness of *not* living in a modern era.

Focusing on the role of artists and intellectuals in the Arab world, Darraj asserts that modernism springs from the life of the society, rather than from intellectual thought or ideas. Modernism, he concludes, must have its roots in a preexisting modernity. It therefore represents reality, and is not an exercise in wish fulfillment. Arab intellectuals may talk about modernism, but this does not represent a reality that they are living and experiencing. Like Rashid al-Da'if and Elias Khoury, Darraj focuses on the necessity of writers creating a language that is modern and reflects the reality of modern life. Significantly, he compares this goal with that of Baudelaire, suggesting that the question of reflecting present reality in literature, so crucial for Arab writers, is the same as that which preoccupied the earliest modernists in the West:

> The modern artist, as Baudelaire saw him, was one who was immersed in the daily life of modern society; the artist became modern due to his contact with the mass of modern humanity rushing and flowing through the wide streets.[42]

Darraj notes that prevailing Arabic literary and cultural discourse focuses on modernism. At the same time, he characterizes the reality within which this prevailing discourse exists as actually resembling pre-modernity. Following Darraj's logic, if we can define Western modernism in terms of the sense of living in a modern era, Arabic modernism might be defined as the awareness of *not* living in a modern era. Arabic postmodernism, then, would presumably reflect the very consciousness of modernity achieved that we find in Western literary modernism.

Darraj is typical of those Arab intellectuals whose viewpoint has undergone a change to a post-Marxist perspective, reflecting the prevailing disillusionment with ideology while still utilizing Marxism for the purpose of social critique. From this perspective, he expresses strong opposition to postmodernism, viewing it as yet another attempt to rob the Arab world of its history. According to Darraj, the idea of an "end of history" is one that fails to grant history to others; it is a purely Western viewpoint. He sees both modernism and postmodernism as having their basis in the European cultural market.

This viewpoint echoes that of Beverly and Oviedo, who cite Octavio Paz to the effect that "Postmodernism is yet another imported *grand récit* . . . that does not fit Latin America," and hence is "a new form of cultural imperialism."[43] This criticism applies equally to postmodern critics such as Said and Malti-Douglas who include practitioners of the "new" Arabic novel within the rubric of postmodernism. In effect, Darraj is arguing that they are transplanting a Western typology that has been applied to a body of literature with a long history of modernist antecedents onto a part of the Arab world that is largely without such antecedents. Darraj is essentially saying that Khoury and other contemporary novelists in the Arab world can be distinguished from postmodern writers in the West in that they are less concerned with the end of modernity than with its implementation or consolidation.

José Joaquín Brunner's article, "Notes on Modernity and Postmodernity in Latin American Culture," supports such a conclusion, while extending the comparison between the Arab world and Latin America. Brunner argues in the article that the postmodern features of political culture in Latin America are allied less with a critique of modernity than with a particular regional form of modernity. He states that the malaise in Latin American culture does not, and could not, spring from the exhaustion of modernity. On the contrary, it arises from exasperation with modernity.

> Condemned to live in a world where all the images of modernity come to us from the outside and become obsolete before we are able to materialize them, we find ourselves trapped in a world where not all solid things, but rather all symbols, melt into air. The sensation of the permanent crisis of everything hides the fact that we live and think in the middle of a modernity in the process of construction, whose dynamic is increasing the heterogeneities of our very perceptions, knowledge, and information.[44]

In this context, Martin makes an observation about Borges that situates him—at least from Borges's own perspective—both at the apex of modernist development and at the brink of postmodernism. "Although Borges," he writes, "sees all writers as part of the same process, all different fragments of the same one face, and that if pressed he will always cautiously include himself in this, it is also possible to infer that he is, as it were, the last of those great writers and great voices, the summit and supreme seer, the end of literature, after which, even if the same process continues, it will be downhill from that focal point of vision. There is there a special edge to John Updike's statement is that Borges is a man for whom literature has 'no future.'" He then adds, almost parenthetically, "We are of course talking about high culture."[45]

The problem inherent in the relationship between high culture and its surrounding milieu has been of crucial importance since the beginning of modernist literary expression in the West. But the problem in the postcolonial world today is more urgent. We are living in the information age. The Internet is ready to replace books, magazines, teachers, lecture halls, even academic institutions. The influence of English as the language of the World Wide Web has enormously increased its relative power over other languages. The incentive for the top writers to write in Arabic today is greatly diminished. Ultimately, we may come to the point where literature is hardly classifiable in cultural terms, but simply melds into a body of global literature. There will still be questions to ask about writers, about their historical and cultural experience, as well as cross-cultural comparisons to be made, but terms such as "modernism" and "postmodernism" may become obsolete for descriptive purposes.

If we wish to bridge the gap between literary perspectives in the Arab world and the West, we need to look at literature in a way that represents the non-Western viewpoint with the least distortion. Since it is inappropriate to respond to the bias of orientalism by creating another bias, what is needed is to convey something of the nature of non-Western literature without reproducing the dichotomy of its expression as the Other.

Aijaz Ahmad, in his critique of Fredric Jameson's article "The Rhetoric of Otherness and the 'National Allegory'" used Marxist principles to argue against the binary opposition between a First and a Third World, asserting that "we live not in three worlds but one."[46] Similarly, Faysal Darraj refers to Frantz Fanon's *The Wretched of the Earth*[47] in concluding that political awareness dictates a theory of multiple modernisms, rather than a single one.[48] Thus, while the investment of postmodernism in postcolonial theory produces a binary vision of the world and a unitary vision of both modernism and postmodernism, our examination of the experimental Arabic novel suggests that a more appropriate response would be to move to a unitary vision of the world and a multiple view of modernism.

No writer offers us as concise a vision of this problem as Borges. In his short story "Averroes' Search," Borges writes: "Few things more beautiful and more pathetic are recorded in history than this Arab physician's dedication to the thoughts of a man [Aristotle] separated from him by fourteen centuries; to the intrinsic difficulties we should add that Averroes, ignorant of Syriac and Greek, was working with the translation of a translation. The night before, two doubtful words had halted him at the beginning of the *Poetics*. These words were tragedy and comedy. He had encountered them years before in the third book of the *Rhetoric;* no one in the whole world of Islam could conjecture what they meant." Borges concludes by turning the problem back on himself. "I felt," he writes, "that Averroes, wanting to imagine what a drama is without ever having suspected what a theater is, was no more absurd than I, wanting to imagine Averroes with no other sources than a few fragments from Renan, Lane, and Asín Palacios."[49]

In this image of Averroes, Borges captures the dilemma of postcolonial literary theorists who attempt to deal with the literatures of cultures of which they do not have firsthand knowledge. The image is applicable to Edward Said, as well. Regardless of his Arab ethnicity and the respect felt toward him for the voice that he has given to the Palestinian cause in the West, Arab writers, literary critics, and scholars tend to regard him as a Western, rather than as an Arab, literary critic. Students of modern Arabic literature cannot, therefore, even rely on the judgment of those who might seem to be the most likely authorities in the West. At the same time, critics such as Faysal Darraj can also be seen as guilty of exaggerating the lack of development in their own society, as much victims of the inferiority complex that typically infects Arab intellectuals as the writers they criticize.

In "The Zahir," Borges writes about obsession in a way that is highly suggestive of both the problem of Arab and Western intellectuals. The Zahir is a Sufi concept. In Borges's words, it signifies "beings or things which possess the terrible property of being unforgettable and whose image finally drives one mad."[50] For the narrator, Borges, the Zahir is a coin—a very ordinary coin. He receives the coin in his change at a bar immediately after attending the wake of a society woman whose death moves him to tears. The next day he gets rid of the coin, but he is unable to rid himself of his obsession. "I remember," Borges writes, "the envy I felt for those whose Zahir was not a coin, but a piece of marble, or a tiger. How easy it would be not to think of a tiger!" He quotes a Sufi commentator who cites a verse of Attar: "The Zahir is the shadow of the Rose, and the Rending of the Veil." "Time, which generally attenuates memories," Borges adds, "only aggravates that of the Zahir. There was a time when I could visualize the obverse, and then the reverse. Now I see them simultaneously."[51]

At the end of "The Zahir," Borges contemplates his old age and death. "They will have to feed and dress me. I shall not know whether it is afternoon or morning. I will not know who Borges was. To call this prospect terrible is a fallacy, for none of its circumstances will exist for me. One might as well say that an anesthetized man feels terrible pain when they open his cranium. I shall no longer perceive the universe: I shall perceive the Zahir. . . . From thousands of images I shall pass to one; from a highly complex dream to a dream of utter simplicity. . . . Others will dream that I am mad; I shall dream of the Zahir."[52]

In this passage, it appears that Borges—at least as narrator—is unable to get past his obsession. He fails to penetrate beyond the veil of the object. But is this a definitive statement on Borges, the writer, or only a fictional gesture? We can point to other works in which Borges masterfully conjures up entire worlds—entire galaxies—based on mere fragments. The symbol of the Zahir is typical of Borges's interest in celebrating the potentiality of the fragment. In this sense, his work can be contrasted with that of T. S. Eliot, in which there is nostalgia for wholeness in a world reduced to fragments.

Thus, Borges offers us something of great value in "The Zahir," and that is obsession itself. But his story also suggests that we must also find our way beyond our obsession. We can't afford to be left with nothing else. In this context, another line of speculation concerning the potential nature of Arabic postmodernism would be that a point would be reached at which the very mechanics of the Arabs' pervasive sense of living in the shadow of the West came to be deconstructed by Arab writers. The self-critical modernist themes of disillusion with inept leadership, corruption, the failure of ideology, and the tragic consequences of acting out political fantasies that abound in the Arabic novel of the past three decades would give way to a transcendence of these themes.

A similar sea change must eventually occur in postcolonial literary criticism. As Aijaz Ahmad notes with respect to Jameson's binary opposition between a First and Third World, "it is impossible to proceed with an examination of his particular propositions regarding the respective literary traditions without first asking whether or not this characterization of the world is theoretically tenable, and whether, therefore, an accurate conception of *literature* can be mapped out on the basis of this binary opposition."[53] Only by disengaging from Western cultural priorities can we develop the objectivity to consider postcolonial modernism as a phenomenon both distinct from, and related to, its Western form, and this will enable us to better appreciate the significance of modernism from a global perspective.

Notes

Introduction: The Experimental Arabic Novel and Comparative Modernisms

1. Malcolm Bradbury, *The Modern British Novel* (Harmondsworth, England: Penguin Books, 1993), 1.
2. Calinescu, *Five Faces of Modernity* (Durham, N.C.: Duke University Press, 1987), 265.
3. Malcolm Bradbury and James McFarlane, eds., *Modernism: 1890-1930* (Harmondsworth, England: Penguin Books, 1991).
4. Brian McHale, *Postmodern Fiction* (London: Routledge, 1994), xii.
5. Roger Allen, *The Arabic Novel: An Historical and Critical Introduction* (Syracuse, N.Y.: Syracuse University Press, 1982), 99.
6. Ibid., 97.
7. Q. D. Leavis, *Fiction and the Reading Public* (London: Bellew Publishing, 1978), 5.
8. Pierre Cachia, *An Overview of Modern Arabic Literature* (Edinburgh: Edinburgh University Press, 1990), 18–19.
9. Roger Allen, "Arabic Fiction and the Quest for Freedom," *Journal of Arabic Literature* 26, nos. 1–2 (March–June 1995): 39.
10. Ibid., 40.
11. Salman Rushdie, *The Satanic Verses* (New York: Viking Press, 1989).
12. Quoted by Aijaz Ahmad in *In Theory: Classes, Nations, Literatures* (London: Verso Press, 1992), 213.
13. Ceza Kassem Draz, "Opaque and Transparent Discourse in Sonallah Ibrahim's Works," in *The View from Within: Writers and Critics on Contemporary Arabic Literature, A Selection from Alif: Journal of Comparative Poetics*, ed. Ferial J. Ghazoul and Barbara Harlow (Cairo: The American University in Cairo Press, 1994), 134–35.
14. Shākir al-Nābulsī, *Madār al-Ṣaḥrā': Dirāsah fī Adab 'Abd al-Raḥmān Munīf* (Beirut: Mu'assasah al-'Arabīyah li al-Dirāsāt wa al-Nashr, 1991), 18.

15. Ibid., 17.

16. Walid Hamarneh, "Some Narrators and Narrative Modes in the Contemporary Arabic Novel," in *The Arabic Novel Since 1950: Critical Essays, Interviews, and Bibliography,* ed. Issa J. Boullata, Mundus Arabicus 5 (Cambridge, Mass: Dar Mahjar Publishing and Distribution, 1994), 210.

17. Ibid., 224.

18. Cachia, 177.

19. Elias Khoury, interview, Beirut, March 1995.

20. Rashid al-Da'if, interview, February 1997.

21. Elias Khoury, interview, Beirut, March 1995.

22. Khūrī, Ilyās, *Al-Dhākirah al-Mafqūdah: Dirāsāt Naqdīyah* (Beirut: Dār al-Ādāb, 1982), 25.

23. Neil Donahue, *Forms of Disruption: Abstraction in Modern German Prose* (Ann Arbor: University of Michigan Press, 1993).

24. Marianne DeKoven, *Rich and Strange: Gender, History, Modernism* (Princeton: Princeton University Press, 1991), 10.

Chapter 1: Modernist Ambivalence and the Beginnings of Narrative Experimentation

1. Ali B. Jad, *Form and Technique in the Egyptian Novel, 1912–1971* (London : Ithaca Press, for the Middle East Centre, St. Antony's College, Oxford, 1983), 406.

2. Ibid.

3. Roger Allen, *The Arabic Novel: An Historical and Critical Introduction,* 2d ed. (Syracuse, N.Y.: Syracuse University Press, 1995), 109.

4. Ibid.

5. Albert Camus, *The Stranger*, trans. Matthew Ward (New York: Vintage Books, 1989).

6. Roger Allen, "Arabic Fiction and the Quest for Freedom," *Journal of Arabic Literature* 26, nos. 1–2 (March–June 1995): 47.

7. Jad, 301.

8. Naguib Mahfouz, *Children of Gebelawi* (London: Heinemann, 1981).

9. Naguib Mahfouz, *The Beginning and the End* (New York: Doubleday, 1989).

10. Mona N. Mikhail, *Studies in the Short Fiction of Mahfouz and Idris* (New York: New York University Press, 1992), 13–14.

11. Naguib Mahfouz, *Miramar*, trans. Fatma Moussa Mahmoud, ed. and rev. Maged el-Kommos and John Rodenbeck (New York: Anchor Books, 1993).

12. William Faulkner, *The Sound and the Fury* (New York: Modern Library, 1992).

13. Jabrā Ibrāhīm Jabrā, *Al-Ṣakhab wa al-'Unf* (Beirut: Al-Mu'assasah al-'Arabīyah li al-Dirāsāt wa al-Nashr, 1983).

14. Yumnā al-'Īd, "Ta'addud al-Mawāqi' fī *Mīrāmār*," in *Al-Rāwi: Al-Mawqi' wa al-Shakl* (Beirut: Mu'assasah al-Abḥāth al-'Arabīyah, 1986), 116.

15. Anjīl Buṭrus Sam'ān, "Wijhah al-Naẓar fī al-Riwāyah al-'Arabīyah" (Point of view in the Arabic novel), *Fuṣūl: Journal of Literary Criticism* 2, no. 2 (January–March 1982): 110.

16. Ṣabrī Ḥāfiẓ, "Al-Tajārub al-Ḥaḍārīyah wa Tafā'ul al-Ru'ā al-Ibdā'īyah: Dirāsah fī Ta'thīr *Al-Ṣakhab wa Al-'Unf* 'alā al-Riwāyah al-'Arabīyah," *Fuṣūl: Journal of Literary Criticism* 3, no. 4 (July–September 1983): 215–29.

17. Ibid., 120.

18. Ibid.

19. Ibid., 116–18.

20. Ibid. 118–19.

21. Sam'ān, 113.

22. Ibid., 111.

23. Ibid., 115.

24. Hamarneh, "Some Narrators and Narrative Modes in the Contemporary Arabic Novel," 213–14.

25. Ghassan Kanafani, *Men in the Sun*, trans. Hilary Kilpatrick (London: Heinemann, 1978).

26. Hilary Kilpatrick, introduction to ibid., 2, 7.

27. Jean-Paul Sartre, *The Wall (Intimacy) and Other Stories* (New York: New Directions, 1969).

28. Albert Camus, "The Guest," in *Exile and the Kingdom*, trans. Justin O'Brien (New York: Vintage Books, 1991).

29. Kilpatrick, 3.

30. Ghassan Kanafani, *All That's Left to You: A Novella and Other Stories*, trans. May Jayyusi and Jeremy Reed, introduction by Roger Allen (Austin: University of Texas Press, 1990.

31. Ḥāfiẓ, 219.

32. Allen, 150.

33. Ibid., 151.

34. Ḥāfiẓ, 220.

35. Allen, 153.

36. Ghassān Kanafānī, *Mā Tabaqqā Lakum*, Silsilah A'māl Ghassān Kanafānī, no. 6 (Beirut: Mu'assasah al-Abḥāth al-'Arabīyah, 1986), 11. See also Roger Allen's introduction to Ghassan Kanafani's *All That's Left to You*, xxi.

37. Ḥāfiẓ, 220.

38. Allen, 150.

39. Jabra Ibrahim Jabra, *The Ship*, trans. Adnan Haydar and Roger Allen (Washington, D.C.: Three Continents Press, 1985).

40. Farūq Wādī, "Jabrā Ibrāhīm Jabrā: Al-Filisṭīnī wa al-Ru'yah al-Burjwāzīyah," in *Thalāth 'Alāmāt fi al-Riwāyah al-Filisṭīnīyah* (Beirut: Mu'assasah al-'Arabīyah li al-Dirāsāt wa al-Nashr, 1981), 147.

41. Jabrā Ibrāhīm Jabrā, *Al-Baḥth 'an Walīd Mas'ūd* (Beirut: Dār al-Ādāb, 1990).

42. Mattityahu Peled, "Sexuality in Jabra's Novel, *In Search of Walid Mas'ud*," in *Love and Sexuality in Modern Arabic Literature*, ed. Roger Allen, Hilary Kilpatrick, and Ed de Moor (London: Saqi Books, 1995), 147.

43. Aḥmad al-Zu'bī, "Al-Īqā' al-Riwā'ī fi *Al-Safinah*," in *Jabrā Ibrāhīm Jabrā, Al-Qalaq wa Tamjīd al-Ḥayāt: Kitāb Takrīm* (Beirut: Al-Mu'assasah al-'Arabīyah li al-Dirāsāt wa al-Nashr, 1995), 125.

44. Roger Allen, introduction to Jabra, *The Ship,* 8.

45. Virginia Woolf, *The Voyage Out* (London and New York: Oxford University Press, 1992).

46. Ibid. 3.

47. Hamarneh, 211.

48. Ibid., 211–12.

49. Conversation with Roger Allen, January 1998.

50. Draz, 135.

51. Taysīr Subūl, *Anta Mundhu al-Yawm* (Beirut: Dār al-Nahār li al-Nashr, 1968.

52. Fakhrī Sāliḥ, *Wahm al-Bidāyāt: Al-Khiṭāb al-Riwā'ī fi al-Urdunn* (Beirut: Al-Mu'assasah al-'Arabīyah li al-Dirāsāt wa al-Nashr, 1993), 27–38.

53. Sun' Allāh Ibrāhīm, *Najmah Aghusṭus* (Damascus: Manshurāt Ittiḥād al-Kuttāb al-'Arabī, 1974).

54. Draz, 136.

55. Maḥmūd Amīn al-'Ālim, *Thulāthīyah al-Rafd wa al-Hazīmah: Dirāsah Naqdīyah li Thalāth Riwāyāt li Ṣun' Allāh Ibrāhīm* (Cairo: Dār al-Mustaqbal al-'Arabī, 1985), 82.

56. Peled, 140. The quote is from Mikhail Bakhtin's book on the poetics of Dostoyevsky.

57. Ibid., 141–42.

58. Fakhrī Sāliḥ, "Al-Riwāyah al-'Arabīyah wa Ashkāl al-Sard al-Turāthīyah," *Suṭūr* (Cairo), no. 2 (January 1997): 76–78.

59. Ibid., 76.

60. Gamal al-Ghitani, *Zayni Barakat*, trans. Farouk Abdel Wahab (London: Viking Press, 1988).

61. Quoted by Ṣāliḥ, 77.

62. Sīzā Qāsim, "Al-Mufāraqah fi al-Qiṣṣ al-'Arabī al-Mu'āṣir," *Fuṣūl: Journal of Literary Criticism* 2, no. 2 (January–March 1982): 147.

63. Hamarneh, "Some Narrators and Narrative Modes in the Contemporary Arabic Novel," 218–19.

64. Qāsim, 147.
65. Hamarneh, 219.
66. Ibid., 220.
67. Fakhrī Ṣāliḥ, "Imīl Ḥabībī: Sayl al-Ḥikāyāt," *Majallah Nazwā* (Muscat, Oman), no. 7 (July 1997): 45.
68. Interview with Ibrahim Nasrallah, Amman, November 1994.
69. Salma Khadra Jayyusi, ed., *Anthology of Modern Palestinian Literature* (New York: Columbia University Press, 1992), 2.
70. Ibid. 3.
71. Emile Habiby, *The Secret Life of Saeed, the Ill-Fated Pessoptimist*, trans. Salma Khadra Jayyusi and Trevor LeGassick (London and New York: Readers International, 1985).
72. Voltaire, *Candide* (New York: Alfred A. Knopf, 1992).
73. Jonathan Swift, *Gulliver's Travels* (Harmondsworth, England: Penguin Books, 1967).
74. Richard F. Burton, *The Arabian Nights' Entertainments, or The Book of the Thousand Nights and a Night* (New York: Modern Library, 1997).
75. Jabra, *Ship*, 26.
76. Jaroslav Hašek, *The Good Soldier Svejk*, trans. Cecil Parrott (Harmondsworth, England: Penguin Books, 1974).
77. Cecil Parrott, *Jaroslav Hašek: A Study of Švejk and the Short Stories* (New York: Cambridge University Press, 1982), 44.
78. Salma Khadra Jayyusi, introduction to Habiby, *Secret Life of Saeed, the Ill-Fated Pessoptimist*, xiv.
79. Ibid.
80. Albert Camus, *The Fall*, trans. Justin O'Brien (New York: Vintage Books, 1991).
81. Shoshana Felman and Dori Laub, M.D., *Testimony: Crises of Witnessing in Literature, Psychoanalysis, and History* (New York: Routledge, 1992), 180.
82. Ibid. 181–82.
83. Camus, *Fall*, trans. O'Brien, 118.
84. Felman and Laub, 185.

Chapter 2: Recovering the Past: The "Arabization" of the Novel

1. Abdelrahman Munif, *Endings*, trans. Roger Allen (London: Quartet Books, 1988).
2. Interview with Abdelrahman Munif ('Abd al-Raḥmān Munīf), Damascus, June 1995.
3. Jean Toomer, *Cane* (New York: Modern Library, 1994).
4. Gertrude Stein, *Three Lives* (Harmondsworth, England: Penguin, 1990).
5. Ernest Hemingway, *In Our Time* (New York: Simon and Schuster, 1996).

6. Muḥammad Kāmil al-Khatīb, *Inkisār al-Aḥlām: Sīrah Riwā'īyah*, Dirāsāt Naqdīyah 'Arabīyah, vol. 1 (Damascus: Manshūrāt Wizārah al-Thiqāfah, 1987), 65.

7. Muhammad Siddiq, "The Making of a Counter-Narrative: Two Examples from Contemporary Arabic and Hebrew Fiction," *Michigan Quarterly Review* 41, no. 4 (fall 1992): 651.

8. Abdelrahman Munif, *Cities of Salt*, trans. Peter Theroux (London: Vintage Books, 1994).

9. Hamarneh, "Some Narrators and Narrative Modes in the Contemporary Arabic Novel," 220.

10. 'Abd al-Raḥman Munīf, *Sharq al-Mutawassiṭ* (Beirut: Dār al-Ṭalī 'ah li al-Ṭibā'ah wa al-Nashr, 1975).

11. Interview with Abdelrahman Munif.

12. Abdelrahman Munif, *Variations on Night and Day*, trans. Peter Theroux (New York: Vintage Books, 1994).

13. From the dust jacket copy of ibid.

14. Interview with Abdelrahman Munif.

15. See *The Encyclopedia of Islam*, vol. 3 (London: E. J. Brill, 1971), 23–28.

16. Jabra, *Ship*, 180.

17. Elizabeth Monroe, *Philby of Arabia* (London: Faber and Faber 1973).

18. Interview with Abdelrahman Munif.

19. Morton P. Levitt, "From Realism to Magic Realism: The Meticulous Modernist Fictions of García Márquez," in *Modern Critical Views: Gabriel García Márquez*, ed. Harold Bloom (New York: Chelsea House, 1989), 241.

20. Salīm Barakāt, *Al-Jundub al-Ḥadīdī* (Beirut: Dār al-Ṭalī'ah li al-Ṭibā'ah wa al-Nashr, 1980).

21. Conversation with Roger Allen, January 1998.

22. Zuhayr Ibn Abī Salmā, in *Sharḥ Shi'r Zuhayr Ibn Abī Salmā*, by Abū al-'Abbās Tha'lab, ed. Fakhr al-Dīn Qabāwah (Beirut: Manshūrāt Dar al-Āfāq al-Jadīdah, 1982), 48.

23. Al-Mutanabbī, in *Sharḥ Dīwān al-Mutanabbī*, by 'Abd al-Raḥmān al-Barqūqi, vol. 4 (Cairo: Maktabah al-Tijārīyah, n.d.), 418.

24. Fakhrī Sāliḥ, "*Fuqahā' al-Ẓalām*: Al-Naṣṣ al-Muttaham," *Al-Mahd*, no. 8 (1986): 37.

25. Issa Boullata, introduction to excerpts from *Sages of Darkness*, by Salīm Barakāt, *Michigan Quarterly Review* 31, no. 4 (fall 1992): 639.

26. Excerpt from *Sages of Darkness*, by Salim Barakat, trans. Issa Boullata, *Michigan Quarterly Review* 31, no. 4 (fall 1992): 648.

27. Salīm Barakāt, *Fuqahā' al-Ẓalām*, *Al-Karmal*, no. 2 (Nicosia, Cyprus: Ittiḥād al-Kuttāb wa al-Ṣaḥāfīyīn al-Filisṭīnīyīn, 1985), 104.

28. Ṣāliḥ, 42.

29. Ibid.

30. Ibid., 45–46.

31. George Lenczowski, *Soviet Advances in the Middle East*, U.S. Interests in the Middle East Series (Washington, D.C.: The American Enterprise Institute for Public Policy Research, 1972), 119.

32. Souraya Botros, "Les Influences Occidentales sur la Nouvelle en Syrie depuis 1946" (diss., University of Paris-Sorbonne, n.d.), 68.

33. See Sabry Hafez, "The Impact of Russian Literature," in *The Genesis of Arabic Narrative Discourse: A Study in the Sociology of Modern Arabic Literature* (London: Saqi Books, 1993), 91–96.

34. Radwan Zaza, "Influences Étrangers dans le Roman et la Nouvelle Arabes en Syrie de 1950 à nos jours" (diss., University of Paris—Sorbonne, 1985).

35. Nabil Sulayman, interview, February 1995.

36. Nihād Sirrīs, *Al-Kūmīdīya al-Fallāḥīyah* (Aleppo: n.p., 1990).

37. Imīl Habībī, *Khurrāfīyah: Sarāyā, Bint al-Ghūl* (Haifa: Arabesque Publishing House, 1991).

38. Fakhrī Sāliḥ, "Imīl Ḥabībī: Sayl al-Ḥikāyāt," *Majallah Nazwā* (Muscat, Oman), no. 7 (July 1997): 48.

39. Fedwa Malti-Douglas, *Woman's Body, Woman's Word: Gender and Discourse in Arabo-Islamic Writing* (Princeton: Princeton University Press, 1991).

40. Ibid., 25.

41. Sāliḥ, "Imīl Ḥabībī, 48.

42. Ramaḍān Ismā'īl al-Rawāshidah, *Min Hayāt Rajul Fāqid al-Dhākirah, Aw: Al-Ḥamrāwī* (Amman: n.p., 1992).

43. Franz Kafka, *The Metamorphosis* (New York: Bantam Books, 1972).

44. Ibrāhīm al-Sa'āfin, *Al-Riwāyah fī al-Urdunn* (Amman: Manshūrāt Lajnah Tārīkh al-Urdunn, 1995), 358.

45. Ibid., 351.

46. Yahya Haqqi, *The Saint's Lamp and Other Stories* (Leiden: E. J. Brill [1973]).

47. Naguib Mahfouz, "Zaabalawi," in *God's World: An Anthology of Short Stories* (Minneapolis, Minn.: Bibliotheca Islamica, 1973).

48. Denys Johnson-Davies, trans., *Modern Arabic Short Stories* (London: Oxford University Press, 1967).

Chapter 3: Rediscovering the Present: The Lebanese Civil War

1. Ghada Samman, *Beirut '75*, trans. Nancy N. Roberts (Fayetteville: University of Arkansas Press, 1995).

2. Ghada Samman, *Beirut Nightmares*, trans. Nancy N. Roberts (London: Quartet Books, 1997).

3. Tawfiq Yusuf Awwad, *Death in Beirut: A Novel* (London: Heinemann Educational, 1976).

4. Nancy N. Roberts, foreword to Samman, *Beirut '75*, vi.

5. Ibid., vii.

6. Joseph T. Zeidan, *Arab Women Novelists: The Formative Years and Beyond* (Albany: State University of New York Press, 1995), 201.

7. The Arabic version consists of 207 "nightmares" followed by one optimistic dream, and concludes with projections of future nightmares.

8. Nancy Roberts, introduction to Samman, *Beirut Nightmares*, iv.

9. Ilyās Khūrī, *Al-Wujūh al-Bayḍā'* (Beirut: Dār Ibn Rushd li al-Ṭibā'ah wa al-Nashr, 1981.

10. John Fletcher and Malcolm Bradbury, "The Introverted Novel," in *Modernism: 1890–1930*, ed. Malcolm Bradbury and James McFarlane (Harmondsworth, England: Penguin Books, 1991), 395.

11. Ernest Hemingway, *In Our Time* (New York: Simon & Schuster, 1996).

12. James Joyce, *Dubliners* (Harmondsworth and New York: Penguin Books, 1979).

13. Samī Suwaydān, "Al-Ḥarb wa al-Naṣṣ: *Al-Wujūh al-Bayḍā'* li Ilyās Khūrī: As'ilah al-Qatl wa al-Qiṣṣ," in *Abḥāth fī al-Naṣṣ al-Riwā'ī al-'Arabī* (Beirut: Mu'assasah al-Abḥāth al-'Arabīyah, 1986), 199.

14. Ibid., 200.

15. Kanafani, *All That's Left to You,* 48.

16. Tayeb Salih, *Season of Migration to the North,* trans. Denys Johnson-Davies (Portsmouth, N.H.: Heinemann, 1989).

17. Joseph Conrad, *Heart of Darkness and The Secret Agent* (New York: Doubleday, 1997).

18. Nawal el-Saadawi, *Woman at Point Zero*, trans. Sherif Hetata (London: Zed Books, 1983).

19. Georges Tarabishi, *Woman Against Her Sex: A Critique of Nawal El-Saadawi*, with a reply by Nawal el-Saadawi, trans. Basil Hatim and Elisabeth Orsini (London: Saqi Books, 1988), 13–14.

20. Miriam Cooke, *War's Other Voices: Women Writers on the Lebanese Civil War* (Cambridge: Cambridge University Press, 1988).

21. Evelyne Accad, *Sexuality and War: Literary Masks of the Middle East* (New York: New York University Press, 1990), 167.

22. Elias Khoury, *La petite montagne* (Paris: Avléa, 1987), 251–52, quoted in ibid., 154–55.

23. Etel Adnan, *Sitt Marie Rose*, translated from the French by Georgina Kleege (Sausalito, Calif.: The Post-Apollo Press, 1982).

24. Hanan al-Shaykh, *The Story of Zahra* (London: Quartet Books, 1986).

25. T. E. Lawrence, *Seven Pillars of Wisdom: A Triumph* (New York: Doubleday, 1991), 445.

26. Hoda Barakat, *The Stone of Laughter*, trans. Sophie Bennett (London: Riad al-Rayyes Books, 1994).

27. Fadia Faqir, introduction to ibid., vi.

28. Ibid., v.

29. Elias Khoury, interview, Beirut, March 1995.

30. Elias Khoury, *Gates of the City*, trans. Paula Haydar (Minneapolis: University of Minnesota Press, 1993).

31. Kahlil Gibran, *The Madman, His Parables and Poems* (New York: Alfred A. Knopf, 1980).

32. Khalil S. Hawi, *Kahlil Gibran: His Background, Character, and Works* (Beirut: The Arab Institute for Research and Publishing, 1972), 196.

33. Gibran, *Madman,* 44.

34. Ibid., 7–8.

35. Muḥammad al-Bāridī, "Al-Tajrīb wa Inhiyār al-Thawābit," *Al- Ādāb*, nos. 5–6 (May–June 1997): 22.

36. Suhayr Salṭī al-Tall, *Al-Mashnaqah wa Qiṣaṣ Ukhrā* (Amman: Al-Mu'assasah al-Waṭanīyah li al-Nashr, 1987).

37. See Gertrude Stein, *A Primer for the Gradual Understanding of Gertrude Stein* (Los Angeles: Black Sparrow Press, 1973).

38. Rashīd al-Ḍa'īf, *Fusḥah Mustahdafah Bayna al-Nu'ās wa al-Nawm* (Beirut: Mukhtārāt, 1986).

39. Mona Takieddine Amyuni, "Style as Politics in the Poems and Novels of Rashid Al-Da'if," *International Journal of Middle East Studies* 28 (1996): 187.

40. Samira Aghacy, "Rachid El Daif's *An Exposed Space between Drowsiness and Sleep*: Abortive Representation," *Journal of Arabic Literature* 27, no. 3 (October 1996): 194.

41. Amyuni, 186 .

42. Aghacy, 195.

43. Rashīd al-Ḍa'īf, *Fusḥah Mustahdafah Bayna al-Nu'ās wa al-Nawm*, 23–24, quoted by Aghacy in "Rachid El Daif's *An Exposed Space between Drowsiness and Sleep*," 196.

44. Ibid., 198.

Chapter 4: Redefining the Future: Questions of Artistic Choice.

1. Ibrahim Nasrallah, in *An Anthology of Modern Palestinian Literature*, edited and introduced by Salma Khadra Jayyusi (New York: Columbia University Press, 1992), 241–42.

2. Ibrahim Nasrallah, interview, Amman, November 1994.

3. Ibid.

4. Mureed Barghouthi [Murid Barghuthi], in Jayyusi, ed., *An Anthology of Modern Palestinian Literature*, 128.

5. Interview with Murid Barghuthi.

6. Ibid.

7. Ibrahim Nasrallah, *Prairies of Fever*, trans. May Jayyusi and Jeremy Reed (New York: Interlink Books, 1993).

8. Hermann Hesse, *Steppenwolf* (New York: Henry Holt and Co., 1990).

9. Thomas Mann, *Death in Venice and Other Tales* (New York: Viking, 1998).

10. Jeremy Reed, translator's foreword to Nasrallah, *Prairies of Fever*, ix.

11. Edgar Allan Poe, *Selected Tales* (New York: Vintage Books, 1991).

12. Ibid., xi–xii.

13. Fedwa Malti-Douglas, introduction to Nasrallah, *Prairies of Fever*, 8.

14. Reed, xi.

15. Kafka, *Metamorphosis*.

16. Franz Kafka, *The Trial* (New York: Alfred A. Knopf, 1992).

17. Paul Bowles, *The Sheltering Sky* (New York: Vintage Books, 1990).

18. Fakhrī Sāliḥ, *Wahm al-Bidāyāt,* 125.

19. Ibid., 129.

20. Sun' Allāh Ibrāhīm, *Najmah Aghusṭus*, 18–19.

21. Ḥasan Dāwūd, *Taḥta Shurfah Ānjī* (Beirut: Dār al-Tanwīr li al-Ṭibā'ah wa al-Nashr, 1984).

22. Rashīd al-Ḍa'īf, *Tiqnīyāt al-Bu's* (Beirut: Mukhtārāt, 1989).

23. Amyuni, "Style as Politics in the Poems and Novels of Rashid Al-Da'if," 188.

24. William Kotzwinkle, *The Fan Man* (New York: Vintage Books, 1974).

25. Amyuni, 188.

26. Interview with Rashid al-Da'if, Beirut, November 1997.

27. Ibid.

28. Yumnā al-'Īd, *Al-Kitābah: Taḥawwul fī al-Taḥawwul: Muqāranah li al-Kitābah al-Adabīyah fī Zaman al-Ḥarb al-Lubnānīyah* (Beirut: Dār al-Ādāb, 1993).

29. Mu'nis al-Razzāz, interview, Amman, October 1994.

30. Mu'nis al-Razzāz, *I'tirāfāt Kātim Ṣawt*, rev. second printing (Amman: Al-Mu'assasah al-'Arabīyah li al-Dirāsāt wa al-Nashr, 1992).

31. Fyodor Dostoyevsky, *Notes from Underground/The Double*, trans. Jessie Coulson (Harmondsworth, England: Penguin Books, 1972).

32. Ralph Ellison, *Invisible Man* (New York: Random House, 1982).

33. Mu'nis al-Razzāz, interview, Amman, October 1994.

34. Fakhrī Sāliḥ, *Wahm al-Bidāyāt*, 96.

35. Italo Svevo, *Confessions of Zeno*, trans. Beryl de Zoete (New York: Vintage Books, 1989).

36. Fakhrī Sāliḥ, *Wahm al-Bidāyāt*, 92.

37. Mu'nis al-Razzāz, *Al-Dhākirah al-Mustabāḥah/Qab'atān wa Ra's Wāḥid* (Beirut: Mu'assasah al-'Arabīyah li al-Dirāsāt wa al-Nashr, 1991).

38. Ibrāhīm al-Sa'āfīn, *Al-Riwāyah fī al-Urdunn* (Amman: Manshūrāt Lajnah Tārīkh al-Urdunn, no. 31, 1995), 305.

39. Elias Khoury, *The Journey of Little Gandhi*, trans. Paula Haydar, foreword by Sabah Ghandour (Minneapolis: University of Minnesota Press, 1994).

40. André Gide, *The Counterfeiters; with Journal of the Counterfeiters* (New York: Alfred A. Knopf, 1951).

41. Samira Aghacy, "Elias Khoury's *The Journey of Little Gandhi:* Fiction and Ideology," *International Journal of Middle East Studies* 28 (1996): 163–76.

42. Gabriel García Márquez, *The Autumn of the Patriarch* (New York: Harper & Row, 1976).

43. Vladimir Nabokov, *Laughter in the Dark* (Harmondsworth, England: Penguin Books, 1982), 5.

44. Edwar al-Kharrat, *Girls of Alexandria*, trans. Frances Liardet (London: Quartet Books, 1993).

45. Frances Liardet, introduction to ibid., viii–ix.

46. Ibid., ix.

47. Ibid., viii.

48. 'Abduh Wāzin, *Ḥadīqah al-Ḥawāss* (Beirut: Dār al-Jadīd, 1993).

49. Bruce Morrissette, "Surfaces and Structures in Robbe-Grillet's Novels," in *Two Novels: Jealousy and In the Labyrinth*, by Alain Robbe-Grillet, trans. Richard Howard (New York: Grove Press, 1965), 7.

50. Nathalie Sarraute, *Tropisms and The Age of Suspicion* (London: Calder and Boyars, 1967).

51. Robbe-Grillet, *Two Novels,* trans. Howard.

52. Christopher Robinson, *French Literature of the Twentieth Century* (Totowa, N.J.: Barnes and Noble, 1980), 268.

53. Samuel Beckett, *Three Novels: Molloy, Malone Dies, The Unnamable,* Everyman's Library (New York: Alfred A. Knopf, 1997).

54. Ibid., 150.

55. Ibid., 146.

56. Ibid.

57. Ibid., 147.

58. Amyuni, 151.

59. Marguerite Duras, *Four Novels* (New York: Grove Press, 1990).

60. Aghacy, "Rachid El Daif's *An Exposed Space between Drowsiness and Sleep,*" 194–99.

61. Ibid., 201.

62. Ibid., 202.

63. Ibid.

64. Ḥasan Dāwūd, *Ayyām Zā'idah* (Beirut: Dār al-Jadīd, 1990).

65. Yumnā al-'Īd, *Al-Kitābah: Taḥawwul fī al-Taḥawwul*, 94.

66. Ibid., 93.

67. Ibid., 95.

68. André Gide, *The Immoralist*, trans. Richard Howard (New York: Vintage Books, 1970).

69. Thomas Mann, *The Magic Mountain – Der Zauberberg* (New York: Alfred A. Knopf, 1977).

70. 'Īd, 98.

71. Ibid.

72. Thomas Mann, *Death in Venice*, trans. and ed. Clayton Koelb (New York: W. W. Norton and Co., 1994), 62.

73. Gabriel García Márquez, *Love in the Time of Cholera* (New York: Alfred A. Knopf, 1988).

74. 'Īd, 99.

75. Interview with Hassan Daoud.

76. Ibid.

77. Conversation with Yumna al-Eid, Beirut, November 1997.

78. See Stein, *Three Lives*.

79. Rashīd al-Ḍa'īf, *'Azīzī al-Sayyid Kawābātā* (Beirut: Mukhtārāt, 1995).

80. Mona Takieddine Amyuni, "Style as Politics in the Poems and Novels of Rashid Al-Da'if," *International Journal of Middle East Studies* 28 (1996): 189.

81. Ibid., 190.

82. Sun' Allāh Ibrāhīm, *Dhāt* (Beirut: Dār al-Mustaqbal al-'Arabī, 1993).

83. John Dos Passos, *U. S.A.* (New York: Library of America, 1996).

84. Muḥammad al-Bāridī, "Al-Tajrīb wa Inhiyār al-Thawābit," *Al-Ādāb*, nos. 5–6 (May–June 1997): 23.

85. Rabī' Jābir, *Rālf Rizq Allāh fī al-Mir'āh* (Beirut: Dar al-Ādāb, 1997).

86. Yumnā al-'Īd, "*Rālf Rizq Allāh fī al-Mir'āh* li Rabī' Jābir: Ḥikāyah Intiḥār fī Dhākirah Mushra'ah 'ala al-As'ilah," *Al-Mulḥaq al-Thiqāfī*, no. 65 (1997).

87. Ibid.

88. Paul Auster, *The New York Trilogy: City of Glass, Ghosts, The Locked Room* (Harmondsworth, England: Penguin Books, 1990).

89. Ibid.

90. Lewis Carroll, *Alice in Wonderland* (New York: W. W. Norton, 1971).

91. James Joyce, *Ulysses* (New York: Modern Library, 1961).

92. Jean-Paul Sartre, *Nausea* (New York: New Directions, 1964).

93. Elias Khoury, *Majma' al-Asrār* (Beirut: Dār al-Ādāb, 1994).

Conclusion: The Experimental Arabic Novel and Postmodern Discourse

1. Edward Said, foreword to *Little Mountain*, by Elias Khoury, trans. Maia Tabet (Manchester, England: Carcanet Press, 1989), xx.
2. Ibid., xvi.
3. Ibid., xii.
4. Ibid.
5. Ibid., xxi.
6. Fakhrī Sāliḥ, "Al-Riwāyah al-'Arabīyah al-Jadīdah: Naz'ah al-Lāyaqīn wa al-Intihāk al-Shaklī," *Suṭūr* (Cairo) 2 (January 1997): 124.
7. Linda Hutcheon, *A Poetics of Postmodernism: History, Theory, Fiction* (New York: Routledge, 1988), 9.
8. Ibid., 84.
9. Patrick Williams and Laura Chrisman, eds., *Colonial Discourse and Post-Colonial Theory: A Reader* (New York: Columbia University Press, 1994), 13.
10. Gregory Jusdanis, *Belated Modernity and Aesthetic Culture: Inventing National Literature* (Minneapolis: University of Minnesota Press, 1991), xiv.
11. Gregory Jusdanis, "Is Postmodernism Possible Outside the 'West'? The Case of Greece," *Byzantine and Modern Greek Studies* 11 (1987): 70.
12. Jusdanis, *Belated Modernity and Aesthetic Culture*, xiv.
13. Roger Allen, *The Arabic Novel: An Historical and Critical Introduction*, 2d ed. (Syracuse, N.Y.: Syracuse University Press, 1995), 65.
14. Malti-Douglas, introduction to Nasrallah, *Prairies of Fever*, 1–2.
15. Amal Amireh, "Ibrahim Nasrallah: *Prairies of Fever*," *World Literature Today* (Norman, Okla.) 69, no. 1 (spring 1994): 419.
16. Malti-Douglas, introduction to Nasrallah, *Prairies of Fever,* 1.
17. Ibid., 10.
18. Aghacy, "Rachid El Daif's *An Exposed Space between Drowsiness and Sleep*," 197.
19. Fakhrī Sāliḥ, *Wahm al-Bidāyāt*, 125.
20. Ibid., 2.
21. Jorge Luis Borges, *Labyrinths: Selected Stories and Other Writings*, ed. Donald A. Yates and James E. Irby (New York: New Directions, 1964).
22. Ibid., 125–26.
23. Georges Dorlian, "Le roman d'expression arabe (après 1975): L'émergence du moi," *Magazine littéraire* (Paris), Supplément: Poètes et romanciers du Liban, no. 359 (November 1997): 107–9.
24. Hassan Daoud, interview, Beirut, November 1997.

25. Fakhrī Sāliḥ, "Al-Riwāyah al-'Arabīyah al-Jadīdah: Naz'ah al-Lāyaqīn wa al-Intihāk al-Shaklī, 124.

26. Ibid., 125.

27. Alfred G. Meyer, "The Political Theory of Pessimism: George Orwell and Herbert Marcuse," in *The Future of Nineteen Eight-Four*, ed. Ejner J. Jensen (Ann Arbor: University of Michigan Press, 1984), 132.

28. Ibrahim Nasrallah, interview, Amman, November 1994.

29. John Beverly and José Oviedo, introduction, *boundary 2*, 20, no. 3 (fall 1993): 5. Special issue, *The Postmodernism Debate in Latin America,* ed. John Beverly and José Oviedo, trans. Michael Aronna (Durham, N.C.: Duke University Press, 1993).

30. Yumnā al-'Īd, *Al-Rāwī: Al-Mawqi' wa al-Shakl* (Beirut: Mu'assasah al-Abḥāth al-'Arabīyah, 1986), 125.

31. Fakhrī Sāliḥ, "*Al-Jabal al-Ṣaghīr:* Buṭālah al-Amkinah wa al-Jamā'āt," *Al-Mahd* (Amman) 2 (1984): 84.

32. Yumnā al-'Īd, "Al-Lāmawqi'? Aw Qaṭl Mafhūm al-Baṭal," in *Al-Rāwī: Al-Mawqi' wa al-Shakl*, 81–86.

33. Mohammed Hussein Haikal (Muḥammad Ḥusayn Haykal), *Mohammed Hussein Haikal's Zainab: The First Egyptian Novel*, trans. John Mohammed Grinsted (London: Darf Publishing, 1989).

34. Naguib Mahfouz, *Palace Walk*, trans. William M. Hutchins and Olive E. Kenny (New York: Doubleday, 1990).

35. Simon Dentith, *Bakhtinian Thought: An Introductory Reader* (London: Routledge, 1995), 42.

36. Ibid., 43.

37. Ann Charters, introduction to Stein, *Three Lives*, xx–xxi.

38. George Martin, *Journeys through the Labyrinth: Latin American Fiction in the Twentieth Century* (New York: Verso, 1989), 164.

39. Ibid.

40. Borges, *Labyrinths,* 181.

41. Fayṣal Darrāj (Faysal Darraj), "Mā Ba'da al-Ḥadāthah fī 'Ālam bilā Ḥadāthaḥ," in *Al-Karmal* (Amman), no. 51 (1997): 82.

42. Ibid., 69.

43. Beverly and Oviedo, 2.

44 José Joaquín Brunner, "Notes on Modernity and Post-modernity in Latin American Culture," *boundary 2: An international journal of literature and culture* 20, no. 3 (fall 1993): 53. Special issue, *The Postmodernism Debate in Latin America,* ed. John Beverly and José Oviedo, trans. Michael Aronna (Durham, N.C.: Duke University Press, 1993).

45. Martin, 163–64.

46. Aijaz Ahmad, *In Theory: Classes, Nations, Literatures* (London: Verso Press, 1992), 98.

47. Frantz Fanon, *The Wretched of the Earth* (New York: Grove Press, 1968).
48. Darrāj, 72.
49. Borges, *Labyrinths,* 149.
50. Ibid., 161.
51. Ibid.
52. Ibid., 164.
53. Ahmad, 98.

Bibliography

PRIMARY TEXTS

Abī Salmā, Zuhayr Ibn. *Sharḥ Shi'r Zuhayr Ibn Abī Salmā*, by Abū al-'Abbās Tha'lab. Edited by Fakhr al-Dīn Qabāwah. Beirut: Manshūrāt Dār al-Āfāq al-Jadīdah, 1982.

Adnan, Etel. *Sitt Marie Rose*. Translated from the French by Georgina Kleege. Sausalito, Calif.: The Post-Apollo Press, 1982.

Awwad, Tawfiq Yusuf [Tawfīq Yūsuf 'Awwād]. *Death in Beirut: A Novel.* London: Heinemann Educational, 1976.

Barakat, Hoda [Hudā Barakāt]. *The Stone of Laughter*. Translated by Sophie Bennett. London: Riad al-Rayyes Books, 1994.

Barakāt, Salīm. *Al-Jundub al-Ḥadīdī*. Beirut: Dār al-Ṭalī'ah li al-Ṭibā'ah wa al-Nashr, 1980.

———. *Fuqahā' al-Ẓalām*, comprising *Al-Karmal*, no. 2. Nicosia, Cyprus: Ittiḥād al-Kuttāb wa al-Ṣiḥāfiyīn al-Filasṭīniyīn, 1985.

Ḍa'īf, Rashīd al- [Rashid al-Da'if]. *Fusḥah Mustahdafah Bayna al-Nu'ās wa al-Nawm*. Beirut: Mukhtārāt, 1986.

———. *Tiqnīyāt al-Bu's*. Beirut: Mukhtārāt, 1989.

———. *'Azīzī al-Sayyid Kawābātā*. Beirut: Mukhtārāt, 1995.

Dāwūd, Ḥasan [Hassan Daoud]. *Taḥta Shurfah Ānjī*. Beirut: Dār al-Tanwīr li al-Ṭibā'ah wa al-Nashr, 1984.

———. *Ayyām Zā'idah*. Beirut: Dār al-Jadīd, 1990.

Ghitani, Gamal al- [Jamāl al-Ghīṭānī]. *Zayni Barakat*. Translated by Farouk Abdel Wahab. London: Viking Press, 1988.

Gibran, Kahlil. *The Madman, His Parables and Poems*. New York: Alfred A. Knopf, 1980.

Ḥabībī, Imīl [Emile Habiby]. *Khurāfiyah: Sarāyā, Bint al-Ghūl*. Haifa: Arabesque Publishing House, 1991.

Habiby, Emile [Ḥabībī, Imīl]. *The Secret Life of Saeed, the Ill-Fated Pessoptimist.* Translated by Salma Khadra Jayyusi and Trevor LeGassick. London and New York: Readers International, 1985.

Haqqi, Yahya [Yaḥyā Ḥaqqī]. *The Saint's Lamp and Other Stories.* Leiden: E. J. Brill, 1973.

Haikal, Mohammed Hussein [Muḥammad Ḥusayn Haykal]. *Mohammed Hussein Haikal's Zainab: The First Egyptian Novel.* Translated by John Mohammed Grinsted. London: Darf Publishing, 1989.

Ibrahim, Sonallah [Ṣun' Allāh Ibrāhīm]. *The Smell of It and Other Stories.* Translated by Denys Johnson-Davies. London: Heinemann, 1971.

Ibrāhīm, Sun' Allāh [Sonallah Ibrahim]. *Najmah Aghusṭus.* Damascus: Manshūrāt Ittiḥād al-Kuttāb al-'Arabī, 1974.

———. *Dhāt.* Beirut: Dār al-Mustaqbal al-'Arabī, 1993.

Idris, Yusuf [Yūsuf Idrīs]. *In the Eye of the Beholder: Tales of Egyptian Life from the Writings of Yusuf Idris.* Edited by Roger Allen. Minneapolis: Biblioteca Islamica, 1978.

Jābir, Rabī' [Rabi' Jaber]. *Rālf Rizq Allāh fī al-Mir'āh.* Beirut: Dār al-Ādāb, 1997.

Jabra, Jabra Ibrahim [Jabrā Ibrāhīm Jabrā]. *The Ship.* Translated by Adnan Haydar and Roger Allen. Washington, D.C.: Three Continents Press, 1985.

Jabrā, Jabrā Ibrāhīm [Jabra Ibrahim Jabra]. *Al-Baḥth 'an Walīd Mas'ūd.* Beirut: Dār al-Ādāb, 1990.

———, trans. *Al-Ṣakhab wa al-'Unf.* Beirut: Al-Mu'assasah al-'Arabīyah li al-Dirāsāt wa al-Nashr, 1983.

Jayyusi, Salma Khadra, ed. *Anthology of Modern Palestinian Literature.* New York: Columbia University Press, 1992.

Johnson-Davies, Denys, trans. *Modern Arabic Short Stories.* London: Oxford University Press, 1967.

Kanafani, Ghassan [Ghassān Kanafānī]. *Men in the Sun.* Translated by Hilary Kilpatrick. London: Heinemann, 1978.

———. *All That's Left to You: A Novella and Other Stories.* Translated by May Jayyusi and Jeremy Reed. Introduction by Roger Allen. Modern Middle East Literature in Translation Series, Center for Middle Eastern Studies. Austin: University of Texas, 1990.

Kanafānī, Ghassān [Ghassan Kanafani]. *Mā Tabaqqā Lakum.* Silsilah A'māl Ghassān Kanafānī, no. 6. Beirut: Mu'assasah al-Abḥāth al-'Arabīyah, 1986.

Kharrat, Edwar al- [Idwār al-Kharrāṭ]. *Girls of Alexandria.* Translated by Frances Liardet. London: Quartet Books, 1993.

Khoury, Elias [Ilyās Khūrī]. *Little Mountain.* Translated by Maia Tabet. Foreword by Edward Said. Manchester, England: Carcanet Press, 1989.

———. *Gates of the City*. Translated by Paula Haydar. Foreword by Sabah Ghandour. Minneapolis: University of Minnesota Press, 1993.

———. *The Journey of Little Gandhi*. Translated by Paula Haydar. Foreword by Sabah Ghandour. Minneapolis: University of Minnesota Press, 1994.

———. *The Kingdom of Strangers*. Translated by Paula Haydar. Fayetteville: University of Arkansas Press, 1996.

Khūrī, Ilyās [Elias Khoury]. *Al-Wujūh al-Bayḍā'*. Beirut: Dār Ibn Rushd li al-Ṭibā'ah wa al-Nashr, 1981.

———. *Majma' al-Asrār*. Beirut: Dār al-Ādāb, 1994.

Mahfouz, Naguib [Najīb Maḥfūẓ]. *God's World: An Anthology of Short Stories*. Minneapolis, Minn.: Bibliotheca Islamica, 1973.

———. *Children of Gebelawi*. London: Heinemann, 1981.

———. *The Beginning and the End*. New York: Doubleday, 1989.

———. *Palace Walk*. Translated by William M. Hutchins and Olive E. Kenny. New York: Doubleday, 1990, c1989.

———. *Miramar*. Translated by Fatma Moussa Mahmoud. Edited and revised by Maged el-Kommos and John Rodenbeck. New York: Doubleday, 1993.

Munīf, 'Abd al-Raḥman [Abdelrahman Munif]. *Sharq al-Mutawassiṭ*. Beirut: Dār al-Ṭalī 'ah li al-Ṭibā'ah wa al-Nashr, 1975.

Munif, Abdelrahman ['Abd al-Raḥman Munīf]. *Endings*. Translated by Roger Allen. London: Quartet Books, 1988.

———. *Cities of Salt*. Translated by Peter Theroux. London: Vintage Books, 1994.

———. *Variations on Night and Day*. Translated by Peter Theroux. New York: Vintage Books, 1994.

Nasrallah, Ibrahim [Ibrāhīm Naṣr Allāh]. *Prairies of Fever*. Translated by May Jayyusi and Jeremy Reed. Introduction by Fedwa Malti-Douglas. New York: Interlink Books, 1993.

Rawāshidah, Ramaḍān al- [Ramadan Rawashdeh]. *Min Hayāt Rajul Fāqid al-Dhākirah, Aw: Al-Ḥamrāwī*. Amman, 1992.

Razzāz, Mu'nis al- [Mu'nis al-Razzaz]. *Al-Dhākirah al-Mustabāḥah / Qab'atān wa Ra's Wāḥid*. Beirut: Al-Mu'assasah al-'Arabīyah li al-Dirāsāt wa al-Nashr, 1991.

———. *I'tirāfāt Kātim Ṣawt*. Revised second printing. Amman: Al-Mu'assasah al-'Arabīyah li al-Dirāsāt wa al-Nashr, 1992.

Saadawi, Nawal el- [Nawāl al-Sa'dāwī]. *Woman at Point Zero*. Translated by Sherif Hetata. London: Zed Books, 1983.

Saleh, Tayeb [Al-Ṭayyib Ṣāliḥ]. *Season of Migration to the North*. Translated by Denys Johnson-Davies. Portsmouth, N.H.: Heinemann, 1989.

Samman, Ghada [Ghādah al-Sammān]. *Beirut '75*. Translated by Nancy N. Roberts. Fayetteville: University of Arkansas Press, 1995.

———. *Beirut Nightmares*. Translated by Nancy N. Roberts. London: Quartet Books, 1997.

Shaykh, Hanan al- [Ḥanān al-Shaykh]. *The Story of Zahra*. London: Quartet Books, 1986.

Sirrīs, Nihād [Nihad Sirris]. *Al-Kūmidīyā al-Fallāḥīyah*. Aleppo: n.p., 1990.

Subūl, Taysīr [Taysir Subul]. *Anta Mundhu al-Yawm*. Beirut: Dār al-Nahār li al-Nashr, 1968.

Tall, Suhayr Salṭī al- [Suhayr al-Tall]. *Al-Mishnaqah wa Qiṣaṣ Ukhrā*. Amman: Al-Mu'assasah al-Waṭanīyah li al-Nashr, 1987.

Wāzin, 'Abduh [Abduh Wazin]. *Ḥadīqah al-Ḥawāss*. Beirut: Dār al-Jadīd, 1993.

CRITICAL AND THEORETICAL WORKS

Accad, Evelyne. *Sexuality and War: Literary Masks of the Middle East*. New York: New York University Press, 1990.

Aghacy, Samira. "Elias Khoury's *The Journey of Little Gandhi*: Fiction and Ideology." *International Journal of Middle East Studies*, no. 28 (1996): 163–76.

Aghacy, Samira. "Rachid El Daif's *An Exposed Space Between Drowsiness and Sleep*: Abortive Representation." *Journal of Arabic Literature* 27, no. 3 (October 1996): 193–203.

Ahmad, Aijaz. *In Theory: Classes, Nations, Literatures*. London: Verso Press, 1992.

'Ālim, Maḥmūd Amīn al- [Mahmud Amin al-'Alim]. *Thulāthīyah al-Rafḍ wa al-Hazīmah: Dirāsah Naqdīyah li Thalāth Riwāyāt li Ṣun' Allāh Ibrāhīm*. Cairo: Dār al-Mustaqbal al-'Arabī, 1985.

Allen, Roger. *The Arabic Novel: An Historical and Critical Introduction*. Syracuse, N.Y.: Syracuse University Press, 1982.

———. "Arabic Fiction and the Quest for Freedom." In *The Quest for Freedom in Modern Arabic Literature*, edited by Robin Ostle, 37–49. Leiden: E. J. Brill, 1995. Special edition of the *Journal of Arabic Literature* 26, nos. 1–2 (March–June 1995).

———. *The Arabic Novel: An Historical and Critical Introduction*. 2d ed. Syracuse, N.Y.: Syracuse University Press, 1995.

———, ed. *Modern Arabic Literature*. A Library of Literary Criticism. New York: Ungar, 1987.

Allen, Roger, Hilary Kilpatrick, and Ed de Moor, eds. *Love and Sexuality in Modern Arabic Literature*. London: Saqi Books, 1995.

Amyuni, Mona Takieddine. "Hadiqat al-Hawass (Garden of the Senses), by Abdo Wazen." Book review. *The Beirut Review*, no. 7 (spring 1994).

———. "Style as Politics in the Poems and Novels of Rashid Al-Da'if." *International Journal of Middle East Studies*, no. 28 (1996): 177–92.

Bāridī, Muḥammad al- [Muhammad al-Baridi]. "Al-Tajrīb wa Inhiyār al-Thawābit" (Experimentalism and the collapse of stability). *Al-Ādāb*, no. 5-6 (May–June 1997): 20–23.

Barqūqī, 'Abd al-Raḥmān al-. *Sharḥ Dīwān al-Mutanabbī*. 2d ed. 1938. Reprint, Cairo: Maktabah al-Tijārah, n.d.

Beverly, John, and José Oviedo, eds. *The Postmodernism Debate in Latin America*. Translated by Michael Aronna. Durham, N.C.: Duke University Press, 1993. Special edition of *boundary 2: An international journal of literature and culture* 20, no. 3 (fall 1993).

Botros, Souraya. "Les Influences Occidentales sur la Nouvelle en Syrie depuis 1946." Dissertation, University of Paris-Sorbonne, n.d.

Boullata, Issa J. "Adonis: Towards a New Arab Culture." Review essay. *International Journal of Middle East Studies* 20 (1988): 109–12.

———. *Trends and Issues in Contemporary Arab Thought*. Albany: State University of New York Press, 1990.

———, ed. *The Arabic Novel Since 1950: Critical Essays, Interviews, and Bibliography*. Mundus Arabicus, vol. 5. Cambridge, Mass.: Dar Mahjar Publishing and Distribution, 1994.

Bradbury, Malcolm. *The Modern British Novel*. Harmondsworth, England: Penguin Books, 1993.

Bradbury, Malcolm, and James McFarlane, eds. *Modernism: 1890–1930*. Harmondsworth, England: Penguin Books, 1991.

Brunner, José Joaquín. "Notes on Modernity and Postmodernity in Latin American Culture." In *The Postmodernism Debate in Latin America*, edited by John Beverly and José Oviedo, translated by Michael Aronna. Durham, N.C.: Duke University Press, 1993. Special edition of *boundary 2: An international journal of literature and culture* 20, no. 3 (fall 1993).

Cachia, Pierre. *An Overview of Modern Arabic Literature*. Edinburgh: Edinburgh University Press, 1990.

Calinescu, Matei. *The Five Faces of Modernity*. Durham, N.C.: Duke University Press, 1987.

Colas, Santiago, *Postmodernity in Latin America: The Argentine Paradigm*,

Post-Contemporary Interventions. Series edited by Stanley Fish and Fredric Jameson. Durham, N.C.: Duke University Press, 1994.

Cooke, Miriam. *War's Other Voices: Women Writers on the Lebanese Civil War.* Cambridge: Cambridge University Press, 1988.

Darrāj, Fayṣal [Faysal Darraj]. "Mā Ba'da al-Ḥadāthah fī 'Ālam bilā Ḥadāthah." *Al-Karmal* (Amman), no. 51 (1997): 64–90.

DeKoven, Marianne. *Rich and Strange: Gender, History, Modernism*. Princeton: Princeton University Press, 1991.

Dentith, Simon. *Bakhtinian Thought: An Introductory Reader*. London: Routledge, 1995.

Dorlian, Georges. "Le roman d'expression arabe (après 1975): L'émergence du moi." *Magazine littéraire* (Paris), Supplément: Poètes et romanciers du Liban, no. 359 (November 1997): 107–9.

Draz, Ceza Kassem. "Opaque and Transparent Discourse in Sonallah Ibrahim's Works." In *The View from Within: Writers and Critics on Contemporary Arabic Literature, A Selection from Alif: Journal of Comparative Poetics*, ed. Ferial J. Ghazoul and Barbara Harlow. Cairo: The American University in Cairo Press, 1994.

Encyclopedia of Islam, The. Vol. 3. Leiden: E. J. Brill, 1971.

Fanon, Frantz. *The Wretched of the Earth*. New York: Grove Press, 1968.

Felman, Shoshana, and Dori Laub, M.D. *Testimony: Crises of Witnessing in Literature, Psychoanalysis, and History*. New York: Routledge, 1992.

Fuṣūl: Journal of Literary Criticism 2, no. 2 (January–March 1982). Special edition, *Fiction and the Art of Narration* (Cairo: General Egyptian Book Organization, January, February, March 1982).

Ghazoul, Ferial J., and Barbara Harlow, eds. *The View from Within: Writers and Critics on Contemporary Arabic Literature, A Selection from Alif: Journal of Comparative Poetics*. Cairo: The American University in Cairo Press, 1994.

Ḥāfiẓ, Ṣabrī [Sabry Hafez]. "Al-Tajārib al-Ḥaḍārīyah wa Tafā'ul al-Ru'ā al-Ibdā'īyah: Dirāsah fī Ta'thīr *Al-Ṣakhab wa al-'Unf* 'alā al-Riwāyah al-'Arabīyah." *Fuṣūl: Journey of Literary Criticism* 3, no. 4 (July–September 1983): 215–29.

Hafez, Sabry [Ṣabrī Ḥāfiẓ]. *The Genesis of Arabic Narrative Discourse: A Study in the Sociology of Modern Arabic Literature*. London: Saqi Books, 1993.

Hawi, Khalil S. *Kahlil Gibran: His Background, Character and Works*. Beirut: The Arab Institute for Research and Publishing, 1972.

Hutcheon, Linda. *A Poetics of Postmodernism: History, Theory, Fiction*. New York: Routledge, 1988.

'Īd, Yumnā al- [Yumna al-Eid]. *Al-Rāwi: Al-Mawqi' wa al-Shakl.* Beirut: Mu'assasah al-Abḥāth al-'Arabīyah, 1986.

———. *Al-Kitābah: Taḥawwul fī al-Taḥawwul: Muqāranah li al-Kitābah al-Adabīyah fī Zaman al-Ḥarb al-Lubnānīyah.* Beirut: Dār al-Ādāb, 1993.

———. "*Rālf Rizq Allāh fī al-Mir'āh* li Rabī' Jābir: Ḥikāyah Intiḥār fī Dhākirah Mushra'ah 'alā al-As'ilah." *Al-Mulḥaq al-Thaqāfī*, no. 65 (1997).

Jabrā Ibrāhīm Jabrā [Jabra Ibrahim Jabra]. *Al-Qalaq wa Tamjīd al-Ḥayāt: Kitāb Takrīm.* Beirut: Al-Mu'assasah al-'Arabīyah li al-Dirāsāt wa al-Nashr, 1995.

Jad, Ali B. *Form and Technique in the Egyptian Novel, 1912-1971.* London: Ithaca Press, for the Middle East Centre, St. Antony's College, Oxford, 1983.

Jusdanis, Gregory. "Is Postmodernism Possible Outside the 'West'? The Case of Greece." *Byzantine and Modern Greek Studies* 11 (1987).

———. *Belated Modernity and Aesthetic Culture: Inventing National Literature.* Theory and History of Literature, vol. 81. Minneapolis: University of Minnesota Press, 1991.

Khaṭīb, Muḥammad Kāmil al- [Muhammad Kamel al-Khatib]. *Inkisār al-Aḥlām: Sīrah Riwā'īyah.* Dirāsāt Naqdīyah 'Arabīyah 1. Damascus: Manshūrāt Wizārah al-Thaqāfah, 1987.

Khūrī, Ilyās [Elias Khoury]. *Al-Dhākirah al-Mafqūdah: Dirāsāt Naqdīyah.* Beirut: Dār al-Ādāb, 1982.

Kundera, Milan. *The Art of the Novel.* London: Faber and Faber, 1988.

Leavis, Q. D. *Fiction and the Reading Public.* London: Bellew Publishing, 1978.

Lenczowski, George. *Soviet Advances in the Middle East.* U.S. Interests in the Middle East Series. Washington, D.C.: The American Enterprise Institute for Public Policy Research, 1972.

Levitt, Morton P. "From Realism to Magic Realism: The Meticulous Modernist Fictions of García Márquez." In *Modern Critical Views: Gabriel García Márquez*, edited by Harold Bloom. New York: Chelsea House, 1989.

Malti-Douglas, Fedwa. *Woman's Body, Woman's Word: Gender and Discourse in Arabo-Islamic Writing.* Princeton: Princeton University Press, 1991.

Martin, Gerald. *Journeys through the Labyrinth: Latin American Fiction in the Twentieth Century.* Critical Studies in Latin American Culture. New York: Verso Press, 1989.

McHale, Brian. *Postmodernist Fiction.* London: Routledge, 1994.

Meyer, Alfred G. "The Political Theory of Pessimism: George Orwell and Herbert Marcuse." In *The Future of Nineteen Eighty-Four*, edited and with an introduction by Ejner J. Jensen. Ann Arbor: University of Michigan Press, 1984.

Mikhail, Mona N. *Studies in the Short Fiction of Mahfouz and Idris*. New York University Studies in Near Eastern Civilization, no. 16. New York: New York University Press, 1992.

Monroe, Elizabeth. *Philby of Arabia*. London: Faber and Faber [1973].

Morrissette, Bruce. "Surfaces and Structures in Robbe-Grillet's Novels." In *Two Novels: Jealousy and In the Labyrinth*, by Alain Robbe-Grillet, trans. Richard Howard. New York: Grove Press, 1965.

Nābulsī, Shākir al- [Shakir al-Nabulsi]. *Madār al-Ṣaḥrā': Dirāsah fī Adab 'Abd al-Raḥmān Munīf*. Beirut: Al-Mu'assasah al-'Arabīyah li al-Dirāsāt wa al-Nashr, 1991.

Parrot, Cecil. *Jaroslav Hašek: A Study of Švejk and the Short Stories*. New York: Cambridge University Press, 1982.

Peled, Mattityahu. "Sexuality in Jabra's Novel, *In Search of Walid Mas'ud*." In *Love and Sexuality in Modern Arabic Literature*, ed. Roger Allen, Hilary Kilpatrick, and Ed de Moor. London: Saqi Books, 1995.

Qāsim, Sīzā. "Al-Mufāraqah fī al-Qiṣṣ al-'Arabī al-Mu'āṣir." *Fuṣūl: Journal of Literary Criticism* 2, no. 2 (January–March 1982).

Razzāz, Mu'nis al- [Mu'nis al-Razzaz], ed. *Al-Ḥadāthah: 'Adad Khāṣṣ*. Amman: Wizārah al-Thaqāfah, Al-Mamlakah al-Urdunnīyah al-Hāshimīyah, 1994. Special edition of the journal *Afkār: Thaqāfīyah Shahrīyah*, no. 118 (August–September 1994).

Robinson, Christopher. *French Literature of the Twentieth Century*. Totowa, N.J.: Barnes and Noble, 1980.

Sa'āfīn, Ibrāhīm al- [Ibrahim al-Sa'afin]. *Taṭawwur al-Riwāyah al-'Arabīyah al-Ḥadāthah fī Bilād al-Shām: 1870–1967*. Beirut: Dār al-Manāhil, [1984?].

———. *Al-Riwāyah fī al-Urdunn*. Amman: Manshūrāt Lajnah Tārīkh al-Urdunn, no. 31, 1995.

Ṣāliḥ, Fakhrī [Fakhri Salih]. "*Al-Jabal al-Ṣaghīr:* Buṭūlah al-Amkinah wa al-Jamā'āt." *Al-Mahd*, no. 2 (1984).

———. "*Fuqahā' al-Ẓalām*: Al-Naṣṣ al-Muttaham." *Al-Mahd*, no. 8 (1986).

———. "Al-Riwāyah al-'Arabīyah al-Jadīdah: Naz'ah al-Lāyaqīn wa al-Intihāk al-Shaklī." *Al-Ṭarīq* (Amman), no. 4 (1993): 123–27.

———. *Wahm al-Bidāyāt: Al-Khiṭāb al-Riwā'ī fī al-Urdunn*. Beirut: Al-Mu'assasah al-'Arabīyah li al-Dirāsāt wa al-Nashr, 1993.

———. "Imīl Ḥabībī: Sayl al-Ḥikāyāt," *Majallah Nazwā* (Muscat, Oman), no. 7 (July 1997): 44–48.

———. "Al-Riwāyah al-'Arabīyah wa Ashkāl al-Sard al-Turāthīyah." *Suṭūr* (Cairo) no. 2 (January 1997): 76–78.

Shammas, Anton, ed. *The Middle East.* Special issue of *Michigan Quarterly Review* 31, no. 4 (fall 1992).

Slavic Review, winter 1995.

Suwaydān, Sāmī [Sami Suwaydan]. *Abḥāth fī al-Naṣṣ al-Riwā'ī al-'Arabī.* Beirut: Mu'assasah al-Abḥāth al-'Arabīyah, 1986.

Al-Tajrīb wa al-Tajdīd fī al-Riwāyah al-'Arabīyah. Special issue of *Al-Ādāb,* nos. 5-6 (May/June 1997).

Tarabishi, Georges. *Woman Against Her Sex: A Critique of Nawal el-Saadawi.* With a reply by Nawal el-Saadawi. Translated by Basil Hatim and Elisabeth Orsini. London: Saqi Books, 1988.

Wādī, Fārūq [Faruq Wadi]. *Thalāth 'Alāmāt fī al-Riwāyah al-Filasṭīnīyah: Ghassān Kanafānī, Imīl Ḥabībī, Jabrā Ibrāhīm Jabrā.* Beirut: Al-Mu'assasah al-'Arabīyah li al-Dirāsāt wa al-Nashr, 1981.

Williams, Patrick, and Laura Chrisman. *Colonial Discourse and Post-Colonial Theory: A Reader.* New York: Columbia University Press, 1994.

Zaza, Radwan. "Influences Étrangers dans le Roman et la Nouvelle Arabes en Syrie de 1950 à nos jours." Diss., University of Paris-Sorbonne, 1985.

Zeidan, Joseph T. *Arab Women Novelists: The Formative Years and Beyond.* Albany: State University of New York Press, 1995.

COMPARATIVE TEXTS

Achebe, Chinua. *Things Fall Apart.* London: Heinemann, [1958].

Auster, Paul. *The New York Trilogy: City of Glass, Ghosts, The Locked Room.* Harmondsworth, England: Penguin Books, 1990.

Beckett, Samuel. *Three Novels: Molloy. Malone Dies, The Unnamable.* Everyman's Library. New York: Alfred A. Knopf, 1997.

Borges, Jorge Luis. *Labyrinths: Selected Stories and Other Writings.* Edited by Donald A. Yates and James E. Irby. New York: New Directions, 1964.

Bowles, Paul. *The Sheltering Sky.* New York: Vintage Books, 1990.

Brecht, Bertolt. *Collected Plays.* Edited by Ralph Manheim and John Willett. New York: Vintage Books, [1971].

Burton, Richard F. *The Arabian Nights' Entertainments, or The Book of the Thousand Nights and a Night.* New York: Modern Library, 1997.

Camus, Albert. *The Stranger.* Translated by Matthew Ward. New York: Vintage Books, 1989.

———. *Exile and the Kingdom*. Translated by Justin O'Brien. New York: Vintage Books, 1991.

———. *The Fall*. Translated by Justin O'Brien. New York: Vintage Books, 1991.

———. *The Plague*. Translated by Stuart Gilbert. New York: Vintage Books, 1991.

Carroll, Lewis. *Alice in Wonderland*. Norton Critical Edition. New York: W. W. Norton and Co., 1971.

Cervantes Saavedra, Miguel de. *Don Quixote*. New York: Modern Library, 1998.

Chekhov, Anton. *Five Great Short Stories*. New York: Dover, 1990.

Conrad, Joseph. *Heart of Darkness and The Secret Agent*. New York: Doubleday, 1997.

Dos Passos, John. *U.S.A.* New York: Library of America, 1996.

Dostoyevsky, Fyodor. *Notes from Underground/The Double*. Translated by Jessie Coulson. Harmondsworth, England: Penguin Books, 1972.

Doughty, Charles Montagu. *Travels in Arabia Deserta*. Gloucester, Mass.: P. Smith, 1968.

Duras, Marguerite. *Four Novels*. New York: Grove Press, 1990.

Durrell, Lawrence. *The Alexandria Quartet: Justine, Balthazar, Mountolive, Clea*. Harmondsworth, England: Penguin Books, 1991.

Ellison, Ralph. *Invisible Man*. New York: Random House, 1982.

Faulkner, William. *The Sound and the Fury*. New York: Modern Library, 1992.

Flaubert, Gustave. *Three Tales*. Oxford and New York: Oxford University Press, 1991.

García Márquez, Gabriel. *The Autumn of the Patriarch*. New York: Harper & Row, 1976.

———. *Love in the Time of Cholera*. New York: Alfred A. Knopf, 1988.

Gide, André. *The Counterfeiters; with Journal of the Counterfeiters*. New York: Alfred A. Knopf, 1951.

———. *The Immoralist*. Translated by Richard Howard. New York: Vintage Books, 1970.

Hašek, Jaroslav. *The Good Soldier Švejk*. Translated by Cecil Parrott. Harmondsworth, England: Penguin Books, 1974.

Hemingway, Ernest. *In Our Time*. New York: Simon & Schuster, 1970.

Hesse, Hermann. *Steppenwolf*. New York: Henry Holt and Co., 1990.

Ionesco, Eugéne. *Rhinoceros, and Other Plays*. Translated by Derek Prouse. New York: Grove Press, [1960].

Joyce, James. *Dubliners*. Harmondsworth and New York: Penguin Books, 1976.

———. *Ulysses*. New York: Vintage Books, 1986.

Kafka, Franz. *The Metamorphosis*. New York: Bantam Books, 1972.

———. *I Am a Memory Come Alive: Autobiographical Writings*. New York: Schocken Books, 1974.

———. *The Trial*. New York: Alfred A. Knopf, 1992.

Kawabata, Yasunari. *Snow Country and A Thousand Cranes*. Translated from the Japanese by Edward G. Seidensticker. Nobel Prize ed. New York: Alfred A. Knopf, 1969.

Kingston, Maxine Hong. *The Woman Warrior: Memoirs of a Girlhood Among Ghosts*. New York: Vintage Books, 1977.

Kotzwinkle, William. *The Fan Man*. New York: Vintage Books, 1994.

Kundera, Milan. *The Book of Laughter and Forgetting*. New York: Alfred A. Knopf, 1980.

Lawrence, D. H. *The Complete Short Stories*. New York: Penguin Books, 1977.

Lawrence, T. E. *Seven Pillars of Wisdom: A Triumph*. New York: Doubleday, 1991.

Mann, Thomas. *The Magic Mountain – Der Zauberberg*. New York: Alfred A. Knopf, 1977.

———. *Death in Venice and Other Tales*. New York: Viking, 1998.

Nabokov, Vladimir. *Laughter in the Dark*. Harmondsworth, England: Penguin Books, 1982.

Poe, Edgar Allan. *Selected Tales*. New York: Vintage Books, 1991.

Proust, Marcel. *Swann's Way: Remembrance of Things Past*. New York: Vintage Books, 1989.

Rilke, Rainer Maria. *The Notebooks of Malte Laurids Brigge*. Translated by Stephen Mitchell. New York: Random House, 1983.

Robbe-Grillet, Alain. *Two Novels: Jealousy and In the Labyrinth*. Translated by Richard Howard. New York: Grove Press, 1977.

Rushdie, Salman. *The Satanic Verses*. New York: Viking, 1989.

Sarraute, Nathalie. *Tropisms and The Age of Suspicion*. London: Calder & Boyars, 1963.

Sartre, Jean-Paul. *Nausea*. New York: New Directions, 1964.

———. *The Wall (Intimacy) and Other Stories*. New York: New Directions, 1969.

Stein, Gertrude. *A Primer for the Gradual Understanding of Gertrude Stein*. Los Angeles: Black Sparrow Press, 1973.

———. *Three Lives*. Harmondsworth, England: Penguin Books, 1990.

Svevo, Italo. *Confessions of Zeno*. Translated by Beryl de Zoete. New York: Vintage Books, 1989.

Swift, Jonathan. *Gulliver's Travels*. Harmondsworth, England: Penguin Books, 1967.

Toomer, Jean. *Cane*. New York: Modern Library, 1994.

Voltaire. *Candide*. New York: Alfred A. Knopf, 1992.

Woolf, Virginia. *Mrs. Dalloway*. San Diego: Harcourt Brace Jovanovich, 1985.

———. *The Voyage Out*. Oxford and New York: Oxford University Press, 1992.

Index

99; *Ayyām Zā'idah* compared to, 235; *'Azīzī al-Sayyid Kāwābātā* compared to, 237; criticism of, 199–201; as experimental novel, 195–96; *Journey of Little Gandhi, The* compared to, 209

Jaber, Rabi', 247–52
Jabra, Jabra Ibrahim: on alienation and exile, 6, 238; background of, 34; context of, 3, 8; identity of, 52; Munif's link to, 85–86; Samman compared to, 118; themes of, 34–37; translation by, 22, 29. *See also Baḥth 'an Walīd Mas'ūd, Al-* (Jabra); *Ship, The* (Jabra)
Jad, Ali B., 16, 19
James, Henry, 7–8, 181, 214, 262
Jameson, Fredric, 277, 279
Japanese literature, interests in, 72
Jayyusi, Salma Khadra, 60–61, 65, 176, 177
Jealousy (Robbe-Grillet), 214
Jordan: author's trial in, 163–64; folk tradition and experimentalism in, 99, 106; politicization in, 194–95; rebellion in, 110; tribal culture in, 107
Journey of Little Gandhi, The (Khoury): *Ayyām Zā'idah* compared to, 235; *'Azīzī al-Sayyid Kāwābātā* compared to, 237; as experimental novel, 201–9; Khoury on, 203, 204, 207–8; *Rālf Rizq Allāh fī al-Mir'āh* compared to, 247
Joyce, James: Kharrat compared to, 213; Khoury compared to, 130, 257; self-conscious novel of, 214; *Star of August, The* compared to, 47; techniques of, 136, 181, 236, 249, 270; works: *Dubliners*, 136; *Ulysses*, 249
Jundub al-Ḥadīdī, Al- (S. Barakat): as experimental narrative, 87–90; *Khurāfīyah: Sarāyā, Bint al-Ghūl* compared to, 101, 103; *Prairies of Fever* compared to, 178, 179
Jurji the monk (legend), 225
Jusdanis, Gregory, 260–61

Kafka, Franz: Jabra on, 85–86; Khoury's reference to, 252; Kundera on, 4; Rawashdeh compared to, 107–8; skepticism of, 267; transformation theme of, 181; works: *Metamorphosis, The*, 107–8, 181; *Trial, The*, 181

Kanafani, Ghassan: on connection/disconnection, 33; context of, 3; generational differences and, 195; Khoury compared to, 270; as modern or postmodern novelist, 264; as modern vs. new novelist, 268; Munif compared to, 77; political views of, 26–27; works: *Men in the Sun*, 27–29, 56, 140. *See also All That's Left to You* (Kanafani)
Kawabata, Yasunari, 236–39
Kharrat, Edwar al-, 225, 259. *See also Girls of Alexandria* (Kharrat)
Khatib, Muhammad Kamil al-, 76
Khoury, Elias: context of, 117, 118; Da'if compared to, 237; Daoud compared to, 226, 228, 235; experimental style of, 129–30, 166–67, 168, 251–53; hero's position undermined by, 268–70; identity of, 272–73; ideology of, 208–9; on language, 11, 274; on modernism, 11, 12; as modern or postmodern novelist, 255–58, 264–65, 271, 275; as modern vs. new novelist, 268–69; on "narrative of interior situations," 160; objectivity and, 270–71; political and artistic committment of, 201–4; works: *Collection of Secrets*, 251–53. *See also Gates of the City* (Khoury); *Journey of Little Gandhi, The* (Khoury); *Kingdom of Strangers, The* (Khoury); *Little Mountain* (Khoury); *Wujūh al-Bayḍā', Al-* (Khoury)
Khurāfīyah: Sarāyā, Bint al-Ghūl (Habiby), 100–106
Kilpatrick, Hilary, 26, 29
Kin'an, Fu'ad, 235
Kingdom of Strangers, The (Khoury): as experimental novel, 114–15, 253; masculine perspective of, 224–26; overview of, 113–14
Kingston, Maxine Hong, 109–10
Kotzwinkle, William, 188–89, 192
Kristeva, Julia, 264
Kūmidīyā al-Fallāḥīyah, Al- (Sirris), 99–100, 107
Kundera, Milan, 3–4, 61
Kurds: experimental autobiography about, 87–90; novel about, 91–95; as unrecognized nationality, 95, 97

language: in *'Azīzī al-Sayyid Kāwābātā* (Da'if), 237; conservative vs. radical